# RADHAKRISHNAN
## A Biography

Radhakrishnan (*courtesy Lotte Meitner-Graf, London*).

# RADHAKRISHNAN
## A Biography

SARVEPALLI GOPAL

DELHI
OXFORD UNIVERSITY PRESS
BOMBAY CALCUTTA MADRAS

*Oxford University Press, Walton Street, Oxford OX2 6DP*

NEW YORK    TORONTO
DELHI   BOMBAY   CALCUTTA   MADRAS   KARACHI
PETALING JAYA   SINGAPORE   HONG KONG   TOKYO
NAIROBI    DAR ES SALAAM
MELBOURNE    AUCKLAND

and associates in
BERLIN   IBADAN

First published 1989
Second impression 1989

SBN 0 19 562351 7

Printed in India at Rekha Printers Pvt. Ltd., New Delhi 110 020
and published by S.K. Mookerjee, Oxford University Press
YMCA Library Building, Jai Singh Road, New Delhi 110001

# CONTENTS

# PLATES

Radhakrishnan (*courtesy Lotte Meitner-Graf, London*) (frontispiece)

(*between pages 150 and 151*)

# PREFACE

Sarvepalli Radhakrishnan was a man of versatile talent and varied achievements. He served India in a number of ways and worked for the reconciliation of mankind at the deepest level. But first and foremost he was a philosopher of the front rank and the final place to encounter and assess him is in his philosophical writings. I being no philosopher, it may seem odd that I should attempt to write about him. But this deficiency is not an insuperable barrier; for he himself wrote copiously and there are, apart from the volume in the Library of Living Philosophers series, many books, monographs and essays on his thought. My own effort is to examine the interaction of thought, life and context and I have touched on his philosophy only to the extent required to follow the growth of his mind and to explain his life.

A greater difficulty has been Radhakrishnan's own deliberate reticence in matters concerning himself. He believed that his work was his best biography. He had said all that he had to say, and the rest was not for public gaze. Such essays as he wrote about himself were solely about his intellectual development. Nor would he agree that his life outside his writings was of interest to anyone. In the summer of 1943, after a serious illness, he jotted down what he termed his 'memories and reflections', but he refused, despite the pressure of friends and publishers, to develop these recollections into a full-scale autobiography. His reply was to quote Samuel Johnson: 'Madam, of the exaltations and depressions of your mind you love to speak and I hate to hear.' And after 1943 there was still much to come.

This is a son's book. The relations between my father and me were closer and more continuous than is usual, in this age, between parents and children; and they brought with it, at times, obscure pains on both sides. Such close association enabled me to be witness to a great deal in the later years that has been recounted here. But I have tried not to be swayed by personal affection and have shirked nothing.

*Madras, 23 November 1988*                                           S. Gopal

# ACKNOWLEDGEMENTS

The writing of this book has been made possible, first, by a Senior Award of the Homi Bhabha Fellowships Council, and second, by a Fellowship of the Nehru Memorial Museum and Library. I am grateful to these two organizations.

# ABBREVIATIONS

| | |
|---|---|
| AICC | All-India Congress Committee |
| IOL | India Office Library |
| MEA | Ministry of External Affairs |
| MSS. EUR. | Manuscripts European |
| NAI | National Archives of India |
| NMML | Nehru Memorial Museum and Library |
| UP | United Provinces (later Uttar Pradesh) |

# Part One

Part One

# PRELUDE

The culture of India under British rule, in the sense of a constitutive social process creating particular ways of life,[1] was a compound of various elements. There was, first of all, imperialism itself, increasingly aggressive after 1857 and engaged in the colonial mode of production without reservations.[2] In this the natural allies of the exploiters were the Christian missionaries. Christianity in India is as old as St Thomas; but with the coming of the Europeans it became inextricably bound up with imperial domination. 'It is no accident that the "great century" of the expansion of the Christian Church was also the great century of European expansion.'[3] Christianity did not make the empire Christian but the empire made Christianity political. It was, above all else, the religion of the white race.[4] When C. F. Andrews came out to Delhi as a conventional young clergyman in 1904 he was told by the British community, 'Never, under any circumstances, give way to a "native", or let him regard himself as your superior. We only rule India in one way—by safeguarding our position. Though you are a missionary you must be an Englishman first, and never forget that you are a Saheb.'[5]

Part of the ruling community and funded considerably by the government, the missionaries acted as sources of intelligence and were prominent in the network of social control. In south India, for example, where in the last quarter of the

[1] This is the meaning suggested by R. Williams, in *Marxism and Literature* (Oxford 1977), p. 19.

[2] H. Alavi, 'The Colonial Mode of Production', *Socialist Register*, 1975; Bipan Chandra, 'Colonialism, Stages of Colonialism and the Colonial State', *Journal of Contemporary Asia*, 1980, pp. 272–85.

[3] S. Neill, 'The Indigenous Church in Self-Governing Countries', *East and West Review*, April 1954, pp. 35–42. Neill was for many years Bishop of Tinnevelly in south India.

[4] W. R. Inge, *Science, Religion and Reality* (London 1926), p. 387.

[5] H. Tinker, 'Between Old and New Delhi', in R. E. Frykenberg (ed.), *Delhi through the Ages* (Delhi 1986), p. 352.

nineteenth century the number of converts to Christianity more than tripled, pride was taken that 'missions as a whole had a share in giving stability and permanence to the British Empire.'[6] It was therefore to be expected that, as criticism of British rule spread in the country, the political antagonism to the Church became more open and direct. Christianity was criticized as an anti-national force, and in turn some publications of missionaries called on Indian Christians not to support the national movement as it was contrary to the spirit of Christ.[7] Bureaucrats, missionaries and racists were all finally on the same side.

The sustenance of imperialism by Christianity was even more effective in areas outside politics and administration. The de-industrialization of the country, the immiseration of artisans, and the subordination of the whole economy to the requirements of colonial power had their own social and intellectual consequences. Stripping bare the mind and spirit of the people fortified imperial rule; and missionaries did what they could to help in the process of damaging the identity of the Indian people. Acting on the assumptions that Christianity was the only true religion and that (whatever the position in the past) by the nineteenth century only the West was the centre of civilization, they saw it as their duty to ensure that the Christian faith and European thought prevailed over all else. Christianity having been vouchsafed the highest truth as yet known to humanity, there was no question of accommodation to other faiths or patterns of thought. 'As long as we claim to be Christians in deed and truth, we must cultivate a certain consciousness of superiority.'[8] Especially after the revolt of 1857 the missionaries, instead of continuing to ignore the beliefs of the Indian population as a mass of iniquitous superstition, studied them carefully—not because there might be grains of truth in them but to combat them better. A change in tactics did not involve a revision of the attitude of condescen-

[6] Editorial Notes, *The Harvest Field* (September 1901), quoted in Y. V. Kumaradoss, 'Protestant Missionary Impact and Quest for National Identity; Tamil Nadu Experience 1900–1923', unpublished Ph.D. thesis, Madras University 1983.

[7] Kumaradoss, pp. 176, 184-5.

[8] H. Frick, 'Is a Conviction of the Superiority of His Message Essential to the Missionary?', *International Review of Missions*, October 1926.

sion. The clinging to the certainty of a unique revelation
ruled out the acceptance of a diversity of belief. To know more
about Hinduism was part of the missionary's equipment; to
show its inadequacy in face of what Christ had to offer was the
missionary's business. India had to be made hungry for Christ
before she received Christ. But until she accepted Christ there
was no hope for her.

Had such a 'permanent organized repression of the cultural
life of the people', which Cabral regarded as the core of colonialism, succeeded, it would have left them with very little.[9]
But they needed to exist in their own eyes, to have some idea
of what they were. All missionary activities—social, educational and philanthropic—had an evangelist objective; and
the more effective these efforts, the more the people lost their
way and became invisible to themselves. Consciousness and
identity were sought to be separated and the Indian people
made to feel, in the phrase of Barthes, 'of myself as other'. But
colonialism, in its drive to destroy all local values, uncon-
sciously exalts that of patriotism; in annihilating all virtues it
promotes that of defiance. Nor does such patriotic defiance
have to be political. For an Englishman, as Orwell noted, there
was no third way; you were either in or out, either a guilty
imperialist or a person dedicated to bringing down the system.
But an Indian could be a non-political nationalist, a seeming
conformist undermining the raj. There were other roads than
collaboration and direct resistance; and some of these feeder
roads were invaluable, maybe even indispensable.

One such road is what Cabral has termed the 'return to the
source'.[10] The past can be a legitimate guarantee of contemporary identity, and it was natural that such Indians as
had begun to smart under British rule should turn to the
solace and strength offered by tradition. For the Hindus, however, this posed a particular problem, as their religion was
without circumference, an amalgamation, under the impact of
extraneous influences, of a large variety of religious beliefs with

[9] Amilcar Cabral, 'The Role of Culture in the Struggle for Independence',
paper for a seminar organized by UNESCO, July 1972.

[10] Quoted by K. N. Panikkar, 'The Intellectual History of Colonial India:
Some Historiographical and Conceptual Questions', in S. Bhattacharya and
R. Thapar (eds.), *Situating Indian History* (Delhi 1986), p. 416.

similar structures into a religious system. Even the general use
of the term Hinduism is a recent phenomenon. There is no
Hindu religion in the sense in which that term is generally
used; but there is an atmosphere, 'a structure of feeling' which
governs the different sects and lifts them to higher levels.
Though conditions change and new ideas are absorbed, some
characteristics persist; a faith, for example, in the oneness and
wholeness of the universe. Such subtle reasoning might not
have percolated to every section of the concerned society; but
a 'common culture is not, at any level, an equal culture'.[11]
There is the lived culture, the recorded culture, and 'the culture of the selective tradition'.

It was the culture of the last category which Indian philosophers, in face of the assaults of Christian preachers, sought to
bring back to prominence. This 'battle for consciousness'[12] was
part of the challenge to colonial domination. Thought and
philosophy, rather than religious belief and practice in the
conventional sense, were the central and conscious parts of
Indian culture, which was really a whole way of life; and they
became integral to the ideology which was distinctive to the
new intelligentsia.[13] Philosophy and politics are not separate
ways of thinking in a colonial society; and in a suffocating
intellectual climate it is difficult for even the least sensitive to
be indifferent. In India, from the second half of the nineteenth
century, even a philosopher could not hope for an autonomous life of the mind, with no commitment to society. For a
bruised community, conscious of its political impotence, a
culture provides both a touch of healing and an element of
defence. It plays an important political role, preserving, re-
fining and idealizing the vision of an independent homeland.
The natural answer to allegations regarding the dying culture
of subjugated people is the assertion that the culture embodies
values which can restore renewed dignity to the people. Hindu-

[11] Raymond Williams, *Culture and Society 1780–1950* (Pelican edition 1963),
p. 305. In this paragraph I have derived much from this book of Williams, as well
as his *The Long Revolution* (Pelican edition 1965), especially pp. 64–6.

[12] R. Miliband, *Marxism and Politics* (Oxford 1977), p. 50.

[13] On the importance of ideology in the formation of this intelligentsia, see
S. Bhattacharya, 'Notes on the Role of the Intelligentsia in Colonial Society:
India from Mid Nineteenth Century', *Studies in History*, vol. 1, no. 1 (Delhi 1979),
pp. 89–104.

ism, as Sir Alfred Lyall, expressing the British viewpoint, observed, was determined to live though doomed to die. Foreign rule had been made possible by the inner disintegration of the people; and pride in their culture was a major aspect of the rescue of the national spirit from apathy and despair. Only those who have no faith in the future hug the past at the cost of all else; but the better part is to accept the best of the past as the beacon to the future. The power of ideas was an important lever for political mobilization. The pressures of colonialism demand a merger of the inner and outer landscapes.

Such a merger had to be effected in the context of an educational system intended primarily to produce clerks for the lower levels of the administration but having also the wider effect of uprooting its products. They were taught the rudiments of a foreign culture in the language of the alien ruler. A few succumbed wholly or rejected it totally, but most emerged half-and-half Indians, caught in the ambivalent interplay of rejection and acceptance. Exposure to an unsettling cultural otherness generated new reflexes, with the best clinging to their old learning and intellectual habit but seeking to improve them by adapting the new teaching. To speak of the clash between tradition and modernity is to oversimplify. The important effort was to revivify tradition with large doses of modernity. Again to use the categories of Raymond Williams, residual and emergent elements were combined to resist an extraneous culture which was seeking to be dominant.[14]

Of course, the medium of instruction itself became an issue. The fact that the nationalist idea was being fostered in the English language was to British imperial apologists in itself sufficient evidence that India was not a nation. For to many theorists of nationalism in Europe in the nineteenth and early-twentieth centuries language was the crucial test. Freeman saw it as the badge of nationality,[15] while Weber spoke of a nation as a 'community of language and literature'.[16] To Indians this

[14] *Marxism and Literature*, pp. 120–7.

[15] E. A. Freeman, 'Race and Language', *Historical Essays*, third series (London 1879), p. 203.

[16] 'The Nation' (written before 1914), H. H. Gerth and C. Wright Mills (eds.), *From Max Weber: Essays in Sociology* (London 1946), pp. 171–9.

was a restricted definition based on European experience. They
preferred to think of a nation, in Acton's phrase, as a moral
and political being,[17] and Renan's description appeared to
them particularly appropriate to themselves: 'l'existence d'une
nation est un plébiscite de tous les jours'.[18] Far from regarding
the expression of their sentiments in the English language as
demeaning, they saw an advantage in strengthening their case
by utilizing the resources which knowledge of English opened
up and carrying the battle to the enemy. Indian languages
were isolated oases which precluded communication with the
outside world. So Herder's advice to his fellow-Germans to
'spit out the green slime of the Seine' seemed to have no
parallel relevance in India. While a few of her thinkers and
politicians, familiar with the language of the oppressor, adopted
a loyalism born of self-interest and hugged the soft fetters of
kitsch, many more expressed their rejection of Britain in
vigorous English. There is no instance in India of such an
incident as that of Jean Joseph Rabéarivels, the poet of Mala-
gasy, who killed himself in 1937 because he could not reconcile
his nationalism with the French language and culture in which
he was obliged to work. Indians saw no contradiction between emotional implication in their own culture and total
ease in a foreign language.[19]

With dual minds held together by a single loyalty, the mana-
gers for legitimation of nationalism provided different mani-
festations in various parts of the country. In southern India
attention centred on religious thought, both because it was less
coloured by Islam here than elsewhere, and because aggressive
Christianity made greater inroads in the south than in other
parts of India. Two men, more than most others, from very
different environments devoted their learning, energy and
will-power to the task described by Yeats as making 'national
feeling noble and enlightened'. Passionately engaged in their
own history and with a new pride in the values and faith of

---

[17] Lord Acton, *Nationality* (1862).

[18] E. Renan, *Qu'est-ce qu' une Nation?* (Paris 1882).

[19] Cf. Chinua Achebe: 'Is it right that a man should abandon his mother tongue
for someone else's? It looks like a dreadful betrayal and produces a guilty feeling.
But for me there is no other choice. I have been given the language and I intend
to use it.' *New Statesman*, 8 August 1986.

PRELUDE

their ancestors, familiar with Western culture but on the edge
of it and apart, they made an effort to pour fresh life into
ancient teachings by coming to terms with the new impulses
created by contact with European thought. These men were
the instruments of historical processes and their expression has
a representative importance. They were too good as scholars to
be limited by the causes of their primary motivation. Contemporary relevance did not preclude universal value, and
there was a smooth movement from specific and national
concerns to a detached search for general truths. Patriotic
involvement could be the base for philosophic detachment. But
their writings start with a lively immediacy. Ananda Coomaraswamy, born of English and Sri Lanka Tamil parents and
trained in Britain in geology, was reclaimed by the haunting
persistence of the past and devoted himself to the service of
ideas which for him was the only service possible to render to
the cause of Indian freedom. It was the work of artists to make
their hearers free; it was they alone who could establish the
status of a nation.[20]

The other, from a much humbler background, was Sarvepalli Radhakrishnan.

---

[20] R. Lipsey, *Coomaraswamy*, volume 3, His Life and Work (Princeton 1977),
pp. 66–7, 84, 90.

# I

## POVERTY AND PHILOSOPHY

Most of the major details about the birth of Sarvepalli Radha-krishnan are uncertain. The official version is that he was born on 5 September 1888 at Tirutani, a very small temple town to the north-west of Madras city, the second son of a poor Brahmin couple, Sarvepalli Veeraswami and his wife Sitamma. However, Radhakrishnan himself was inclined to believe that the date of his birth was in fact 20 September 1887. More important is the doubt whether Veeraswami was his father. Parental responsibility lay, according to village rumour, with an itinerant Vaishnavite official. Sitamma's brother, who served in the local administration, was thought to have arranged the rendezvous to oblige a superior officer. Credence is lent to the story by the difficulty in believing that Radha-krishnan and his four brothers and sister belonged to the same genetic pool. Intellectual endowment and physical appearance both suggested that Radhakrishnan belonged to different stock. Radhakrishnan himself accepted this version and, critical of his mother's conduct, always, throughout her long life, kept her at a distance. But he was attached to the man who passed for his father.

Veeraswami's ancestors had moved, sometime in the middle of the eighteenth century, from the village of Sarvepalli in the east coast about two hundred miles to the north of Madras, westward to North Arcot district, but retained the word Sarvepalli in their names to indicate their place of origin. Veeraswami, a subordinate revenue official in the service of a local zamindar, was hard put to it to maintain his large family and send his children to school. Radhakrishnan joined the primary Board High School at Tirutani at the age of four and spent about four years there, learning elementary English,

Telugu, arithmetic, geography and Indian history. He was then, in 1896, shifted to the Hermansburg Evangelical Lutheran Mission School at Tirupati. This school was run, till the outbreak of the First World War, by German missionaries; and Radhakrishnan had his first lessons in the Bible. This came as a supplement to a sense of Hindu religion, inculcated at home by regular practice of ritual and visits to temples. But the introduction to both creeds was mechanical and with no noticeable impact.

There was, in fact, nothing remarkable about Radhakrishnan as a schoolboy. Little of introspection or intellectuality is to be found in his childhood. He was clever enough to win scholarships but was by no means studious; nor was he interested in games. His main activity was to play truant and walk long distances from village to village, utilizing the scholarship money and whatever was sent from home to pay for his food en route. It was on one such trek that a highwayman led him to the side of a well and searched him for gold ornaments such as were traditionally worn by Brahmin boys in those days. Finding that Radhakrishnan had on him nothing but a small bag of peanuts the robber let him go rather than push him into the well.

Such waywardness did not seem to make for academic progress. In fact, on the day when students were to fill the forms for the Lower Secondary examinations (which was in those days a public examination) for promotion to the next class, Radhakrishnan was absent; but a discerning headmaster, breaking the rules, filled the form for him. Radhakrishnan was sensible enough to turn up for the examinations themselves.

Radhakrishnan's parents knew no English and had no clear idea of his performance at school. But, hearing of his erratic behaviour, they moved him in 1900, after four years at the school at Tirupati, to Vellore, a nearby town, where a distant uncle of his happened to be on the teaching staff of the local missionary college. Radhakrishnan now drifted out of the lonely wildness of his boyhood and his studies became more regular. After two years he passed the matriculation examination of the University of Madras and won a scholarship to Voorhee's College. He was again asked to memorize passages from the Bible and secured a certificate of merit for proficiency in the scriptures. But this still meant very little. He was more influenced by a surreptitious reading of the letters of Swami Vivekananda, with their eloquent appeal to India's youth to evince pride and self-respect; and this vague sense of nationalism was further quickened by the reading, also in clandestine circulation, of V. D. Savarkar's *The First War of Indian Independence.*

From Vivekananda and Savarkar, Radhakrishnan moved on to other authors of a more general kind. It was during the years at Vellore that he showed the first signs of enthusiasm for reading and started buying books. This was the seeding of a habit which endured. Radhakrishnan was always, deep down, a shy and lonely man, and over the years he developed his inner resources and private interests to engage the solitude which he increasingly sought. But there was also, at all times, a social side to him; and this too was first to be seen at Vellore. He never, throughout his life, smoked tobacco or tasted liquor; and his die. was always vegetarian of the simplest kind. But he liked company; and what was left, after paying his fees and buying books, out of the 60 to 100 rupees he was given every term as a scholarship, was either given away to even poorer boys or spent in entertaining friends. Concerts and the street theatre were his forms of relaxation and, averse to confessing that he himself was not too well off, he was sometimes prone to extravagance. Sex does not seem to have interested him at this stage, though there is a curious comment in his notes written in 1943:

No disasters overtook me. Though I was held back from the grossest 'sins', there was much in my student life that could be recalled only with shame and self-accusation. Though I was free from the puerility which scrawls indecencies on the walls of lavatories, I was not a moral snob to complain about it. Both these may be due to cowardice and not moral sense or courage.

While still a student at Vellore, in May 1903, at the age of sixteen, Radhakrishnan was married to a distant cousin, Sivakamu, aged ten. The marriage was arranged by his parents. Radhakrishnan's reputation, won during his schooldays, for being a shirker had not been overborne by his more attentive ways at Vellore. As one of his uncles remarked, when there was some talk of his making for himself a satisfactory career, 'this creeper is not likely to climb that scaffolding'. So parents in search of promising sons-in-law did not look in his direction. Sivakamu's father, a railway station-master, had died in her infancy, and her mother was in no position to seek or buy for her a young man who was heir to property or of established ability. Radhakrishnan and Sivakamu were chosen for each other because they seemed hardly fitted for anyone else.

They made, as they grew up, a handsome, physically dissonant couple. Sivakamu, or Padma as her husband called her, was short, fair, inclined to be plump but with a pleasant face. Radhakrishnan was darker, tall—5 foot 10 inches—spare, fairly muscular, with thick hair which soon turned grey and then white, bright brown eyes, an aquiline nose and a full, pouting mouth, shadowed, till 1919, by a bushy moustache. Strangers when they were married, Sivakamu joined Radhakrishnan three years after their wedding, and they gradually grew into each other. Their first child, a daughter, was born in 1908; and then, during the next fifteen years, they had six more children: two daughters, a son who died a fortnight after birth, two more daughters and a son.

In the early years of their marriage Radhakrishnan and Sivakamu found it mutually satisfying and infused with all the warmth and humour of intimate companionship. As he developed intellectual interests and ambitions which she could not share, there was no multi-level communion. But she accepted the poverty and the struggle and provided him with a stable home life such as enabled him to be wrapped up in himself and in his own work. Her feeling for him was not so much an obtrusive passion as an unquestioning dedication and rock-like loyalty. She made no claim to understand him but was involved in his hopes and disappointments, hinting to him, through the steady, drab routine of everyday life, that her commitment to him was enduring. He, on his part, took pride in bringing home his medals and prizes won at college and university and assuring her that there would be no shortage of these, at any rate, in the years to come. He also borrowed in order to buy the ornaments for which the young housewife craved.

As Radhakrishnan's intellectual and public life widened and as he travelled, from the mid twenties, incessantly and far afield, his wife took over silently the responsibilities of the family. Radhakrishnan began, too, to show an interest in other women; but like many Indians of his generation (and since) it did not seem to him that love and infidelity were incompatible.[1] He would not accept, even to himself, that his loyalty to her was tarnished by his extra-marital adventures. He recognized that she was the foundation of his life and genuinely believed that she was the only woman who had ever mattered to him and the greatest single influence on him. He was fond of quoting Hegel's remark that a man has made up his account with this life when he has work that suits him and a wife whom he loves. Marriage was to him a game seldom played according to the rules, and a happy marriage, as he saw it, did not require the husband's monogamous attitude. He always regarded himself as happily married. It is of some doubt whether, especially in her later years, his wife felt the same. She was a devoted wife by any standards; he was a devoted husband according to his lights.

In 1904 Radhakrishnan passed the first arts examination in the first class, with distinctions in mathematics, psychology and history, and won a scholarship to the Christian College at Madras for the BA courses. Asked to choose his specialization, he was inclined towards the physical sciences but ultimately decided on philosophy solely because a cousin who had just graduated passed on to him his textbooks in psychology, logic and ethics, thus saving Radhakrishnan considerable expense. So, clearly, Radhakrishnan had no deep sense of vocation for philosophy. His choice of subject was more by accident than by design; and time and again during his life, Radhakrishnan tried to get away from the main pursuit of philosophy only to be foiled by circumstances. Till 1949, when public life became his primary interest, he studied philosophy with great assiduity and lectured and wrote on it with breadth, fluency and vision; but it was not a study undertaken as a matter of conscious

---

[1] Nor is this an attitude unknown outside India. Margaret Cole, for example, describing herself as 'made monogamous, but not faithful', was content in her marriage to G. D. H. Cole. B. D. Vernon, *Margaret Cole 1893–1980* (London 1986), p. 75.

inevitability. The fact that he was pushed into it and attained, in the process, deep scholarship and a world-wide reputation convinced him that his career was the handiwork of a power not himself, call it Nature, Fate, Providence, God or whatever. As his success blossomed Radhakrishnan was increasingly convinced that his life was being shaped by an unseen hand, much as he might try to mould it in different patterns; and more and more he committed himself, his decisions and his judgement, to his star.

The Christian College had at this time a high reputation. William Miller, one of the best-known missionaries of the nineteenth century in India, was still on the staff and taught Shakespeare to all students of the college. Of the teachers of philosophy, Radhakrishnan was touched by the kindness of William Skinner, to whom he later dedicated one of his books, and influenced by the rigorous analysis and wide learning of A. G. Hogg. Neither of these men published much; but they imparted to Radhakrishnan a sense of tolerance, the importance of accurate scholarship and a broad view of philosophy as an understanding of the nature and ends of human life, of the search for a synoptic grasp of reality and of man's place in it. Hogg was so meticulous a thinker that in his lectures and writings, and even in informal conversations, there was throughout a restrained hesitation of thought, a qualified moderation, a scrupulous regard for all sides of a case and an anxiety to ensure all the qualifications for any statement. A dedicated missionary with an unshakeable belief in the person of Christ and in the indispensability of belonging to the visible Church, Hogg was yet flexible in matters of doctrine and regarded himself as more a philosopher than a theologian;[2] and Radhakrishnan always acknowledged the permanent mark on his own mind of Hogg's influence, in both response and reaction.

At the end of 1906 Radhakrishnan obtained the BA degree with first class honours and was the best student of that year in philosophy. He thought of switching to the law but this assumed financial resources which he did not possess. Veeraswami had by now retired and Radhakrishnan had to send him money, as well as support his mother and his three younger brothers

[2] G. Sharpe, *The Theology of A. G. Hogg* (Madras 1971).

who had joined him and his wife in Madras. From 1906 began
his years of grinding, if genteel, poverty; and it was now that
he began to incur large debts. So there was really no option but
to accept the studentship of Rs 25 per month (supplemented
by what he could earn by giving private tuition) and move on
to the MA classes in philosophy.

## II

In his lectures on ethics to the MA classes Hogg spoke rather
disparagingly of the ascetic and otherworldly tendencies of the
Bhagavad Gita. These remarks, as well as the general atmosphere of the college, roused Radhakrishnan to examine for
himself the religious beliefs of the Hindus. He wondered if
it was the intellectual incoherence and ethical inadequacy of
these beliefs which had brought about the political downfall
of India. 'I remember the cold sense of reality, the depressing
feeling of defeat that crept over me, as a causal relation between the anaemic Hindu religion and our political failure
forced itself on my mind during those years.'[3] Though he had
read Vivekananda's writings, it had been the nationalist spirit
rather than the exposition of religion in them which had impressed him; and now he started on his own research. His lifelong trek in the study of Indian thought began with the
purchase of three primers, Barnett's *Hinduism*, Wilbernitz's
study of the Bhagavad Gita, and Swami Abhedananda's three
lectures on the religion of the Vedanta. Indian philosophy not
being a part of the syllabus in Madras or indeed in any of the
Indian universities, this was a self-imposed task; and in partial
fulfilment of the requirements of the MA degree, Radhakrishnan submitted a dissertation titled 'The Ethics of the
Vedanta and Its Metaphysical Presuppositions'. It underlines
his moral strength that he should have chosen a subject which
was outside the purview of the courses and for which he would
have to rely on his own intellectual resources, just as it speaks
for the tolerance of Hogg and his colleagues that they permitted Radhakrishnan to write on this theme, of which they
could not have approved, and gave him such guidance as they

[3] S. Radhakrishnan, 'The Spirit in Man', in *Contemporary Indian Philosophy*
(London 1936), p. 476.

could. Radhakrishnan's performance in the BA examination had brought him to Hogg's notice, and he now received some personal attention. Had Radhakrishnan chosen a topic more to the liking of the university authorities (among whom the missionaries predominated) he might not have dropped to a second class in the final examinations. But Hogg himself was broadminded enough to commend the thesis for its 'remarkable understanding' of the main aspects of the philosophical problem and its capacity for handling easily a complex argument, besides its author's higher than average mastery of good English. A more general assessment by another of his teachers, William Meston, is of interest for its perception:

He has displayed a power of clear thought, an independence of judgment and a capacity of accurate and rapid assimilation of what he has read which mark him out as possessed of high intellectual bent and attainments. Whatever he deals with goes through the mill of his own mind, and undigested opinion has no place with him.[4]

The thesis was published in a limited edition by a local press and is now a collector's piece. Radhakrishnan in later years dismissed it as a juvenile production which he would not wish to be taken seriously. It is certainly coloured with purple patches and is overstocked with quotations from poets and philosophers. It also starts with an unsophisticated assertion of nationalist sentiment, boasting that Indians were philosophical at a time when other peoples were tattooing their bodies and eating raw animal flesh; and it was pointed out that even Jesus had spoken of brother delivering up brother to death, and the father his child. But the thesis progresses to become a book of courage, confidence and conviction, and lays down the lines of Radhakrishnan's future development. Spreading much beyond its title, the book drew upon a wide knowledge of European thought to formulate ideas which were the germs of Radhakrishnan's writings for nearly sixty years. There are soundings of themes treated grandly later, and clear hints of the powers to come. Radhakrishnan accepted the Christian

[4] For Hogg's opinion, see S. Radhakrishnan, 'My Search for Truth', in V. Ferm (ed.), *Religion in Transition* (London 1937), p. 20; Meston's assessment of 26 January 1909 is to be found in Madras govt. file, home dept (education), 14 December 1920, nos. 1500–1, Miscellaneous, Tamil Nadu Archives.

criticisms of Hindu practices and social institutions. Rules could and had to be changed if they did not serve their purpose. In a short work of ninety-three pages he quotes twice the adage that the Sabbath is made for man and not man for the Sabbath. It was because India had failed to adapt practice to life that her society had retrograded and the country lagged behind the other nations of the world. But the evils of priestcraft which distorted the interpretation of scriptures were not a phenomenon restricted to India: 'more than half the wars, half the sin, misery and all the religious persecutions, the massacres, burnings, torturings that have occurred in this world are attributable to its baneful influence.'

Yet, Radhakrishnan goes on to argue, ideals are not invalidated by their imperfect embodiments. He outlines the history of Indian philosophy which to him culminates in the philosophy of Samkara: 'The grandeur of spiritual oneness which very few thinkers can appreciate is brought out most sublimely.' Samkara's system is to him a combination of religion, metaphysics and ethics; and Radhakrishnan contends that, contrary to general assumption, in this philosophy are to be found the elements of an ethical science though not a perfected system of ethics. It is rationalistic, a type of moderate rationalism. Karma is not preordained destiny, precluding free will. Our actions in past lives result in certain fixed tendencies or natural dispositions; and free will lies in rising above these. Reason has the choice to make what it pleases with the given material. Men's duty is to make the lower sensuous self yield to the higher rational self. The senses are a bar to morality and religion, yet they are to be not destroyed but controlled. By life according to reason the Vedanta ethics does not mean a passionless life but one in which passion is transcended. The individual has to develop a character out of the lines laid down by his nature and ordained circumstances. To realize the oneness of the self with the Absolute is the goal of Vedanta ethics.

Opportunity, therefore, makes the hero. Writing as a student of a Christian institution and knowing that among his examiners were Christian priests, Radhakrishnan boldly and explicitly rejected the uniqueness of Christ. The life, death and resurrection of Christ were not a solitary or a special portent

but the supreme vindication of a universal spiritual law. It was
no more than a dramatization of a normal psychological experience open to all. The crucifixion was the death of the
lower egohood, the resurrection the rise of the true self.

So, beneath the obscurantism and superstition, Radhakrishnan discerned vital sparks in the Hindu tradition—an
acceptance of spiritual values and a compulsion to social
service. Cultivation of the spirit of non-difference and universal
brotherhood was the primary axiom of the ethics of the Vedanta. The corollary of inward peace was work for the welfare
of humanity. Moksha and dharma were the two poles of
religion. Wisdom and love, insight into the Supreme and
fellowship with other human beings had to go together. To
revere God was to respect mankind. Conscious of the failure,
discord and impotence of finite existence, the mystic was inclined to enter into the solitude of the soul; but such an
escape was to risk depriving religion of much of its content. For
the inward life of the spirit was the essence of religion but not
the whole of it. With faith in the ultimate spirituality of the
universe, the mystic should sally forth into the world to bend
the facts of nature to the will of God.[5]

When he had obtained his MA degree in January 1909, it
was suggested to Radhakrishnan that he apply for one of the
scholarships offered every year by the Government of India for
Indian students to study at Oxford or Cambridge. The necessity of providing for the family ruled out any prolonged absence
from Madras, but Radhakrishnan covered whatever disappointment he might have felt with the boast that if he ever
went to Oxford it would be not to study but to teach. He
needed employment desperately and tried for various jobs in
Madras without success. Skinner finally gave him a letter of
introduction to the Director of Public Instruction, recommending him—'one of the best men we have had of recent years'—for
the post of lecturer in the educational service. As a result, there
being no suitable teaching vacancy, Radhakrishnan was appointed to a substantive post of sub-assistant inspector of
schools in an area far from the city but directed to fill a
temporary vacancy as Malayalam Master in the Presidency

[5] S. Radhakrishnan, BA, *The Ethics of the Vedanta and Its Metaphysical Presuppositions* (Guardian Press, Madras, 1908).

College at Madras on a salary of Rs 60, in the scale of Rs 60–80 per month. He knew no Malayalam but was expected to teach philosophy. So he joined official service and started, for want of anything else, on a teaching career.

In 1910, a few months after hc had begun lecturing, Radhakrishnan was deputed to the teacher's training college at Saidapet on a monthly half-salary of Rs 37.50 to obtain a diploma in teaching. This was a year of real hardship and the time when Radhakrishnan's household, on one occasion, unable to afford even the banana leaves on which food is served, washed the floor and ate off it. He auctioned his university medals and in addition borrowed more money. Unable in the following years even to pay the interest on these debts, Radhakrishnan found himself dragged to court in 1913 in a civil suit. To earn extra money he, apart from continuing private tuition, took on as many examinerships as he could get and went through vast piles of answer papers in logic for the university. Financial necessity was also responsible for the writing of his next book. He put together his class lectures on psychology and *Essentials of Psychology*, a small book of seventy-five pages, was printed at the Clarendon Press in Oxford and brought out in 1912 by the Indian branch of the Oxford University Press as its first publication. Radhakrishnan sold all his rights in the book for the lump sum of Rs 500. The work made no claim to originality but provided a broad and lucid survey of the basic principles of the subject and the various schools of thought within it. It was received well in India and was popular with students, so the publishers had no reason to regret their purchase. Such reviews as appeared in Britain were friendly but condescending. The *Athenaeum* saw in it an indication that the gulf between Indian and European minds was not so great as had often been asserted.[6] 'Nevertheless', commented *The Bookman*, 'if the native Indian may not hope to write anything enduring in English, he writes a good deal in it that is interesting and valuable.'[7]

This book indicates the strength of Radhakrishnan as a teacher. He was always a very clear expositor of even the most abstruse topic. This ability he manifested from the start of his career. Preferring to rely on his memory rather than on notes,

[6] August 1912, p. 223.     [7] September 1912, p. 252.

he knew what he wanted to say and said it with the utmost
directness. Even while under training at Saidapet, he was
asked, in the absence on leave of the regular teacher, to give
to the other trainees some lectures on philosophy, 'very
successful and much appreciated'.[8] The principal attended
these lectures and said to Radhakrishnan 'you lecture as I do',
an empty compliment, as he did not lecture at all. More surprisingly, considering Radhakrishnan's lifelong aversion to
any form of strenuous exercise, the diploma awarded him on
the completion of this training course refers to his 'very good'
performance at drill.

Returning to the Presidency College in 1911, Radhakrishnan
served there for the next five years, first as additional assistant
professor and then, from 1914, as assistant professor of philosophy. The subjects handled by him, apart from psychology,
were European thought and political philosophy; and his
reputation for clarity and comprehensiveness was so widespread that students of other colleges attended his classes. Hogg
himself made very clear that his students would attend the
lectures on political philosophy in the Presidency College only
if Radhakrishnan delivered them.[9]

Radhakrishnan's influence with his students was, however,
not based only on his mastery of the material and facility of
expression. Poverty did not preclude his working out for himself a dress which suited his figure and his personality—a long
silk coat buttoned up at the neck and reaching down to his
knees, a white dhoti with a black border, black slippers and a
turban of white muslin. This was his attire in India for the rest
of his life, whatever his position; and sartorial elegance became
a part of his personality.

Distinction of appearance did not, however, imply stand-
offishness. His informality and warmheartedness reached out
to all who came in contact with him, and the 'boy professor', as
he was known, was exceedingly popular, not only with his own
students but throughout the college. This trait was to continue
and even intensify throughout the years of his association with
various Indian universities, as professor or vice-chancellor. It

[8] Letter of A. S. Hall, principal, Teachers College, Saidapet, 22 December
1910.
[9] A. G. Hogg to Radhakrishnan, 12 and 16 November 1914.

was the students who made his reputation long before his writings and speeches had made an impact.

This popularity with the young was partly responsible for an unusual encounter. One evening in 1914, as Radhakrishnan was poring over Sanskrit texts by the light of a lantern in his dingy home, there was a knock on the door. He opened it to find a stranger, a short, dark and stocky young man, accompanied by one of Radhakrishnan's students. 'I am leaving for Cambridge', said the stranger, 'and, as instructed by the goddess Bhavani in a dream, I have come to seek your blessing.' Radhakrishnan asked him in, the young man introduced himself and they had a short and desultory conversation. The two men never met again. The visitor was Srinivasa Ramanujan.[10]

Unlike in the years at Vellore, in his student days at Madras Radhakrishnan made no great friendships. He was generally known as a promising scholar; but family life rather than the social round appears to have engaged his attention. Alladi Krishnaswami, later to become one of India's leading lawyers, was senior to Radhakrishnan; though acquainted at this time, their close friendship developed only from the early twenties. Among his contemporaries with whom Radhakrishnan kept up in later years were Satyamurti, who became one of the most articulate leaders of the Congress; Subbaraya Aiyer, the lawyer and philanthropist; and the large, friendly, but academically backward Mahomed Usman. 'Help me', said Usman to Radhakrishnan, 'to pass the BA examination, and there is no telling what I shall achieve.' So Radhakrishnan gave him lessons in logic and Usman, true to his word, became in turn officiating governor of Madras, vice-chancellor of Madras University, and member of the viceroy's council. But there was affection rather than depth in these relationships.

At Saidapet, however, Radhakrishnan met T. K. Doraiswami, a fellow-trainee and specialist in economics; and from then till his death in 1961 Doraiswami was devoted to Radhakrishnan. From 1911 till Radhakrishnan was transferred to the districts five years later, they were colleagues in the Presidency

---

[10] I relate the story as told to me by Radhakrishnan. The mention of a deity which was not Ramanujan's traditional one adds to the credence of the story. A fantasy would have been smoother.

College, shared a small house in Madras, lent each other money and were generally inseparable. Doraiswami did not claim to be Radhakrishnan's intellectual equal but looked after his finances in these early years when Radhakrishnan had to worry about them. In the thirties Doraiswami developed an obsession, which Radhakrishnan did not share, about the mindless and mercenary instincts of the 'lawyers of Mylapore' (a middle-class residential area of Madras); but this did not weaken their mutual affection. Indeed, Doraiswami's unselfish dedication to Radhakrishnan was to many his saving grace.

Radhakrishnan also, when appointed to the Presidency College, joined the Cosmopolitan Club in the city and was to be found there almost every evening on his way home from the college. This might, considering his financial position, seem an extravagance. Like his attention to teaching and immersion in study, it was part of the effort to escape from the dreariness of daily life; but it was rationalized by the access to newspapers and journals from Britain. Hard pressed as he was for money, Radhakrishnan yet entertained in moderate measure both at home and in the club. He was also drawn to that part of the city's wider society which centred round the sisters of Sarojini Naidu. Sympathetic to the national movement and interested in the arts, they conducted a fashionable soirée; and Radhakrishnan enjoyed the flirtatious conversation.[11]

Radhakrishnan's link with this world was his other great friend of these years, M. A. Candeth. Though himself in straitened circumstances, Radhakrishnan unhesitatingly gave a loan of Rs 50 when requested by a colleague, whom he did not know, in the history department of the college. Thereafter the friendship strengthened rapidly. Candeth, fresh from Cambridge, where he had been a friend of Jawaharlal Nehru, and recruited directly to the Indian Educational Service, had a sharp wit, wide interests and considerable skill as a raconteur. Basically patriotic and giving free rein to his views on a range of varied topics, he was probably Radhakrishnan's first intellectual companion, and they became closely attached. From 1916, when Radhakrishnan was posted outside Madras, they maintained a steady correspondence, and Candeth, a prolific

[11] For an account of this salon, see K. M. Panikkar, *An Autobiography* (English translation, Madras 1977), appendix 3, pp. 355 ff.

3

letter-writer, kept Radhakrishnan abreast of official and other
gossip. Later, however, Candeth left the Presidency College for
educational administration and was sucked into the local politics of Madras, and the intellectual and personal trust on
which their close association was based slowly collapsed. They
began to flinch away from one another and the friendship was
reduced to fragmentary contacts until Candeth died, tragically
young, in 1934.

## III

Along with teaching and an active social life, Radhakrishnan
persevered with his studies. His years in Christian institutions
had given him a firm grounding in the Bible, European thought
and English literature; and on these he never ceased to build.
It is astonishing to see the sweep of his purchase of books during
these years as a student and a young lecturer, when he had to
count every pie. Many of his books were lost, borrowed permanently by his friends or destroyed by termites; but even
those which survive establish a wide range. Apart from philosophy—Plato, Aristotle, Augustine, Kant, Locke, Mill, there
was poetry—Chaucer, Blake, Longfellow; history—Plutarch,
Froude, Carlyle; the standard textbooks in psychology and
ethics, the writings of Darwin, the collected essays of Thomas
Huxley, and a contemporary scientific series. Besides his reading in libraries, these were some of the books he wished to own,
even if this meant forgoing much else.

What attracts lay readers to Radhakrishnan's learned works
is not only the smooth handling of the English language and the
vigour and clarity of the style, but also the literary allusions
and the striking quotations from creative writers. However, if
he were to establish with any conviction that Hinduism was a
living tradition he needed firsthand knowledge of the ancient
texts which he was seeking to interpret on modern lines. So
he set himself, during his years at the Presidency College, to
learn Sanskrit with the help of pandits and then studied the
classics, the Upanishads and the Bhagavad Gita, and the com-
mentaries on them. With Pali he was not as familiar, but read
in English the Buddhist texts as well as those of Jainism. Lecturing now on Indian philosophy, which had been introduced as
a subject for the honours course, as well as on contemporary

philosophy, Radhakrishnan found that there was no standard
textbook for the former subject, while the latter was to the
students rootless, for it was shallow to lecture on Bergson or
William James or whoever else was in current fashion in the
West without linking it with Greek or medieval philosophy.

However futile the attempt to teach modern European
thought to students, for Radhakrishnan himself the benefits of
the courses he taught were marked. In addition to his study of
the primary sources of Indian philosophy, he was obliged to
ground himself in Western classics and also to keep abreast of
the latest developments in Western thought. The advantageous
consequence of this multiple effort was his development into
what J. H. Muirhead termed later a 'philosophical bilinguist'.[12]
No one else in the world of philosophy in the twentieth century
could rival him in his knowledge of both Eastern and Western
philosophical and religious thought.

Radhakrishnan was, from the start, not satisfied merely to
counter the Christian missionaries in India, as he had done in
his thesis, or to remind the Hindus that they had to revise their
practices and that their religion at its best preached, as did
Plato, that both egoism and altruism were parts of man's
nature.[13] With a vague but powerful ambition to secure recognition for the validity of the intrinsic elements of Hindu
thought in the world outside, Radhakrishnan was keen to
publish his articles in the philosophical journals of the West.
His first efforts were returned by the editors of *Mind* and the
*Hibbert Journal*; but in 1911 the *International Journal of Ethics*
published an article by him called 'The Ethics of the Bhagavad
Gita and Kant'. Elaborating the teachings and practical
aspects as found in the Gita, Radhakrishnan compared them
with Kant's views on free will, the moral problem and the law
of duty, and suggested the superiority of the Hindu position.
For while to Kant man was determined with regard to his
relations as a member of the phenomenal realm but free in the
noumenal realm, the Vedanta allowed freedom even in the
phenomenal realm with a choice to resist impulses, check passions and lead a life regulated by reason.

[12] *Hibbert Journal*, October 1932.
[13] S. Radhakrishnan, ' "Nature" and "Convention" in Greek Ethics', *Calcutta
Review*, January 1910, pp. 9–23; 'Religion and Life', leaflet no. 15, issued by The
Theistic Endeavour Society of Madras, November 1915.

The same journal also published, three years later, two articles on aspects of the Vedanta. While conceding that the Vedanta did not put forward an articulate code of morality, Radhakrishnan contended, as he had in his thesis, that inherent in a metaphysics which repudiated separateness was an ethic which led naturally to an ideal of love and brotherhood. The Vedanta required every person to work out his own spiritual destiny by struggle and effort; and 'the drugged conscience of the average Hindu mind' should wake up to the necessity of practical energy and strength of character. Radhakrishnan added that, according to the ethics of the Vedanta, everyone should contribute a quota of earnest effort to the national strength. It was by the adoption of such a gospel of work that the nation could grow.

Clearly, whatever be the real nature of the Vedanta, there was nothing otherworldly about Radhakrishnan's interpretation of it. As in the utterances of Swami Vivekananda, it had a practical and even nationalist tinge. While the teachings of Hinduism seemed to him basically sound, he blamed its current practices for India's political weakness and abject condition. Indeed, the increasing scholarship of the philosopher did not abate the interest in the politics of the day. In his last year as a student he had, like many others, been agitated by the deportation of Lala Lajpat Rai from the Punjab; he had read avidly the statements of Tilak in court in defence against the charge of sedition; and he had attended the session of the Indian National Congress at Madras in December 1908 and listened to Malaviya, Gokhale, Rash Bihari Ghose and Surendranath Banerjee. But the orator who thrilled him was Annie Besant, and he went to every lecture of hers in Madras to listen to her panegyrics on India and on Hinduism. So a high point to him of these years was her friendly acknowledgement of a reprint of his article on the Vedanta and a generous reference to it in her journal.[14]

Such visceral nationalism must in those days have been a painful affair. This was obvious even in faraway London to a perceptive observer like Bertrand Russell: 'It must be appallingly tragic to be civilized and educated and belong to such a country as India.'[15] The bitterness and self-indulgent pride

[14] *The Commonweal*, 6 March 1914.
[15] 27 February 1916, *Autobiography*, volume II (London 1968), p. 61.

which possessed Radhakrishnan come through in two *articles
agissants* which he sent to *The Asiatic Review* in 1915; the first was
published but the second, dealing mainly with India, was with-
held by the censor.[16] After condemning the European spirit,
the material will to possess, which had brought about the
world war, Radhakrishnan saw saving grace in that it had
opened the eyes of those in India who had been eager to
imitate it: 'India thanks her bright star that she has had the
opportunity to know in good time how hollow and unsubstan-
tial Western civilization is.' All that she needed was drastic
social change without becoming a spiritual vassal of the West.
Both Britain and Germany were playing the same game of
imperialism, and *ententes* were only 'a sort of cat friendship,
paw today and claw tomorrow; velvet gloves, then iron fists'.
In the pursuit of outward ends and material aims Europe had
lost the inward vision and the spiritual impulse. She was
Christian only in name. But the civilization of India was still
spiritual and her support of Britain in the war was an indication
of this. If a man like Tilak had called upon the people to
suspend agitation and stand by Britain in her hour of danger,
it was because of faith that Britain would act rightly at least
after the war. Though without the political freedom which she
would and must have, India was not petty or poor in spirit.
Foreign attacks and spiritual vicissitudes had not deprived her
of her spiritual vitality and her people did not repay wrong by
wrong. Christ was forsaken in Europe but was alive in India.
Her people needed more energy and enterprise but these
should be fostered in the shadow of their own civilization.
They should try to spiritualize matter instead of materializing
spirit.

In the course of his argument Radhakrishnan paid tribute to
Gandhi's work in South Africa; but when he met Gandhi in
Madras at this time, the interview was not a success. The man
whom he was later to regard as greater than Annie Besant and
Tilak, indeed as the greatest person living and as the centre of
life in India, had at this first meeting a negative impact. After a
discussion solely on non-political matters, Radhakrishnan came
back with the impression that Gandhi had a medieval attitude

[16] The published essay: 'A View from India on the War', *The Asiatic Review*,
15 May 1915, pp. 369–74.

of mind. Gandhi directed him not to drink milk, which was the essence of beef; Radhakrishnan retorted that it followed that all human beings were cannibals for mother's milk could be described in the same way as the essence of human flesh. Gandhi said, 'you are too logical'; and his host, G. A. Natesan, remarked, 'Don't you know he is a professor of logic?' The conversation then turned to medical relief. Gandhi observed that there was little need for doctors; for example, in the jungle thousands of births took place without medical assistance. Thousands, commented Radhakrishnan, also died in the jungle. 'How do you know?' said Gandhi. 'How do *you* know?' was the reply. The conversation ended.[17]

A more positive response was evoked by Tilak when he wrote from Mandalay gaol asking for a reprint of Radhakrishnan's article on the Gita and later affirmed publicly that his own work on the subject was on the same lines as Radhakrishnan's approach.[18] Radhakrishnan's reply to Tilak was charged with emotion and showed, for an impecunious lecturer struggling in the subordinate ranks of the official service, extraordinary courage; for he knew that his letter would be read by the authorities in the mail.

Revered Sir,

I cannot say how much I feel honoured by your kind reference to me in your monumental work on the Bhagavadgita. The recognition of my humble work in the field of Indian philosophy, at the hands of one so very able and learned like yourself, has encouraged me a good deal. Being unacquainted with the Marathi language, I am not able to make out what you say about my papers. I am anxiously awaiting the issue of an English edition.

With my namaskarams

> I remain
> Revered Sir
> Yours devotedly
> S. Radhakrishnan[19]

[17] The gist of this conversation is recorded in Pyarelal, 'Gandhiji's "Krishna" ', *The Radhakrishnan Number* (Madras 1962), p. 55.

[18] *Bhagavad Gita–Rahasya* (Marathi edition, Pune, June 1915; English edition, Pune 1935), p. liv.

[19] Radhakrishnan to B. G. Tilak, 4 November 1915, Tilak papers.

## IV

However, as the articles written in 1915 make clear, it was with
Rabindranath Tagore that Radhakrishnan at this time was
most fully in accord. In 1912 he had begun to read such works
of Tagore as had been translated into English, and, unlike most
of Tagore's readers, was absorbed more in the prose than in the
verse. Irritated by the claims made in the West, especially
after the award of the Nobel Prize for Literature in 1913, that
Tagore's outlook was deeply influenced by Christianity,
Radhakrishnan set out to establish, by putting together and
spelling out the views implicit in Tagore's writings, that he was
in essence a Hindu Vedantist, in line with the thinkers of the
Vedas and the Upanishads but in tune with his own times and
therefore re-emphasizing what was of value and relevance in
ancient tradition and discarding the rest.[20] Radhakrishnan's
explanation of Tagore's eminence brings to mind the belief of
Coleridge that no man was ever a great poet without being at
the same time a profound philosopher; for to Radhakrishnan
Tagore's work was the outcome and expression of the Indian
ideals of philosophy, religion and art. It was a mystical torrent,
clearing a path towards transcendence and inward grace while
yet being of this world. It was false to allege that Hinduism
regarded the world as an illusion and contemplation as the
way of escape, and to deduce from this that if Tagore were a
poet of affirmation this was the consequence of non-Hindu
influences. Radhakrishnan contended that the true Hindu outlook demands that finite man should strive for the infinite and
seek to reconcile the self and the not-self. One can progress into
the other because they are not opposed; nature and spirit are
both parts of the universal principle. The external world, the
creation of God's joy, is not foreign to us. Intellect misses the
unity which intuitive insight discerns. The Absolute which
does not lend itself to intellectual description and the personal
God of mystic religion whom Tagore celebrated both had a
place in the Vedanta system; and those who made Tagore a
borrower from Christianity betrayed to Radhakrishnan an
astonishing lack of 'historic conscience'. Christianity laid stress
on man's natural sinfulness and his salvation by Divine grace;

[20] *The Philosophy of Rabindranath Tagore* (London 1918).

but the Vedanta takes the opposite view, which is to be found in Tagore, that God is in man, waiting to be realized by the removal of ignorance and selfishness.

Intuitive insight was to be attained, according to Radhakrishnan's understanding of the Hindu faith—and which he also saw in Tagore—through renunciation and surrender of the will to God. As such a complete integration might not be achieved in one life, we have to go through the cycle of births and deaths. Nature and the world are not evil and hostile but instruments to be utilized for progress to eternal life. Such eternal life was not, however, beyond time, and the God-possessed soul would spend itself in the service of man. The consciousness of divine immanence demands social justice, the acceptance of every human being as not a means but an end. The mystic's feeling of solidarity with the universe expresses itself in work for a happier humanity. To Radhakrishnan both the Vedanta and Tagore stood for practical mysticism, a 'synthetic idealism' which, while not avoiding the temporal and the finite, still has a hold on the Eternal Spirit.

Radhakrishnan always attached importance to suffering as the way of salvation, the chance offered by God to draw man to his real destiny. This was to him the message of Hinduism and of Christianity as well; and he found echoes of this in Tagore. But there was also another aspect of suffering, that caused by selfishness. The war, still raging when Radhakrishnan commenced his work on Tagore, was to him a result of materialism and of the greed that manifested itself in selfish nationalism, realpolitik and imperialism; but he hoped that out of the war would emerge a new internationalism based on self-sacrifice and disinterestedness, a philosophy of spirit and a civilization founded on love and justice. Unless the spirit of nationalism was ended, there would soon be an end of nations; unless the gospel of imperialism was permanently laid to rest, there was no hope for the world. The ideal was balanced harmony between the materialism of the West and the spirituality of the East. An integrated human being needed both the calm of contemplation and the stress of life, the joy of self-abandonment as well as the pride of creativity.

In the longest chapter of the book, Radhakrishnan elaborated what he saw as Tagore's message to India. For him

Tagore spoke to as well as for India, interpreting her ancient thought as brought up-to-date so as to instil in her sinking heart faith in herself, in her future and in the world. 'It is the sign that God has not lost all hope of India that Rabindranath is born in this age.' The religious future of a people with many faiths lay in an intuitive grasp of the Divine in diverse ways without quarrel or misunderstanding. 'Stick to religion, let religions go.' This was to Radhakrishnan the essence of Hindu teaching and he claimed to find it in Tagore. India could withstand the onslaught of Western civilization, religion and culture provided that she rid herself of dogmatism and superstition. Radhakrishnan harks back to the concept of Indian and Western civilizations as a contrast of opposites— just as Gandhi had done in 1909 in *Hind Swaraj*—with the preponderance of wisdom on the Indian side. It seemed to him that the materialist influence was growing steadily and eating subtly into the very substance of the Indian soul, and he blamed educated Indians for seeking to graft on it the soul of the West. To accept Western culture and to forget that the Indian spirit was still alive was, in Tagore's later phrase, to buy eye-glasses at the cost of one's eyes.

Elsewhere in the book, however, Radhakrishnan shifted the emphasis from confrontation to each civilization absorbing the best of the other, and pleaded more for the assimilative synthesis which he thought had always been the characteristic of India—the integration of the old and the new, of the East and the West. What he really had in mind was the necessity of India building herself up from within, recovering her soul, regaining her self-confidence, conserving the idealism and spiritual vision of the past and basing on them progress and reform. Caste, for example, Radhakrishnan regarded as a system not without rationale and indeed inspired by a right hierarchy of values, as against Western society motivated by economic principles and structured on class; but life had departed from the caste system and it needed drastic overhaul. The prevalent system of education too seemed to him to drown the artistic, the moral and the spiritual sides of man's nature in the study of scientific formulae and social laws. In an implied criticism of the kind of education he himself had received, he favoured the replacement of English by the regional languages as the

medium of instruction and wanted a stress on the teaching of
Indian history and literature. The purpose of education was
the culture of the soul and not merely the feeding of intellect
or the cramming of memory, resulting in a materialistic mind
and a commercialistic outlook.

Radhakrishnan thought it possible to achieve such a revival
of the Indian spirit. 'Heaven does not send such men as
Rabindranath Tagore to underserving nations.' Life in India,
slovenly, disgusting and joyless, could be transformed through
a religious movement of the kind for which Tagore stood.
Purity of heart, harmony with the universe and concern for all
humanity, which had all been choked in India over a long
period of time, would have to be resuscitated to arrest the
decline of the country. But Radhakrishnan, like Tagore, recognized that this was not enough. For poverty was another
major obstacle and it had roots elsewhere. The social action
required to deal with this also called for national consciousness
and devotion. Only self-government could enable Indians to
rise to their full moral and spiritual stature. India was responsible for her own degradation. Life could not be broken into
fragments, and a demand for political freedom was incompatible with the acceptance of a cruel tyranny in social life. The
colonial condition was the penalty which India paid for the
corruption of centuries. Radhakrishnan agreed with Tagore
that if India had to be subject to foreign domination it were
better British than any other. But the liberation of spirit
produced by contact with Britain had to be taken to its logical
conclusion. Spiritual liberation meant political freedom. It was
Britain's duty to grant freedom to India; and if she did so with
intelligent sympathy and practical guidance, the union between Britain and India would be a permanent one. As to
what Indians should do in the matter, Radhakrishnan had no
sympathy with either the constitutional agitation of the Mod-
erates or the violent activities of the terrorists but favoured
independent action, 'earnest spiritual work' which would convince the British of the justice of the Indian cause. What such
work should be is not made clear. He spoke of 'a royal road
through strength and suffering' but did not define it precisely.
He revered Tilak but did not support his political stance; and
he was as yet no admirer of Gandhi, who had still not formu-

lated his policy in the Indian context. Neither Tagore nor Radhakrishnan had by this time gone beyond a vague nationalist sentiment; and the only positive step proposed by Radhakrishnan was the weak suggestion that the government should open more avenues for public service.

Ernest Rhys, who had himself written on Tagore and who had had a chance to glance through Radhakrishnan's manuscript, expressed an interest in having it published by Dent, a firm with which he was associated. But Radhakrishnan preferred to send it to Macmillan, who were Tagore's publishers; and the London office forwarded the manuscript to their reader, Sir Henry Jones. His report was, on the whole, favourable. He commended Radhakrishnan for his vigour of thought and style, his freedom from the 'Eastern vice' of slavish borrowing and making up a book out of quotations and shadows of quotations, his 'white heat' of love for Tagore and for India and his understanding of Tagore's religion. He thought the work lacked philosophical wholeness and unity; but this to him was compensated by '*one* atmosphere and that a very interesting one'. The most serious defect, in Jones's view, was that the author did not keep distinct his own thoughts and moods from those of Tagore. But all told, the book, 'though *not* on the highest plane', was decisively too good to be rejected.[21]

It is possible that Radhakrishnan, working from the English translations which at that time covered only a fraction of Tagore's writings, was asserting and claiming where Tagore often did no more than hint. Indeed, Tagore was basically a poet of Bengal, and for Radhakrishnan to interpret his philosophy without being able to read Bengali would seem a senseless act of courage. But the young author, still in his late twenties, was not short of self-confidence. 'My acquaintance with the soul of India', runs a breathtaking sentence in the preface, 'from which Sir Rabindranath draws his inspiration has helped me in the work of exposition.' It should be added that the poet himself was more than satisfied with the interpretation. In 1917, when Radhakrishnan published two articles in *The Quest* on Tagore's philosophy of life, the latter wrote on his own expressing 'grateful admiration' for what he thought to be one of the

[21] Report of Sir Henry Jones, 7 October 1917. Macmillan Archive, British Library, London, section x, third series 55988, folios 110 and 111.

best critical essays that had yet appeared on the subject, 'full of sympathetic understanding and lucid exposition'. Encouraged by this, Radhakrishnan requested Tagore for a foreword to the book he was planning in elaboration of these articles. From this Tagore cried off, pleading want of time; but he permitted the book to be dedicated to him and promised to read the proofs.[22] When these arrived, Tagore passed on the task to C. F. Andrews, who did no more than correct some factual inaccuracies. This careful abstention from open involvement in Radhakrishnan's effort Tagore justified by saying that

about my philosophy I am like M. Jourdain who had been talking prose all his life without knowing it. It may tickle my vanity to be told that my writings carry dissolved in their stream pure gold of philosophical speculation, and that gold bricks can be made by washing its sands and melting the precious fragments—but yet it is for the readers to find it out and it would be a perilous responsibility on my part to give assurance to the seekers and stand guarantee for its realization.[23]

Such caution, however, he did not persist in when the book was published, but expressed his delight and said it had surpassed his expectations: 'The earnestness of your endeavour and your penetration have amazed me in this book and I am thankful to you for the literary grace of its language which is so beautifully free from all technical jargons and a mere display of scholarship.'[24] Part of the explanation for such encomia perhaps lies in Tagore's desire to present himself to the Western world as primarily a religious mystic and not the poet of nature and love which predominate in his Bengali songs; and Radhakrishnan's book helped in this endeavour.

Though the book came out at the time of the armistice in November 1918, it was widely noticed. The reviews were as expected. Radhakrishnan's clear, epigrammatic style was generally commended, though one critic charged him with occasional word-spinning and elaboration of the obvious.[25] His account of Christianity and refusal to accept major Christian

[22] Tagore to Radhakrishnan, 12 May, 16 May and 17 December 1917.
[23] Ibid., 9 May 1918.
[24] Tagore to Radhakrishnan, 28 December 1918.
[25] *Yorkshire Post*, 8 January 1919.

influence on Tagore naturally did not secure unqualifed approval. The *Times of India*, the British-owned newspaper of Bombay, went further: 'We confess to some impatience of the author's persistent depreciation of Western civilization and thought.'[26] On the other hand, a missionary critic, accepting Radhakrishnan's view that Tagore's basic premisses were Vedantic, commented that 'we are left cold by the exposition of his philosophy, which seems to us a philosophy of conceit, concentrated selfishness and essential untruth.'[27] But Professor Muirhead, who was to be Radhakrishnan's staunchest ally and promoter over the years, shrewdly discerned beneath the polemic surface of the book the presence of what became a major strand in Radhakrishnan's life-work: 'May I venture to hope that one of the first effects of the new order [after the war] will be the closer union of the thought and feeling of East and West, to which your book is a notable contribution.'[28]

As the years passed and more of Tagore's works appeared in English translation and he himself wrote and lectured in English, Radhakrishnan found no reason to revise his interpretation.[29] In fact, it is now accepted that the Upanishads meant more to Tagore than any other literature, that he stressed the common truths in all religions and that he insisted on social and cultural renewal in India preceding political independence.[30] But the book itself Radhakrishnan allowed to go out of print after 1919 as being too youthful and effusive; and its publication again in 1961 with a fresh introduction by Radhakrishnan narrating his friendly relations with Tagore over the years was intended by him more as a token of remembrance in the centenary year than as an unqualified reiteration of the argument. For while Radhakrishnan held firm to its core, he was less satisfied with certain subsidiary aspects. To assert, for example, that poetry was creative and

[26] 12 February 1919.

[27] Quoted in the *Hindustan Review*, July 1919.

[28] J. H. Muirhead to S. Radhakrishnan, 12 November 1918.

[29] See, for example, his speech at the celebrations of Tagore's seventieth birthday in Calcutta, December 1931, printed in *East and West in Religion* (London 1933), pp. 129–43, and his article, 'Most Dear to All the Muses', in *Rabindranath Tagore: A Centenary Volume* (Delhi 1961), pp. xvii–xxiv.

[30] See William Radice's introduction in Rabindranath Tagore, *Selected Poems* (Penguin edition 1985).

prose was narrative or that religious poetry was the only type worth consideration was to beg the question. It was odd too for Radhakrishnan to defend Tagore's departure from the conventions of poetic form in English when Tagore was primarily writing in Bengali. The contrast between the outlooks of Europe and India was depicted at some places in too stark and combative a fashion, and Europe was sharply told that her chance after the war lay in her adoption of Eastern ideals. More important than all these, Radhakrishnan realized that his conceptual analysis was insufficiently refined. The shortcomings, as he later saw it, of this book lay not so much in the analysis of Tagore's writings as in his own constructive philosophical system. The philosophy of Samkara had been portrayed, with lack of full understanding, as stern and based on negation, and Tagore was said to be at 'war to the knife' with it. The teaching of the Buddha too was criticized as being in favour of seeming asceticism and inaction; and the concept of intuition was seen in opposition to intellect and not as a forward movement from it. On all these subjects Radhakrishnan developed in later years more subtle and comprehensive approaches.

# 2

# MYSORE

Radhakrishnan was happy with his work in the Presidency College and turned down the offer of a more lucrative post at Pachaiyappa's College, a private institution in the city. Presidency College was at this time the premier educational institution in southern India and enjoyed a higher academic status than even the University of Madras, which as yet had no department of philosophy; and Radhakrishnan got on well with most of his colleagues, both British and Indian, and found his students responsive and most appreciative. So he would happily have spent the rest of his professional life in this place. After five years, in 1916, he was transferred to Anantapur, in the western part of the Andhra area, as a junior lecturer; but this exile lasted only for three months and he returned to Presidency College in September 1916 as professor of philosophy. Radhakrishnan looked forward to nothing more and expected to hold that post for the next thirty years. His ambition, from the viewpoint of a career, had been fulfilled.

His destiny, however, had other plans. These were the days of the intensification of caste politics in the Madras presidency and Radhakrishnan was abruptly, in the summer of 1917, confirmed as professor but transferred from the Presidency College to the college at Rajahmundry to make way for a non-Brahmin, accepted by all as less able but senior to him in the service. To Radhakrishnan this was, of course, a disappointment, though he set out to make the best of it. His long contact, for the first time in his adulthood, with his own Telugu-speaking people established links which were to become closer in later years. A special friend was Duggirala Gopalakrishnayya, a graduate of Edinburgh, a keen student of Sanskrit, a friend of Ananda Coomaraswamy, an ardent nationalist, a gifted singer and a warm-hearted personality.

Yet Radhakrishnan was unhappy out of Madras and, seeing
no chance of getting back soon to the Presidency College, began
seriously to consider moving to the newly-founded university
in the state of Mysore. Even the year before, when Radhakrishnan was still in Madras, the vice-chancellor had, with the
approval of the university council, invited him to accept the
chair in philosophy; and Radhakrishnan had offered to resign
from the Madras service and join if probation were waived
and he were appointed permanently on a much higher salary
than what he was drawing. It does not seem that Radhakrishnan was serious about this and deliberately pitched his
demands so high as to make them unacceptable. What would
he have done if they had, in fact, been agreed to? The question
remained hypothetical, for the Mysore government overruled
the university authorities and, holding against Radhakrishnan
the fact that he had not been educated abroad, appointed
A. R. Wadia, a graduate from Cambridge, to the chair.[1]
C. R. Reddy, the principal of the Maharaja's College, who was
strongly in favour of Radhakrishnan, was unwilling to let the
matter rest and persuaded the university council to recommend
the creation of a second chair in philosophy and the appointment to it of Radhakrishnan. By this time out of the Presidency
College, Radhakrishnan was keener to join and reduced his
terms; he was now willing to come even on a temporary basis.
Again the Mysore government were reluctant; they first
objected to a second chair and, even after agreeing to it,
offered it to two scholars in Bengal. It was only on their declining that Radhakrishnan's name was finally approved.[2] The
anti-Brahmin feeling had now spread to Mysore state as well.[3]
Reddy, while prominent in the ranks of this movement, did
not, to his credit, allow it to colour his judgement of Radhakrishnan at this time; but Visvesvarayya, the dewan, although
a Brahmin, went along with caste currents on this issue.

So Radhakrishnan moved from Rajahmundry to Mysore as

[1] File 69 of 1917–18, Mysore University Archives: vice-chancellor of Mysore
University to Radhakrishnan, 3 October 1916.

[2] File 8 of 1917, General and Review Secretariat, Karnataka State Archives,
Bangalore.

[3] J. Manor, *Political Change in an Indian State: Mysore 1917–1950* (Delhi 1977),
pp. 14, 59.

additional professor of philosophy in July 1918. The appointment was for five years on a fixed monthly salary of Rs 500.
Recruited for being strong in Indian as well as the European
systems of philosophy, he lectured in both subjects and laid
down for himself a stiff course of study. He spent hours studying
the Sanskrit texts with the local pandits and then switched to
the continuance of an analysis of the writings of contemporary
thinkers on which he had already begun work before coming
to Mysore.

If Radhakrishnan's study of Tagore was in many ways the
product of a patriotic Indian scholar, his next publication in
1920 with a clumsy title, *The Reign of Religion in Contemporary
Philosophy* (hereafter *The Reign*), was a very professional effort.
His thesis was that philosophy, taken to its logical conclusion,
leads to absolute idealism and, if various forms of pluralistic
theism were prevalent in the Western world, it was because of
the subconscious interference of dogmatic religion with the
intellectual pursuit of philosophy. Though he did not say so,
Radhakrishnan was in fact criticizing the influence of Christianity. This was more explicit in the article written at about the
same time, where Radhakrishnan was scathing about the difficulties into which a philosopher like Clement Webb was led by
his belief in the personal God of Christianity, and suggested
that the philosophy of the Upanishads was more satisfying.[4] In
the final, constructive, section of the book too he contended
that the only religion consistent with philosophy was a spiritual, absolutist, non-dogmatic view of religion such as the
Vedanta. But this argument was not fully worked out and
forms the weakest section of the book, which was basically an
assault on the role of a religion dependent on authority. In a
sense, Radhakrishnan was an absolute idealist in the Western
tradition before he became a sympathetic exponent of the
Vedanta. A more precise title of the book would have been
'The Reign of the Christian Religion in Contemporary
Western Philosophy'.

As a philosophical work *The Reign* is a *tour de force*. A young
Indian who was hardly known took on all the leading thinkers
of the contemporary world and, playing expertly the game of
metaphysics, pointed out with originality and power what he

[4] 'The Future of Religion', *Mysore University Magazine*, July 1920.

4

felt to be their inadequacies. Reversing the trend of Eastern metaphysical speculations being viewed with European condescension, Radhakrishnan examined current schools of Western thought and found them inferior to the Upanishads. It is the intellectual confidence which astonishes. He wrote with the authority of one determined to make his readers take him at his own valuation. He was liberated from the domination of European thought and did not indulge in sycophantic paraphrase. He sent the relevant proof sheets to Bertrand Russell, James Ward, F. C. S. Schiller, Hastings Rashdall and Wildon Carr, the leading authority on Bergson in the English-speaking world; and such was the academic fraternity of those days that they all wrote back to the unknown professor from Mysore listing the points where they believed he had misconstrued them, but recognizing his right to his argument and not interfering with its substance.

Radhakrishnan later paid little attention to this book. It is not even mentioned in his account of his philosophical development written in 1950. He would probably have agreed with an American philosopher's later description of The Reign as part of Radhakrishnan's 'intellectual measles and wild oats'.[5] But it is not to be underrated, for it shows tough mental muscle and logical skill. Philosophy to him was an intellectual attempt to organize the whole of experience, and religion must not influence philosophy but be justified by it. Even religious feeling must pass through the fire of metaphysical thinking. Instead of trying to make philosophy religious, we should if possible make religion philosophical. No religious dogma should prejudice philosophy, which must, however, reckon with religious experience. Thought should help to support our beliefs but beliefs should not colour our thoughts. Religion is not the starting-point but the terminus of philosophy. Ethical and religious conclusions should not control philosophical discussions but philosophy must see whether they can be justified by hard reasoning.

True philosophy would result in true religion and to Radhakrishnan this was the Advaita Vedanta. This was the only philosophical religion which could be justified by logical

[5] G. P. Conger, 'Radhakrishnan's World', in P. A. Schilpp (ed.), The Philosophy of Sarvepalli Radhakrishnan (New York 1952), p. 87.

seriousness and not just by soft thinking, emotional fervour or moral earnestness. It was justified by reason and supported by philosophy. The religion of the spirit alone has a base in logic.

The book glittered with metaphysical brilliance and was written with wit and irony. Hogg toned down what seemed to him at times unnecessary abrasiveness, but even so there was enough polemic to give the book bite. Bergson was reproved for a 'cheap and facile monism', Ward's 'tender and sensitive fibres' were scorned, and contemporary Western philosophy in general was castigated for pandering to the common taste. 'If he requires a God, philosophy supplies him with one; if a ghost, it will also be supplied.' William James, Bergson and Russell were charged with producing 'romances of philosophy'.

When published in the summer of 1920, *The Reign* received considerable attention. Christian theologians were concerned by his implicit attack on Christianity. Clement Webb was critical in the *Times Literary Supplement* and advised Radhakrishnan to return to the subject after a more careful study of the past history and present character of the dominant religions of Europe and America. The reviewer in the *Glasgow Herald* had no use at all for Radhakrishnan's analysis. 'It is all rather wearisome, rather wooden, rather learned and quite unconvincing.'[6] But in philosophical circles the book was more favourably considered and was prescribed for study in a number of British and American universities as providing a clear and able exposition and discussion of the fundamentals of contemporary philosophy. Lord Haldane was impressed by Radhakrishnan's grasp of the Hegelian principle as well as by his extension to qualitative measurement of Einstein's theory of relativity by applying the principle of degrees in knowledge and reality.[7] McTaggart and Margoliouth congratulated him on his command of the English language.[8] Professor J. E. Turner of Liverpool, in a long review, found the viewpoint refreshing: 'The absolutist heavy artillery has re-opened with a well-directed barrage and not without having learned some valuable lessons from the tactics of its opponents.'[9] Professor

---

[6] *Glasgow Herald*, 26 June 1920.

[7] Lord Haldane to Radhakrishnan, 11 June 1920.

[8] J. E. McTaggart in the *Cambridge Review*, 19 November 1920; D. S. Margoliouth in *Church Family Newspaper*.　　[9] *Journal of Philosophy*, 3 March 1921.

E. L. Hinman chose as the subject of his presidential address to the western division of the American Philosophical Association in March 1921 idealism as delineated by Bosanquet and Radhakrishnan. For a young philosopher in a remote Indian university who had never visited the West to be linked on such a special occasion with one of the leading figures of British philosophy was in itself a signal distinction. 'To be coupled with Bosanquet', as Radhakrishnan wrote later, 'is an honour which more eminent men would covet.'[10] Hinman thought *The Reign* to be the best available book on the issues raised in the debate between absolute idealism and its opponents. Exceptionally well written, this defence of idealism by 'a champion of notable power' was 'mighty good reading'. But Hinman did not regard Radhakrishnan as irreligious; rather he had expounded a form of concrete idealism, a version of Samkara's Advaita as adapted by Western philosophical ideas and stressing development, growth and gradual progress towards perfection.[11]

Hinman's main criticism of the book was that the elements of a speculative theism which were inevitably involved in Radhakrishnan's position were not developed but rather quietly suppressed. Such validity as there is in this criticism was the result perhaps of the underlying contradiction in that position. All of Radhakrishnan's trenchant arguments against the distortions produced in philosophical thinking by religious faith could be used even against him. He was not such a total believer in logic as his comments on other philosophers suggest. He was no advocate of a personal God and had yet to reach an understanding of the relationship between God and the Absolute. He was, however, already essaying the explanation, which he was later to develop very fully, of intuition as being not in contrast to the intellect but the crown of the intellectual process, a completion of its labour, a comprehension which sees things as a whole. Unguided by reason, intuition becomes instinct, but when supported by it becomes divine. Intuition does not cease to be rational merely because reason is tran-

10 'My Search for Truth', in Ferm, p. 24.

11 E. L. Hinman, review of *The Reign*, and presidential address, 'Modern Idealism and the Logos Teaching', *The Philosophical Review*, November 1920, pp. 582–6, and July 1921, pp. 333–51, respectively.

scended. But this is a slippery argument which requires much greater attention than Radhakrishnan was able to give in *The Reign*; and this becomes more noticeable because Radhakrishnan, writing before the publication of Bergson's *The Two Sources of Morality and Religion*, was severely critical of Bergson's concept of intuition. Indeed, no one puts the argument against intuition better than he does at one point: 'There is no need to surrender hard thinking and take to intuition and such other doubtful remedies.'[12]

The other element in this book which draws away from Radhakrishnan's vigorous defence of reason and logic is his unqualified appreciation of what he describes as true mysticism as against magic and occultism. Such mystics, he says, can speak with direct authority in matters of religious belief. They have known reality at first hand and, living at different times and places, corroborate each other. Radhakrishnan argued that absolute idealism can contain the mystic element in man and is not in disagreement with the conclusion of the mystics that spirit is the all-inclusive reality and the world a divine manifestation. But the non-rational element in mysticism went against the whole drift of Radhakrishnan's approach.

*The Reign*, therefore, is a germinal book but not a mature one. It was a pyrotechnic display, compelling Western readers to recognize that Indian philosophers not merely, as was generally thought, 'collected opinions', but in original reflection and acuteness of analysis were as good as anyone else in the world.[13] Though many of the bricks with which Radhakrishnan was to erect in later years his philosophical system are to be found here—absolute idealism, an adapted form of Advaita Vedanta, intuition unopposed to intellect, the mystic grasp of truth— much integration was still required. There were a number of loose ends and seemingly contradictory positions in a path-clearing work. But he had marked out for himself a special place among the different schools of philosophical thought then prevailing, and in the years to come he consolidated this position as an absolute idealist, anchored in the tradition of

[12] *The Reign*, p. 267.
[13] See the comment of Sir Henry Jones on S. N. Dasgupta's manuscript on Indian philosophy, 19 April 1920, Macmillan Archive, section x, Readers' Reports, third series 55988, folio 155.

the Upanishads but open to other influences.

Yet perhaps *The Reign* is important not just for its substance or even for its significance in Radhakrishnan's philosophical development. It symbolizes the new robustness and confidence of Indian thinkers, a fresh step in the shaking off of the mental shackles of the raj. This assertion of the spirit of independent enquiry from the Indian standpoint was of immense importance to the further achievement of modern Indian thought.

## II

During his years in Mysore Radhakrishnan was bubbling over with creative energy and, even while putting together his effort in metaphysics, startlingly tried his hand at a novel. The plot of 'The Crime of Leela' is simple. There are seven interacting characters, six of them highly educated. Chandra, a Cambridge graduate and a civil servant, is married to Leela. Though deeply in love, they married by arrangement and have a child on whom they dote. Their friend Sekhar is the professor of philosophy at the local university. Patriotic, a fearless visionary though no hater of the British, a clever orator and interested primarily in matters of the mind and spirit, he is attractive to women. Rohini, Chandra's sister, also a product of Cambridge and a student of philosophy, falls in love with him; but Sekhar is married and determined to be faithful. He is the version of the New Man, recently described as 'passive and exemplary'.[14] The comic relief is provided by Narad, Sekhar's colleague in the university. Obscurantist yet ambitious, pompous and worldly wise, a poor scholar who makes his way in the world by flaunting the spurious glories of ancient India while all the time toadying to British authority, Narad is also the villain of the story. Attached to his wife Kamala but resentful of her desire to be treated as an equal, he traces what he regards as her new-fangled and erroneous ideas to Leela's influence and in revenge hints to Chandra that his wife is having an affair with Sekhar. The gullible Chandra is taken in and sends Leela back to her parents. By the time he is convinced that she is innocent, it is too late; the pining Leela has died of sorrow.

[14] D. Kiberd, *Men and Feminism in Modern Literature* (London 1985).

This is by no means a gripping tale; and the writing is not stylish, falters at times in idiom and occasionally descends to cheap melodrama. For example: 'He gave her a look of fire, bit his lips and passed out of her presence like whirlwind.' But it is only fair to add that we are discussing a draft and Radhakrishnan would no doubt have chiselled the text before dispatching it to the publishers. The characters too are not complex or vividly drawn. There is obviously much of the author himself in Sekhar; and the other characters are clearly based on friends and acquaintances in Madras and Mysore. But Radhakrishnan was attempting a novel of ideas, and the main interest is expected to lie not in the narrative or the depiction of personalities but in the dialogue and the exchange of thoughts. The action takes place between the years 1905, when the swadeshi movement was inaugurated, and 1915 or 1916, after the world war has broken out; and the locale is Bengal, of which Radhakrishnan had at this time no firsthand knowledge but which he regarded as the most forward-looking province in India. The politics are broadly nationalist. Terrorism is rejected, and support to Britain in the war is recommended because she is expected to implement certain ideals in India. The country's weaknesses were a rigid caste system, an anti-democratic outlook, a false sense of fatality which deprived human beings of spirit and spontaneity, and a wrong view of human nature which held asceticism to be the goal of existence. The views which Radhakrishnan put forward consistently throughout his life on the subject of religion are also to be found here; that there is no one way to God, that true religion is not renunciation but love and service, that Hinduism should discard dead ideals and lifeless beliefs and nurture the true values of spirit. The classical scriptures provided emotional satisfaction, moral inspiration and spiritual solace; but their vital essence was being almost smothered by accidental accretions, and these had to be chopped off. So long as there was a premium on blind credulity, abject dependence and dumb acquiescence to authority, India could not attain freedom.

The main theme of the novel, however, is the role of women. Radhakrishnan was steeped in Tagore and had obviously been impressed by Ibsen and Shaw. Tagore's novel *Gora* had not yet

been translated into English but Radhakrishnan was aware of
its general drift and familiar with Tagore's portrayal of the
Bengali woman caught in the cross-currents of tradition and
reform. The influence of these three writers can clearly be seen
in Radhakrishnan's characterization of the New Woman in the
Indian context. Four women dominate the story, Leela,
Rohini, Kamala and Sekhar's wife, who does not appear but,
though absent, is a powerful influence. Leela is the mixture of
the old and the new and modelled on Nora in Ibsen's *A
Doll's House*. She wishes to marry for love but floats a lamp on
the Ganga to ascertain the decree of destiny. She regards a
loveless marriage as unclean traffic in souls, but opts for a conventional approach to the man she favours and places the
responsibility for her conduct on God. The author justifies this.
'To the people of India, the commonplace world of commerce
and industry, law and politics, is a gigantic dream while the
world of the Unseen is the supreme reality. The Hindu woman
is in touch with this Unseen World.' After marriage, she seeks
to please her husband in all things—'To me there is no other
God but you'—but regards herself as an equal comrade and
companion. Motherhood is her greatest joy; but her effort to
combine 'the natural eloquence of wifely devotion' with a
frank and open demeanour ends in tragedy.

Her sister-in-law, Rohini, starts at the other end. She
returns from Cambridge a free thinker with an undisciplined
intelligence. 'Some support', comments the author disapprov-
ingly, 'is necessary for life rather than none though that be a
chain or a prison.' She throws herself at Sekhar with the
argument that a man may live for himself but not a woman;
she who tries to do so has yet to learn the secret of life. Sekhar
spurns her because his marriage is important to him, a sacred
bond, the holiest relation in life. Rohini then offers to be his
mistress; her radicalism leads her to the view that morality is
moonshine. Again Sekhar declines; and when Rohini cites
Ibsen and Shaw in her own favour, he replies that they are
'mystical anarchists' and to act on their assertion of individual
wills would make a madness of this earth. To him there can be
no love of a woman outside marriage. Rohini quietly yields,
accepts sexless love and is even triumphant about it: 'A new
spirit is being born within my being.' She talks of India's

ancient heroines and preaches to Leela the virtues of suffering: 'the child of love, the dearest thing in God's universe ... Sadness helps us to put our souls in order.' One should accept one's fate with faith in the underlying harmony of the universe.

Perhaps Radhakrishnan was in Rohini carrying the argument much further than he himself believed; for he combined faith with a rejection of determinism. A more sympathetically drawn character is Narad's wife, Kamala. She is an unselfconscious, uneducated girl from the village, 'a woman of a soft heart and an impressionable nature, clever without cunning, simple without being petty and good-natured without being aware of it'. She is loyal to her husband but, after meeting Leela and Sekhar, demands that Narad share his work with her and give her a chance to develop. She wishes to be treated as a human being and not as a female animal. By acting on the premiss that if the bondage of women were lifted the whole social fabric would collapse, he was killing the woman in her. There was joy when two hearts lived a complete life in ardent love, fervent hope and sweet faith. Joy was not just a selfish aim at pleasure, the wretched gospel of the sensualist, but the motive power of the universe, a good that all ought to desire.[15]

Radhakrishnan, with indefatigable zest, planned a series of novels depicting the changing India, of how, in his view, the people should react to the contact with Western ideas and absorb these into Indian tradition. The blend of the new with the old should result in securing the best of both worlds. The title page of 'The Crime of Leela' designates it as the first of the stories of Indian life in transition. Radhakrishnan wished the novel to appear under a pseudonym, 'R.S.', probably because he felt it would seem undignified for a professor of philosophy to be writing romantic novels. The best of philosophers clearly like to be both Spinoza and Stendhal; but in the India of that time this was not easily acceptable. It is said that Radhakrishnan's publishers—at this stage Macmillan—would only consider it if the author's name was disclosed, so the idea of publication fell through. Meantime, Muirhead suggested to Radhakrishnan that he prepare a standard and comprehensive

[15] In analysing this novel I have had the benefit of a discussion with Keshav Desiraju.

account of Indian philosophical development, and this entailed such detailed study that Radhakrishnan let drop his
plans for parallel writing of fiction. It was just as well that he
concentrated his talents on philosophy, for he had not the
imagination and style appropriate to a novelist. His first effort
was thin and anaemic. Radhakrishnan's experience of the
world was still limited, and wide reading is no substitute. He
could not in this novel move out of academic élitism. All the
characters are bloodless and one-dimensional. One of them,
for example, when having nothing to do, casually picks up a
copy of Mind. The writing too lacks verve. It is replete with
quotations—among the authors cited are Nietzsche, Renan,
Hardy and Browning, apart from Ibsen and Shaw, Kalidasa
and Tagore; but the narrative does not take off on its own.
The novel certainly did not come up to the standards Radhakrishnan later set for creative literature—that it should be
not intellectual but spiritual, that it should bring out the full
meaning of life, and shake, exhaust and cleanse the reader.
'The Crime of Leela' suffers, to use Radhakrishnan's words on
a later occasion and in another context, from a secret sterility.[16]

The sole interest of the manuscript today is the light it
throws on Radhakrishnan's views and opinions. He was a
nationalist and felt that, while Indians were able, generous,
clever and patriotic, all these qualities were like a feather in the
balance because most Indians were lacking in character. This
emphasis on the importance of character runs through all his
utterances in the coming years. Similarly, his views on women
as delineated in this novel also remained basically unaltered.
Radhakrishnan recognized that women were the equals of men
and there was no justification for sexual discrimination. Indeed
he argued that this was enjoined in the ancient scriptures which
provided women with the rights to education and to seek their
own fulfilment. But he also believed that by nature they were
endowed with an immense capacity for suffering and their
natural vocation was service rather than achievement. Men are
lost in the routine of activity with no time for reflection and self-
awareness; and it is the task of women, with their capacity for

[16] An Idealist View of Life (London 1932), p. 161; 'Moral Values in Literature',
speech at the first All-India Writers Conference 1945, Indian Writers in Council
(Bombay 1947), p. 89.

restraint and patience, to refine men. Women should not become masculine in temperament and behaviour; they were made to love. Double standards were really a compliment to women, for by this was accepted their natural superiority. In the language of feminists this is 'pedestal treatment', romanticizing women so that they remain unaware of their condition.[17]

Radhakrishnan was also of the view that the service of which women were capable was best performed within the bond of marriage. The normal life for women was marriage and motherhood. It is of interest that he arranged the marriages of his five daughters when they were between eleven and sixteen years of age without bothering to secure their consent, and indeed sometimes even without his having seen the bridegroom before the day of the ceremony. This was partly because he assumed that marriages were made in heaven, and to an extent because he was confident he could take care of the careers of the men lucky enough to be chosen, so that his daughters need never lack in comfort. But his attitude also indicates that, whatever his utterances, his instinctive outlook was that women were made for men. In this he was very much an Indian of his generation, with the difference that he could clothe his conservative views in noble sentiment:

India in every generation has produced millions of women who have never found fame, but whose daily existence has helped to civilize the race, and whose warmth of heart, self-sacrificing zeal, unassuming loyalty and strength in suffering, when subjected to trials of extreme severity, are among the glories of this ancient race.[18]

But before we move to judgement we would do well to recall that even a radical thinker nearer our own times, Sartre, believed that the woman's role was on the emotional plane; it was a question not of inferiority but of different dispositions. Because of various material and social relations, women retained their sensibility unimpaired.[19] Simone de Beauvoir herself agreed that certain 'feminine' qualities, such as a healthy distance from hierarchies, tolerance of competition, patience

[17] Juliet Mitchell, *Women: The Longest Revolution* (London 1984), p. 104.
[18] *Religion and Society* (London 1947), pp. 197–8.
[19] Simone de Beauvoir, *Adieux: A Farewell to Sartre* (London 1984), pp. 298–9.

and a straightforward manner, though products of oppression, ought to be retained after liberation.[20]

## III

Such unbending commitment to philosophical and creative writing proclaims a remarkable intensity of purpose. As Trollope says of one of his characters, he was a man who had long resolved that his life should be a success. But in Radhakrishnan this driving will did not have a crippling effect and divest him of distracting interests. There was a human side to the philosopher and he did not retreat from life. Too high-spirited to hide himself behind his work, he attracted and dominated those round him by his infectious vitality and a sense of fun which was never still. He had no close companions; but Hiriyanna, the Sanskrit scholar, was a respected colleague; and Wadia in the department of philosophy and K. T. Shah, the professor of commerce, were good friends. In their company Radhakrishnan went for walks, played bridge, and disclosed the element of play about him, the sparkle of mischief which found little room in the wider sprawl of Madras or the limited environs of Rajahmundry. While earlier he had been known for his kindheartedness and sense of friendship, it was Mysore which for the first time provided scope for his social graces, tending at times even to mild exuberance.

It was also at Mysore that Radhakrishnan, no longer compelled to concentrate on making his way in an inhospitable world, found time for sexual adventurousness. Till now he and his wife had been held close by the ordinary difficulties of living; in Mysore, with relative success and an ampler life, there was room for a wandering of desires. The affair with the neighbour's wife was to set the pattern for the long series of involvements of which this was the first. As time passed they formed a fairly constant undercurrent to the decorum of his outward life. But self-indulgence carried with it no emotional investment; he showed his mistresses consideration and, while the relationship lasted, was generous with time, support and money; but he never gave them even the semblance of love.

[20] A Schwarzer, *Simone de Beauvoir Today: Conversations 1972-1982* (London 1984), p. 78.

He looked, in these marginal and temporary attachments of the senses, for no intellectual partnership; all the women whom he accepted in his life were of superficial mind, some enjoyed dubious reputations and many were dominating and hysterical. Radhakrishnan's liaisons put one in mind of Cyril Connolly's remark that the punishment of continual philandering resides in the successes even more than in the failures. One's wonder at how Radhakrishnan could have endured such women is tempered by the knowledge that, having embarked on these affairs, he ended them at the first opportunity, though such an opportunity was often long in coming. The company of women, of which he was a compulsive seeker, was like gossip and light reading, an agreeable way of passing the time in the intervals of concentrated work and thought. H. G. Wells summed up this requirement: 'To make love periodically, with some grace and pride and freshness, seems to be, for most of us, a necessary condition to efficient working.'[21] But to Radhakrishnan, as for Wells, these affairs diversified but did not disorganize his life. They did not deflect him from his serious purposes and he did not expect them to upset his marital harmony. The women who moved in and out of his life were bit-players, acting against the backdrop of a stable marriage and a wife with whom he had his only deep and lasting relationship. While various women helped to keep him youthful, he was of the same view as Bernard Shaw: 'The deeper fidelities are, however, untouched.'[22]

An air of general friendliness and a new interest in women did not encompass the whole of Radhakrishnan's social efforts in Mysore. His main constituency was the students. His lectures, clear and lightened with touches of humour, drew many from other departments. But a teacher's reputation depends on much more than teaching alone. Radhakrishnan commanded attention and affection by the atmosphere created by his personality. Striking in appearance, with the definite features of a finely modelled face revealed more clearly by the removal of his moustache in 1919, dressed with elegant distinction and erect of carriage, Radhakrishnan looked the embodiment of humane

[21] G. P. Wells (ed.), *H. G. Wells in Love* (London 1984), p. 67.
[22] Bernard Shaw to Lillah McCarthy, *circa* 2 August 1912. *Collected Letters 1911–1925* (London 1985), p. 101.

authority. His powerful memory enabled him to recognize each one of his students and he was natural with them, treating them with an unaffected familiarity and concerning himself with their problems. Though still unable to afford even small luxuries, he was generous with money. While he never talked about his early years of steep poverty, the memory of them made assistance to all who sought it an unquestioned habit. He kept an open house. On special occasions anyone could join his family for a meal, and many frequently did. But it was recognized that there was more to Radhakrishnan than a beguiling and unemphatic charm. The modest exterior could not conceal the person aware of his powers and content to be himself; the gentleness and nobility were rooted in the poise and confidence of the inner life.

Nor did he care, especially after the massacre at Amritsar in April 1919, to conceal his opinions on political issues. In these days and in the years to follow he often felt the urge to jump into the political struggle, but was held back by the need to earn a living and look after a large and growing family. But there was comfort in the thought that even his philosophical writings were a form of committed political action. Radhakrishnan was confident that his work, born of faith in himself and inspired by the pride of patriotism, had its own contribution to make to the national effort. Every individual can best help the cause by using his own weapons. In his classes, while laying stress on spiritual values and intellectual standards, he also drew attention to the strength and validity of the essentials of Indian culture, grieved at the country's misfortunes and rejoiced at the signs of revival. 'He captivated us by his elusiveness, and one could never understand him fully; unperceived excellences were always coming into view and genius was stamped on every one of his actions; he was uncommon in everything.'[23] In November 1919, when the students showed

---

[23] Professor M. V. Krishna Rao, 'Our Alma Mater through One Hundred Years', *Maharaja's College Centenary Commemoration Volume* (Mysore 1951), p. 43. For Radhakrishnan's relations with his students in Mysore I have also relied on three books in Kannada: V. Sitaramayya, *College Dinagalu* (Bangalore 1971); S. K. Sarma, *Dipa Mala* (Dharwar 1971); and A. N. Moorthy Rao, *Chitra-galu Patra-galu* (Bangalore 1983). I have had too the benefit of conversations with Nittoor Srinivasa Rao.

some reluctance to observe silence for two minutes on Armistice Day, Radhakrishnan persuaded them to do so by asking them to think also of the men and women who had been killed by British soldiers in the Punjab. Testimony to his hold over the students was provided the next year by his election as vice-president of the newly constituted union, the president being the principal *ex officio*.

# 3

## THE GEORGE V CHAIR

For all his engrossment in the higher reaches of philosophy, Radhakrishnan was a shrewd man of the world. His letters to his publishers reveal a knowing interest in the sales of his books; and he had a sound grasp of the mechanics of dignified career-making. While well-regarded by his colleagues and esteemed by the students at the University of Mysore, he was aware that the Government of Mysore were not appreciative of his work. They had, for example, made no move to secure his services on a permanent basis. So, when in 1920, the post of professor of philosophy in the Presidency College was allotted to the Indian Educational Service, Radhakrishnan let the Government of Madras know that, if promoted from the provincial service and offered that professorship, he was prepared to return from Mysore. His claims were now stronger than before because since 1917 he had written a number of articles in such journals as *Mind* and published two major works which had received wide and favourable notice. He had also in Candeth a vigorous lobbyist in Madras. But the British officials in the department of education were still unwilling to set aside the claims of the person who had displaced Radhakrishnan in the Presidency College in 1917. He contended that he was not only a non-Brahmin but, as a Jain, a non-Hindu; and, as Candeth observed privately to Radhakrishnan, the British officials, being mostly mediocre, had no wish to see seniority overlooked because that was the main argument on which they themselves relied. So Radhakrishnan appealed over their heads to Lionel Davidson, the member of the governor's council in charge of education. All he wanted was to teach philosophy at the Presidency College; if offered that opportunity he was willing to come back even as a member of the provincial service.

On the other hand, if promoted to the all-India service but
posted elsewhere he would stay out of the Madras presidency
till a second professorship was created at the Presidency
College.[1] Davidson did not set aside the promotion of the other
claimant to the all-India service or his posting to the Presidency
College; but he secured the appointment of Radhakrishnan as
well to the higher service and the offer to him of a posting
either at another college in Madras or at Rajahmundry. That
Davidson went out of his way to give Radhakrishnan at least
part of what he had sought was due neither to Radhakrishnan's
representations nor to the impression made by his books nor
to Candeth's bluff that Radhakrishnan had been offered a
chair at Calcutta. The decision was brought about by the
accident of the British philosopher J. S. Mackenzie passing
through Madras on his way home from Colombo and, dining
at Government House, finding himself seated next to Davidson.
Making conversation, Davidson asked Mackenzie for his opinion of Radhakrishnan as well as of his rival. Mackenzie
replied that Radhakrishnan was the ablest philosopher in
India but he had not heard of the other man. To Davidson
this clinched the matter. As for Radhakrishnan, true to his
word, as he had been denied the post at the Presidency
College, he never returned to teaching service in the Madras
presidency.

The story of Candeth about the chair in Calcutta was not a
total fantasy. The first holder of the King George V professorship of mental and moral sciences, Brajendranath Seal, was, in
the summer of 1920, appointed vice-chancellor of Mysore University; and Sir Ashutosh Mukherjee, the vice-chancellor of
Calcutta University, was keen on getting the best man in
India as Seal's successor. Travelling south that autumn he was
told by his host in Madras, Sir P. S. Sivaswami Iyer, who was
always supportive of Radhakrishnan, that he should pull
Radhakrishnan out of Mysore. Mukherjee seems also to have
consulted the British missionary philosophers in Bengal, particularly George Howells and W. S. Urquhart, and they approved of the suggestion. Urquhart had recently written a

[1] S. Radhakrishnan to L. Davidson, 11 and 30 October 1920. Madras Govt.
Home Dept. (Education) file, 14 December 1920, nos. 1500–1. Miscellaneous.
Tamil Nadu Archives.

5

warm review of *The Reign* in the *Calcutta Review* and, while
obviously not in full agreement with Radhakrishnan's views,
thought highly of his intellectual powers.

So Mukherjee decided to appoint Radhakrishnan, just
thirty-two years of age, on the basis of the creative promise of
his two books. He sent word to Radhakrishnan that it would
be difficult to invite him to accept the appointment because
many older men were in the running but that he should
formally apply when the chair was advertised.[2] Radhakrishnan complied, for a posting to the Presidency College was still
uncertain. The University of Mysore woke up to the probabi-
lity of losing Radhakrishnan and hastily thought of offering him
a permanent appointment coupled with a steep rise in salary.
But the Mysore government deferred a decision till the University of Calcutta had made an appointment and, unaware
that Radhakrishnan's application was a formality, pettily
failed to forward along with it the commendation by the vice-
chancellor of Mysore of Radhakrishnan's work as a teacher.
Radhakrishnan, however, came to know of this from a friend
in the registrar's office and, after protesting to the government,
persuaded the university to send it direct to Calcutta.[3]

In November 1920, therefore, with his appointment to the
George V chair and the decision to promote him to the Indian
Educational Service, Radhakrishnan had at last, from the
viewpoint of his professional career, arrived. The struggle for
acceptance was finally over. His star quality was manifest and
he was set on a rapidly rising curve of recognition. The George
V professorship was the most prestigious chair in philosophy in
India and doubled his salary from Rs 500 to Rs 1000 a month.
It pushed a little into the background the vicissitudes of
ordinary life from which he had so far suffered—poverty,
domestic obligations, the wear-and-tear of the struggle for
economic security. Both his youthful confidence in the future
and his sturdy confidence in his fate seemed justified. The
remarkable assurance in his own intellectual capacity and in
his staying power had carried him through very hard times.

Yet, after telling Davidson proudly that he would not come
back to Madras and requesting the University of Mysore to

relieve him by the end of February 1921, Radhakrishnan felt slightly uneasy at the thought of shifting to Calcutta. Life in Bengal in a position of dignity offered wider horizons than in Mysore; and Bengal was to him, as his novel showed, that part of the country which provided imaginative and emotional stimulus. Above all, it was the home of Tagore. But he had not even travelled north of Rajahmundry and was accustomed to sheltered employment and the local landscape. He had now to face moving, with his wife, five daughters and a crowd of dependants to a place which seemed over the edge of the world, whose language he did not speak and where he knew no one. His diffidence was increased by anonymous letters, obviously inspired by unsuccessful aspirants to the chair, warning him that non-Bengalis were not welcome in Calcutta and no one who did not eat fish could hope to survive in that city. 'I had literally', said Reddy later, 'to bundle Radhakrishnan out of Mysore.'[4] Radhakrishnan even wrote to Sir Ashutosh Mukherjee that he was young and could afford to wait for a while before aspiring to what was virtually the Regius chair in philosophy in India, only to get the terse but cordial reply that the vice-chancellor was expecting to see Radhakrishnan in Calcutta by March 1921.

So Radhakrishnan, subduing his nervousness and misgivings, migrated from Mysore to Calcutta. In the last week of February 1921 he handed over charge; and, as he had declined to attend any formal functions to bid him farewell, the students converted the occasion of his departure into such a function. That scene has become a part of the history of Mysore city. The horses were detached from his carriage and students in harness pulled it to the station. There the platform was wreathed with flowers and the compartment packed with roses. Almost the whole university, faculty and students, turned up to see Radhakrishnan off. The traffic on all roads leading to the station was held up for hours and the crowd was such that other passengers found it extremely difficult to get through. As the train pulled out, hours late, to resounding cheers, Radhakrishnan, like many others present, was moved to tears. 'There is no saying', wrote J. C. Rollo, the professor

---

[4] C. R. Reddy to K. Iswara Dutt, quoted in K. I. Dutt (ed.), *Sarvepalli Radhakrishnan* (Delhi 1966), p. 89.

of English, 'what distinction Mr. Radhakrishnan will attain to,
but he will never receive more convincing honours than were
bestowed on him that night.'[5] That was true enough. Long
years after, towards the end of his life, Radhakrishnan recognized that of the many gatherings in various parts of the
world that had assembled in his honour, the farewell at Mysore
station in 1921 stood way ahead.

## II

To introduce Radhakrishnan to Calcutta, Sir Ashutosh
Mukherjee arranged for him to deliver a public lecture on a
philosophical topic. The large Senate Hall was crowded and
Radhakrishnan made the expected impact with his wide range
and quick fluency. But he felt a coolness in the department
among the senior members, much older to him and, in addition, disappointed applicants for the chair; and their feelings
found voice in the snarling of a section of the local press. So
Radhakrishnan withdrew into himself and did no more in the
university than what was required of the holder of the chair.
Till 1926 he was not even a member of the senate and ignored
Mukherjee's hints that he concern himself more with the
business of the university. Even on the vice-chancellor he
called only thrice during the three years from 1921 till Mukherjee's death in 1924. Kiron Mukherji and Basanta Kumar
Mallik, two younger philosophers, shared with Radhakrishnan
an interest in European philosophy; but the close bond with
Mallik emerged only in the late twenties. Radhakrishnan's
only friend at this time was the physicist C. V. Raman, also
still not fully at home in Calcutta and a fellow-victim of such
resentment as there was of non-Bengalis. When not in the
department Radhakrishnan remained mostly at home. But the
modest houses he rented during those years in various parts of
Calcutta were always full of people. Hospitable beyond his
means, there were at all times one or two poor students staying
with him, while visitors from the south, be it tourists or delegates to academic conferences or Congress sessions, used his
residence as a camping place. Radhakrishnan also had a
dutiful sense of obligation to his brothers and sister as well as

5 *Mysore University Magazine*, May 1921, p. 85.

to his now widowed mother, and usually some of them were with him in Calcutta. It was only in 1938, after his elder brother's betrayal of trust and recourse to litigation on ridiculous charges, that Radhakrishnan secured a formal dissolution of the joint family.

Teeming with people as the house usually was, it did not distract Radhakrishnan from the work he had begun at Mysore on a survey of Indian philosophy. He never in his life studied at a desk; in later days, whenever he could, he lay in bed. In these years, stretched out on a mat, insatiable in his appetite for work, he read and wrote for long hours. A flood of paper, in chaotic bits and pieces which often only he could read, fell from the cataract of his pen. He sifted and pared intensely in search of clarity, smoothness, the easy flow of argument, the exact word, the striking parallel. This was contented absorption; and a saying of the Buddha, 'concentration is the joy of the mind', was always one of his favourite quotations. The intense work on hand also left no time for sensual discursiveness; and the early years in Calcutta marked a new phase of closeness between husband and wife. But the unremitting toil, rigorous logic and racking thought took their toll, and Radhakrishnan began now to suffer from insomnia, a torture which was to plague him for the rest of his life.

*Indian Philosophy* was a massive work in two volumes, the first published in 1923 and the second in 1927. Muirhead, who had planned to include them in the distinguished 'Library of Philosophy' series of which he was the editor, was himself so taken aback by the size and the cost of printing, with Sanskrit passages in Roman script and diacritical marks, that he left the final decision to the publishers, George Allen and Unwin. The head of the firm, Stanley Unwin, was shrewd enough to see the potential of this work and recognized that steady sales over the years would soon cover the heavy costs at the start. So he agreed to bring out the two volumes, totalling about 1480 pages, in full, as they stood. This was the beginning of a long association between Radhakrishnan and Allen and Unwin. They published most of his later works, and consulted him on manuscripts by Indians or about India submitted to them. Radhakrishnan was an astute man of business and, clearheaded about the printing and sales of his own works, gave opinions on the commercial aspects of the writings of other persons which proved 'so extraordinarily exact'.[6] Out of these transactions developed a close personal friendship between Radhakrishnan and Sir Stanley Unwin and his nephew Philip Unwin; and, whatever the office he held, no visit of Radhakrishnan to London was complete without a visit to the offices of Allen and Unwin in Museum Street. He would first make suggestions about his books without insisting on them—'Well, see to the thing, will you?'—and then settle down to a relaxing discussion on the state of the world.[7]

Radhakrishnan did not call his work a history of Indian philosophy, not so much because Dasgupta was at this time bringing out a series of volumes with that title as because he regarded his own effort as an interpretative survey rather than a chronicle. His purpose was, with neither looseness nor pedantry, to set Indian thinkers in their context, look at the world through their eyes and interpret them at their best, discarding what was dated and drawing attention to the enduring elements in their thought. Philosophers, even religious teachers, do not exist in a vacuum; they do not step out of history and are subject to their time. All thought is a dialogue with circumstance, and philosophical systems can be understood only in relation to their time and place. They are visions of reality reflected in the mirrors of men's minds. They can only be grasped if we take into account the habits of thought on which they are based and the viewpoints from which they look at the world. Every great thinker works out a hypothesis which seeks to satisfy the aspirations of the time and harmonize the results of current knowledge and new insights. A teacher like the Buddha is at once a prophet and the exponent of the time spirit; he focuses the strivings of his age and gives voice to the unsystematized thinking of his contemporaries. One does not have to accept any one school and reject others; each is an approximation of the truth and its study can prove rewarding.

So Radhakrishnan, unlike earlier European writers who wrote as antiquarians of early India as a perished civilization,

---

[6] Philip Unwin to S. Radhakrishnan, 22 December 1936.

[7] Stanley Unwin, *The Truth about a Publisher* (London 1960), p. 199; Philip Unwin, *The Publishing Unwins* (London 1972), pp. 101–2, 142; M. C. Chagla, *Roses in December* (Bombay 1973), p. 321.

recreated the atmosphere in which each thinker functioned, and leavened the pure world of scholarship with a feeling for life. He reconstructed the arguments of the ancient texts and assessed them in relation both to the debates which formed their original context and to modern controversies. The text is the point of mediation between two minds, and the interpretation must not only satisfy the curiosity but disturb the consciousness of the present-day reader. Though Radhakrishnan disclaimed being a historian this was intellectual history of a high quality: the re-enactment of past thought in the historian's mind, his forming a judgement of its value in the context of his own knowledge. It is not to be wondered at that Collingwood, the foremost exponent of this method in the English-speaking world, became an unreserved admirer of Radhakrishnan's learning, understanding, sympathy and insight.

In studying the philosophical thought of the past Radhakrishnan regarded as senseless the notion of an uninterpreted text. One should not see only with the eyes of the dead. Great thinkers are of their time without being walled in by it; they are liberating forces as well as representative of their age. Mere exposition, or erudition, running, in Marc Bloch's phrase, in neutral gear, was of scant use. One should be faithful to the spirit rather than to the letter and with 'creative logic', as distinct from linguistic analysis, piece together the living truth in those doctrines. The historian of philosophy should be a critic and an interpreter and not merely a mechanical ragpicker.[8] The recounting of texts was a small part of the task; one had to draw inferences, suggest meanings and formulate theories which would introduce some order into the vast and shapeless mass of unrelated facts. There was no point in a dead study of 'inert ideas', defined by Whitehead as ideas received without being utilized and tested or thrown into fresh combination and so forming the enemy of all intellectual culture.

In such interpretation Radhakrishnan's endeavour was to expound Indian thought in terms which related it to the Western tradition. Ignorance in other countries of the philosophy of India was mainly due to the unattractive clothing in

[8] 'Indian Philosophy: Some Problems', *Mind*, April 1926, reprinted as an appendix in *Indian Philosophy*, volume 1 (second edition 1929), pp. 671–703.

which it was set out.[9] Radhakrishnan tried to avoid jargon, to explain the special terms used in Indian texts which were not easily rendered into English, to draw parallels with Western thought and cite from European literature. He compared the teachings of the Buddha and of Bergson, explained Hinayana Buddhism with a quotation from Ibsen and, while discussing Buddhism, on one page cited Kant, Schopenhauer, Berkeley and Leibniz. His inner nature, as *The Reign* had shown, was akin both to the philosophy of his own people and to that of the West; he thus sought to demonstrate that Indian thought was not an esoteric creation of interest only to pandits but a bright chapter in the history of the human mind which should be a part of every man's heritage and enter into the blood-stream of world culture. European missionaries had studied Indian thought with a preconceived determination to confirm the superiority of Christian civilization, while in reaction some Indian scholars had made up their minds to prove that, in matters of philosophy and religion at any rate, India was far superior. But neither imperialist nor nationalist attitudes were safe guides in comparative studies. Only mutual respect could enable an understanding which would reveal what was still vital in Indian thought. 'There is hardly any height of spiritual insight or rational philosophy attained in the world that has not its parallel in the vast stretch that lies between the early Vedic seers and the modern Naiyayikas.'[10] The thinkers of ancient India had grappled with the basic problems of life and formulated theories which had not lost their value. These could be discussed in terms of modern thought and related to the living issues of philosophy and religion without playing tricks with the evidence or substituting current arguments for ancient lines of thought. The modern interpreter had to re-capture the spirit of life and convert it to fresh purposes. Scholarship required such vitality to loosen the choking hold of traditions and recall attention to the inner core of truth.

Some readers felt that Radhakrishnan tended to lay too much emphasis on the similarities between Indian and Western thought and, in his desire to find parallels, pressed

[9] Radhakrishnan to Bertrand Russell, 3 October 1923, Russell Archives, McMaster University Library.
[10] *Indian Philosophy*, volume I, p. 8.

THE GEORGE V CHAIR

too much meaning out of the original texts. But, on the whole, it was recognized that he had provided impressive witness to the universality of certain fundamental truths.[11] Bertrand Russell, already interested in Buddhism, was particularly attracted by Radhakrishnan's exposition.[12] It was here that Radhakrishnan first put forward the thesis to which he adhered all his life, that the Buddha's silence on metaphysical questions should not be interpreted as atheism or agnosticism. Russell gave the book a friendly review[13] and, nearly forty years later, commended Radhakrishnan not only for the precision and high intelligence he had brought to world problems but for having served to make the culture of India one of the glories of human achievement.[14]

Hinduism, unlike the Semitic religions, lacks a structure, is not linear, has no single sacred text, is not organized by a church. Even the term Hinduism came into vogue only in the nineteenth century as a portmanteau word to cover a diversity of sects.[15] Radhakrishnan was aware of this and so carefully entitled his work not Hindu but Indian philosophy, a survey of the ideas of Brahminical Hinduism and of the reactions to them before the advent to the country of Islam and Christianity. He did not make the absurd claim that they had seeped down through all the layers of society, but he did see in the development of these ideas in the highest reaches of Hinduism, even if understood only by a few men at the top, an organic intellectual growth rather than a random succession of change on change. In tracing this evolution of thought Radhakrishnan did not fly a banner or strive to establish preferences. But, like all good historians, he did not deny his sympathies or suppress his viewpoint; and it is clear that to him the Advaita system of Samkara, for which he could find no full parallel in Western philosophy, was the most satisfying. He was also convinced, at the end of his studies, that in the India of those years philosophy had been a religious voca-

[11] Evelyn Underhill in *Daily News*, 24 September 1923.
[12] B. Russell to Radhakrishnan, 26 August 1923.
[13] In the *Nation and Athenaeum*, 15 September 1923.
[14] *The Radhakrishnan Number* (Madras 1962), p. 5.
[15] See R. Thapar, 'Syndicated Moksha?', *Seminar* (Delhi), issue 313, September 1985.

tion, and that the foundation of her thought was spiritual experience, not in the sense of involving the exercise of supernatural powers but as insisting on a discipline of human nature which could lead to the realization of the spiritual: 'The one fact of life in India is the Eternal Being of God.'[16] He believed that this was felt by very many more than those who comprehended it with their minds.

In India the criticisms of Radhakrishnan's volumes were that 'creative logic' was no more than pure imagination,[17] that he sometimes tortured texts to wrest the meanings he desired, that he relied heavily on translations of Sanskrit texts, that he did not mention every reference and his bibliographies were not exhaustive. In fact, Radhakrishnan, though making no claims to be a pandit, had a good working knowledge of the Sanskrit language; and he was writing not a catalogue but a history, a work not of description but about significance. In seeking to provide a clear and rational account he did not delight in the ambiguities and high artifice of learned parlance. To the audiences outside India of not only professional scholars but educated persons his reasoning and persuasive straightforwardness helped to make the conceptions of Indian thinkers a part of the structure of modern philosophy. It was his reading of Radhakrishnan that led T. S. Eliot to comment on Indian philosophers that 'their subtleties make most of the great European philosophers look like schoolboys.'[18] The critical comments in the West were that Radhakrishnan had too facile a pen and the book suffered from verboseness; a good editor could easily have reduced the length of the two volumes taken together by about a third without diminishing its impact. But the major criticism was that in his effort to combat the general Christian attitude—that philosophy in India was a crass compilation of the crude and the fatuous—Radhakrishnan tended to be aggressive in defence. Representative of this attitude was Stephen Mackenna: 'I bought Rhada-Krishnan's [sic] Indian Philosophy, first vol.; you'd be interested in it; it's rather overwritten and distinctly propagandist, pro-Indian and down-the-foolish West, but is taken to be very sufficiently authoritative

[16] *Indian Philosophy*, volume I, p. 42.
[17] P. Chandra, *The Hindu Mind* (Delhi 1977), p. 86.
[18] *After Strange Gods* (London 1934), p. 43.

and is very fairly easy reading even to my muddy poor brain.'[19]

The commitment to India need not, however, have surprised anybody. Like the thinkers whom he discussed, Radhakrishnan belonged to his time and place. He was an Indian in a colonial setting justifying his people both to themselves and to the outside world. If Mackenna had gone on to read the second volume, he would have found in the last chapter an explicit statement by Radhakrishnan of his position. He regretted that the philosophic impulse, which he had shown to be so vigorous and varied, had had an attack of lethargy with the coming of Islam and Christianity and the consequent clash of cultures. Hindus by and large ceased to think, took refuge in authority and barred entry to invading ideas. In the words of Marx, which Radhakrishnan would have regarded as fully applicable to India: 'the tradition of the dead generations weighs like a nightmare on the minds of the living.'[20] Loyalty to tradition smothered devotion to truth. Reverence for authority was another name for the imprisonment of the human spirit. At the time he was writing, with the full impact of Western ideas, tradition had become fluid again. But even non-political activity could not thrive in the absence of political freedom. The spirit of man craves the right to work out one's own salvation even at the cost of infinite trial and tribulation. A bureaucratic despotism which forgot spiritual ends could not evoke any living response from the people. When the founts of life were drying up, when the ideals of millenniums were decaying, it was no wonder that the Indian was conscious only of the crushing burden of British imperialism and not of any good that it might have done. Intellectual sterility in India was to no small extent due to the shock caused by the Western spirit and the shame of subjection. India had no sympathy with the British policy of cultural imperialism. She wished to dwell in her own spiritual house. Political subjection which interfered with this inner freedom was felt as a gross humiliation; and the demand for swaraj was the outer expression of the anxiety to preserve the provinces of the soul.

[19] To Henry Hall, July 1929, in E. R. Dodds (ed.), *Journal and Letters of Stephen Mackenna* (London 1936), p. 264.

[20] *The Eighteenth Brumaire of Louis Bonaparte* (1852).

Yet, once India gained her freedom, the Western spirit would be of great help to her mind. India had never developed a Monroe doctrine in matters of culture. Along with an appreciation of past achievements, Radhakrishnan had a forward-looking faith in the power of Indian thinkers to renew the spirit of truth by discarding old forms if given the right conditions. Radicals in India wished to forget the past even as conservatives were convinced of its glory; but the right path lay in between, building on old foundations while responsive to new influences: 'Those who condemn Indian culture as useless are ignorant of it, while those who commend it as perfect are ignorant of any other.' India should absorb other cultures and fuse them with the best in her own. That could only happen when India was free and politics did not absorb the energies of some of the best minds in the country.[21] But even in 1923, long before the achievement of independence, he was optimistic: 'Perhaps the philosophy of India which lost its strength and vigour when her political fortunes met with defeat may derive fresh inspiration and a new impulse from the era just dawning upon her.' If her thinkers combined a love of the old with a thirst for the true, Indian philosophy could have a future as glorious as its past.[22]

Nearly sixty years after publication, the two volumes of *Indian Philosophy*, despite the outdated political rhetoric and, at places, the weakness of being wordy and repetitive, have not been displaced. The presentation—with creative power, density of content and a high level of sophistication—of Indian thought in its whole range and variety has not been equalled. Radhakrishnan rescued the country's intellectual tradition from mistreatment by inexpert Western enthusiasts and ignorant Indian pedants, and established the presence, behind all the divergences, of interest in perennial problems. He showed, with forceful clarity and critical insight, how philosophical inquiry in India had led to the emergence of ideas which confirm similarities in the responses of the human spirit in various parts of the world and proclaim the oneness of the human mind. Radhakrishnan was working in the light of other people's ideas; and creative force expressed entirely through

[21] *Indian Philosophy*, volume II, pp. 773–81.
[22] Ibid., volume I, p. 53.

such discussion necessarily lacks completion. The great philosopher and thinker is not quite there yet; the full display of
creative intellect was yet to come. But one can feel him near.
Meantime, the commanding control of the vast material by a
single sensibility without subduing it to a single view, the
packed array of ideas, the fertility and penetration of thought,
the sustained argument stretching and stimulating the reader's
mind, the wealth of cross reference and literary allusion, all
combined to establish his hegemony in the field. He himself
was modest about this enduring achievement:

I know there are deeper students of philosophy and greater scholars
of Sanskrit in this country. My ambition is not only to chronicle
but to interpret and to reveal the movement of the mind and unfold
the sources of India in the profound plane of human nature. There
was a time when Indian philosophy was regarded as something
quaint, strange, antiquated and incapable of playing a part in the
world's spiritual awakening. That impression is slowly disappearing.[23]

## III

Radhakrishnan's only relaxation from the writing of Indian
Philosophy was to plan books on a minor scale on two other
topics. When he joined Calcutta University in March 1921
the students were on strike in obedience to Gandhi's call; and
Sir Ashutosh Mukherjee was having problems with the
Government of Bengal. On both counts Radhakrishnan's sympathy was naturally against the authorities; but he did not
whack the nationalist drum. In fact, in an article on Gandhi
and Tagore, written under a pseudonym because he was still
a government servant, he accepted that Gandhi was the
greatest living person because of his spiritual ideals but was
unenthusiastic about a political campaign that assumed all
its followers to be heroes, an economic programme that
required the burning and boycott of foreign cloth, and, above
all, an educational policy that called on students to leave
schools and colleges. It seemed to Radhakrishnan a mental
derangement on the part of Indians to believe that Gandhi
was an authority in economics and education and social reform
and everything else merely because he happened to be a spiri-

[23] Speech at Madras, 31 March, The Statesman, 2 April 1936.

tual saint. Radhakrishnan's heart was still with Tagore who, while as much a patriot as Gandhi, had a greater sense of joy in life and of the freedom of the spirit.[24]

The swing in Radhakrishnan's attitude to Gandhi came early the next year, when Gandhi called off the campaign of civil disobedience because of the burning of a few policemen by a riotous mob and, arrested soon after, made a moving statement in court. Radhakrishnan was now convinced that the movement which Gandhi had initiated was deeply spiritual; non-co-operation was a war of principle waged with the strength of spirit. To co-operate with the British government was to submit to sin; to take up the sword was to stab the soul. The assumption, which he had earlier doubted, that the followers of Gandhi should behave like heroes, now seemed to him confirmed. The action of a few could not invalidate the transformation which Gandhi had wrought in the country. There had been a rebirth of mind and character in India, a new feeling of freedom and service. Failure to appropriate the powers and privileges of the kingdom within us could only be because of weakness; but nothing was impossible with God. Gandhi was no mere worldly politician depending on mechanical devices for the attainment of self-government. He applied religion to politics and sought to convert the world of nations to the higher law of love. The central interest of the movement in India was a religious one. No one could say if Gandhi would succeed but at least the votaries of spirit should pray for the success of a holy experiment not so much for the sake of India as for the future of the world.[25]

In this mood, Radhakrishnan was outraged by the publication of a letter by the synod of bishops of the Church of England in India denouncing Gandhi's non-violence as unchristian and contrary to the teachings of Jesus, and calling on their followers to obey the government without question. In a series of unsigned articles he tore apart the arguments of the bishops. To say that suffering was not to Christ a method but only a passing incident was to misinterpret his teachings. The cross was no accident in his life. To argue that Christ had not concerned himself with the political struggles round him

[24] CSR, 'Gandhi and Tagore', *Calcutta Review*, October 1921, pp. 14–29.
[25] This paragraph is based on Radhakrishnan's notes written in February 1922.

was to ignore that he had called on his followers to resist evil
but to do so, as Gandhi did, in a non-violent manner. Responding to hatred with love was the governing principle of the life
of Jesus. In Gandhi the sufferer could be recognized the true
image of Christ, while those who wore his uniform had become cogs in the imperial machine. Gandhi was interpreting
the religion of Jesus which was a complete denial of the practice of Christendom. The bishops, instead of indulging in hair-
splitting discussion in order to justify fighting for empire,
should promote a Christian reconciliation between India and
Britain.

The brisk, assertive prose attracted such attention that the
articles were published later as a booklet.[26] Because the articles, with their extensive knowledge of the Christian scriptures,
had been attributed to various missionaries such as C. F.
Andrews, the editor of the *Indian Social Reformer*, where the
articles first appeared, added a note stating that 'the author is
a Hindu with a profound reverence for Jesus Christ'. Radhakrishnan felt encouraged by such wide notice to develop this
pamphlet into a book. 'Gandhi and the Indian Problem' was
planned as a philosophical analysis of Gandhi's ideas with
little reference to politics. Haldane had liked the articles: 'We
British, Bishops or otherwise, are not strongly gifted with imagination. Therefore we fail in sympathy.'[27] He now agreed to
write a foreword to the larger work. As Radhakrishnan
intended to publish this book under his own name, he wrote to
the Government of Madras, as he was obliged to do, for permission. They directed him to submit the proofs to them before they took a decision.[28] This Radhakrishnan was not prepared to do and so abandoned the project.


## IV

The answer to the bishops also led Radhakrishnan to consider
a full-scale work on Christianity in India. Educated throughout
in Christian institutions, taught by redoubtable Christian theo-

[26] *Gandhi and the Anglican Bishops* (Madras 1922).
[27] Lord Haldane to Radhakrishnan, 25 December 1922.
[28] Order of the director of public instruction, Madras, 8 June 1922, law
department education file no. 704 of 1922, Miscellaneous. Tamil Nadu Archives.

logians and influenced by their personalities, steeped in the
Bible and familiar with the writings of Christian thinkers,
Radhakrishnan had reacted defensively to the criticisms and
disparagement of Hinduism so common in the early years of
this century and to the argument that there was no hope for
India unless it accepted Christianity. He had then gradually
moved on to the offensive. The censure in *The Reign* on the distortions induced by religious prejudice in contemporary philosophy was in fact a criticism of the influence of Christian
dogma in Western thought. Christians in India should not be
servile imitators of this attitude which was alien to their
country. They should move away from rule, ritual and ceremony, abide by the national traditions and kindle the spiritual
sense, thus helping people to respect each other's faith. 'Let
us adopt the old ideals and wipe away the accumulated shame
from which we are now suffering.'[29]

Radhakrishnan later suggested that Christianity properly
understood had much in common with the fundamentals of
Hindu thought. The belief in divine immanence rather than in
a transcendent God could be found in the teachings of Jesus if
shorn of Jewish tradition. The growth of religion consisted in
an ever-increasing approximation of our ideas of God to the
truth: 'An honest God is the noblest work of man.' Christian
doctrine was not fully aware of the implications of the indwelling of God in all; but there was no reason why there should
not be an evolution of the Christian conception of God. Christ
himself was a striking example of the son of man raising himself to be the son of God. He was a man in whom God dwelt
with singular closeness and intimacy and who responded to the
graces which he received with unfailing fidelity. If such a view
were taken, there was no need to assume that he was uni-
quely conceived, performed miracles or rose from the tomb.
Christ was the way in the sense that each one has to live
through a similar process of redemption through suffering. The
Hindu admired in Christ his spirit of love and sacrifice; but he
noted too that the Christ was formed in him, for, especially in
his early years, he was at times impatient, violent and provincial and often condemned without extenuation. But if it were

[29] Letter to K. C. Chacko, sometime in 1920, printed in the Alwaye Christian
College magazine, January 1941.

assumed that Christ possessed non-human elements which enabled him to reach perfection, then his life could not be an example to lesser mortals. Other religions too provided examples of mystics and spiritual leaders whose lives and teachings had much in common with those of Jesus; and a man like Gandhi was a much better human being than many in the Western world who professed to believe in the Sermon on the Mount. The claim that the revelation of God in Jesus was complete and unparalleled set his Christian followers apart from all others and led to intolerance with all its consequences.

So Radhakrishnan pleaded that Christians, particularly in India, should not stress the aspects of Christian dogma which spoke of the special character of Jesus, of grace to the elect and of eternal torment of the rest, but emphasize those elements which were common to all the great religions. Christianity should help Hinduism to enrich its spirit not by giving of itself but by helping Hinduism to discover what lay in it undeveloped. Hinduism was attempting to slough off its superstitions and purify itself and there was no greater mission for Christians than to help in this process. If the best features of Hinduism and Christianity were brought together, it was not India alone that would be the gainer by this 'Hindu Christianity'. Indeed, were the Indian Christian to relate the message of salvation in Christ to the larger spiritual background of India, it might help also to revivify Christianity not only in India but in the world at large. What humanity needed was not conversion to a single faith or a pale syncretism but an intelligent understanding of the deeper unity of principle among all religions. Almost all religious misunderstandings were due to a false sense of a monopoly of truth.[30]

This was, of course, not acceptable to orthodox Christian theologians to whom Christ was not just one of the prophets but unique, 'the one God'.[31] The difference of viewpoint was fundamental. But although in his later writings Radhakrishnan

---

[30] 'Religious Unity', *Mysore University Magazine*, September 1923, pp. 187–98; 'Hindu Thought and Christian Doctrine', *Madras Christian College Magazine*, 1924, reprinted in *The Heart of Hindustan* (Madras 1932), pp. 89–122; address to the Calcutta Missionary Conference, 7 September 1925, *The Guardian* (Calcutta), 24 September 1925.

[31] C. C. J. Webb to Radhakrishnan, 18 March 1924.

came back to this subject, <u>he never completed the book which</u> <u>he had contemplated on Christianity and the religious situa-</u> <u>tion in India.</u>

## V

Radhakrishnan's disappointment at the failure to write books on Gandhi and on Christian missions was more than balanced by the success of his two-volume *Indian Philosophy*; and he could derive satisfaction too from the enduring achievement of the organization of the <u>Indian Philosophical Congress</u>. He had been feeling for some time the need for the philosophers of the country to meet once a year to exchange ideas on the state of research in various branches of the discipline; and from the vantage point of the George V chair he first formed an executive committee with the leading scholars, British and Indian, as members. He himself was the chairman of this committee as well as of the reception committee at the first session of the Congress in Calcutta in December 1925. The first president was Rabindranath Tagore, again the choice of Radhakrishnan, selected primarily to demonstrate that the roots of philosophy in India had always lain outside classrooms and cloisters. Since then the Indian Philosophical Congress has assembled every year in different parts of the country and established itself as a leading academic association in India.

# 4

# FIRST VISIT TO THE WEST

In 1926 Calcutta University nominated Radhakrishnan as its representative at the Congress of Universities of the British Empire which was to meet in London. Radhakrishnan was not eager to go out of India, and arrival in London at the height of the general strike was not the best introduction to England. But there were other compensations. Haldane, who even in 1923 had foretold a great future for . Radhakrishnan in the realm of thought,[1] was keen on taking full advantage of his presence, and encouraged L. P. Jacks, the principal of Manchester College at Oxford, to invite him to deliver the Upton Lectures, outlining the essential features and central values of Hinduism without getting involved in technical details. Though Manchester College was an institution for the training of Christian clergymen, Jacks had been seeking to keep it untied denominationally and to involve it in the work of synthesis and reconciliation which seemed to him sorely needed in the religious world. The work of the Reformation would only be completed when the spiritual wisdom of the East and the West had joined hands. For Radhakrishnan this was an opportunity to present to a non-Hindu audience the fundamentals of the Hindu religion. The common element in the faith which bound together those who called themselves Hindu in the various parts of India Radhakrishnan defined as the acceptance of religion as experience, the direct apprehension of the reality of the one supreme Universal Spirit. Hinduism was not a creed but a unified mass of thought collected round the Vedanta, stressing not belief but conduct, accepting

[1] Tej Bahadur Sapru to Radhakrishnan, 22 November 1933, reporting conversation with Haldane ten years earlier, vice-chancellor's files, Andhra University.

graduated levels of comprehension and seeking to deepen understanding and refine the existing content. Respect for all men and devotion to truth meant that there would be no hunting of heresy but an acceptance of other viewpoints on the premiss of diverse roads to the summit. It was a missionary but not a proselytizing religion and, by its emphasis not on a common creed but on a common quest, offered the best promise for a world seeking religious concord.

Radhakrishnan then dealt with some problems raised by Hindu thought and practice. The doctrine of maya did not imply that the world was an illusion but that it was unreal in contrast to the Ultimate Reality, and that the link between God and the world was a mystery. The theory of karma did not preclude free will but suggested that men had to exercise it within given conditions such as heredity. It was—though Radhakrishnan did not say it—very similar to Marx's definition of freedom as the recognition of necessity. In a passage which has been often quoted and has found its way into numerous anthologies, Radhakrishnan likened life to playing a hand at bridge: 'The cards in the game of life are given to us. We do not select them. They are traced to our past Karma, but we can call as we please, lead what suit we will and, as we play, we gain or lose. And there is freedom.'[2] We may not like the way in which the cards have been shuffled and dealt; but we like the game and we want to play; and it depends on us whether we play well or badly. To reckon with a universe that is marked by order and regularity is not to deny freedom.

To assert that Hinduism was more a way of life than a form of thought, to insist that it was not a static but a resilient religion, 'a movement, not a position; a process, not a result; a growing tradition, not a fixed revelation',[3] meant that Radhakrishnan had to concern himself with Hindu organization and behaviour as well as with its theoretical attractiveness. Hindu dharma, or right action, recognized, according to him, the different cravings of a human being, and provided for them all: the sexual and parental instincts, the love of power and wealth, the desire for the common good and the hunger for communion with the unseen. A person passes accordingly through four stages in life: the periods of training, of work

[2] *The Hindu View of Life* (London 1927), p. 75.          [3] Ibid., p. 129.

as a householder, of retreat and of renunciation. A happy monogamy was the ideal and, while the functions of women are distinguished from those of men, there was no suggestion of inferiority.

However, what interested Radhakrishnan's audience most in this connection was obviously the institution of caste; and Radhakrishnan explained its origin as part of the Aryan effort to absorb the various racial groups with whom they came in contact. As against the extermination of the aboriginals and the Red Indians, caste was the superior method of harmonization. It recognized local custom and affirmed the infinite diversity of human groups. It stood 'for the ordered complexity, the harmonized multiplicity, the many in one which is the clue to the structure of the universe'.[4] On its social side, each caste had its own purpose and function. Each pursued its own aims free from interference by others and contributed to the prosperity of the whole. It conformed to that law of social life which provided for harmony and co-operation and not cold and cruel competition. In his lectures on the same subject in the United States Radhakrishnan drew a comparison more familiar to his audiences, and broadly compared the caste system in India with the monopolies in types of jobs which had developed in the United States. The policemen in New York were predominantly Irish, most street cleaners were Italian, Greeks specialized in quick-lunch counters, and blacks monopolized the jobs as janitors and attendants in Pullman cars.

Fluently delivered, the four lectures on the Hindu view of life drew packed audiences in Oxford even during 'Eights' week, and later, when published, the book, easy to read, sold widely, running quickly into several impressions. Hinduism as elaborated by Radhakrishnan appealed to many. Jacks, in his concluding remarks, said that while listening to Radhakrishnan he had often felt inclined to exclaim that he too was a Hindu.[5] The religion expounded by Radhakrishnan 'may be said to have illustrated the principles of Manchester College on a scale of which those acquainted only with Western religion have no knowledge.'[6] Years later Jacks wrote of the transforma-

---

[4] Ibid., p. 105.
[5] Report in the *Indian Social Reformer* (Bombay), 7 August 1926.
[6] Report of Manchester College for 1926.

tion which Radhakrishnan's writings had wrought in his life. 'Here was a new window as well as a new wind. I felt the ventilation greatly improved and began to breathe more freely.'[7] Haldane was impressed by the vitality of Hinduism, and the testimony the book bore to philosophy in the East and the West constituting one whole under different forms.[8] The businessman Gordon Selfridge listed it among the three books which had most influenced his life.[9] 'I have been reading', wrote Sir Francis Younghusband, 'your *Hindu View of Life* with the greatest joy and wish you had been born forty years earlier so that I could have had it when I was first in India.'[10] In India, as was to be expected, the book was received very favourably. It helped the Hindu majority, sunk in subjection and wretchedness, to bolster their self-respect by suggesting the rationalism and superiority of their religion. The young Jawaharlal Nehru had no use for conventional religion; but he read *The Hindu View* with approval twice in prison, recommended it to his friends and, over thirty years later, as prime minister, could quote bits of it from memory. The time when Radhakrishnan delivered these lectures was obviously one when in India religion and politics could not be kept apart. Radhakrishnan was a sensitive patriot and his work was intended as much to assert the primacy of India in matters of faith and spirit as to delineate the main principles of Hinduism.

Not that Radhakrishnan was wholly uncritical. He acknowledged that, in the name of toleration, Hindus had carefully protected superstitious rites and customs, and that the doctrine of karma was frequently confused with a fatalist outlook. There had been in recent years a failure of nerve, a reluctance to curb such practices as child marriages and the prohibition of the remarriage of widows. Above all, the institution of caste, whatever its healthy spirit of synthesis in remote times, had degenerated into an instrument of oppression, enforcing ideas of superiority and inferiority. Political vicissitudes had brought about an attitude of listlessness which it was the duty of reformers to check. But basically *The Hindu View of Life* was an

---

[7] L. P. Jacks, *The Confessions of an Octogenarian* (London 1942), p. 182.
[8] To S. Radhakrishnan, 6 March 1927.
[9] *The Spectator*, 17 December 1927.
[10] To S. Radhakrishnan, 19 March 1930.

eloquent statement of Hinduism as it perhaps was at some time, and as it should be, and not as it prevailed in the mid twenties. Radhakrishnan's justification was that the student of any religion should dive beneath the froth and scum on the surface of the waters and look for what really counted, the silent stream running below with its own impetus, its own velocity and in its own direction. But Estlin Carpenter, a pioneer scholar of comparative religion at Oxford, wrote to Radhakrishnan, after reading the typescript of the first two lectures which he had been unable to attend, that some at least of his hearers would like to know something about the present aspects of the problem; for example, 'how it is possible to worship Kali as the Supreme Deity, and to bow before an image of her garlanded with a necklace of skulls'.[11]

Christian missionaries in particular took alarm at what seemed to them an anti-Christian strain and at this persuasive exposition of Hinduism by 'an apologist who refuses to face the facts and substitutes an idealized picture for the less attractive reality'.[12] It was pointed out that instances of religious persecution were not unknown in Indian history, that Hindu women had few rights, and that caste as it existed had no justification. By softening 'the harsh outlines' of traditional Hindu thought and practice Radhakrishnan was making it easier for civilized persons to hold to the Hindu faith and to resist the attractions of Christianity. Certainly historians and sociologists today would have much to dissent from in Radhakrishnan's account of the origins of caste; and, even in his description of the way it had developed, he asserted his belief in a natural elite, set little store by intercaste marriages, and failed, while speaking of the flexibility of the caste system, to take adequate account of the fact that a person's caste is determined by birth. He also virtually ignored the practice of untouchability, leading a Christian writer to remark recently that the book 'reads very much like a justification of apartheid'.[13] Indeed, Radhakrishnan himself moved away in later years to positions which were explicitly more qualified. He thought that caste as originally

[11] J. Estlin Carpenter to S. Radhakrishnan, 4 July 1926.
[12] Introduction of Bishop Westcott of Calcutta to C. Mukerji, *A Modern Hindu View of Life* (S.P.C.K, London 1930).
[13] Duncan Forrester, *Caste and Christianity* (London 1980), p. 165.

conceived had had an exalted objective; but ideas degenerate and also become futile when the social order alters. The caste system had fallen out of harmony with changed conditions, and new institutions in accordance with the growing conscience of the community were required.[14] In 1936 he publicly castigated the compulsory degradation of a large part of mankind as revolting to those who have a sense of the dignity of man and respect for the preciousness of human life.[15] Five years later, speaking to an Indian audience, he called for the riddance of the caste spirit and the innumerable castes and outcastes.[16] After independence he explained the fourfold order as placing emphasis on aptitude and function and not on birth. The caste system had changed its character in the process of history and could no longer be regarded as anything more than an insistence on a variety of ways in which the social purpose should be carried out. It was a matter of deep humiliation and shame to every sensible Hindu to think that attempts were sometimes still being made to justify untouchability.[17] In office as vice-president and then president, the urgency of abolishing caste and of atoning for the 'sin of untouchability' was a constant refrain in his speeches and writings.[18] In his own personal life he at no stage attached any importance to the restrictions and practices ordained by caste. Even his strict vegetarianism was a matter of concern for other forms of life and of what he, like Bernard Shaw, regarded as cleanliness rather than the result of any taboos: 'We must never cause death or suffering beyond what we absolutely must.'[19]

Though the Upton Lectures at Oxford formed the main event of the visit to Britain, Radhakrishnan was in much demand elsewhere. He spoke at the Moral Sciences Club in Cambridge on Bradley and Samkara, and gave three lectures in London on the philosophic basis of Hinduism. C. E. M. Joad

[14] To M. P. Gopala Menon, 30 August 1935.

[15] 'The Individual and the Social Order in Hinduism', in E. R. Hughes (ed.), *The Individual in East and West* (Oxford 1937), p. 147.

[16] *Religion and Society* (London 1947), p. 133.

[17] *The Bhagavad Gita* (London 1948), pp. 160–1, and p. 253 n.

[18] This is what makes unfair Forrester's criticism that Radhakrishnan's arguments on caste have an air of irrelevance because they so rarely impinge on any practical issue. See Forrester, p. 168.

[19] *Religion and Society* (London 1947), p. 204.

was in the audience and was bowled over:

Those of us who had the good fortune to attend will remember the
alert and vivid personality of the lecturer, a spare figure, with flashing eyes and a beautifully modulated voice, conveying in a series of
exquisitely turned phrases an equal mastery of the intricacies of the
English language and Hindu metaphysics. As one followed him
through the mazes of what must be reckoned the most ambiguous
system of thought which the ingenuity of the human mind has yet
evolved, one was struck by what the Professor will, I hope, forgive
me for calling the Western incisiveness of his mind. The subject was
so obscure, the exposition so clear, the metaphysic so other-worldly,
the treatment so matter-of-fact, that whatever one might think of
the merits of Hindu philosophy, there could be no two opinions
about those of the Professor.[20]

Of personal friends there were few at this time in Britain.
Shyama Prasad Mukherjee, whom Radhakrishnan had known
in Calcutta as the son of Sir Ashutosh, was in London reading
for the Bar, and, though Shyama Prasad was much younger in
years, they met frequently. From this time grew a friendship
which deepened with the years. Muirhead, with whom Radhakrishnan had corresponded for many years, was away in the
United States, and Mackenzie was the only British philosopher whom he had met earlier. But personal contacts developed with others. There was a quiet dinner with Haldane, a
talk with Russell, and tea with Balfour and with Moore, Keynes and Lowes Dickinson, who asked him seriously if Indians
were capable of scientific work. Radhakrishnan's retort was to
quote Acton's remark about the lack of perspective shown in
judging a people by the last four hundred years, forgetting the
last four thousand. It was when India's political fortunes
suffered that even her non-political qualities had deteriorated.
   The same staunchness characterized his interventions at the
Universities Congress. He deplored the role of the government
in Indian universities. It was not interference but domination.
The universities were not only aided but controlled to a large
extent by the state, and this resulted in producing graduates
suited mostly for law and the public services. Macaulay's
policy of providing Indians with an outlook oriented to the
West, while it drew India into the current of world thought,

<hr>

[20] *The Spectator*, 16 February 1929.

sought to 'borrow souls as we barter goods' and tempted Indians to ignore the value of their own culture. When the Congress discussed co-operation in research, Radhakrishnan complained that India was being looked upon as a field of exploitation and British graduates had become part of the general export trade. He also wished that co-operation should be interpreted in the true spirit of university fellowship and extended even to political problems so that the British empire became a step towards the achievement of world unity.

From Britain Radhakrishnan moved on to the United States. Confronted by journalists at New York harbour who were looking for the spiritual teacher Krishnamurti, he joked, 'even a Cunard liner is too small to hold two messiahs.' He witnessed by chance in New York the spectacle of the funeral of Rudolph Valentino before visiting the leading universities, colleges and theological centres on the east coast. The Haskell Lectures at Chicago on the philosophy of the Hindu religion have not been published; but clearly Radhakrishnan drew attention to what he saw as its universalist character and the necessity of moving away from a spirit of narrow dogmatism and exclusiveness. To him truly religious men, to whatever denomination they might belong, were of the same kin. Harry Emerson Fosdick, one of the leading Christian ministers in the United States, wrote thirty years later of the afternoon he spent with Radhakrishnan and Dean Gilkey of Chicago: 'That day in a small sailboat, when Gilkey, Radhakrishnan and I had a few hours of intimate conversation about the meaning of religion, is one of my most unforgettable recollections. I felt much closer to him, Hindu though he was, than to many Christians.'[21]

The highlight of Radhakrishnan's visit to the United States was his performance at the International Congress of Philosophy at Harvard. Always, from his first years as a teacher, a fluent yet ordered speaker, Radhakrishnan had developed into a remarkable orator. He gave much thought to his addresses but disliked reading from a written script. Rather, standing straight with his hands in the side pockets of his long coat, with no gestures, he would draw on his powers of total recall to elucidate at great speed the most abstruse topics of philosophy and religion in a way which held his audiences spellbound. He

[21] H. E. Fosdick, *The Living of These Days* (New York 1956), p. 116.

could also adapt his style to the audience, giving a serious
lecture packed with argument when the occasion demanded it,
but interspersing his thoughts with wit and humour when that
seemed more appropriate. At Harvard he was asked to speak
at an open session, along with Etienne Gilson, Dewey and
Croce, on the role of philosophy in the history of civilization.
Nothing suited Radhakrishnan better. Every civilization, he
said, needed a metaphysic, its own synoptic vision of reality; a
civilization was a philosophy concretized. Any system of philosophy, if it were to be adequate and alive, had to be relevant
to the problems of the day. It had to take account of science,
the shrinkage of space, the upsetting of traditional codes and
the undermining of orthodox theology. If philosophy were not
to abdicate its function, it should meet these challenges and
provide a spiritual view of the universe, broad-based on the
results of the sciences and the aspirations of humanity. The
subjection of the cosmic process to law and its tendency to
produce higher values indicated the reality of an Ultimate
Spirit. Man had the power to understand his place in this
scheme and play his role consciously and with a spiritual
attitude.[22]

This short address, serious in substance, delivered without
notes and without hesitation, full of striking phrases and
punctuated with humour, carried the audience.

Now making the capacious audience roar with laughter at a witty
reference to the instability of marriage in the Western world, and
then holding it so silently attentive that the creaking of a chair
sounded large, Professor Radhakrishnan . . . leaned toward the up-
turned faces and gave them one flashing criticism after another . . .
Even greater applause than followed Professor Dewey's address
greeted Professor Radhakrishnan. He half rose from his chair two
or three times to acknowledge it. After the meeting there was a
buzz of admiring comment about him.[23]

Reports of Radhakrishnan's activities in the West preceded
his return and ensured welcome receptions at Bombay, Madras
and Calcutta. At a time when the political tide was at an ebb,

[22] 'The Role of Philosophy in the History of Civilization', *Proceedings of the
Sixth International Congress of Philosophy* (New York 1927), pp. 543–50.
[23] *The Boston Globe*, 16 September 1926.

the recognition won by Radhakrishnan in the academic world was gratifying to sensitive Indians, though his friend Candeth was aggrieved that in Madras the Brahmins seemed set on making of him a Brahmin hero.[24] But to Indians Radhakrishnan stressed that they were lapsing from the ideals which he had presented abroad. The world belonged to the living and what India needed was not just the thought of the past but thinkers of the present day. Glorification of the past was no compensation for the bitter present. The vital principles of the Hindu faith had to be applied anew in every generation. Obsolete dogmas could not reshape society. But he also criticized the educational policy of the government for not generating in students a sense of national pride and self-respect. The university system in India was divorced from the culture of the country and a huge national effort in the matter of education was required for religious reform, economic advance and political stability. Universities should be free from interference by the state as well as by politicians.[25]

[24] Diary entry, 16 November 1926, M. A. Candeth diaries, Nehru Memorial Museum and Library (NMML).

[25] Interview at Bombay, *The Indian Daily Mail*, 14 and 15 November 1926; speeches at Madras, *The Hindu*, 16 November 1926.

# CALCUTTA AND OXFORD

On his return to Calcutta in November 1926 Radhakrishnan found his university at a high pitch of excitement. The historian Jadunath Sarkar had been brought from Bihar by the Bengal government to serve as vice-chancellor. The appointment was resented by all the members of the syndicate except the Acting Director of Public Instruction, who felt that, as an official, he should support every decision of the government. The professors of the university too disliked the choice of Sarkar, for he had made public attacks on some of them and had no greater claims to the vice-chancellorship than many of them. Even his predecessor in office, Sir Ewart Greaves, a highly respected judge of the High Court, had been driven to criticize the appointment at a meeting of the senate as an indication of the government's 'callous indifference to the feelings of the University'.[1]

The tension continued throughout Sarkar's term of office for two years. He regarded those loyal to the memory of Sir Ashutosh Mukherjee as chiefly responsible for this, and viewed Radhakrishnan, widely liked by the teachers and by now a close friend of Sir Ashutosh's son Shyama Prasad Mukherjee, as a key figure of the opposition. Nor was Radhakrishnan any longer a recluse within the university. So, though Sarkar had had glowing accounts of Radhakrishnan's lectures from the heads of institutions abroad, he made no reference to this in the annual report of the university, which was devoted mainly to loyal praise of the government.[2] In contrast was Radhakrishnan's forthright criticism of the official attitude to

[1] See Sir Ewart Greaves to Lord Lytton, governor of Bengal, 20 December 1926, Lytton papers, India Office Library, London (IOL), EUR. MSS. F. 160, vol. 29.     [2] See J. Sarkar to Radhakrishnan, 16 November 1926.

education. His presidential address at the second conference of
the All-Bengal College and University Teachers' Association,
though concerned primarily with the problems of Bengal and
particularly of Calcutta University, raised such fundamental
issues that it attracted attention throughout the country, and
almost every nationalist newspaper commented editorially. In
his first major address in India on education Radhakrishnan
laid down principles which he consistently sponsored for the
next forty years.

Radhakrishnan at the outset denounced a policy which
trained students to serve as efficient and docile tools of an
external authority but did not help them to become self-
respecting citizens of a free nation. Rather than imbuing the
young with a burning passion to remove the conditions which
prevented them from assuming control of their destinies, they
were being taught that the history of India was a record of
failure. The attitude to Indian thought was one of hazy emotional reverence and not that of historical analysis and critical
evaluation: 'The living faith of the dead has become the dead
faith of the living.' Nor could such education make any contribution to culture: 'As a rule our literature is puerile, our
art thin and affected, our science second-hand and shallow and
our philosophy—it does not exist.' University education in
India discouraged free mental life and intellectual adventure.
Remodelling was essential from the school level upwards, and
Radhakrishnan favoured guidance of secondary education also
by the university, which itself should be dominated by professors and teachers. The state should give the university liberal
grants, but these should be statutory and not dependent on
votes in the legislature, for universities should be free from the
control and interference of the government, whether British or
Indian. In conclusion, Radhakrishnan suggested adequate
salaries and reasonable security of tenure for university and
college teachers.[3]

So fierce was the indictment that even *Forward*, a newspaper
with a Congress viewpoint, advised its readers not to be swept
away by Radhakrishnan's vehemence and eloquence.[4] But the
speech, combined with reports of Radhakrishnan's recent

[3] 'Educational Reform', address delivered at Calcutta, 3 April 1927, and published in *The Calcutta Review*, May 1927, pp. 143–54.    [4] 9 April 1927.

triumphs in the West, placed him at the head of independent academic opinion in the province, in contrast to the timid loyalism of the vice-chancellor. One consequence of this was seen a few months later, when Radhakrishnan was unanimously elected by the concerned faculties as President of the Postgraduate Council of Arts. Till then the vice-chancellor had been elected to this post also; but Sarkar, who was present, sensing the mood of the meeting, did not even have his name proposed. At the same meeting he did allow suggestions that he be coopted to four boards of studies; but each time the proposal was defeated by vote. Even the board for history, which was his field of research, would not have him. The lines between the vice-chancellor and the teaching staff were thus clearly drawn, and when Radhakrishnan, thanking the teachers for his election, spoke of the vital need for autonomy and independence in the postgraduate departments,[5] it was a fair assumption that he had in mind independence not only from the government but also from the vice-chancellor. Certainly he found himself deeply involved in all the clashes that followed in the senate and other university bodies, and was regarded as the leading champion of the teachers and students of Calcutta University against all who sought to encroach on their interests. Even the nationalist press of Bengal took sides, the *Bengalee* supporting Sarkar, the *Forward* those who regarded him as subservient to the government, and the *Amrita Bazar Patrika* adopting a middle line, conceding Sarkar's inadequacy but pleading that he be shown at least the ordinary courtesies such as membership of the boards of studies.

The skirmishing continued into 1928. The students hooted out the vice-chancellor when he came to preside over the prestigious Kamala Lectures delivered by Sarojini Naidu, and Radhakrishnan had to take the chair. The differences between Sarkar on the one hand and the staff and students on the other also expanded to become part of a general confrontation between the government and the public. To deal with the demonstrations against the Simon Commission on its arrival in Calcutta in February 1928 the vice-chancellor sought the support of the police, who beat up the protesting students. Radhakrishnan was appointed by the syndicate (despite the

[5] *New Empire* (Calcutta), 3 August 1927.

vice-chancellor) to conduct an enquiry, and he reported that the attack on the students was unprovoked and unjustified. He could find no excuse for armoured cars chasing students. The senate adopted the report and instructed the vice-chancellor to bring the matter to the notice of the chancellor, who was also governor of the province. Little could be expected of him, for, immediately after the disturbances, he had issued a threat, criticized even by the British-owned *Statesman*, that grants to the university might be suspended.[6] This increased the pertinence of Radhakrishnan's demand since 1926 for genuine autonomy and freedom from official interference for Indian universities, and he now once again at a public meeting moved a resolution calling for the reconstruction of Calcutta University on a wide, elective basis. Only then could that institution play its vital role in keeping alive the national self-consciousness of a suppressed people.

Such extensive activity in university affairs went along with lecturing for eight hours a week, supervising research, carrying out administrative duties as President of the Postgraduate Council, and even participation in the social side of academic life by founding an Arts Faculty Club and encouraging the postgraduate faculty and teachers from the various colleges scattered round Calcutta to get together informally. Radhakrishnan was also to be seen more often at functions in the city. Till 1928 he had gone to College Square by bus and by tram; but in that year he indulged in the extravagance of buying a second-hand car, which he replaced two years later with a brand-new one. This made him more mobile and also enabled him to take his family on outings. A visit to Whiteaway's on Thursday afternoons for fruit salad and ice cream became an established treat.

These diverse commitments would have explained at least a short suspension of philosophical study and writing. However, early in 1928, at the request of Bishop David of Liverpool, Radhakrishnan wrote a short pamphlet, *The Religion We Need*, for the Affirmations Series, 'God and the Modern World', published by Ernest Benn. The purpose of this series was to encourage open discussion of religious problems in order to help Christians make better sense of the world; and Radhakrishnan

[6] *Statesman*, 12 February 1928.

fell in line with the scheme to the extent that he stated general propositions and kept Hindu thought well in the background. With educated men and women moving away from conventional beliefs, those who were still anxious for religion were building for themselves different ways of escape. But Radhakrishnan believed that the growing dissatisfaction with established religion was the prelude to the rise of a truer, more spiritual, and so more universal, religion. Science, rightly understood, was essentially spiritual in its temper and outlook. It had no sympathy with revealed religion but instead of abolishing the mysteries of the world, deepened them.

From his undergraduate days Radhakrishnan had been interested in theories of evolution and he now examined them from his own point of view. The hypothesis of evolution substituted the theory of development for that of creation; but it was silent on the question of ultimate causation and was not inconsistent with the highest idealism. It assumed an element behind all evolution which was not the product of evolution, though its ultimate ground and driving power. There were sudden and considerable qualitative leaps, from matter to life, from life to mind, from mind to intelligence, which were inexplicable.[7] From this Radhakrishnan concluded, with Bergson of the early years and Bernard Shaw, that evolution was not blind and mechanical but the expression of a purposive force. Where he went beyond them was to assume not just a life-force but the reality of a single supreme spirit at work in the whole cosmos. They believed, as Gide was to put it later, 'that, instead of existing already, God was *becoming* and that it depended on each one of us that he should become . . .'[8] But Radhakrishnan believed that the divine was already present in the self and the goal of cosmic evolution was the release of the imprisoned splendour in all men and women. God was not an emergent deity but the immanent spirit working in and through all. The argument of Bergson in his later work, *The*

[7] Some years later J. B. S. Haldane, the well-known Marxist biologist, expressed a similar view. When anything, he wrote, increased to a certain point, there was sudden change; and such creative change was always the result of struggle. The most important conflicts and contradictions were internal; the most important changes came from inside. *What I Believe* (London 1940), pp. 111–12.

[8] Andre Gide in 1942, quoted in J. O'Brien's Introduction, *The Journals of Andre Gide*, volume 1 (London 1947), p. xv.

*Two Sources of Morality and Religion,* is much nearer to this position. For in this work Bergson speaks not only of a static but also of a dynamic force of religion, which springs from the experience of union with a supernatural spirit whose law is love. Individuals have a sense of participation in the onward creative movement of reality. The great mystics have been in instinctive touch with the pulse of creative life and inspired by the emotion thus generated. The evolutionary process thus appears in this work as the manifestation not of natural force but of creative love. The universe is seen as the work of a creative spirit, the creator of creators, whose purpose is the making of gods.

As both the soul of man and the God whom it seeks are infinite in character and with unlimited possibilities, it follows that any number of ways of approach and address can be envisaged. Provincialism in religion is an obvious sign of crudity. The mystics of the world belonged to the same tradition and asked us to get behind all outward churches and worship the nameless who is above every name. The illogical idea of a single religion for mankind was the product of unreason and the parent of intolerance. Every religion was an integral element of the society in which it was found, an expression of its spiritual experience, a record of its evolution. But the essence of religious life was spiritual certainty, the conviction that love and justice are at the heart of the universe, that the spirit which gave rise to men will further his perfection. So the truly religious soul will be prepared to suffer, with faith 'that though the waves on the shore may be broken, the ocean conquers nevertheless'; and his aim will be human brotherhood. A more vivid, a deeper sense of the one universal God was the profoundest need of the age.

The social side of such a religion was spelt out by Radhakrishnan in a short book written immediately after and published the next year. Before the advent of the paperback, 'Today and Tomorrow' was a popular series on futurology in which well-known authors wrote on their special interests, with titles drawn from mythology. For example, Russell and Haldane each wrote on science, Liddell Hart on war and Gerald Heard on clothes. Radhakrishnan was invited to write on the future of civilization and he dashed it off during a fortnight's vacation in Darjeeling in the summer of 1928. The primary purpose of the trip was to lobby with the Bengal government for the selection of the next vice-chancellor from among the members of the Mukherjee group. The *Forward* pressed for Radhakrishnan, while the *Modern Review*, edited by Ramananda Chatterjee, who had a dislike of Sir Ashutosh Mukherjee and all his men, urged that Sarkar be given a second term. Radhakrishnan's name had also been suggested (without his knowledge) by Sir Ewart Greaves, along with that of the principal of a missionary college;[9] and the government, playing safe, selected the latter. But the vice-chancellorship was not Radhakrishnan's sole preoccupation. He could always switch easily from the clatter of politics and detail of daily life to austere metaphysical thinking and back again. As he preached, so in life, he was deeply involved, yet ever detached; and, in the intervals between lunches and teas with ministers and officials in Darjeeling, he completed the manuscript he had agreed to write.

In *Kalki* (the title chosen by Radhakrishnan from the name in Hindu mythology for the tenth and last avatar to be expected when the world has touched the depths of decadence), Radhakrishnan expanded his address at the International Congress of Philosophy two years earlier. He drew attention to the contrast between the growing closeness of the world outwardly and the lack of an inner unity of mind and spirit. The breakdown of traditional systems of thought, belief and practice could be the prelude to such a unity; but meantime one saw a laxity in standards in family life, the expansion of economic and political systems which suppressed the finer instincts, and the intensification of warmongering in international relations. Human nature was body, mind and spirit, and harmony of the three was the aim of civilization. It was within ourselves, in our moral conceptions, religious ideas and social outlook. But, while we had asserted mind over life and matter, the spirit had yet to subdue mind, life and body. By transforming ourselves we should be able to transform the world. Each of us can participate in the process of creating a better world by understanding the purpose of the universe and identifying ourselves with it.

[9] W. E. Greaves to Radhakrishnan, 11 December 1928.

The law of moral progress was defined by Radhakrishnan as
one of acceptance and adventure. We have to accept the given
and build higher on its basis. The essence of moral life consisted not so much in adjusting to the environment as in changing it in accordance with our ideals. The objective was not self-
perfection but social redemption. If we believed in the divine
possibilities of all human beings, we could not rest until the
whole world was redeemed. No one was truly saved until the
world was saved.

Morality was but the current brand of social customs and all
progress was due to the rebels. Life was an adventure and not
a set scheme. It was a game of which we could never know the
rules precisely. 'In the sphere of morality, the lights are dim
and the stars wander.' It seemed to Radhakrishnan that the
trouble with the world was a deadly mediocrity and a marked
triviality in life and thinking. An ample expression of all sides
of human nature in their highest forms, economic organization animated by community of feeling, a democratic system
supported by education and striving for the least inequality of
opportunity and the fostering of oneness of outlook and feeling
as the basis of international relations—these were the goals of a
truly religious person, whatever his denomination; and religious idealism was to Radhakrishnan the most hopeful political
instrument for peace which the world had ever seen.

He also, at this time, wrote a long article on Indian philosophy for the new (fourteenth) edition of the *Encyclopaedia
Britannica.* The decision to have for the first time a separate
section on this topic was in itself, in a way, recognition of
Radhakrishnan's work. He was prepared too to undertake less
professional writing. Jawaharlal Nehru, in Calcutta that winter
for the annual session of the Congress party, called on Radhakrishnan. This was the first meeting between the two men who
were many years later to work so closely together. The purpose
of Nehru's visit was not only to make the acquaintance of the
man whose books he had read in prison but to interest Radhakrishnan in a project for a series of books which he, as secretary
of the Congress party, was seeking to promote. Radhakrishnan
was still technically in government service and therefore not a
member of the Congress; but in the light of his forthright
speeches and writings this tended to be forgotten. Thus, when

he attended the Congress session in Calcutta as a visitor, approaches were made to him by various members to speak for or against resolutions. To Nehru's suggestion he was responsive and offered to help in editing a volume on 'The Soul of India' dealing with the scientific and cultural history of India, with special reference to current issues. The very best Indians should be asked to write, even if they were not 'Congressmen in the technical sense of the term'—a description which Radhakrishnan no doubt regarded as appropriate to himself.[10] This project finally did not materialize. But more fruitful was Radhakrishnan's counter-request to Nehru: that he write for the quarterly The New Era, started by Radhakrishnan's eldest son-in-law in Madras and of which Radhakrishnan was the driving force. Nehru complied and wrote a seminal article, based on his experiences during his recent stay in Europe, elaborating the need for the Indian national movement to look beyond its frontiers.[11]

## II

Towards the end of 1928 L. P. Jacks offered Radhakrishnan the lecturership at Manchester College in comparative religion, held till then by Estlin Carpenter, on a permanent basis or for five years. Radhakrishnan declined, for this would have meant leaving Calcutta University, but agreed to take the post for a year, starting from January 1929. However, he was elected a member of the syndicate, with all sides voting for a person 'distinguished alike for his scholarship, his administrative ability and his moderating influence';[12] and he did not feel he could leave till the report of the University Organization Committee, of which he was a prominent member, had been completed. So he postponed his departure till September and spent the academic year 1929–30 at Oxford. He also agreed to deliver, during that year, the Hibbert Lectures at the universities of

[10] See Radhakrishnan to B. A. Mirza, 20 May 1929, AICC file, G4–1929, NMML.

[11] 'India and the Need for International Contacts', written on 13 May 1929, published in The New Era and reprinted in Selected Works of Jawaharlal Nehru, vol. 3 (Delhi 1972), pp. 379–86.

[12] R. B. Ramsbotham, principal, Presidency College, to Radhakrishnan, 28 January 1929.

Manchester and London. This gave him the opportunity to construct his own metaphysical system. Regarded till now as basically an exponent of other men's ideas, he broke new ground by setting forth his personal philosophy, the product of many years of reflection and conscientious scholarship. *The Religion We Need* had been a preliminary canter; now Radhakrishnan, master of two philosophical worlds and yet sworn to the texts of neither, provided to the twentieth century, in rounded and detailed form, 'a vital religion, a live philosophy, which will reconstruct the bases of conviction and devise a scheme of life which men can follow with self-respect and joy'.[13] His aim was to show that the universe had value, a meaning and a purpose, and that humanity needed a religion which provided a vital contact with reality, measured up to rigorous metaphysical requirements, satisfied the scientific approach and met the spiritual demands of the time.

Radhakrishnan began by stating the case against conventional religions at their best. Science demands proof which such religions cannot offer; astronomy reveals the insignificance of the earth while theories of evolution provided more rational grounds than any theology for human life. Ethics could be seen as social convenience and not the embodiment of eternal values, and behaviourism contended that man was a mere nexus between stimuli and responses: 'We can make a god out of glands, if only we set about it.'[14] The new science of psychoanalysis suggested that religion was an illusion, and the disciplines of comparative religion and social anthropology showed all religions to be man-made. On the other hand, all proofs of the existence of God were deficient in one way or the other; and what made this worse was the practical inefficiency, the moral ineffectiveness and the disastrous political consequences of all established religious faiths: 'Nothing is so hostile to religion as other religions ... The world would be a much more religious place if all religions were removed from it.'[15]

If the modern challenge to belief was formidable the substitutes were inadequate. Naturalistic atheism, agnosticism, scepticism, humanism, pragmatism, modernism and authoritarianism all left the mind and spirit unsatisfied: 'Today many

---

[13] *An Idealist View of Life* (London 1932), p. 65.
[14] Ibid., p. 22.      [15] Ibid., p. 34.

of those who deny God are unable to dispense with ghosts.'[16] They were weak replacements for a religion which takes us deeper than intellect and re-establishes the vital relationship already at work between men and nature. Such religious experience was as wide as human nature. Philosophy of religion was religion come to an understanding of itself and, if it were to be scientific, it had to become empirical and base itself on religious experience. It should adopt a scientific view of such experience and examine with detachment and impartiality the spiritual inheritance of all humanity irrespective of creeds.

Such religious experience is mystical and intuitive. There is deep in the self of man an affinity to the Supreme. In the moment of its highest insight, the self becomes aware not only of its own existence but also of an omnipresent spirit of which it is, as it were, the focusing. We see the one spirit overarching us and recognize the unity of the universe. Meditation is the way to self-discovery and establishment of contact with the creative centre; but, from the moment of insight, the reborn person returns to the world. The spiritual is not an essence apart, to be protected from the rest of the world; it pervades and refines the whole life of the individual. Such a person is now world-conscious and works for the redemption of others.

At once the question arises of the validity of intuitive knowledge. Western systems of thought are generally characterized by an adherence to critical intelligence and find it more difficult than the East to recognize creative intuition. The logical intellect is regarded as the supreme instrument of knowledge. But to Radhakrishnan sense experience and logical analysis were in themselves inadequate; it was the creative effort of the whole man as distinct from mere intellectual effort that alone could comprehend the nature of reality: 'A set of qualities is not a sunset.'[17] The deepest things of life are known only through intuitive apprehension. Certainty and not communicability is the truest test of knowledge. Such intuition, as explained by Radhakrishnan, was not opposed to intellect but lay beyond it. Intuition stood to intellect as intellect stood to sense. Reflective knowledge was a preparation for integral experience. This was reached after a long process of discursive analysis and, once attained, was prolonged into an intellectual ordering of images

[16] Ibid., p. 47.       [17] Ibid., p. 107.

and concepts. All dynamic acts of thinking are controlled by an intuitive grasp of the situation as a whole. There was no break of continuity between intuition and intellect. In moving from intellect to intuition we are not moving in the direction of unreason but getting into the deepest rationality of which human nature is capable. Intuitive knowledge is not non-rational but non-conceptual.

In *The Reign* Radhakrishnan had written of reason-philo-sophers and faith-philosophers. In 1918 he was in the first category; by 1929 he had moved to the second. He who had criticized Western philosophers for allowing belief to cloud their intellectual analysis now spoke of philosophy as being an exposition and explanation of religious experience. Of all his philosophical writings, *An Idealist View* was his most personal utterance. What had happened between 1918 and 1929 to lead Radhakrishnan to shift the axis of his thought? If he had had any signal experiences he never spoke of them, for he was of firm opinion that these were not matters one talked about. He had had no mystical vision; but religious experience is not restricted to that type of insight.

There is an illuminating note to be found in his papers written sometime in the thirties:

Religious experience need not always be of the mystic character. There are many religious men who are innocent of ecstasies but pass their lives in a spirit of utter faith in a trend behind phenomena, a Power behind appearances to whom they are responsible and owe reverence. Their lives are passed against such a religious background. These are also the possessors of religious experience though it may not be of an exciting or catastrophic character.

This passage speaks much about himself. The presence of God is not something to be seen or touched but to be felt. Radha-krishnan always felt the presence of the Unseen Reality and was confident that he was being led by a Higher Power. He wrote in the evening of his life of his

conviction based on experience that a great pilot is guiding and taking us from one stage to another. All that he calls for in return is complete surrender. Consciousness of the pervading presence of the Divine has helped me all these days. I have never had any sud-den flash or experience of any other type.[18]

[18] To Dilip Kumar Roy, 29 September 1962.

This feeling of guidance and an inevitability of direction obviously intensified in the twenties to such an extent as to change the stresses in his philosophical outlook. His thinking, as he acknowledged many years later, was born of spiritual experience rather than deduced from logically ascertained premises.[19] 'If you ask me whether my conviction about the reality of God is intellectual or spiritual, it is difficult to answer. It is something deep-rooted, suggested perhaps by the intellect and confirmed by the whole nature.'[20] He carried out in the Hibbert Lectures the task which he had stated in 1926 to be that of every person who has been given a glimpse of what seemed to be the truth: 'the religious seer is compelled to justify his inmost convictions in a way that satisfies the thought of the age.'[21]

It followed that while in *The Reign* Radhakrishnan had criticized religion for distorting philosophy, he now gave a lower role to philosophy. It was to him at this time interpretative rather than creative, not so much an intellectual reconstruction as an exhibition of insights. As conceptual knowing it was a preparation for intuitive understanding and an exposition of it when it was secured. The great truths of philosophy were not proved but seen. The philosophers conveyed visions to others by the machinery of logical proof. The task of the critics of philosophy was to find out whether the views were partial or total, pure or impure. No one could be a philosopher whose non-logical sides were not well developed. If modern philosophers were not as influential as before, it was because the pursuit of wisdom had become dependent on the possession of a technique. Though philosophy is a system of thought, the experience it organizes must be both rich and comprehensive. The vision of the philosopher was the reaction of his whole personality to the nature of the experienced world. It was a mistake to think that the only qualifications for elucidating truth in the sphere of philosophy were purely intellectual. The form in which analytical philosophy comprehends reality is less adequate to the true nature of reality than is the form under which religious intuition grasps it. All that dialectic and philosophy do is to clarify our intuitions.

Radhakrishnan also contended that all creative work in

[19] 'Fragments of a Confession', in Schilpp, p. 10.
[20] To M. C. Ray, 22 July 1954.          [21] *The Hindu View of Life*, p. 15.

science, philosophy and art was inspired by intuitive experience. The great scientific discoveries were the result not of a patient collection of facts or the plodding processes of the intellect but of the inventive genius of the creative thinkers, of a sudden discovery of new meaning in well-known facts. 'Apples had been falling to the ground a long time before Newton worked out the law of gravitation.'[22] But the insight requires previous study. Great intuitions arise out of a matrix of rationality and have to be set forth as a rational synthesis. We invent by intuition and prove by logic. Mere intuitions are blind while intellectual work by itself is empty. A work of art too is creative contemplation which is a process of travail of the spirit. A poem is the image of a vision; and unless the poet speaks from the depths he cannot engage the depths in others. What matters is not the massiveness of thought or the importance of the subject but the purity and profundity of the experience. By these standards, Radhakrishnan regarded the literature of his time as essentially trivial. Even the greatest masters, Shaw, Wells and Bridges, did not seem to him to touch the heights of genius. They were predominantly intellectual and dealt with the tumult and not the depth of the soul. Their works lacked emotional intensity and sustained inspiration.[23]

To Radhakrishnan intuitive insight was essential also for the highest reaches of ethical life. The art of living was not the mechanical observance of rules or the barren rehearsal of stale roles. The moral hero follows his deeper nature, an inner rhythm which guides him on to obey his destiny, fulfil his self. There is intuitive apprehension of the path of duty. But even greater than such men and women who had found themselves on a higher level were those of religious genius, the prophets with the creative spirit. They are free from the dogmas of religious intellectualism. They are lonely, with the sweet dignity, quiet resignation and patient faith of those who dwell in another world. 'Poets and prophets do not go into committees.'[24] They invite the soul to its lonely pilgrimage and give it

---

[22] Ibid., p. 139.
[23] At the time this criticism created a flutter, but is now more generally prevalent. See, for example, W. W. Robson, *Modern English Literature* (Oxford 1984).
[24] *The Hindu View of Life*, p. 162.

absolute freedom in the faith that a free adaptation of the divine into oneself is the essential condition of spiritual life. When the spirit in man inspires the intellect we have genius, when it stirs the will we have heroism, when it flows through the heart we have love, and when it transforms our being the son of man becomes the son of God: 'Put the fire of spirit on any altar, it blazes up to heaven.'[25] Science and criticism have nothing to say against a religion which proclaims an invisible church of spirit which will be a community of men and women of good will, who find nothing hateful but hypocrisy and nothing immoral except hardheartedness.

That all men and women could at some time attain to such greatness was a hope which Radhakrishnan based on his understanding of the theory of evolution. The ideas of Darwin, Wallace and Huxley could be interpreted to take in his concept of the universal spirit in all human beings. Even as the anthropoid ape became the human being, the human could become the divine. According to both Hindu and Buddhist thought, the world is movement and being is process. Modern physics was in line with this, for it regarded matter as a form of energy and nature as a complex of events. There follow life, instinct, intelligence—in Radhakrishnan's phrase, grades of experience. Human progress lies in an increasing awareness of the universal working in the human being. The individual frames ideals, strives after values and struggles to build a world of unity and harmony. The truth of the universe is not a mathematical equation or a kinematical system or a biological adjustment or a psychological pluralism or ethical individualism, but a spiritual organism. From consciousness in the animal world (perception and action) and self-consciousness in the human (intelligence and will), we can move on to superconsciousness, an awareness of the substance of spirit. The spiritualized person is a new genus exhibiting a new quality of life. Cosmic history is working towards its highest moment when the universal tendency towards spiritual life is realized in all. The liberated souls continue to participate in the cosmic process till everyone is redeemed.

What happens then? Human thought, said Radhakrishnan, cannot go beyond this point where the quest ends. But, after

[25] Ibid.

pointing out the flaws in other theories of the universe current at that time, Radhakrishnan offered one of his own. The historical world of becoming is incapable of explanation from within itself; and the reality of God experienced by the mystics is compatible with scientific facts and logical reasoning based on them. Radhakrishnan thought that spirit and not, as Bergson and Shaw suggested, a vital force, was the crucial element. The immanent purposiveness of the world was not inconsistent with the presence of evil, ugliness and error; for it was man's task to transmute them into goodness, beauty and truth. In communicating his nature to us, God makes us sharers in his creative power. The realization of the end of the world depends on human co-operation and is, therefore, unpredictable.[26]

There was still the problem of reconciling Radhakrishnan's religion with his philosophy, even if the latter were only interpreting religious experience. If God is the whole reality which intuitive knowledge affirms, this had to be fitted in with monism and the Ultimate Reality as the ground of all Being. The Upanishads give no definite answer and indeed do not face the question directly.[27] But spiritual idealism required an explanation of the relation between God and the Absolute. In 1926 Radhakrishnan had favoured a wise agnosticism even in the matter of the relation between God and the actual world process. The history of philosophy in India as well as in Europe had been one long illustration of the inability of the human mind to solve this problem, and the greatest thinkers were those who recognized this lack of omniscience. This maya, mystery, should be accepted and one should bow before the impenetrable veil. One knew both God and the world; as for the link between them, Radhakrishnan thought with Bossuet, 'Hold fast both ends and do not try to find out where the lines meet.' If the world were a transformation of God, then, if the whole of God, it became lower pantheism; and if of a part of God, which part? 'We cannot take half a fowl for cooking, leaving the other half for laying eggs.' So the most modest course for philosophers would be to admit a mystery at the

[26] Cf. Bishop Jenkins of Durham: 'I should think God is a supreme artist and we are trying to be collaborative artists.' *The Listener*, 19 June 1986.
[27] *Indian Philosophy*, volume 1, pp. 184–5.

centre of things and recognize that we do not know how the world rests in God.[28]

Yet, as Radhakrishnan added, the logical mind is unwilling to admit defeat. It cannot rest in the idea that the Absolute is incomprehensible and that the world hangs on it somehow. This was as true of him as of any other philosopher. Although in 1926 he had repeatedly advocated the honest acceptance of lack of understanding, and even in 1928 conceded that the relation between the universal spirit and the cosmic process was enveloped in impenetrable mystery,[29] obviously this problem continued to nag him and in 1929 he came up with a possible answer. God is organic with the world. Life beyond time may take us to the Absolute, but God is essentially bound up with the life in time. The process of the world is emergence under the guidance of God, who is immanent in the process but not identical with the world. The creative impulse is active in the world constantly but not predeterminedly. While the Absolute is pure consciousness and pure freedom and infinite possibility, it appears to be God from the point of view of the specific possibility which has become actualized. As to why this particular possibility and not any other has been realized is still a mystery. It is much too difficult for us in the pit to know what is happening behind the screens. But once the infinite Absolute has created a finite universe, it develops, though in no predetermined forms. Man's free will comes into play and he yearns towards God, in whom he finds self-completion. When universal salvation has been achieved, time ends and the universe unites with its source. When the present order of things passes away there will be others, for the possibilities of the Absolute are infinite. If the present universe is running down like a clock, it must have been wound up in the beginning, and if it was wound up once, it can be wound up again. The motionless Absolute and the energizing God are complementary and inseparable. The Absolute is the pre-cosmic nature of God, and God is the Absolute from the

[28] *The Hindu View of Life*, pp. 66–9; 'The Doctrine of Maya: Some Problems', *Proceedings of the Sixth International Congress of Philosophy* (New York 1927), pp. 683–9. For a recent analysis of Radhakrishnan's views on this subject, see R. D. Tuck, *The Concept of Maya in Samkara and Radhakrishnan* (Delhi 1986).

[29] *The Religion We Need*, p. 26.

human end, the cosmic point of view.[30]

This was not a complete metaphysical system and had not been worked out in-detail; 'indeed', suggested Evelyn Underhill, herself a distinguished student of mysticism, 'he shows his genuine spirituality by a humble refusal to try to make all the pieces of our puzzle fit.'[31] As Radhakrishnan later observed, perhaps a complete system is not only unattainable but undesirable. A problem completely solved is no problem, a God that is fully understood is no God at all.[32] But even as it stands the system as elaborated in *An Idealist View* constitutes Radhakrishnan's major effort at constructive and original thinking. The Absolute with its playful freedom, as envisaged by him, was midway between the Pure Being of Samkara and the Concrete Absolute Spirit of Hegel. As a review in the *Times Literary Supplement* pointed out, he had boldly confronted the problem which had haunted Bradley and come forward with a solution which fused Indian and Western thought and envisaged creation being at once ransomed and annulled by the perfection of all spirits and the cessation of the impulse to individuate:

This is no place to discuss the case for and against a subtle and elevated philosophical system; but it at least behoves every inquirer to ask himself whether the gulf between this eschatology and that which asserts the 'value and destiny of the individual' is or is not one which is ultimately bridgeable. Those who feel able to reply in the affirmative may well accept Radhakrishnan, not merely as the distinguished exponent of a lofty spiritual philosophy (as he assuredly is), but as the initiator of a new synthesis.[33]

The lectures themselves, swift and forceful in delivery, rich in substance, astonishingly wide in their range of learning and philosophical grasp, and crackling with epigram and wit, drew large audiences both in Manchester and London. They

[30] *An Idealist View of Life*, pp. 263–73; 'Fragments of a Confession' and 'Reply to Critics', in Schilpp, pp. 44-7 and 796–9 respectively.

[31] *The Spectator*, 22 December 1933.

[32] Speech at Parliament of Religions in Bombay, 7 May 1936, *Times of India*, 8 May 1936. Cf. A. N. Whitehead: 'Philosophy begins in wonder. And, at the end, when philosophic thought has done its best, the wonder remains. There have been added, however, some grasp of the immensity of things, some purification of emotion by understanding.' *Nature and Life* (Chicago University Press 1934).

[33] 3 May 1934. We now know that the reviewer was Lawrence Hyde.

were the largest gatherings seen at either place since the First World War at public lectures on a philosophical subject; and the striking feature was that most of those present were young men and women straight from classrooms, offices and factories, 'listening to a profoundly religious man expounding to a generation which has largely lost its religion a profoundly religious view of life'.[34] After the last lecture in London the audience lined up to shake hands with the speaker; and many whom he did not know wrote to thank him for his utterance: 'In you a great dream is realized—the East bringing its own message in our own language thro' one who knows all about Western thought.'[35]

If the young were there in their hundreds, it was to some extent because Radhakrishnan was so eloquent and, to British audiences, an unusual speaker. They were captivated by this gushing stream of perfectly balanced sentences, poured forth without a note or a gesture, and conveying lightly a profundity of thought. They would have been even more surprised had they known that at Manchester Radhakrishnan did not even have his papers with him to refresh his memory before the lectures, for the British Railways had misplaced his luggage. No one else at this time anywhere in the world enjoyed this command of Western and Eastern philosophy, awareness of current thought and problems, felicity of phrase and fluency of expression. Sir Francis Younghusband, who listened to the lectures in London, wrote that

in the delivery of his addresses he gives the same impression of grace and finish that 'Ranji' gives to cricketers. As 'Ranji' had the quickness of eye and suppleness of wrist to play strokes which delighted onlookers by their consummate ease and mastery, so Radhakrishnan will, in perfect English and with great rapidity, give an address on the profoundest problems of existence which will enchant all those who hear it.[36]

But there was more to Radhakrishnan than mesmerism of speech. He appealed to many who, while willing to look in-

[34] C. E. M. Joad in *The Spectator*, 16 February 1930.

[35] J. Tyssul Davis (of the London Unitarian Ministers Group) to Radhakrishnan, 21 January 1930.

[36] F. Younghusband, *Dawn in India* (London 1930), p. 282.

wards, yet found themselves incapable of traditional belief. Typical was the reaction of an undergraduate at St Hugh's College in Oxford: 'I think I almost hated you last term, because you had so completely smashed up everything I had believed in. I'm only just beginning to thank you, but it is hard to begin to build everything up again ... you've raised up a kind of volcano inside me, and you ought to understand ...'[37]

The spoken word and impact of personality soon pass. Yet, when *An Idealist View of Life* was published in 1932, the book secured even greater attention than the lectures had done. His friends and fellow idealists, Muirhead and Mackenzie, were, as was to be expected, enthusiastic. Muirhead compared him with Bergson and found behind the doctrinal differences a certain unity of spirit;[38] and Mackenzie commended a 'very brilliant' book.[39] Bertrand Russell, while unsympathetic to the approach, recognized that it was 'the greatest influence for religion in this crisis'.[40] Samuel Alexander, who had listened to the lectures in Manchester, thought that Radhakrishnan tended to be summary in his criticisms of other schools of philosophy and was much better in working out his own positions;[41] and Dean Inge, unlike others who too easily cast Radhakrishnan in the role of an Eastern sage and relished the book's oriental flavour, discerned that Radhakrishnan was fully steeped in a tradition which was not solely Indian but had among its forebears Plato, Plotinus, Augustine and Eckhart. So the book was 'a brilliant and cogent exposition of what spiritual religion means to the modern mind'.[42] A more orthodox Christian reviewer, while disputing a number of Radhakrishnan's interpretations, saluted the 'beautiful religious spirit' and found that the persuasive gentleness and clarity and grace of style had made the reading of the book a pleasure. Radhakrishnan seemed to have read almost everything of any importance written in the English language, and in most cases set forth the main contention with more lucidity than the

[37] 15 May 1930.      [38] *Hibbert Journal*, October 1932.
[39] *Mind*, October 1932.
[40] *The Literary Guide*, New York.
[41] *Manchester Guardian*, 10 August 1932.
[42] *The Week-End Review*, 4 November 1933.

original writers. 'Even Professor Whitehead he leads gently in the ways of simplicity.'[43]

As in the case of the lectures, for the book too the circle of appreciation extended far beyond professional scholars. *The New York Times* found it 'startling in its timeliness', and the editor of *Everyman* commended it for showing how ordinary men and women could start where they were in practising the religious life and using their own familiar circumstances as the material out of which the perfect life could be made.[44] Hugh Fausset was impressed by Radhakrishnan's real spiritual insight which freed him from the provincialism of the intellectual, the dogmatist or the sectarian. Such a rare combination of spiritual and scientific knowledge represented a collaboration between East and West which was full of fertile promise.[45]

For a serious philosophical work the book sold widely, was repeatedly reprinted and went into a paperback edition in 1961. C. E. M. Joad, a popular expositor with no religious preconceptions and an avowed agnostic as far as the established religions were concerned, was so entranced by Radhakrishnan's eloquence and readability that he wrote a full-scale work about the substance and significance of his philosophy, titled *Counter-Attack from the East*. This is a warm-hearted book with a personal approach. Joad paid tribute to Radhakrishnan's integrated personality, his gift of sustained elucidation, the capacity for brilliant statement and the illuminating phrase, the synoptic vision and social awareness. To a Western world afflicted with scepticism in belief, guidelessness in matters of conduct and indifference in regard to values, Radhakrishnan offered a reasoned defence of religion. Joad termed it a counter-attack from the East because it seemed to him that Radhakrishnan was seeking a new synthesis of thought expressing itself alike in religion, politics and civilization. While calling on fellow-Indians to set their own house in order and throw off the shackles of the dead past, Radhakrishnan provided to the West a spiritual view of the universe as possessing values and thereby withstood the attacks of various currents of modern thought.

Joad was sympathetic but not unquestioning. He remained a pluralist and was not convinced that Radhakrishnan's monism

---

[43] John Oman in *The Journal of Theological Studies*, April 1933.
[44] *Everyman*, 21 July 1932.         [45] *Yorkshire Post*, 3 August 1932.

had explained away the dualism of subjects and objects. Nor was he persuaded by Radhakrishnan's explanation of the problem of evil as part of the drama of man's striving by free will towards perfection. He was, moreover, ready to acknowledge that he himself had had no religious experience and could, therefore, only say, not that Radhakrishnan's analysis was true, but that it may be true. Yet the simplified précis of Radhakrishnan's thought primarily as expressed in *An Idealist View of Life* brought it to the notice of an even wider audience than Radhakrishnan's own work had reached; and in the thirties Radhakrishnan became almost a cult figure in Europe and America.

This was to Radhakrishnan's extreme distaste. Regarding the self's encounter with the inner spirit as the only valid form of experience, he had little use for human teachers and gurus and was often suspicious of their intentions. A favourite crack in his lectures was, 'A *sadhu* has been seen in Swat, and the police are after him.' So it did not please him to see himself placed in the role of a spiritual guide rather than a philosophical analyst. He was also not much impressed by the quality of Joad's book, regarding it as belonging to the higher category of journalism. He felt that Joad had flattened out the subtleties and smothered the nuances of his thought. It was, too, a distortion to lay emphasis on the suggestion that he was launching a counter-attack from the East; while his system had been considerably influenced by Indian philosophy and he was persuaded that the Hindu approach to religion was the most appropriate for the modern world, basically Radhakrishnan was in the mainstream of the idealist tradition and his standpoint was very similar to that which some Western philosophers were working out for themselves without the help of the Upanishads. For Radhakrishnan, whose main hope was to give a new vitality to the religious outlook everywhere by assimilating the latest developments in all branches of intellectual discipline, it was irritating to be portrayed as advocating that men and women should cease to think and act and learn to sit back and feel. Yet it was this parody of his views that gained general credence and wide support.[46] Indeed this trend went so far that Radha-

---

[46] R. Graves and A. Hodge, *The Long Week-End: A Social History of Great Britain 1919-1939* (London 1940), pp. 202-3.

krishnan found himself, to his amusement as well as chagrin, figuring in a novel by a story-teller of romances in imperial contexts.[47] The ruler of a border province in India turns the pages of *An Idealist View* in the midst of his administrative chores, is captivated by Radhakrishnan's wit as well as wisdom, and is convinced that the 'newer Hinduism' which he preaches offers a noble philosophy of thought and life to any thinking man of any creed. Radhakrishnan was lauded as one of the few builders of the 'rainbow bridge' between the age-old wisdom of India and all the new knowledge of the West that, without wisdom, could only bring destruction.

Such vulgar popularization of a serious philosophical work was bound to produce a reaction. That orthodox Christian thinkers complained that Radhakrishnan appeared to be unaware of a God of grace did not surprise him. But more challenging was the charge that by his emphasis on intuition he had demoted reason from pride of place. J. S. Collis, basing himself on Joad's book, criticized Radhakrishnan as one 'who, while undoubtedly a true mystic in Eastern fashion, spends most of his time on the circumference of the problem, luxuriating in intellectual irrelevancies'.[48] Religion was but a surmise which could not possibly be influenced by science. On the same lines but even sharper, and again on the basis of Joad's exposition, was the criticism of Leonard Woolf. The dethronement of reason was a common phenomenon at the ebb of all civilizations and Woolf castigated Radhakrishnan's philosophy as belonging to that category. What Radhakrishnan elaborated could be neither proved nor communicated and was therefore no more than 'loud quackery'. When Joad protested that he had not contended that Radhakrishnan's claims for mysticism must be true and only that they might be true, Woolf replied that he could see no point in writing in high praise of an inexplicable and incommunicable message unless it was believed that there was truth in what was said.[49]

Joad clearly got the worse of these exchanges, and Woolf

[47] Maud Diver, *The Dream Prevails* (London 1938).
[48] J. S. Collis, *Farewell to Argument* (London 1935), p. 148.
[49] L. Woolf, 'Quack Quack! Or Having It Both Ways', *New Statesman and Nation*, 2 December 1933; Joad's reply and Woolf's rejoinder, ibid., 9 December 1933, and Joad's second reply, ibid., 16 December 1933.

expanded his criticism into a full-scale work, denouncing intellectual quackery in all its forms in Europe in the thirties. If Hitler and Mussolini represented the political assault on reason and intelligence, Spengler and Bergson provided the philosophical counterpart; and to their names he added that of Radhakrishnan, whose philosophy he considered an extreme form of metaphysical mumbo-jumbo. It was to him sterile oriental mysticism, refurbished by a writer of considerable intellectual power and decorated with the flowers and fruit of Western rationalism. Woolf did not regard all mysticism as spurious; he objected only to efforts to impose such views on those who had not had similar experience. This formed for him the metaphysical revolt against reason which was part of the decivilizing process.[50] He paid insufficient attention to Radhakrishnan's argument that intuition supplemented reason and did not supplant it. A possible explanation of Woolf's sharpness in criticism is that a combination of the rational and the intuitive was at the base of his own wife's attitude.

Witty and stinging, linking the attack of the dictators on liberty with the discount placed by some philosophers on reason, Woolf's book was a bestseller in the summer of 1935. Radhakrishnan, feeling that it had been unfair of Woolf to depict him as a shaman or medicine-man on the basis of Joad's commentary, sent him a copy of *An Idealist View*. He protested that he was not anti-intellectual, as Woolf had made him out to be, and added that if after reading the book Woolf still felt that he had revolted against reason, there would be need for rethinking on his part. Woolf thanked him for 'an extraordinarily nice letter' and for the book, gestures of Radhakrishnan which made him 'feel as if coals of fire are being heaped on my head'; but, after reading the book, he found no grounds to revise his assessment. In fact, he had been shocked that Radhakrishnan could believe what he did and make the statements which he had. Reason and intelligence could make no sense of the universe, and the claim of Radhakrishnan that direct perceptions provided understanding opened 'an unfathomable gulf' between them. It was impossible, as Radhakrishnan conceded, to bridge this gulf through correspondence

---

[50] Leonard Woolf, *Quack, Quack!* (London 1935).

when hundreds of pages were unable to do so.[51]

Though the critics were not converted, *An Idealist View* was the most distinguished of Radhakrishnan's writings and his major claim on posterity. He drew a complete map of current knowledge, used it in a fresh way to support his arguments and rounded it off with an original hypothesis. Above all, he spoke from the depths and clearly with the intuitive insight which was to him basic. But, after more than fifty years, does the system elaborated with subtlety and combative forcefulness in *An Idealist View* still stand up, or is the book now read chiefly for its literary excellence and the passages of eloquence and power? The epigrams glint as brightly today as when they were first written—but is that all? The book, of course, served a specific need in the temper of the inter-War years, 'devoid of faith, yet terrified of scepticism';[52] but it also offers a response to the religious impulse which is continuous in human nature. For questing minds in a changing world it still provides a spiritual philosophy that withstands both scientific naturalism and religious dogmatism. Belief in God and the Absolute was not inconsistent with or demolished by other systems through which we gain coherent knowledge of the world in which we live. The general character of the universe as known was reconcilable with the intuited certainty of God. There was no reason why the rational man should not rely on his own religious experience.

By the late twenties, the dualistic, mechanistic view of the world had been destroyed by the new theories of relativity and quantum physics. An aggregate of distinct units was replaced by waves, differentials of time and curvature of space. Uncertainty and indeterminacy were the new paradigms. Joseph Needham, though professing Marxism, recognized that to penetrate to the 'alogical' core of the world philosophy and religion as well as science were needed, plus 'moments of insight, of mystical experience closely allied to the apprehen-

[51] Radhakrishnan to Woolf, 22 July 1935; Woolf to Radhakrishnan, 23 July 1935; Radhakrishnan to Woolf, 24 July 1935; Woolf to Radhakrishnan, 4 August 1935; and Radhakrishnan to Woolf, 8 August 1935. Radhakrishnan's letters are in the Woolf papers at the Sussex University Library, and Woolf's letters in the Radhakrishnan papers.

[52] J. S. Mill, *On Liberty.*

sion of the beautiful which all three of them give us'.[53] Radhakrishnan utilized these new perceptions of science to support his views; and the advances in science since that time have strengthened his position by further dematerializing the universe. Physicists have long given up a mechanical approach to the cosmos and are moving to a concept of an ordered whole.[54] 'A physicist who rejects the testimony of saints and mystics is no better than a tone-deaf man deriding the power of music.'[55] Radhakrishnan tended to make a number of *ex cathedra* statements on subjects like immortality and rebirth. He spoke, for example, of the 'mistaken view' of the rebirth of human beings in the form of animals and added that simply because we do not understand the process we cannot deny the fact.[56] How, one is bound to wonder with Woolf, does he know even the fact? Despite the apparatus of argument, Radhakrishnan in essence communicates a vision; and to accept his contention that this vision is true is to take with him at a crucial point a leap of faith. But the core of his system, the universe as spirit, has, to put it at the minimum, gained further corroboration from science since the time he wrote. More and more scientists are coming round to the view that the world we know is not just a gigantic accident, one chance in a billion and that there is an element of design in some generalized sense.[57] As for attaining knowledge of this reality, the observations of Bertrand Russell, normally indifferent to religion, are of interest. He recognized the existence of 'side by side the two truths, the truth of science and the truth of vision', and believed 'that, by sufficient restraint, there is an element of wisdom to be learned from the mystical way of feeling, which does not seem to be attainable in any other manner'. The vice in philosophers was due to their determination to find religion;

[53] *The Sceptical Biologist* (London 1929), p. 65.
[54] P. Davies, *God and the New Physics* (London 1983), pp. 64, 221.
[55] Brian Pippard in the *Times Literary Supplement*, 29 July 1983.
[56] *An Idealist View of Life*, p. 234.
[57] Cf. W. H. Thorpe: 'Indeed one can say that the "Argument from Design" has been brought back to a central position in our thought, from which it was banished by the theory of "evolution by natural selection" more than a century ago. There seems now to be justification for assuming that from its first moment the universe was "ordered" or programmed—was in fact Cosmos, not Chaos.' *Purpose in a World of Chance* (Oxford 1978), pp. 11–12.

but mysticism could be commended as an attitude towards life even if not as a creed about the world.[58]

Theories of evolution seemed to Radhakrishnan to fit neatly into the framework of his philosophy. The Upanishads had spoken of the five stages of the cosmic process—matter, life, instinct, reflective consciousness and spiritual consciousness; and it was the last stage which had now to be reached. Humanity had to work for this. The meaning of history was to Radhakrishnan the establishment of a kingdom of free spirits. But scientists today are not agreed that what the Buddha termed 'the ladder of being' leads automatically to the topmost rung of spiritual freedom. Radhakrishnan's assumption that the nature of evolution presumes a deeper law of inward striving after higher forms of life and a persistent tendency to self-perfection would be regarded by some as what has been recently described as 'the escalation fallacy'.[59] But to Radhakrishnan, with his faith in an indwelling God, evolution was a moral and a spiritual process. He is more with Lamarck and Spencer than with Darwin and Huxley.

As for his emphasis on intuition, Radhakrishnan always contended that he was not an anti-intellectual intellectual, providing rational justification for a basically anti-rational attitude. His ideas were based on the notion in the Upanishads of the comradeship of scientific knowledge and intuitive experience. Intuition can throw light on the dark places which intellect cannot penetrate; but the results of mystic intuition should be subjected to logical analysis. The results of intellect will be fragmentary and incomplete without the help of intuition while intuitional insights would be blind and dumb without intellectual confirmation.[60] Intuition was not a euphemism for instinct. It was dependent on thought, took up reason and went beyond it. In his later writings Radhakrishnan emphasized that the human mind does not function in fractions. The concept of personality as a bundle of faculties, instinct and emotion, desire and will, intellect and intuition, was misleading. The

[58] G. G. Leithauser, 'The Romantic Russell and the Legacy of Shelley', and N. Griffin, 'Bertrand Russell's Crisis of Faith', in M. Moran and C. Spadoni, *Intellect and Social Conscience* (Hamilton 1984), p. 33 and pp. 113–16 respectively.

[59] M. Midgley, *Evolution as a Religion* (London 1985), p. 6.

[60] *Indian Philosophy*, volume I, pp. 179–81.

various faculties shade off one into another by imperceptible gradations. To use Sartre's language, the individual is a totality and not a collection. In all knowledge the whole personality is at work. We can distinguish between the various faculties of the human being in thought but not in fact. So any coherent philosophy should take into account observed data, rational reflection and intuitive insight. Such insight comes only to such persons as have thought hard and long on a subject. Intuitive knowledge is verified by its capacity to bring order and harmony into systems framed by the intellect. It is also intellect which tests the validity of intuitions, supports and clarifies spiritual experience and communicates the results to others.[61]

That intuition or inspiration, or whatever it be called, is a means of forwarding our understanding is now generally accepted. Great art is known to be, in the words of Daniel Weiss, the intuitive grasp of the nature of things, while inferior art is the studied grasp of these relations. E. M. Forster distinguished carefully between thought, logic and what is indefinable but he called 'pure creation'.[62] Russell too recognized the existence of an element deeper than conscious thought:

I haven't the vaguest idea either how I think or how one ought to think. The process, so far as I know it, is as instinctive and unconscious as digestion. I fill my mind with whatever relevant knowledge I can find, and just wait. With luck, there comes a moment when the work is done, but in the meantime my conscious mind has been occupied with other things.[63]

Eliot believed that poetic composition was not an activity that could be consciously controlled.[64] Lévi-Strauss has denied responsibility for his books; they get written through him by 'poetic intuition'.[65] Sir Peter Medawar, who scorned 'philosophy fiction' and regarded it as an 'elevated kind of barminess',

[61] 'Reply to Critics', in Schilpp, pp. 790–5; *Recovery of Faith* (London 1956), p. 107.
[62] *Commonplace Book* (Scolar Press 1985), p. 52.
[63] To Gilbert Murray, 15 January 1939. *Autobiography*, volume II (London 1968), p. 246.
[64] Peter Ackroyd, *T. S. Eliot* (London 1984), p. 261.
[65] R. Needham, 'The Truth of the Meaningful', *Times Literary Supplement*, 13 April 1984.

yet conceded that the necessity of reason did not mean the
sufficiency of reason, rejected the reductionist view of the complete accountability of science to reason, and recognized that
'in science a creative imagination is the privilege of the rare
spirit who achieves in a blaze of intuition what the rest of us
can only do by rote or by "analytic industry".'[66] Max Perutz
has described scientific research as an imaginative activity,
dependent on qualities of mind that are beyond our comprehension: 'There is no linear progression from the appearance of a problem to its solution.'[67]

Radhakrishnan felt no need in later years, in the light of
new knowledge and experience, to revise the essentials of his
philosophical system.[68] It has also gained more general acceptance today than even in the thirties. Philosophy is a fashion-
bound discipline, and fewer believe now than some years ago
that all knowledge must be based on sensation. Metaphysics
has once again become acceptable and is not regarded as just,
in Sir Alfred Ayer's phrase, 'woolly uplift'. Commonsense provides only an inadequate approximation to the truth; one
needs recourse to many ways to get at the whole. Jung has
pleaded for a widening of consciousness beyond the narrow
limits set by a tyrannical intellect;[69] and to Jaspers actual cognition or knowledge is a synthesis of thought and intuition in one
apprehension.[70] 'Philosophy', said Wittgenstein, 'is like trying
to open a safe with a combination lock; each little adjustment
of the dials seems to achieve nothing, only when everything is
in place does the door open.'[71] Radhakrishnan would have
agreed.

If, then, his philosophy has current validity, his religious
teachings have real immediacy. It is not merely that he felt to
the full the difficulties of faith and the force of modern criticism
in an age of doubt and provided satisfying rejoinders. He was
himself one of the prophet souls of whom he spoke.

[66] *Pluto's Republic* (Oxford 1982), pp. 45, 249, 328–9.

[67] 'Spying Made Easy', *London Review of Books*, 25 June 1987.

[68] See his 'Reply to Critics', in Schilpp, pp. 789–842, and his introduction to
*The Brahma Sutra* (London 1960), especially pp. 103–223.

[69] Cited by H. Coward, *Jung and Eastern Thought* (New York 1985), p. 8.

[70] W. Earle, 'Anthropology in the Philosophy of Karl Jaspers', in P. A. Schilpp
(ed.), *The Philosophy of Karl Jaspers* (New York 1957), p. 527.

[71] R. Rhees (ed.), *Recollections of Wittgenstein* (Oxford 1984), p. 81.

The original man of understanding, and not the priest or the mechanical imitator of inherited habits, is needed to help our wandering generation to fashion a goal for itself. With the growing retreat from dogmatic faith to the humanist core of idealism, with an objective God and a sense of sin becoming increasingly outmoded, more and more are turning to the approach and the values which Radhakrishnan outlined. The convincing nature of its philosophical and religious systems as well as its literary attractiveness give *An Idealist View of Life* the quality of timeless pertinence which proclaims the live classic.

## III

During this year at Oxford Radhakrishnan had much else to do besides delivering the Hibbert Lectures. In his courses on comparative religion at Manchester College he gave the discipline a new slant. Till then it had been developed as a branch of apologetics to reaffirm, in contrast to other sets of beliefs, that one's own religion was superior and had a monopoly of truth. In this context Radhakrishnan was severe, not on Christianity as taught by Christ but on the Christian churches as organized, rigid and chauvinist institutions. He was particularly critical of missionaries in India and did not hesitate to describe the Anglican church as linked up with British imperialism. The study of other religions, indispensable for the proper understanding of one's own, had to be based on the assumption that one religion was as good as another and none was final or perfect. All religions were quickened by the same spirit and the different systems were tentative adjustments, more or less satisfactory, to spiritual reality. Inner religious consciousness was similar everywhere and the different religions had a common background and had borrowed from each other. Radhakrishnan thought that, generally speaking, the dominant features of Eastern thought were its insistence on creative intuition and the life of spirit, a non-dogmatic approach, an attitude of 'spiritual good manners', and statements of religious ideas in terms of masks and symbols, while the Western systems were characterized by a greater adherence to critical intelligence, an eagerness for definition and form, and an insistence on the divine personality. But there were prominent exceptions to these generalizations, and there was much that the East and the West could learn from each other. Every living religion had a part to play in the spiritual education of humanity and, for any religious internationalism, a comparative study of religions was indispensable. The unity of the modern world demanded a new spiritual and cultural basis, so that the whole of humanity was bound by one spirit, though not by one name.[72]

Between these lectures, to which he was committed, and during the vacations, Radhakrishnan agreed to requests to speak in various parts of Britain, and, towards the end of his stay in the spring and summer of 1930, he was giving a major address almost every day. His friend Bishop David invited him to Liverpool to preach at the cathedral in that city; the Quakers at Birmingham wished him to talk to them over a weekend; Stanton Coit persuaded him to speak at a service in the Ethical Church in London.

But, as was to be expected of Radhakrishnan, all his activities were not solely spiritual. He agreed to mediate between two rival societies of Indian students in Britain and asked the chief disputants to meet him at the waiting-room in Paddington station. There he met V. K. Krishna Menon again, whom he had known years before as a student in Madras. The two groups accepted Radhakrishnan's suggestion that they merge their organizations in the newly-formed National Union of Indian Students, of which Radhakrishnan was elected chairman for the few months that he was in Britain so that he could get it going. It followed that he was asked to be the chief speaker at the tenth anniversary of the Indian Students Hostel in London in February 1930. The political situation in India was by now heading to a crisis. The Congress party had declared its objective to be complete independence and Mahatma Gandhi was preparing for a campaign of civil disobedience. Radhakrishnan's membership of the Indian Educational Service bound him to make no political speech, but by now he had ceased to care. Asserting that it was natural for educated Indians to want to be free and to feel bitterly the shame of bondage, he thought that no sensible person in Britain would want to see India pledge herself to perpetual subordination,

[72] For Radhakrishnan's lectures on comparative religion in 1929–30, see his *East and West in Religion* (London 1933), pp. 13–70.

just as no Indian would wish to sever the British connection if it earned its right to be preserved. The cry for independence was to him a cry of despair. If Britain genuinely desired partnership with India, he was confident that the Indian leaders would respond. Justice, common sense, a perception of the realities of the case and the cause of world peace all demanded freedom for India, and it was the duty of the clear-sighted and the forward-looking in Britain to foster it.[73]

Even more telling was Radhakrishnan's sermon at Manchester College on 8 June. By then civil disobedience in India was in full swing and Gandhi was in prison. Radhakrishnan felt keenly his being on the sidelines while others accepted prison and suffering. There was a touch of personal guilt in the remark he is reported to have made at a party in Bangalore a few years before, even before civil disobedience had started, that while every family in Europe had sent a husband or son to the war, in India no one was willing even to resign a job.[74] That sense of identification with the movement which Gandhi had started comes through in the sermon at Oxford. Choosing as his text a passage in Ezekiel which prophesied incessant upheaval till the right order prevailed, Radhakrishnan preached revolution through suffering and love. In an address sparkling in style and in thought, and charged with emotion, Radhakrishnan spoke of the believers in God who possess the faith that rebels and who bring not peace but dissension, for they steer by stars which the world cannot see. Caught by a purpose greater than their own, they cannot turn back until the goal is reached. He who took upon himself a nation's shame was the true leader. The world belonged to the unarmed challengers of the mighty, the meek resisters who put truth above policy, humanity above country, love above force.[75] Patently it was Gandhi whom Radhakrishnan had chiefly in mind, though he did not mention him by name; and the intensity of his utterance carried its own conviction: 'Though the Indian preacher had the marvellous power to weave a magic web of thought, imagination and language, the real

[73] Much of the text of this speech has been printed in S. Radhakrishnan, *Freedom and Culture* (Madras 1936), pp. 146–52.

[74] See C. R. Reddy to Radhakrishnan, 6 July 1930.

[75] 'Revolution through Suffering', *East and West in Religion*, pp. 101–25.

greatness of his sermon resides in some indefinable spiritual quality which arrests attention, moves the heart, and lifts us into an ampler air.'[76]

With so many demands, entailing much hard work and constant travelling, Radhakrishnan was by the end longing to be back at rest in his little corner in Calcutta: 'I am most unhappy here, feeling absolutely homesick. A lonely love-starved life is not worth much and one who is being mistaken for a religious man has to be more cautious in his behaviour. So I am looking homewards and living up to my reputation here!'[77] When his friend J. C. Ghosh teased him that he was too well-known a person to accost the attractive girls in the streets of Oxford, Radhakrishnan retorted, 'Do you think I can't go and fall in love with the next girl? I can, but I won't.'[78] But such willed self-denial was not unqualified. There had been an admiring girl training to be a teacher in Manchester, as well as the wife of an Indian official in London. Emotional deprivation, such as it was, had not been Radhakrishnan's real torment. It was worry of an entirely different nature that caused him much inner anguish, though he gave no outward sign of it in this year of triumphs.

## IV

The *Modern Review* was an English monthly published from Calcutta, and with a wide circulation throughout India; and its editor, Ramananda Chatterjee, was respected for his many years of service to journalism and his nationalist stance. It was in the *Modern Review*, for example, that Jawaharlal Nehru chose to publish his unsigned article in 1936 criticizing himself for developing dictatorial tendencies. But Chatterjee and the firm-minded vice-chancellor of Calcutta University, Sir Ashutosh Mukherjee, could not get on; and there was constant sniping in the pages of the *Modern Review* at the way in which the affairs

[76] Report in an Oxford daily quoted by Radhakrishnan, 'My Search for Truth', in Ferm, p. 42.

[77] To Shyama Prasad Mukherjee, 17 April 1930, S. P. Mukherjee papers, NMML.

[78] Hiren Mukherjee, 'Reminiscences of Radhakrishnan', *Mainstream* (Delhi), 26 April 1975.

of the university were being conducted. A particular target was Mukherjee's recruitment of non-Bengalis to senior positions; and this grouse was made even more explicit in the sister journal in Bengali, the *Prabasi*. Snide remarks were made about the appointment of such persons from outside the province as Bhandarkar the orientalist, and C. V. Raman. It could be expected, therefore, that Mukherjee's selection of Radhakrishnan for the chair of philosophy would be received with consternation; and from April 1921, within a few weeks of Radhakrishnan's arrival in Calcutta, there were regular attacks on his writings. Having declined to publish a favourable review of *The Reign of Religion* by R. D. Ranade, a scholar from Allahabad who was himself an authority on Indian philosophy, Chatterjee carried over the years long articles accusing Radhakrishnan, among other things, of faulty English, ignorance of Bengali, lack of Sanskrit learning, imperfect acquaintance with Western philosophy, and careless and inadequate references. The barrage was then extended to insinuate that Radhakrishnan had served, till Ashutosh Mukherjee's death in 1924, as a courtier of the vice-chancellor in the counsels of the university.[79] Radhakrishnan, in turn, unwittingly gave Chatterjee special cause for dislike. He had secured for the inaugural issue of *The New Era* a poem by Sarojini Naidu; and later issues carried articles from a wide variety of distinguished figures from India and abroad. Though *The New Era* folded up after four years, Chatterjee saw in it at this time a threat to the primacy of the *Modern Review* as the leading journal in English under Indian editorship; and he held Radhakrishnan responsible for such success as *The New Era* enjoyed.

This was fertile ground for Radhakrishnan's opponents to move in—and of opponents he had created many by his unusually quick rise to renown and appointment to a prestigious chair. The conspiracy was hatched by Surendranath Dasgupta, the self-proclaimed rival of Radhakrishnan, who had been the local candidate for the chair; Brajendranath Seal, whom Radhakrishnan had succeeded as George V Professor and of whose writings he had been critical; and Jadunath Sarkar, who belonged to the anti-Mukherjee cabal in the university. An

[79] *Modern Review*, May 1927, pp. 655–6.

instrument at hand for the plotters was Jadunath Sinha, a young postgraduate scholar working on Indian systems of psychology. He had submitted a thesis which Radhakrishnan had examined for the doctorate degree; and Sinha claimed to see in the second volume of *Indian Philosophy*, published in 1927, passages identical to some in his unpublished thesis, submitted two years earlier. The issue of the *Modern Review* for January 1929 carried a long letter from Sinha charging Radhakrishnan with plagiarism and citing passages from the thesis and Radhakrishnan's book. Perhaps it was thought that Radhakrishnan would let this go unchallenged, for he had till now been silent in the face of the *Modern Review's* sustained vendetta; and anyway he had been expected to leave for Oxford on a year's leave at the end of 1928. But it so happened that Radhakrishnan had postponed his departure by a few months; and when not merely his scholarship and intelligence but his honour and integrity were impugned, Radhakrishnan was driven to reply. He pointed out that he had been studying these Sanskrit texts and lecturing on them for many years and had indeed been assisting his students in translating them. Notes taken at his lectures in Madras, Mysore and Calcutta were in great demand and Sinha could well have seen them. Moreover, in translating Sanskrit texts into English it was natural that the same words were often used; indeed, it would be difficult to find other words even if one wished to do so. In fact, Sinha himself had furnished translations of some texts identical with those given by Ganganatha Jha some years before. The manuscript of the second volume of *Indian Philosophy* had been sent to the publishers much before Sinha's submission of the thesis, even though it had appeared only in 1927.

Radhakrishnan, it may be said, was particularly open to charges of plagiarism. His omnivorous reading, combined with his power of total recall, meant that sometimes in his speeches he would repeat word for word passages he had read many years before without being aware that he was indulging in direct quotation. An absorbent memory is sometimes a disadvantage. But in this specific case he was innocent of even unconscious borrowing from another author, and his reply would seem to have dealt effectively with Sinha's allegations. But Ramananda Chatterjee, while publishing Radhakrishnan's letter, had refused to publish a letter from Nalin Ganguly, an old student of Radhakrishnan, corroborating that Radhakrishnan had provided him with translations of the concerned texts as early as 1922.[80] On the other hand, Chatterjee continued to publish further letters from Sinha reiterating his charges, and took the unusual—and, for a journalist, unethical—step of publishing an editorial note making clear that he sided with Sinha.

The matter could obviously not rest here. Chatterjee permitted Sinha's letters to be reprinted elsewhere, notably by *Justice*, the organ of the non-Brahmin party in Madras; and it was clear that a systematic effort was being made by dedicated detractors to destroy Radhakrishnan's reputation as a scholar and public figure. So Radhakrishnan had no option but, in the summer of 1929, to file, in the Calcutta High Court, a plaint for defamation against Jadunath Sinha and Ramananda Chatterjee, and seek Rs 100,000 as damages. Sinha promptly lodged a counter-claim of Rs 20,000 for literary piracy. The cases were finally taken up four years later, in the spring of 1933. For Radhakrishnan the years between formed a time of much mental agony and waste of time and labour. The serenity of mind indispensable for his kind of creative work was disturbed. But the expenses normally entailed by such litigation were reduced by his legal counsel refusing to charge fees. Indeed the lawyers appearing for him spread across the political spectrum of Bengal, from Sir N. N. Sirkar, advocate-general of Bengal and later law member of the Government of India; Asoka Roy, who followed Sirkar in both these posts; to Sarat Bose, brother of Subhas Bose and one of the leading Congressmen of the province; and Shyama Prasad Mukherjee, the future leader of the Jan Sangh. His solicitor was Dhiren Mitra, the future solicitor-general to the Government of India. When Radhakrishnan offered to pay this galaxy their standard fees, Sirkar replied on their behalf, 'You are the guest of Bengal and have brought honour to this province; it is our duty to look after you.' Obviously the Bengali chauvinism which corroded Chatterjee's spirit was not a widespread disease. Radhakrishnan himself was deeply moved by this response of friendship at a crisis in his career, and always felt more at home in Bengal than in any other part of India.

[80] Ganguly's letter was later published in *The Calcutta Review*, March 1929.

While waiting for the cases to be reached, efforts were made by third parties to secure a compromise. Tagore, a friend of Chatterjee and a well-wisher of Radhakrishnan, was helpless in the matter; and the other mediators could only report failure. When the cases came up in court the two most eminent living Sanskritists, Ganganatha Jha and Kuppuswami Sastri, voluntarily came to Calcutta to give evidence in support of Radhakrishnan; and it became clear that Sinha had little chance of success. At this stage, therefore, he was advised by his friends to settle out of court; and Radhakrishnan, despite being in a strong position, was generous enough to forget all the trouble to which he had been put and to agree to a compromise. In April 1933 both the plaints, about defamation and piracy, were simultaneously withdrawn.

# 6

# THE ANDHRA UNIVERSITY

Born in a Tamil town, educated (apart from Tirupati) in the Tamil area, fluent in reading and speaking the language, happy studying and teaching in Madras city, it was in the Tamil country that the foundations of Radhakrishnan's intellectual life were laid. Yet he never ignored his Andhra ancestry and was well-versed in Telugu literature, and it was in that script that, till he acquired a working knowledge of Sanskrit, he read the classic philosophical texts. He had not particularly enjoyed his short postings in the government colleges in Rajahmundry and Anantapur; but his first adult experience of life in the Andhra districts did not kill his sense of attachment to the Telugu-speaking people. In 1925, when the establishment of a university in the Andhra area was in the air, he toyed with the idea of returning from Calcutta as its first professor of philosophy; but nothing came of this.[1] In December 1927, at the invitation of the vice-chancellor, C. R. Reddy, he delivered the address at the first convocation of the new university. It was also the first of the many convocation addresses delivered by Radhakrishnan over the years, and set the tone for what became his general approach to young people in India. He expected them to cultivate as students a liberty of mind, spirit of self-criticism and a rejection of conformity. He preached the middle way between reaction and radicalism, a 'constructive conservatism' which would retain what was valuable in the past and restate old knowledge in new forms adapted to present needs. This would enable them to contribute to a national life distracted by the feuds of creeds and communities. It was the task of universities to break down narrowness and bigotry and

[1] See R. Littehailes, director of public instruction, Madras, to Radhakrishnan, 11 November 1925.

reshape the thought and temper of the age.

Yet, towards the end of the address, Radhakrishnan descended from the heights to deal with the specific problems of the Andhra University, still groping to find its feet. He warned against the replacement of English by Telugu as the medium of instruction. He favoured a residential rather than a purely affiliating university and wished, in addition to the central campus, the undergraduate colleges of Rajahmundry and Anantapur (of which he had experience) to be developed as postgraduate centres. But he did not sympathize with the proposal to develop the arts and the sciences in different centres; they should be promoted in all places to complete, correct and balance each other. Radhakrishnan rejected the idea of the two cultures long before the phrase became a cliché. He stressed that merit should be the sole criterion in the choice of professors, for only they—if they had a zeal for research which would create a zest in teaching—could develop the atmosphere of scientific habit which imparted value to university training. He chided the leaders of Andhra opinion for bickering about the location of the university and thus delaying its inauguration, drew a picture of more than one university for the Telugu-speaking people, and urged the chancellor (who was also the governor of the province) to see to it that the government was not parsimonious: 'If we do not wash our hands, we are dirty; if we do, we are wasting water. You cannot stint money and then complain that the Andhra University is a second-class institution, if not a failure.'[2]

The address roused considerable enthusiasm, and hints were thrown out that Radhakrishnan should take over as vice-chancellor to put his ideas into practice. Radhakrishnan did not dismiss the suggestion out of hand but promptly informed Reddy of it and made clear that he would consider it only if Reddy intended to step down at the end of his first term in April 1928. Since their collaboration in Mysore Radhakrishnan and Reddy had remained on cordial terms, and indeed, recognizing that they were the two leading Andhra educationists, worked in tandem. Reddy wished to remain in office but appreciated Radhakrishnan's gesture; and in 1928, at his

[2] For the full text of the convocation address, see S. Radhakrishnan, *Freedom and Culture* (Madras 1936), pp. 2–28.

instance, Radhakrishnan received from the Andhra university
his first honorary degree.[3] On this visit to the Andhra areas
Radhakrishnan was involved in more than academic activity.
He presided over both the Andhra students' conference at
Guntur and the session of the Andhra Mahasabha at Nandyal.
In addition to the issues regarding the location and jurisdiction
of the Andhra University, the first stirrings of the desire for a
separate Andhra province could also be discerned; and what is
of interest in the proceedings of the Andhra Mahasabha is the
willingness of redoubtable politicians like Prakasam to authorize
decisions to be taken by a philosopher from Calcutta. Radhakrishnan had obviously won recognition in his own parish.

Eighteen months later, in July 1930, Reddy, frustrated by
his failure to move forward in the matter of developing the
university, took advantage of the political situation in the
country to proceed on leave with intent to resign. He explained
that the harsh measures taken by the authorities to suppress the
campaign for civil disobedience made it impossible for him to
continue. At the same time he wrote to Radhakrishnan suggesting that he officiate as vice-chancellor. Radhakrishnan declined, for Reddy had said he would withdraw his resignation if
there were a political settlement. Radhakrishnan preferred to
wait for a permanent vacancy and election by the senate for a
term of three years rather than accept selection by the syndicate
for a temporary and uncertain period. Reddy resigned in
December and the election took place in March 1931, ironi-
cally the day after Gandhi and the viceroy reached a settlement. The other candidate was Venkatratnam Naidu, much
older than Radhakrishnan, veteran leader of the Brahmo
Samaj movement in the Andhra districts and former vice-
chancellor of Madras University. While Venkatratnam could
rely on the fanatical members of the non-Brahmin movement,
the vote was not solely on caste lines. Some Brahmin supporters
of the Brahmo Samaj voted for him, while the non-Brahmin
vote was split by the rivalry between the zamindars of Pitha-
puram (of the Brahmo group) and Bobbili. Radhakrishnan
could also count on the support of a large number of university
and college teachers, Congressmen—who regarded him as a

[3] Radhakrishnan to Reddy, 24 December 1927: Reddy to Radhakrishnan,
29 December 1927; and Radhakrishnan to Reddy, 3 January 1928.

nationalist sympathizer as against a supporter of the loyalist Justice party and canvassed for him even from within prison—and British officials and missionaries, who were impressed by his international standing. But it was a close contest, Radhakrishnan being declared elected by thirty-three votes as against twenty-eight.

Radhakrishnan's election was generally welcomed. The British-owned *Madras Mail*, for example, congratulated the senate on its decision:

Under his influence this young University, whose infancy has been so sorely troubled with political and factious strife, may develop into a true home of learning, a place where character is developed and knowledge increased. We wish him every success in a most difficult task, certain that he will not spare himself in the endeavour to save the Andhra University from the plight into which undue concession to public clamour has plunged others.[4]

But the size of the opposition to him startled Radhakrishnan and made him reluctant to assume the vice-chancellorship. He knew that though a Muslim loyalist had been chosen by the government in 1930 to head Calcutta University, they could not continue to ignore his own claims when the post fell vacant again two years later; and he would have preferred to continue in Calcutta and govern with wide popular support an established university rather than accept in a new place a post which had been so keenly contested. He was also deeply involved in negotiations with the Bengal government on the future of the postgraduate departments, for the official grants earmarked for this purpose had lapsed in 1930. But, urged by his supporters in Waltair not to let them down, he took up the Andhra vice-chancellorship in May 1931.

The five years of his tenure got the university going and gave it a momentum which stood it for long in good stead. Though the university had been in existence for five years, Radhakrishnan had virtually to start from scratch. Nothing had been done; only one decision had been taken, and that too by the government in 1930, to move the headquarters from Vijayawada further north to Waltair (Visakhapatnam). The protest of the senate against this shift was overruled. It was thought by

[4] Editorial in *The Madras Mail*, 10 March 1931.

some that the official intention was to make sure that Chittoor and what were then known as the ceded districts (in western Andhra), which had been disaffiliated in 1929 from the Andhra University, would find Waltair too distant and would prefer to retain their connections with Madras University rather than return to the Andhra fold. But, whatever the motive, the choice of Waltair proved in the long run a happy one. The town was climatically pleasant and offered scope for development. Radhakrishnan, though he had originally favoured Rajah-mundry or Anantapur, which already had government col-leges, now wasted no time on regrets. He had long given thought to the lines on which the university should be built up, and, even in 1927, had urged from Calcutta that honours and postgraduate courses, 'which constitute the basis for all univer-sity education', should be established as soon as possible; for surely it was no one's opinion that the new university should be merely an administrative convenience. The other prime requisite was the recognition of the university as a national institution, above the strife of parties and free from interference from the government. Appointments should be made on purely academic grounds and all academic and administrative ques-tions should be left to the university: 'I am strongly of opinion that the University at least should be kept absolutely free from the breath of partisanship which is so blighting to academic ideals.'[5]

Four years later, given the opportunity, Radhakrishnan acted promptly. At the first meeting of the syndicate a fort-night after taking charge, he secured the appointment of temporary staff in English, Telugu, French and history; and the College of Arts, with postgraduate courses in history and Telugu, was opened on 1 July 1931. As there were no buildings, classes were started in Bobbili Hall, the palace of the pro-chancellor, who was a supporter of Radhakrishnan; and rooms for the students were reserved in the hostels of the local colleges. Now also began the recruitment of permanent staff and for this, during the next five years, Radhakrishnan looked round the country and beyond for the best available persons. The list of recruits to the faculty of the Andhra University in the thirties

[5] Radhakrishnan to the registrar, Andhra University, 16 February 1927, file R. Dis., no. 55C/27, Andhra University Records.

is a roll-call of distinguished Indians in the sixties and seventies. Humayun Kabir, who later became a cabinet minister, and Hiren Mukherjee, now better known as a left-wing parliamentarian, were among the first to be chosen. Radhakrishnan had known them both as students at Calcutta, helped them to secure government scholarships for study abroad, and offered them posts at Waltair while they were still at Oxford. 'I cannot think', wrote Kabir, 'of anyone else in India who would have done this for me.'[6] He invited, on Harold Laski's recommendation, Krishna Menon to join the department of politics and offered to his friend from Madras days, John Matthai, just then retiring from the tariff commission, the professorship of economics, and was disappointed that both Menon and Matthai were disinclined to come to Waltair. Among the last of Radhakrishnan's selections was that of V. K. R. V. Rao, then still at Cambridge, and, many years after, the national professor of economics.

It was also decided in 1931 to start honours courses in physics and chemistry from 1 July 1932 and to organize honours courses the year after in technology. C. V. Raman, the first name in science in India, was co-opted as a member of the syndicate, took charge of the drafting of the syllabuses in science and was appointed honorary professor of physics, while M. Visveswarayya, the doyen of Indian engineering, took responsibility for the studies in technology, which the university was the first institution in southern India to offer. A brilliant young mathematician, S. C. Chawla, was brought from Lahore, and for chemistry Radhakrishnan, after consulting Raman and Nils Bohr, secured Ludwig Wolf, the professor at Berlin University who was driven by Hitler into exile, with T. R. Seshadri, who later became Fellow of the Royal Society, being appointed to his first post as lecturer.

By his determination and ability to get to Waltair the most promising talent available in the country, irrespective of all other considerations, Radhakrishnan within two years made the Andhra University, located in a remote place, one of the most exciting academic centres in India. But his achievements were not solely academic. Within days of assuming office in 1931 he acquired for the university about fifty-four acres in the

[6] H. Kabir to Radhakrishnan, 27 January 1932.

upland areas, appointed an architect to draw plans for colleges
of arts and of science and two hostels, called for tenders, selected
a construction firm in consultation with the chief engineers of
Madras and Bengal, and saw to it that work began. By 1934
the two colleges and one hostel had been completed; two more
hostels were ready the next year and, by the time of Radhakrishnan's departure in 1936, the construction of the library
and the clock tower had been completed. As Raman remarked
in 1934, it was like a story from the Arabian nights; Radhakrishnan had waved his wand and a university complete with
buildings and staff had sprung up.[7]

Having got the best available men to function in a proper
setting, Radhakrishnan set about creating the proper atmosphere for intellectual activity. He shielded from the wrath of the
authorities those members of the staff who were known sym-
pathizers with the Congress and asserted the rights of teachers
to freedom of opinion and of expression. Andhra was among the
first universities in India to introduce tenure in place of contract for professors; and the salaries were also placed on a time-
scale with a maximum of Rs 1000 a month—at that time no
university in India paid more. He also secured in 1935 sanction
for the payment of advance increments in recognition of
research of quality. 'It was open', he said, 'to the Senate to
refuse these increments and thus discourage special work or
accept them and encourage the teachers in doing something
more than their routine duties. They might do as they pleased.'[8]
The senate approved. That same year, apart from the research
work of the staff, the first degrees in research were awarded.

Radhakrishnan also, on the model of Oxford, attached every
student in the university colleges to a tutor to exercise general
supervision—a pioneering step in India, made feasible by the
small numbers in a university that had, for all practical
purposes, been just set up. All students, of whatever caste or
creed, lived and ate together; but only vegetarian food was
served. This was an informal arrangement which the senate
approved, but, on Radhakrishnan's advice, did not formalize
as it was best done on the initiative of the management and
students. Tennis courts, a football ground and a cricket field

[7] Speech at the Andhra University Students Union, 24 February 1934, *The
Hindu*, 27 February 1934.     [8] Minutes of the senate, 30 March 1935.

were laid down and Radhakrishnan negotiated with C. K. Nayudu, India's test captain in cricket in 1932 and an Andhra by birth, to come to Waltair as a coach. The idea fizzled out after Radhakrishnan's departure, but from this time may be dated Radhakrishnan's special interest in the game. He watched test matches in India and abroad and even played cricket with his grandchildren.

With the first postgraduates of the university passing out in 1934, an employment bureau to assist them in securing jobs was created. Radhakrishnan always kept in mind this economic problem. It was with this in view that a college of commerce was instituted and the courses in technology oriented to industry. The objectives of an institution of higher learning were not ignored:

I know some universities very richly endowed and dominated by utilitarian considerations which give instruction even in subjects like scoutmastership, hotel management, composition of lyrical poetry and social conversation. We have no desire of turning our University into a Selfridge's stores exhibiting all odds and ends.[9]

But the need for graduates of the university to make their way in the world was also not forgotten.

To the library Radhakrishnan, as was to be expected, gave special attention. He drew up a list of the journals in the humanities and the social sciences to which the university should subscribe and asked Raman to assume responsibility for scientific periodicals. A special feature of the Andhra University library in these years was its collection of Marxist literature —easily the best in any public library in India. On his summer visits to Europe Radhakrishnan purchased books which were proscribed in India, and the Director of the Intelligence Bureau, in recognition of Radhakrishnan's scholarship, allowed them entry.[10] There was no effort at concealment. Subhas Bose's *The Indian Struggle*, for example, which had clandestine circulation elsewhere in India, was presented by Radhakrishnan to the library and accessioned. Unfortunately, after Radhakrishnan's departure in 1936 the university administra-

---

[9] Radhakrishnan's address to the convocation, December 1932.
[10] H. Williamson, director, intelligence bureau, to Radhakrishnan, 16 November 1935.

tion, in a calculated fit of loyalty, presented the whole collection
of proscribed literature to the government.

Radhakrishnan was ever conscious of the role of the university
in society. He instituted a prize to be given by the university to
the best work written in Telugu in fiction or on science or
public health. Also, without revising his opinion about the value
of English as the medium of instruction, he agreed in 1933 to
the commissioning of the writing of textbooks in Telugu and,
three years later, established a committee for drawing up
Telugu glossaries in the various sciences. Members of the staff
were encouraged to give extension lectures in Waltair as well
as in other Andhra towns. To make staff and students aware of
intellectual activity in the outside world the Indian Philosophical Congress was invited to hold its annual session in
Waltair in 1934. The vice-chancellor also persuaded his friend,
Alladi Krishnaswami, to endow a series of lectures to be given
in Waltair by eminent Indians. Radhakrishnan set his sights
high. Mahatma Gandhi was invited. He could not come; but
Tagore did, and not only spoke but directed a dance drama.
Sapru and Srinivasa Sastri were among the others whom
Radhakrishnan planned to bring to Waltair.

Radhakrishnan also constituted a high-powered commission, including Raman and the palaeo-botanist Birbal Sahni,
to visit the affiliated colleges, which had been forgotten for
years, and formulate proposals for the improvement of teaching standards. In 1934 undergraduate courses were started at
the headquarters of the university, but, to avoid competition
with the affiliated colleges, fees were fixed at a higher level and
the number of admissions limited.

All these diverse projects required considerable funds.
Radhakrishnan was on friendly terms with the two chancel-
lors of his time, Sir George Stanley and Lord Erskine, who were
also, as governors, at the head of the provincial government.
Stanley was especially appreciative of Radhakrishnan's work
at Waltair, and, on the eve of laying down office, endowed not
at Madras University but at the much younger institution in
Waltair a prize in his name for proficiency in English. The
local collectors, who were at this time always Englishmen, also
were helpful and E. C. Wood, who was in charge of the district
during the penultimate years of Radhakrishnan's term, be-

came a personal friend. The chief minister was the raja of Bobbili, a friend of Radhakrishnan and pro-chancellor of the university. One would therefore have expected substantial financial assistance from the Madras government. But these were years of depression and retrenchment and official funds were not as readily forthcoming as the vice-chancellor had expected. In this context, he declined to consider reduction of examination fees; one could not expand activities and at the same time reduce a source of income.[11] But his main hope was donations from the rich zamindars of the area. Within a fortnight of his arrival in Waltair he secured the assent of the raja of Jeypore, who had literary and philosophical interests, to provide a lakh of rupees every year for the college of science till such time as the capital sum amounted to fifteen lakhs. This required the approval of the government; and to avoid discussion in the legislature Radhakrishnan sought to make it an act of the executive. The officials, however, dragged their feet and Radhakrishnan had to secure Sir George Stanley's intervention. At a conference in January 1933, after Radhakrishnan made an impassioned intervention accusing the government of preferring zamindars who spent their money on women and at the race-course, the details were settled. But his arrangement was affected by the constitutional changes of 1937, when Jeypore found itself part of the province of Orissa.

Radhakrishnan also sought to consolidate and expand the jurisdiction of the university. The medical college at Visakhapatnam was still affiliated to Madras University. Radhakrishnan took steps to tone up the teaching at the college in accordance with the proposals of the Indian Medical Council and in 1935 the college was able to hold its own examinations. Even this was achieved only after some straight talking by Radhakrishnan to the governor and the finance member. On 19 May 1936, the day before Radhakrishnan handed over charge, the Government of Madras wrote to the Medical Council recommending recognition of medical degrees conferred by the Andhra University. So all but the last formal step had been taken. But Radhakrishnan was not so successful in securing the restoration of the jurisdiction of the university over Chittoor and the ceded districts. Towards the end of 1933 a non-official

[11] Address to the senate, 18 December 1934.

bill to this effect had been introduced in the legislature in Madras and the vice-chancellor wrote to the government supporting the proposal—'in the interests of the cultural unity of the Andhradesa as well as the efficiency of the University'.[12] He secured the support of the syndicate and the senate in offering to reserve a percentage of admissions and scholarships for students from these areas in the colleges of the university, and held out the baits of a law college at Anantapur and the holding of every second meeting of the senate in that town. Radhakrishnan followed this up by a visit to Anantapur to rally public opinion. He pointed out that a separate university for that area did not seem financially feasible and promised that the Andhra University would give their interests special attention. There were differences enough among the Telugu-speaking people, and, instead of adding to them, they should all help to build up a solid unity and draw closer in spirit and mind.[13] But there was opposition from the Kannada-speaking groups in these districts and the government allowed the non-official bill to lapse.

In his five years at Waltair, Radhakrishnan laid the foundations in every sense of the Andhra University. His administrative and organizational talents, working on the basis that only the best will do, were seen at their best. His assessment of academic worth was sounder than his judgement of human character in general; and he publicly asserted that, with a staff of superior quality, he planned not mass production of ordinary graduates but well-trained men and women much above the average: 'Democracy can save itself only by becoming aristocratic. Its leaders must be men of integrity and independence, of discernment and devotion to truth.'[14]

There was, enveloping all the hard work and planning, the exhilaration of adventure. His old friend Candeth visited him in Waltair in 1933. During the past two years they had slowly drifted apart. Radhakrishnan felt that Candeth, now the deputy director of public instruction, under the influence of caste politics in Madras, was treating their mutual friend Dorai-

[12] Radhakrishnan to D. M. Boulton, deputy secretary to Government of Madras, 15 January 1934, file R. Dis., no. 78/C 34, Andhra University Records.

[13] Report of speech at Anantapur in *The Hindu*, 28 January 1934.

[14] Address to the convocation of Andhra University, December 1935.

swami shabbily; and he could not have liked Candeth's active role, in partnership with Christian missionaries, in persuading the Academic Council of Madras University to reject the proposal of the board of studies in English to prescribe a collection of Radhakrishnan's essays, published by a local firm under the title *The Heart of Hindustan*, as one of the books for study in undergraduate classes. Candeth felt the lack of the old warmth when they met but was impressed by Radhakrishnan's 'distinct success as Vice-Chancellor. Understands his men and gets into real touch with them.'[15] Raman too has borne witness to Radhakrishnan's unbelievable hold on all the members of the staff of the university: 'He does not carry much in pounds avoirdupois; but in that frail body is enshrined a great spirit— a great spirit which we have all learned to revere and admire, even to worship.'[16]

Elected vice-chancellor in 1931 for three years, Radhakrishnan was unanimously re-elected in 1934. This would have taken him on till February 1937, and Waltair, half-way between Madras and Calcutta, was a pleasant place to live in. Radhakrishnan resided in a large house near the beach and had time to spend with his growing children. He was reticent by nature, but did not conceal the wordless affection. He played games with them and talked to them without strain about their own problems as well as matters which were to him important. He created in the house an atmosphere of scholarship and human values and impressed on his children the necessity of faith and the virtue of kindness. Yet, by the summer of 1935, Radhakrishnan began to feel that he should consider leaving Waltair, however idyllic, and handing over the vice-chancellorship to someone else. He had achieved much in the university and set in motion a great deal; and a new hand at the helm was perhaps desirable. Before the meetings of university bodies Radhakrishnan studied his papers carefully and guided, with a sharp sense of time, the discussions towards the decisions he desired; and this had led to talk of his autocratic ways. There were also murmurs of resentment at his emphasis on merit. It was felt that, particularly in the recruitment of academic staff, he did not give preference to Andhras or attach importance to con-

15 Candeth's diary entry, 10 May 1933.
16 Speech at Waltair, 29 March 1936, *Madras Mail*, 31 March 1936.

siderations of caste. That the Andhra University had, for a short while at least, become a national institution and its vice-chancellor an international personality were not developments which were favoured by all. Of what advantage to the university, asked a member of the senate as early as 1932, was the fact that the vice-chancellor was a member of the International Committee for Intellectual Co-operation; and the answer, 'there are no material benefits and non-material benefits cannot be defined', all did not find satisfying.[17] Two candidates for election from the senate to the syndicate, whom the vice-chancellor was said to favour, were defeated.

So Radhakrishnan decided that the time to move on was approaching. There were two alternatives. H. N. Spalding, who had listened to the Hibbert Lectures in 1930 and had been won over by Radhakrishnan's personality as well as by his teachings, endowed in the autumn of 1935 at Oxford a chair for the study of eastern religions and ethics; and Radhakrishnan let his interest be known. But the thought of living permanently abroad was not attractive, especially as he had just built a house in Madras. Till 1931, despite the fact that he had for ten years earned what was then regarded as a high salary for a professor of Rs 1000 per month, Radhakrishnan could save no money. But as vice-chancellor his emoluments had doubled and he had been able to set aside half of it; and with this accumulated amount he bought a plot of land in 1934 in the residential area of Mylapore in Madras, and, within a year, constructed a house on it. Named 'Girija' (like his wife's name another name of the goddess Parvati), it was, by the standards of those days, a spacious bungalow; and Radhakrishnan looked forward very much to residing in it and continuing the comfortable life with his family which he had established in Waltair. So he informed the governor of Madras that he would be interested in serving as the director of public instruction in the state. Still a member of the Indian Educational Service, Radhakrishnan was entitled to be considered for this post. What is astonishing is that he preferred to work in the provincial arena as a civil servant with no scope for public utterances to being the first Indian, indeed the first Asian, to hold a chair at Oxford. It shows both the innate modesty of Radhakrishnan and the lack of any sense of

[17] Minutes of the senate, 6 December 1932.

mission to preach his philosophy to the world. But Providence came to his rescue. The Government of Madras informed him that they could not consider him for the post he desired so long as an Englishman senior to him in service was available;[18] and Radhakrishnan, relieved to be rid of administration while regretting his inability to dwell in his new home, accepted the chair at Oxford. That the Government of Madras had virtually driven him out of the country by refusing to appoint him director of public instruction became known and invited adverse comment.[19] But the turn of events only strengthened his conviction that the major decisions of his life were being taken by a higher power. He was struck by a remark made to him long after by Oswald Couldrey, the Englishman who had been his principal at Rajahmundry and had stood in the way of his promotion: 'There is no obstructing the man of destiny.'

So, in February 1936, Radhakrishnan informed the senate of the Andhra University that he would lay down office in May and steps should be taken to elect his successor. Reddy was now once again adrift, with success in politics eluding him; and Radhakrishnan worked to see that the ball passed back to him. The two leading educationists of the Andhra country were still on cordial terms. It was only in the forties, when Radhakrishnan moved on to planes to which his friend could not even hope to aspire, that Reddy's attitude soured. Reddy never quite recovered from having been a clever and successful young man at Cambridge, and, as the years passed without his achieving the kind of recognition he felt to be his due (and, in a sense, deserved), he became increasingly embittered.

## II

The political commitment which Radhakrishnan had not hesitated to show in Britain did not waver on his return to India in the summer of 1930. Inaugurating the students' parliament of Calcutta University he welcomed the fact that the students were not free from 'the blessed contagion' of unrest, and asked them to live 'a dedicated life' with no thought of personal com-

[18] Lord Erskine, governor of Madras, to Radhakrishnan, 16 January 1936.
[19] See speech of Srinivasa Sastri, 31 March 1936, *The Hindu*, 1 April 1936; editorial in *The Hindu*, 1 April 1936.

fort. He was a member of the committee which condemned the
police for entering the university on 9 September and assaulting
students for no reason; and the chancellor was obliged to
promise redress. His reputation as scholar and speaker led to
requests from various universities for the delivery of convocation addresses, and Radhakrishnan accepted most of these invitations, for he thought it of importance to communicate with
educated young men and women. India needed an enlightened
spirit of rebellious youth; and it was from the ranks of these new
graduates that the future leadership would be drawn. Democracy to him had an aristocratic slant in the sense that he believed that the people should be led by trained experts chosen
by them.

At these convocations, while speaking of the ideals of a
university, Radhakrishnan did not forbear from touching on
political topics. At Mysore he reminded his audience that freedom was won from within and not given from without. They
should not renounce the Indian tradition but adapt it to
modern needs. But the British rulers also had a duty. National
feeling could not be wished away. Contact with the West had
strengthened in India the sense of pride and self-respect. Association between Britain and India could become an expression
of the ultimate synthesis between the East and the West if both
sides acted up to their responsibilities. The delegates at the
Round Table Conference meeting in London should remember
that India was not a subject to be administered but a nation
seeking its soul. While the British seemed to exaggerate the
demands of security, the Indians emphasized the right to
liberty. They stressed the shame of subjection and the lines of
sorrow which even the best Indians bore on their faces. Britain
should rise to the height of her vast opportunities, take occasion
by the hand and make the bounds of freedom wider yet.[20] The
vice-chancellor of the university, who was an Englishman,
after seeing a typescript of the address, requested Radhakrishnan to omit the paragraphs about the Round Table Conference, but Radhakrishnan declined.[21]

Very soon after came the address at Lahore. Here Radha-

[20] Convocation address at Mysore University, 16 October 1930, *Freedom and
Culture*, pp. 29–47.
[21] E. P. Metcalfe to Radhakrishnan, 8 October 1930.

krishnan, assuming that India's freedom was bound to come, stressed that universities should train the young for leadership. Indian nationalism owed much to the West but it should not surrender its individuality. In the minds of many Indian leaders antagonism to British rule was strangely mixed up with a love of British institutions. Between the abstract rationalism of the revolutionary making a clean sweep of the past and the equally abstract historicism of the reactionary making a clean sweep of the present, India was losing her inward unity. To strengthen national feeling by building a sense of like-mindedness and community of interests, universities should be able to function in an atmosphere of freedom. Whether it be between Indian and British or Hindu and Muslim, the difficulty in India was want of understanding.[22]

This convocation was reported on the front page of every newspaper in India because, as the speakers were leaving the hall, a young man rose, bowed to Radhakrishnan, and then, pulling out a revolver, fired at the chancellor, wounding him. Later, asked why he had failed in his attempt to wound the governor fatally, the young man answered that one main reason was that he had wished to avoid hurting Radhakrishnan.[23] Clearly even terrorists, who could expect no sympathy from Radhakrishnan, respected him. But so too apparently did the government. The term of Sir Jagadish Bose as India's representative on the International Committee of Intellectual Cooperation, a body set up by the League of Nations, was coming to an end. Srinivasa Sastri, at this time in London for the Round Table Conference, had been much impressed by reports of Radhakrishnan's lectures in Britain—'You are worth a lakh of us any day'[24]—and spoke to Wedgwood Benn, secretary of state in the Labour government, recommending Radhakrishnan as Bose's successor. Gilbert Murray, the chairman of the Committee, having heard from Jacks about Radhakrishnan's ability, informed the British government that Radhakrishnan would be suitable. Benn consulted the viceroy, Lord Irwin, who in turn asked his law member, Sir B. L. Mitter, for

[22] Convocation address at Punjab University, Lahore, 23 December 1930, *Freedom and Culture*, pp. 48–63.
[23] See 'Pathan Harikishan' by 'Sukalesh', *Organiser* (Delhi), 26 June 1966.
[24] V. S. Srinivasa Sastri to Radhakrishnan, 8 May 1930.

his opinion. Mitter knew enough about Radhakrishnan's standing in Calcutta to support his selection.[25] And so Radhakrishnan's name was sponsored by the British government and accepted by the Committee and the League of Nations.

Irwin, rare among viceroys for his interest in matters of the mind and spirit, decided also that Radhakrishnan's stature as a philosopher merited official recognition. Rejecting a suggestion that Radhakrishnan be given some lower title,[26] he consulted the governor of Bengal, Sir Stanley Jackson, on the award of a knighthood. Jackson, who had been seeing Radhakrishnan frequently during these months in connection with the reorganization of the university, replied, 'All the police reports are against him, but I like him.'[27] So the announcement was made in June 1931. 'It is rare', commented Sir Geoffrey de Montmorency, the governor of the Punjab who had presided as chancellor over the convocation at Lahore and had been shot at, 'for a man to receive at once an honour from the king and the homage of a revolutionary.'[28] The government did not apparently think it necessary to obtain Radhakrishnan's consent as he was still a member of the Indian Educational Service. Radhakrishnan was embarrassed by this appendage, which was not of his seeking and seemed to stamp him as acceptable to the establishment, though it turned out to be useful in providing added leverage in his dealings as vice-chancellor with officials. It made no difference to his outspoken views but gave an opportunity for critics to suggest that he was making the best of both worlds. His friends of course rejoiced; but one of the oldest of them noted, 'Radhakrishnan has been knighted. Am afraid it will make him a real Bore.'[29]

With the assumption of office in Britain of a National Government which was predominantly Conservative, the second Round Table Conference ended in failure. Gandhi returned to India a disappointed man and was promptly

[25] Irwin to Benn, 3 November, and Benn to Irwin, 24 November 1930, Halifax papers, IOL, vol. 6.

[26] B. L. Mitter to private secretary to viceroy, 25 February 1931, Halifax papers, vol. 26.

[27] See K. P. S. Menon, *Memories and Musings* (Delhi 1979), p. 35.

[28] Quoted by K. P. S. Menon, 'Radhakrishnan as Diplomat', in K. I. Dutt (ed.), *Sarvepalli Radhakrishnan* (Delhi 1966), p. 65.

[29] Candeth's diary entry, 3 June 1931.

arrested by Willingdon, who had taken over as viceroy from Irwin and regarded the crushing of the Congress to be his chief objective. Radhakrishnan, despite the encumbrance of a knighthood, left no doubt as to where he stood. He paid his 'homage of love' to Mahatma Gandhi for his example of self-respect and moral courage.[30] He defined the duty of universities to be the handing on of the lighted torch of culture, which stirs upheavals and starts conflagrations. A university education should not be hampered by obsolete thought and tradition, for its essence was the spirit of criticism and understanding. Any university that produced graduates who played for safety and cared for comfort had failed in its essential task. Timidity and conservatism were the greatest dangers to society. The passion for political freedom was the greatest ferment at work in India, and the condition of mental and moral decay consequent on political subjection and economic depression was the problem. Repression could not stop the growth of the legitimate aspiration for freedom, even as violence could not further it. The products of universities should work for this as well as think ahead of a more just social order:

If we are to preserve ourselves, we must use the lighted torch, the cleansing fire, the spirit that rebels ... We hear on all sides about the revolt of youth. I am afraid I have a good deal of sympathy with this attitude of revolt, and my complaint is that it is not sufficiently widespread.[31]

For a vice-chancellor to advocate a spirit of rebellion among the students might seem foolhardy; but Radhakrishnan was confident that he could, by his personality, control his own flock at Waltair. Even there he urged the need for drastic change in India, for political freedom and social revolution. It was the duty of intellectuals to see that loyalty to the living and vital elements of the past was not confused with bondage to dead encrustations and accretions. He wanted the members of his university to combine the Greek spirit of youth with the Indian emphasis on spiritual values.[32]

[30] Speech at Calcutta, 2 October, *Amrita Bazar Patrika*, 3 October 1931.
[31] Convocation address at Lucknow University, 5 December 1931, reprinted in *Freedom and Culture*, pp. 64–80.
[32] Speech at Waltair, 17 April 1932, *The Hindu*, 19 April 1932.

His sympathy for the Congress, now being pushed hard by the government, he continued to brandish. In a foreword to a collection of essays on the politicians of southern India, many of whom were Liberals with a desire to seek favours from the British, he spoke with a trace of contempt of their

exaggerated sense of balance and proportion, hardly consistent with great faith in or even enthusiasm for radical changes. A few of them, it is clear from these sketches, illustrate the paradox that intellectual understanding of or sentimental attachment to ideals may well coincide with moral inertia and personal evasion. It is a law of life that our desires can be accomplished only by fighting and making sacrifices for them.[33]

Srinivasa Sastri, a personal friend of Radhakrishnan, was hurt by the criticism of inertia and evasion and Radhakrishnan allowed the author to reprint the book after deleting the offending sentence.[34] But his views were unchanged and deepened with the years, leading the moderate Liberals to dub him an 'academic extremist'.[35]

In particular, the attachment to Mahatma Gandhi, now embarked on a campaign to improve the lot of the 'untouchables' in Hindu society, grew stronger. Tagore came twice to Waltair as Radhakrishnan's guest, in the winter of 1933 and the spring of 1934, and in their long private conversations the two found themselves in agreement that Gandhi was the one person whom India had produced in the last two hundred years who was possessed of the ethereal fire. When Radhakrishnan invited Gandhi for a contribution to a volume on contemporary Indian philosophy, Gandhi was reluctant: 'The fact that I have affected the thought and practice of our times does not make me fit to give expression to the philosophy that may lie behind it. To give a philosophical interpretation of the phenomenon must be reserved for men like you.'[36] Radhakrishnan's address to the convocation of Allahabad University two months later was in a sense a response to this challenge. He

[33] Foreword to K. Chandrasekharan, *Persons and Personalities* (Madras 1932).

[34] K. Chandrasekharan to Radhakrishnan, 15 October 1932; Chandrasekharan in conversation with the author, 15 May 1984.

[35] C. Y. Chintamani to K. Iswara Dutt, quoted in K. I. Dutt, *Sarvepalli Radhakrishnan* (Delhi 1966), p. 91.

[36] M. K. Gandhi to Radhakrishnan, 16 September 1934.

asserted that, in an age witnessing the triumph of dictatorships and an increase in armaments, Gandhi's contention that he would never accept self-government if brought about by violence was 'like a ray of heavenly light let into a world of deep darkness'. In placing the interests of universal truth before those of national politics, Gandhi had lit a candle that would not easily be put out. Its light would have a far penetration in time and space and would be seen and welcomed by all honest and sincere people the world over. His appeal would stand by the side of utterances of great national leaders as well as religious reformers; for his was one of the immortal voices of the human race in all that related to the highest effort of men and nations.

Nations, added Radhakrishnan, like individuals, wield lasting influence by their attachment to a purpose larger than their immediate advantage, and he hoped that Britain would realize that the time had come for paternalism to be replaced by a partnership held together by the free consent of self-governing peoples. But India too had to deserve such an arrangement. A society which tolerated untouchability had no right to call itself civilized. No education which inculcated caste superiority and communal contempt could be regarded as successful. Social stability presumed social justice.[37]

The address, given by one who was not a regular politician and at a time when the government's offensive against the Congress was sweeping the country, startled and delighted Indian opinion. Jawaharlal Nehru, in a nearby prison, cut out the report in the newspapers and stuck it in his notebook. Rajagopalachari—the chief follower of Gandhi in south India— who was till now no more than an acquaintance of Radhakrishnan, read the report while travelling from Pune to Madras and was moved to dash off an enthusiastic letter from a wayside station.

Dear Sir Radhakrishnan,

It was undoubted satisfaction to read the beautiful references in your convocation address to Gandhiji's message to the relation between Britain and India and the removal of untouchability. Nothing less could have been expected from an illustrious thinker

[37] Address at the convocation of Allahabad University, 13 November 1934, *Freedom and Culture*, pp. 100–16.

like you, but it was good that among the vast array of things to be referred to, you chose these among other things for the occasion.

With deepest regards,

I remain
Yours sincerely,
C. Rajagopalachari[38]

Thereafter, in the years to come, while Rajagopalachari and Radhakrishnan often failed to agree and moved on divergent paths, their personal relations never lacked cordiality.

As for the British officials, they preferred to ignore the address—with one outstanding exception. Sir Malcolm Hailey was in the last weeks of his long years of service in India, and, as chancellor of the university, presided over the convocation. He had the vision and breadth of spirit to appreciate the wisdom of Radhakrishnan's opinions and went out of his way 'to express my admiration of your very eloquent and thoughtful' address.[39]

If, however, to Radhakrishnan Gandhi was one of those rare souls endowed with genius who appear from time to time in this world with the capacity to find out what is wrong and the ability, courage and faith to lead the people to set it right, he himself wanted more positive action by the state in economic affairs than Gandhi would have approved. In this insistence on control of private interests and regulation of social forces for the development of the individual[40] he had more in common with Nehru whom, even by 1933, he had seen as the leader of the future.[41]

## III

The International Committee for Intellectual Co-operation, of which Radhakrishnan was a member for eight years from 1931, was for him an ideal forum. The broader sweep had, as much as academic donnery and political commitment, engaged him

[38] 14 November 1934.

[39] Sir Malcolm Hailey to Radhakrishnan, 22 November 1934.

[40] Addresses at the Andhra University convocation, November 1935, and at the jubilee celebrations of Morris College, Nagpur, December 1935, *Freedom and Culture*, pp. 117–39.

[41] Interview in the *Daily News* (Colombo), 12 October 1933.

from his earliest years; and he was now brought into contact with fifteen distinguished persons of learning and science from various parts of the world—among them Einstein, Madame Curie, Valery and Huizinga, apart from Murray himself. As the Committee's composition was not determined by the politics of the League and they had a member from the United States, Radhakrishnan suggested that someone from the Soviet Union should also be invited. Maxim Gorky, for example, would do honour to any committee. While politics and economics often divided countries, art and letters united them. Misunderstandings throve in the dark but perished in the light.[42] The agenda of the Committee comprised items with an international context; but Radhakrishnan lost no time in drawing the Committee's attention to the fact that the League was regarded in Asia as legalizing and consecrating imperialism; and this explained the indifference, if not hostility, to the League and its activities in his own country. The Committee should take notice of developments in India and of the efforts being made by some of her rarest spirits to restore honour and meaning to national life. Membership of the Committee was acceptable to him only because he and the member from Britain sat as equals, unlike in the political organs of the League where India was treated as a subordinate of Britain.

Radhakrishnan sought to promote an interest in India in the Committee's activities by forming, as in some other countries, a national commission of persons of scholarship and science drawn from all parts of India, 'the cultural counterpart to the political federation to be'.[43] But this required the support of the state, and the government vetoed it on the plea of lack of funds.[44] As a compromise arrangement, in 1935 Radhakrishnan persuaded the Inter-University Board of India to function also as a national commission. But Radhakrishnan's efforts in Geneva throughout these years were wholly individual. Speaking on moral disarmament, a phrase obviously coined to match the fashionable 'moral rearmament' of the Oxford Group, he contended that an education which was purely intellectual was

[42] Reports of Radhakrishnan's speeches at Geneva, *The Hindu*, 10 August 1931.

[43] Radhakrishnan to private secretary to viceroy, 5 February 1932.

[44] Letter from department of education, Government of India, to Radhakrishnan, 23 April 1932.

no longer adequate. A world that had become one physically required an international mind, a fundamental re-creation of the human being. The development of a world culture which would express itself in a world citizenship was our only hope. That a large number of sovereign states governed the world which had become very nearly one civilized society resulted in the prevalent anarchy and a normal condition of war with two phases, static and belligerent—probably the first clear reference in international discussion to what we now term the 'cold war'. In every nation there should arise men and women with the mental agility to proclaim the ideals of peace and human brotherhood and the moral courage to suffer for them. Such loyalty to the human community also imposed an obligation to exert moral pressure on all who exploited other peoples. The peoples of India and China, for example, were by training, temperament and conviction pacifist; but their subjection was making them wonder if militarism was not perhaps right. Before they abandoned their non-violent approach the League should seek to enforce justice and equality among all nations. How, for example, could the League close its eyes to thousands of political prisoners in India?[45]

In Radhakrishnan, therefore, as in Nehru, nationalism and internationalism were never apart. As reactionary policy intensified in India, Radhakrishnan's speeches at Geneva became even more forthright. He implored his colleagues on the Committee to move on from abstract discussions on first principles which led nowhere to real problems without being afraid of treading on the sensitive spots of nations. Racial and national prejudices were much to the fore in the East as well as in the West, and in India pride and prestige were making fair-dealing and justice difficult if not impossible. In working groups set up by the Committee, not those who loved every country except their own—a clear dig at loyalists—or who had set opinions, but rather nationalists who were at the same time devoted to the international community, should be appointed. Nor should the Committee dismiss with ignorant contempt the cultures of India and China merely because of the political weaknesses of those

[45] Speech at Geneva, 21 July 1932, reported in *The Indian Social Reformer* (Bombay), 20 August 1932; speech at International Students Union, Geneva, July 1933, *Daily News* (Colombo), 21 September 1933.

countries. Those cultures were still alive and had much to contribute to the concord of minds which was the objective of the
International Committee: 'Men not depraved in their morals,
not perverse in their judgments, not inferior to the highest types
of other countries in their tastes and life plead guilty to belonging to these cultures.'[46] Mme Curie asked him whether the
peoples of the East were happier than those of the West; recounting this the next year, after Mme Curie's death, Radhakrishnan added that this melancholy question was one which
needed further investigation.[47]

Sometime during these years, when Radhakrishnan was
spending the summers in Europe, he met 'Cheiro', the best-
known palmist of his day. 'Cheiro' studied Radhakrishnan's
palms and forecast that he would reach the top, be the head of a
state, but would, before his death, lose his mind. Both these pro-
phecies seemed at the time so wildly off the mark that they
became a family joke.

# IV

These varied activities in India and abroad in the early thirties precluded sustained philosophical effort. Radhakrishnan
planned a second series of Hibbert Lectures with an emphasis
on the influence of his philosophy of religion on moral life. He
also considered writing, as a sequel to *Kalki*, a book on the
moral law, entitled 'Acceptance and Adventure'. It was his
thesis that such a law followed logically from the kind of metaphysics common to Plato and the Upanishads, which regarded
the Supreme Spirit as expressing itself in and through the cosmic
process. As stated by Plato, 'The Idea of the Good is the Universal Author of all things beautiful and good, Parent of Light,
and the immediate source of reason and truth.'[48] We should
accept our given endowment; but mere acceptance is not
enough. In the history of the human race, as in that of the individual, progress is achieved by a spirit of adventure. Inertia is
a natural temptation, but life is a continuous struggle between
inertia and movement. The life force weakens if burdened by

[46] Speeches at Geneva, July 1933, *The Indian Social Reformer*, 12 August 1933.
[47] Minutes of the meeting of the International Committee, 16 July 1934.
[48] *The Republic*, v, 17.

the heavy weight of accumulated wastage. True happiness is not a satisfaction of individual wants but an unceasing effort for the realization in the world of the kingdom of ends.

However, Radhakrishnan did not get down to writing this book. Rather, his energies were engaged in writing chapters on Hinduism for *The Legacy of India*, published by the Clarendon Press, and for a volume on *Modern India and the West* sponsored by Chatham House. He was also busy editing, with Muirhead, a collection of essays on *Contemporary Indian Philosophy* and himself provided for it, as a statement of his philosophical position, a terse summary of his views as expounded in *An Idealist View of Life*.

More sparkling in phrase and gripping in theme than all these was a short biographical account which Radhakrishnan wrote in 1934 for an American editor who was putting together such expositions by leaders of religious thought.[49] Radhakrishnan always shied away from talking about himself. Basically he was too private a person; he believed that the best of him was to be found in his writings, and other aspects of his life, however important to himself, could be of little interest to others. It is this general reluctance to lift the veil that makes this essay wrenched out of him all the more interesting and revelatory of Radhakrishnan in mid career. He explains his interest in Hinduism, his conception of religion as experience and inter-meshed with living, his concern for other people. He sees himself as not solely an academic philosopher but a compassionate humanist. Entitled 'My Search for Truth', thus deliberately raising echoes of Gandhi's famous autobiography which also spoke of experiments in a similar quest, Radhakrishnan's essay is moving in its sensitivity of feeling even if, at places, slightly soggy in its complacency.

---

[49] V. Ferm (ed.), *Religion in Transition* (London 1937).

# 7

# THE SPALDING CHAIR

In the summer of 1936, therefore, Radhakrishnan shifted his
base to Britain, and there it remained for the next three years,
till the outbreak of war in September 1939. Although, under the
terms of his contract, he was obliged to spend only two terms
every year at Oxford and was in India for the other six months
of the year, functioning again as a professor at Calcutta, Radhakrishnan's primary role was in British academic life. The
appointment at Oxford was obviously of more than professional significance. In India, to a people sensitive to their
subject status, it gave much pleasure as acceptance that in
fields outside politics and economics the country could boast of
achievements as good as any elsewhere. If the *Indian Social
Reformer* believed that Radhakrishnan's appointment at Oxford
was of deeper significance than the appointment of half-a-
dozen Indian governors or even an Indian viceroy and would
help in a right understanding and closer relations between the
Indian and English peoples,[1] it was because of the prestige and
the recognition which the election of Radhakrishnan implied.
Moreover, Radhakrishnan had never been a secluded philosopher. His patriotism had stood out both in his stress on the
vitality of Indian thought and in his non-philosophical
addresses. Now he himself underlined the wider aspects of his
appointment: 'You may rest assured that my own work will be
directly to propagate philosophy and indirectly to convince all
that India is not a subject to be administered but is a nation
seeking its soul.'[2]

In Britain too, much was expected from Radhakrishnan's
presence. Harold Nicolson, meeting him at lunch with Joad,

[1] *Indian Social Reformer*, 9 January 1937.
[2] Speech at Madras, 31 March 1936, *The Hindu*, 1 April 1936.

had his doubts: 'He is a gentle, reasonable and, I should imagine, unreliable person.'[3] But this was very much an isolated
opinion. Radhakrishnan was a well-known figure, generally
respected for his learning and lucid eloquence and liked as a
personality. That he should now be available to speak with
authority on India's culture and her problems was to many
an event of crucial importance: 'In his new post at Oxford he
will have a position which is in its way as important as that of
the Viceroy of India.'[4]

On political issues Radhakrishnan continued to support the
leadership of Gandhi and, in addition, felt increasingly in
sympathy with Nehru. This was the effect of *An Autobiography*,
published that summer and read by Radhakrishnan from cover
to cover over a weekend: 'Finished Nehru's *Autobiography*. A
noble piece of work and has done a good deal for educating the
people of England about India, more than the conferences and
papers and interviews in London. Puts us all to shame for our
selfishness and careerist tendencies.'[5] Radhakrishnan himself
was now a freer man, having retired from the Indian Educational Service on moving to Oxford. He could not afford to
resign earlier and forgo the pension; for having used up all his
savings in building a house, he was now again in debt. But
retirement at the first opportunity rid him of the last shackles;
and thereafter, even in his speeches on religious and philosophical topics, he contrived opportunities to affirm the necessity
of political freedom for India and to extol the leadership of
Gandhi who bore witness in politics to the cult of the spirit and
had provided in non-violent struggle a moral equivalent to war.
Later that year, at the time of the abdication of Edward VIII
in December 1936, it was Radhakrishnan who protested at the
failure of the British government to consult India as they had
the dominions.[6] Even the Congress did not take up this issue,
which provided a precedent for the more serious failure three
years later to consult Indian opinion about the declaration
of war.

[3] Diary entry, 15 June 1936, Nicolson diaries, Balliol College, Oxford.
[4] Major F. Yeats-Brown in *The Spectator*, 12 June 1936.
[5] Diary entry, 21 June 1936. Radhakrishnan kept a diary for a few months
at this time.
[6] Speech at London, 19 December, *The Statesman*, 21 December 1936.

Discriminatory treatment of India and the reluctance of the Conservative government to hasten the advance of self-government were part, as Nehru constantly insisted, of a general crisis which was overshadowing the world from the mid thirties. Fascism, dictatorships, imperialism, aggressive nationalism and the kind of education which prepared youth for war were all intertwined and Radhakrishnan, like Nehru, had no doubt that the fundamental conditions of the existing order had to be altered to pave the way for a new society with civil liberties for all individuals and independence for all nations. But this was to him not just a matter of political and economic adjustments. Science and technology had drawn the world closer; and even in social and political thinking there was among the best minds an increasing community of ideas and ideals. Human beings could no more escape being members of a world society than they could jump out of their skins. Yet physical proximity and mental approximation had not been followed by a closer spiritual unity. The failure, in the striking words of the title of Radhakrishnan's inaugural lecture at Oxford, of 'the world's unborn soul' to emerge resulted in the existing uncertainty of outlook, the sense of uneasiness that humanity was hastening confusedly to unknown ends.

Radhakrishnan's solution for this problem of the disparity between the processes of life and the attitude to life was a return to the religion of the spirit, the mystic tradition which was to be found in all the living religions. Radhakrishnan was never an advocate of a world religion, or any effort to amalgamate bits and pieces of various beliefs. He favoured a pluralistic world with no universal churches. Multiplicity of approaches was acceptable, for he believed that they all led to the same summit. He certainly disliked proselytization. 'Who', as he had said, 'wished to have the gracious and magnetic personality of the Buddha superseded by some Old Testament worthy?'[7] Even in 1930 in London he had spoken of the need for a 'spiritual League of Nations'; in Bombay before he sailed for Europe in 1936 he had presided over a parliament of religions; and now in London he was one of the leading figures at the World Congress of Faiths sponsored by Sir Francis Younghusband.

It was Radhakrishnan's thesis that one need not change the

[7] Speech at Cambridge, reported in *The Inquirer,* 22 February 1930.

religion in which one happened to be born. It was only necessary to move away from organized churches which insisted on
exclusive truth, sought to impose such truth on others and were
generally narrow-minded, and to go back to the sources which
favoured spiritual experience and intuitive apprehension of the
living reality of God. Such realization, deeper than theology or
morality, was in tune with the natural instinct for human
fellowship and in accord with the world spirit. But, though
this was the vital teaching of all religious faiths, Radhakrishnan
felt that Hinduism and Buddhism laid particular stress on it.
Greek civilization had given excessive emphasis to rationalism,
humanism and the patriotic spirit; Judaism and Christianity
had taken their stand on revelation, with the consequent bias
towards exclusiveness and enforcement; and, since the Renais-
sance in Europe, the welcome weakening of dogmatic religion
had had, as corollaries, the growing faith in the infallibility of
scientific reasoning and the increased spread of agnosticism.
The result was a world lacking in moral unity and fellowship
among nations. But Hinduism and Buddhism gave primacy
not to revelation or shallow intellectualism but to effort and
experience, creative thinking and the discovery of the self, the
reality of the unseen world and the call of the spiritual life. They
regarded the aim of all human living as the reaching down,
through the turmoil of empirical happenings, to the substantial
permanence possessed by each finite life.

This to Radhakrishnan was the religion of the future. It had,
contrary to general belief in the West, a social and ethical commitment. To say that the world was maya was to suggest not
that it was an illusion but that it was not ultimate. The person
who has seen the reality returns to the world a complete human
being, conscious of the universal life of which all individuals,
peoples and races are specific articulations. The Church
Invisible—comprising all those, whatever their denominations,
who seek God—works for the kingdom of ends. A right relationship with God can only be realized through a right relationship with other human beings. Spiritual advancement is not a
refuge from reality or the hope of paradise in the future but the
furtherance of human welfare. In Edward Caird's favourite
phrase, which Radhakrishnan echoed, it was 'dying to live'—
one died to selfish ends and passions in order to live for the

higher life of reason and morality. Religious experience was born in solitude but showed its existence by awareness and sympathy, love and lack of fear. Religion starts with the individual but culminates in fellowship. It does not provide a body of knowledge but prescribes a life to be lived. In the anxiety to have no temporal possessions and to spend one's days in communion with spirit, Indians had frequently tended to neglect the duty of service; but this was a travesty of the teachings of Hinduism. True spiritual religion, in Radhakrishnan's formulation, was characterized by social virtue.

Radhakrishnan was confident that, to a shrinking world without a vision and to the growing world consciousness without a soul, his generation would be able to provide spiritual oneness and create an integrated human community. He and Nehru were both, in their own ways in that pre-nuclear age, optimists. Radhakrishnan believed that the universe had a sovereign purpose and history was a meaningful process. At rock bottom things were good and there was a power which was ceaselessly overcoming evil and transforming it into good. Mankind was still in the making, and if the existing civilization proved inadequate the central drive of the universe would replace it with a better one. Nature moved in her own triumphant way and the slow dying of the old order need not cause despair. The spiritual revolution which he envisaged was bound to come.[8]

These lectures attracted considerable attention. Many in his audiences at the World Congress of Faiths were already converted. But agreement or rejection was secondary; what mattered was contact with a profoundly spiritual person speaking with impassioned conviction. His fluency was never confusing and did not cloud the clarity of his complicated thought. There was no deliberate attempt at eloquence; rather, it seemed, as Younghusband believed, that it was only with such lightning rapidity that he could keep his thoughts together.[9] 'I wish', wrote Agatha Harrison, herself devoted to the cause of

[8] 'Religion and Religions', address to the World Congress of Faiths (July 1936); 'The Supreme Spiritual Ideal: The Hindu View', address to the World Congress of Faiths, *Hibbert Journal*, October 1936; 'The World's Unborn Soul' (Oxford 1936). The last two lectures have been reprinted in *Eastern Religions and Western Thought* (Oxford 1939), pp. 1–57.

[9] Article in the *Asiatic Review*, July 1936; *A Venture of Faith* (London 1937), p. 247.

India, 'you could have heard some of the comments of the people around me after you had spoken. One said that if the Conference had been organized for the *sole* purpose of hearing what you said yesterday it would have been worth it.'

From the viewpoint of public speaking, Radhakrishnan had been disappointed by his inaugural lecture at Oxford. Told that it was customary on such occasions to read from the text, he started doing so and, finding this uncongenial, half-way through the lecture threw away the printed pages and reverted to his normal practice of rapid delivery without notes. Radhakrishnan was upset by this; but the audience itself was impressed by the range of thought, the high seriousness of spirit, the eloquence of language and the manner of delivery.[10] Eric Williams, the future prime minister of Trinidad, then an undergraduate, has written of the pride felt by many from what we now term the Third World at the inaugural performance of the first professor to be chosen from Asia.[11] Reading the text later, Herbert Samuel thought that this lecture 'alone would be a sufficient justification, if any were needed, of your appointment to the new Chair at Oxford.'[12] It was this lecture, summing up all that Radhakrishnan had been expounding and contending for nearly two decades, which persuaded Aldous Huxley and Gerald Heard, long before they migrated to California, that modern civilization could be sustained only by an insight into religion of the type for which Radhakrishnan stood. Such a synthesis of Asian and European thought could be a foundation for a world civilization and a culture embracing humanity.[13] But the most moving testimony of the way in which this inaugural lecture could turn and transform people's lives is that of a Soviet citizen. A member of the troupe of the Moscow Academic Theatre in London in the summer of 1936, he met Radhakrishnan, 'A man—like a lion.' He then read 'The World's Unborn Soul' by the light of a street-lamp on the Embankment. The call in that lecture to resistance to all kinds of spiritual and moral tyranny and the development of a full and comprehensive view of life led him to renounce his career as an actor,

[10] For example, Professor C. C. J. Webb to Radhakrishnan, 24 October 1936.
[11] Eric Williams, *Inward Hunger* (London 1969), p. 53.
[12] Sir Herbert Samuel to Radhakrishnan, 12 November 1936.
[13] Gerald Heard to Radhakrishnan, 26 July and 24 October 1936.

1. One of the few photographs of Radhakrishnan with a moustache.

2. With A. R. Wadia and K. T. Shah, Mysore, January 1921.

3. Radhakrishnan, 1921.

4. With Suren Sen and Shyama Prasad Mukherjee, Paris, 13 July 1926.

5. With his wife, Calcutta, 1929.

6. London, 1930.

7. Geneva, 1932.

8. London, 1936.

9. With Tagore at the special convocation
of Oxford University at Shantiniketan,
7 August 1940.

10. Receiving Mahatma Gandhi at his residence, Banaras, 20 January 1942.

11.  Banaras, September 1941.

12.  Outside All Souls College, Oxford, March 1946.

13. With Swami Ranganathananda, Karachi,
14 September 1946.

14. Moscow, September 1950.

15. Delhi, 12 May 1952.

16. With Sheikh Abdullah, Srinagar, July 1952.

17. Broadcasting with Bertrand Russell, London, 28 October 1952.

18. With Zhou en-lai, Delhi, June 1954.

19. President of the General Conference of
UNESCO, Paris, 12 November 1952.

20. With his wife, Delhi, June 1953.

21. Cricket with the grandchildren.

22. Delhi, 1955.

23. Delhi, 1955.

24. Welcome by Ho Chi Minh, Hanoi, 12 September 1957.

25. With Khruschev, Delhi, February 1960.

26. Assuming office as President of India, 12 May 1962.

27. With Rajagopalachari at Madras airport, 27 May 1962.

28. Delhi, 5 September 1962.

29. Arrival at the White House, Washington D.C., 2 June 1963.

30. Arrival at Victoria Station, London, 12 June 1963.

31. Receiving the Fellowship of the
Sahitya Akademi, Madras, 10 September 1968;
Radhakrishnan's last public appearance.

break off the tour and return to the Soviet Union to lead a new kind of life. He ended up in a penal camp in Siberia.[14]

## II

In his first year at Oxford Radhakrishnan had had with him his wife and some of his children. He had brought his son to Britain to give him the best education possible. Failing to place him at short notice in Eton he had admitted him to Mill Hill, chosen primarily because the headmaster was a son of Radhakrishnan's old friend, L. P. Jacks. His wife and the two youngest daughters joined him a few weeks later and Radhakrishnan took a house at the end of Woodstock Road. They were in Oxford for a year, till the summer of 1937; and this turned out to be the last time that Radhakrishnan and his wife stayed together for any length of time.

But, despite the comfort of home life, Radhakrishnan was not in a relaxed and settled mood. With his philosophical work and public activity he had no cause to be dissatisfied, for he was doing exactly what he wished to do. Nor was he bothered by the mists of gossip that floated at this time round his personal life. He expressed this general confidence in a jotting written in 1936:

If I were to choose any words with which to conclude, I would choose the words that Browning put into the mouth of Andrea del Sarto,

> 'I, painting from myself and to myself,
> Know what I do, am unmoved by men's blame
> Or their praise either.'

But he was concerned about his future at Oxford. The chair had been established only for five years and Radhakrishnan, still under fifty years of age, naturally worried about the lack of permanent tenure. In 1937 Spalding provided funds to maintain the chair for fifteen years and Radhakrishnan's tenure was correspondingly extended. But no college fellowship was attached to it and Radhakrishnan was only made a member of

[14] W. Schwarz, 'Philosopher and Teacher from India', *Munchner Merkur*, 23 October 1961.

the common room of All Souls. Apart from detracting from the prestige of the chair it also caused Radhakrishnan physical inconvenience for, after the departure of the family, instead of moving into a college, he had to find rooms in the city. Bardwell Court, where he resided when in Oxford during the two years till the outbreak of war, was comfortable; but it meant much journeying by taxi and bus.

Also, after the inaugural lecture, while Radhakrishnan had enough time for his own work, the unavoidable routine of teaching and supervising students was not exciting. Radhakrishnan, frequently in later years, expressed the opinion that a person was best in instructing the young till the age of fifty. His lectures were devoted to comparative religion and the influence, in the ancient past, of Indian thought on Greece, Rome and Palestine.[15] While he gave them much thought and attention, lecturing to students now seems to have become a slight chore. He was very careful, as always, to conceal his real feelings; but a comment to a friend in India gives us a glimpse of his mood within a week of the inaugural lecture: 'I am getting on with this work and hope that it will prove less taxing and more interesting in time to come.'[16] But, being a good lecturer and a striking personality, he drew students from various disciplines even though the subject had little to do with examination syllabuses, and his audiences were of a respectable size. 'I admire', wrote his friend and colleague Edward Thompson, 'his intellect, scholarship, spirit. His mind is alive at every moment. His lectures at Oxford, by universal admission, have been astonishingly clear and vivid.'[17]

To many senior members of the university too, the very presence of Radhakrishnan offered the prospect of new approaches to traditional subjects and unexpected insights in well-traversed fields of study. Much could be expected from a scholar equally at home in the thought of the West as well as of the East, 'whose genius embraces the whole world of thought'.[18] Professor Col-

[15] See *Eastern Religions and Western Thought* (Oxford 1939).
[16] To Birbal Sahni in Lucknow, 26 October 1936, Sahni papers, NMML.
[17] Edward Thompson, 'Inheritance from India', *The Observer* (London), 30 May 1937.
[18] Review of *Contemporary Indian Philosophy* in *The Inquirer* (London), 26 December 1936.

lingwood thanked Spalding for making it possible for Radhakrishnan to continue for more than five years in Oxford: 'He
is a great man and I love him. I don't know how much effect he
is having on Oxford (we are rather a generation of deaf adders)
but whatever effect he has can only be good. Let us, I beg, have
him amongst us for as long as possible.'[19] Canon Raven, Professor of Divinity and former vice-chancellor of Cambridge,
said that the lack of a similar chair was giving his own university an inferiority complex. The period in which the Christian
religion could be studied successfully in isolation was over and
Radhakrishnan had set a standard for the discipline of comparative religion in Oxford to which other universities in Britain
could look forward.[20]

In fact, it was the influence which Radhakrishnan exercised
not just in Oxford but from there throughout Britain and the
Western world that was of significance in these years. As in the
year 1929-30, he was more of a public figure than the average
don and was frequently on the move delivering public addresses, speaking to groups of scholars and philosophers and
preaching in churches, chapels and synagogues. A busy nurse
who happened to hear him lecture in April 1937 found that
occasion to be the turning-point in her life. Thereafter she read
his books; but 'I feel I should never have got near the core of
your thought—had I only *read* and never *heard* you.'[21] There
were probably many more who felt the same way but remained
silent; and Radhakrishnan was not always certain whether he
was making sufficient impact. Younghusband, who took care to
attend every address of Radhakrishnan in London, once finding
him despondent at the reaction of his audience, acknowledged
that

it must seem uphill work for you over here as we are not very de-
monstrative and not overmuch devoted to spiritual things. But I
can tell you for certain that what you have done already is greatly
appreciated. You have already made your mark with those of real
influence in the country and through them your work will spread

[19] Quoted by H. N. Spalding to Radhakrishnan, 4 November 1937.
[20] Speech at Cambridge, 24 June 1938, *The Renascence of Religion* (London
1938), p. 5.
[21] Hermione Gepp to Radhakrishnan, 2 June 1939.

... Just go ahead then ... With great gratitude for all you are doing for England ...[22]

And even from beyond Britain there were some sustaining letters from less well-known men and women, such as the lady from Brooklyn who wrote to say that if 'moments of discouragement come to you also, I hope at that time the thought will persist that there must be many who are somewhat stronger because you are here among men.'[23]

Knowledge of this pervasive influence which Radhakrishnan was steadily acquiring gradually percolated to India and naturally gave pleasure in many circles. 'India, I think', wrote Tagore, 'is now suffering from a surfeit of itinerant professors and preachers in English and the various Continental Universities. There is one hope for me that *you* are there.'[24] Radhakrishnan's other great Indian contemporary was also of a similar view: 'My experience makes me more and more convinced that we have not done justice to the inheritance left to us by our ancestors. We have been too lazy to understand its value for us and the world. I am glad therefore that you are successfully trying to interpret ancient Indian wisdom to the West.'[25] But to less lofty spirits in India Radhakrishnan's philosophical mission was of less account than the fact that an Indian was on equal terms with the most eminent scholars of the Western world and could tell them how Indian culture could be of help to stricken humanity. This was salve to the soul of an oppressed people.

The religious philosophy which Radhakrishnan expounded could not in Indian eyes be divorced from national sentiment. His 'all-embracing knowledge and penetration' were grounded in Hinduism.[26] When Radhakrishnan, on his return to India in 1937, told his people that Indian civilization based on religious values was enduring, unlike the more materialist civilization of the West, and that the world, drawing closer together, was looking to the vaster and stronger inheritance of the East for self-preservation, it was not only religious-minded persons in

[22] Sir Francis Younghusband to Radhakrishnan, 20 January 1937.
[23] May Reid to Radhakrishnan, 26 November 1937.
[24] Tagore to Radhakrishnan, 23 November 1936. Emphasis in original.
[25] Mahatma Gandhi to Radhakrishnan, 13 May 1937.
[26] Professor F. W. Thomas in the *Hibbert Journal*, October 1937.

India who responded.[27] Such satisfaction was strengthened, of
course, by the fact that Radhakrishnan himself gave expression
to his patriotism on suitable occasions. He who commended to
Europe non-violence, patience and tolerance and asked India
not to turn to force and hatred in emulation of the West also
reminded the British that no individual nation can be trusted
with the charge of another.[28]

In August 1937 Radhakrishnan was invited by the British
Academy to deliver the next year the Master Mind Lecture on
the Buddha. That for the first time an Asian was selected as the
subject and an Asian asked to speak on it was a measure of the
inroads which Radhakrishnan had made into conservative
British academic thinking. The lecture itself, given in June
1938, was a combination of historical insight and philosophic
force. It forms the most authoritative exposition of Radhakrishnan's consistent view that the Buddha was a reformer of the
Hindu faith rather than a breakaway innovator, and that his
silence on ultimate problems implied neither agnosticism nor
atheism but a refusal to speak of the Absolute of which he was
aware because it was not directly relevant to ethical ways of
living. Delivered as was his custom without any notes or single
hesitation, the lecture was one of Radhakrishnan's more sparkling efforts. It was particularly spectacular because the chairman, Sir David Ross, in introducing Radhakrishnan to a large
and distinguished audience (which included T. S. Eliot), rather
brusquely reminded the speaker that he should not take more
than an hour as many in the hall had trains to catch. In
obedience to this directive, Radhakrishnan wound up his
virtuoso performance as the clock struck six; and Ross, in his
concluding remarks, made amends for his seeming rudeness.
They had heard, he said, a lecture not only on a master mind
but by a master mind.[29] Doubtless this lecture smoothed the
way to Radhakrishnan's election a year later to the fellowship
of the Academy. He was once again a pioneer, being the first
Indian to be so honoured.

[27] Statement to the press at Bombay, 13 August 1937, *The Hindu*, 16 August
1937.
[28] Speech at the annual dinner of Sri Lanka students in Britain, 8 June, *Ceylon
Daily News* (Colombo), 10 June 1937.
[29] Sir Francis Younghusband, 'Our Debt to India', *Times Literary Supplement*,
7 September 1940.

## III

Such academic recognition did not lighten for Radhakrishnan the ever-present shadow of India's subordinate condition:

If you watch closely and catch a face in repose of any intelligent young man or woman, you will see there a shade which is not quite natural to youth, an under-current of sorrow that he belongs to a country, vast, populous and ancient, that is still a subject nation. It is there, that impersonal, detached shadow, and will be there so long as the present condition continues. The shame of subjection is written across the faces of young intelligent Indians and that is what gives meaning to the demand for independence.[30]

With the Congress in office in many provinces, Radhakrishnan's hope was that the British government would display imagination and sympathy in responding to this co-operative attitude. He tried to convince the British that Gandhi was their best friend, reported to Zetland, the secretary of state, that he had talked to Gandhi, who was in a receptive mood, and urged the British to settle matters regarding federation with Gandhi while he was still around and in charge.[31] The election of Subhas Bose as president of the Congress should be a warning to them. But he was not optimistic: 'In spite of the tense situation here, the unwillingness to do the right thing is simply astounding.'[32]

At the same interview with Gandhi at Wardha in December 1938, Radhakrishnan, who had been elected president of the Andhra Mahasabha for a second time, secured Gandhi's written support for the immediate formation of a separate Andhra province.[33] He also spoke to Gandhi of his intent to edit a collection of essays and reflections on Gandhi's life and work to be presented to him on his seventieth birthday in October 1939. Gandhi gave his permission and Radhakrishnan went

[30] Speech at Madras, 15 July 1938, printed in S. Radhakrishnan, *Education, Politics and War* (Pune 1944), p. 5.

[31] Radhakrishnan's letters to *The Times* (London), 19 February and 30 September 1938; speech at Madras 15 July 1938, *Education, Politics and War*, p. 6; interview with Zetland, reported in Zetland's letter to Linlithgow, 5 February 1939, Zetland papers, IOL, MSS. EUR. D609, vol. 11.

[32] Radhakrishnan to Nehru, 30 January 1939, Nehru papers.

[33] Mahatma Gandhi to Radhakrishnan, 23 December 1938.

ahead. Though there was not much time left, Radhakrishnan
sought to make it a representative volume and sent a circular
inviting articles from politicians, scholars, intellectuals and
literary figures in various parts of the world. Shaw, Russell and
Archbishop Temple of York declined for they had reservations
about Gandhi. Wells was emphatic in his refusal: 'I will not
write a line to boost up that old publicity bore.' Others like
Gide and Santayana excused themselves for various reasons, as
did Keynes with a charming comment. 'What a boy Gandhi
is! I imagined that he was immensely older than seventy.' Yet,
despite these negative responses, Radhakrishnan secured over
sixty contributions from a wide range of personalities of many
nationalities and almost every creed. This arresting company
included Smuts and Hofmeyr from South Africa, where Gandhi
had made his entry into political struggles; C. F. Andrews and
Edward Thompson, the Englishmen who knew Gandhi best;
Einstein and Romain Rolland; and Llewelyn Powys and Laur-
ence Binyon. Never before had any public figure of any country
received during his lifetime such varied and abundant testimony to his principles and character. Even many who disagreed
with him acknowledged Gandhi's stature.

Radhakrishnan had been particularly anxious to receive
comments and assessments from prominent figures in British
public life so as to establish the basic goodwill inspiring both
sides in the freedom struggle in India. Lord Sankey and Herbert
Samuel agreed to write, but the members of the Conservative
party in power were less co-operative. Linlithgow, the viceroy,
refused and prevailed on Zetland, the secretary of state, also
to decline; but the foreign secretary, Halifax, who as viceroy
had negotiated with Gandhi, withstood their pressure and sent
a short letter recognizing Gandhi's quality and the deep spiritual force by which he was activated.

From India the contributions were many and diverse; but
the big gap was the lack of an article by Jawaharlal Nehru. He
had at first taken interest in the project, promised to write and
thought in terms of a public function, presided over by Tagore,
at which the volume would be presented to Gandhi. But finally
he suffered from writer's block:

I am too closely associated with Gandhiji in our day to day work
for me to write anything of value without saying something which

I ought not to say. And I do not want to write a collection of pious platitudes. Hence my difficulty. I do not suppose I shall get over it for some time. Meanwhile my mind is not in a fit condition for any creative work.[34]

Radhakrishnan himself, in a long introduction, developed the deeper thought and meaning of Gandhi's life and work. To him Gandhi was essentially a religious person who had become a political worker because his religious outlook meant a commitment to the whole of humanity. This explained his activities in South Africa and India as well as his economic programme. Non-violence was the only possible means for such a religious person, and satyagraha the only practical way of applying non-violence. Though opposed to imperialism, Gandhi was a friend of the British. Writing in the early months of 1939, Radhakrishnan felt that such an approach availed no more than the whistling of the wind; but he hoped that British public opinion would assert itself to force the British government to do the right thing while Gandhi was still alive. Radhakrishnan was also, even though it was clear by then that war could not be avoided, optimist enough to assert that on the whole humanity was moving ahead; and in this advance Gandhi was one of the foremost leaders. He was the prophet of a liberated life.[35]

The political significance of this essay could not be missed. Writing at a time when Gandhi was in the thick of the struggle, Radhakrishnan was certainly, by tracing the principles which underlay Gandhi's activities and providing a unity between theory and practice, raising both the leader and the movement to a loftier plane. The only critical note, and that too in a low key, was the protest that Gandhi's insistence on celibacy was beyond the reach of most men and women. But the case for Gandhi, and for India, had never, on the level of philosophical and spiritual ideals, been more powerfully argued: 'One of Gandhi's successes has been securing the devotion of a man like Radhakrishnan who, if he has less experience in the rough and tumble of political life, has higher intellectual attainments and perhaps a finer quality of soul than Gandhi himself.'[36] Muir-

[34] Nehru to Radhakrishnan, 16 May 1939.

[35] S. Radhakrishnan (ed.), *Mahatma Gandhi: Essays and Reflections on His Life and Work* (London 1939).    [36] Review in *Times Literary Supplement*.

head thought that Radhakrishnan had excelled himself in the writing of it; it could not have been better done by anyone alive, and Gandhi ought to be immensely pleased with it.[37]

## IV

Gandhi vetoed the proposal to have a public meeting for presenting the volume to him; he could not, he said, attend merely to hear his praises sung. So the book was sent to him by a special messenger. Once this had been decided, Radhakrishnan planned to spend most of the year 1939 out of India. The Easter vacation took him to South Africa in response to a joint invitation from the Indian agent-general, the South African Indian Congress and the universities of Capetown and the Witwatersrand. The purpose was to strengthen the morale of the Indian settlers and to weaken the prejudice against Indians among the 'white' population by providing fresh testimony that India had a rich and ancient culture, and that her best scholars were held in high esteem by the West.

The latter criterion Radhakrishnan certainly at this time fulfilled to a high degree. *Eastern Religions and Western Thought*, based on his lectures at Oxford and elsewhere, had just been published and received with enthusiasm. He had argued, with style, scholarship and much spiritual feeling, that the problem of contemporary civilization was to gain a unity of soul; and this challenge could be met if a philosophy could be developed which combined the best of European humanism and Asian religion. In the past such interaction could be seen in the influence of Hindu thought on early Greek philosophy and on the development of Christian speculation; and now again living religions could draw together under the inspiring example of mystics who were spiritual kinsmen, whatever their particular denominations. Radhakrishnan drew attention to the common elements in Christianity and Hinduism and emphasized the points in which they moved in the same direction. With an unshakeable faith in the ultimate goodness of the universe, he accepted all that was best in Western religious thought and asked his readers to take advantage of the rich treasures of the spirit which India had to offer. There was no incompatibility

[37] J. H. Muirhead to Radhakrishnan, 5 October 1939.

between Hinduism and Christianity if the latter moved away from dogmatism and institutionalization and became genuinely Christlike.

Radhakrishnan's journey through the centuries, covering a vast range of thought and religious experience and stressing the affinities of approach among Greeks, Hebrews, Romans, Christians and Indians, made, to serious-minded persons, interesting and even exciting reading. Orthodox Christians felt that he stressed the best points, the ideals, of Hinduism and compared them with the weaknesses and failures of Christianity. It seemed to them that Radhakrishnan, while emphasizing the common points of religions, implicitly assumed that Hinduism was superior to all others; and they were irritated by his assertion that he could not regard the substitution of a credal religion even for atheistic materialism as a spiritual good. But most others found the book of vital significance. The reviewer in the *Times Literary Supplement* thought it might well mark a turning-point in Western civilization—it certainly should; and the same issue which carried this front-page review also had a leader on the subject.[38] To those who believed that only a blending of East and West could give modern civilization a philosophy, Radhakrishnan's work 'has been one of the outstanding arches on which such a road may be carried'.[39] But the appeal of the book spread far beyond professional scholars and learned intellectuals. 'Most of us', Edward Hulton advised readers of *Picture Post*, 'would do well to sell all our books and get this one, for it is a guide book to the treasury of man's approach to truth down the ages.'[40] Sir Siegmund Warburg, one of the leading merchant bankers of London, was so impressed that he wrote to Radhakrishnan suggesting the starting of a movement transcending any separate religious community: 'Has not the time come to get a group of persons together who think out this problem as a small community and as a nucleus for the new religious congregation which must come?'[41]

So Radhakrishnan arrived in Durban with a formidable reputation, recently enhanced. His addresses on comparative

[38] 8 April 1939.    [39] Gerald Heard to Radhakrishnan, 9 May 1939.
[40] *Picture Post*, 11 May 1940.
[41] Sir Siegmund Warburg to Radhakrishnan, 7 October 1940.

religion at the universities were given to audiences which over-
flowed into other rooms,[42] while his general talks to Indian
societies, African schools and rotary and ladies' clubs drew considerable numbers despite the reluctance of the European press
to give publicity to him and his visit. While the set lectures
demonstrated, in Jan Hofmeyr's words, that the Indians in
South Africa were not a small and isolated group but the out-
post of a great and large nation,[43] the tenor of Radhakrishnan's
more informal speeches was to warn the European population
that no sound social structure could be founded on racial discrimination. One could not chain others without at the same
time chaining oneself; and any injury done to the very least of
humanity was injury done to the whole. Running a whole
country for the benefit of one section of the community was to
invite destruction. The spirit of man could not be entombed for
all time. It was no use involving God in defending an unjust
society; every religion was a burning flame of human service,
and beauty fouled and humanity oppressed proved a lack of
faith in spiritual values. To worship man was to worship God,
and the highest religion was the recognition of the fundamental
right of all human beings to develop their possibilities.[44] On
the other hand, he expected the Indian community to look on
South Africa as their home without forgetting their cultural
background, to work together with Africans against common
humiliation and to stand up, on the lines which Gandhi had
shown them, for the right, whatever the consequences.[45]

*Indian Opinion*, the journal started by Mahatma Gandhi and
at this time edited by his son, wrote that Radhakrishnan's
short visit to South Africa was like a flash of light from heaven.[46]
But the only tangible result was a renewed, and short-lived,
effort by the various Indian associations to work in harmony.[47]
The leaders of 'white' opinion in the government and outside

[42] Report in *Johannesburg Star*, 4 April 1939.
[43] Speech at Durban, 10 April, *Natal Mercury*, 11 April 1939.
[44] Speech at Durban, 19 March 1939, and speeches at Maritzburg, 9 and 10
April 1939, *Natal Witness*, 20 March and 10 and 11 April 1939, respectively;
interview in *Natal Daily News*, 5 April 1939.
[45] Speech at Johannesburg, 28 March 1939, *Rand Daily Mail*, 29 March 1939;
farewell message, 14 April 1939, *Natal Mercury*, 15 April 1939.
[46] *Indian Opinion*, 14 April 1939.
[47] Ibid., 13 October 1939.

treated Radhakrishnan with respect. Smuts and Hofmeyr in particular showed great warmth and Radhakrishnan secured their assent to contribute to the birthday volume for Gandhi. But his advocacy of far-sighted and liberal statemanship so as to make the different communities feel that they belonged to South Africa met with no response; and Smuts and Hofmeyr themselves were soon to be replaced by even more diehard elements. In the long history of South Africa's determined drive to disaster the efforts of Radhakrishnan on his short visit form a forlorn venture. The flash of light from heaven lasted hardly an hour.

# 8

# BANARAS

When, with the outbreak of war in September 1939, Indian politics headed for stormy waters, there was no doubt as to where Radhakrishnan's sympathy lay. He pressed Britain to transfer the substance of self-government immediately and supported the demand of the Congress for a clear statement of Britain's objectives. She should grant self-government to India not because there was a state of war, but because that was the right thing to do.[1] Even a declaration that this would be done as soon as possible would serve to touch the imagination of the Indian people and strengthen the hands of Gandhi and his colleagues in binding India and Britain together in an abiding loyalty to common ideals and principles.[2] But on the question of a constituent assembly to determine India's future he was more moderate than the Congress, in that he was willing to allow representation to the government as then existing as well as to important trading interests and did not envisage full self-government for at least thirty years. Not to do even this would be to weaken Britain's moral case.[3] But the British government had no intention of giving any undertaking.[4] Zetland noted that Radhakrishnan's position differed from that of the Congress in an effort to placate the British, but commented airily that 'political Indians, as has so often happened in the past, have fallen victims once more to the seductive attractions of mere phrases, the actual significance of which they have not troubled themselves to think out.'[5]

[1] Statements to the press, 3 and 16 September 1939, *Education, Politics and War*, pp. 60–2; statement, 5 September 1939, *The Statesman*, 6 September 1939.
[2] Speech at Calcutta, 29 September 1939, *The Hindu*, 30 September 1939.
[3] Statement to the press, 27 October 1939, *Education, Politics and War*, pp. 63–5; letter to Zetland, 29 October 1939.
[4] Zetland to Radhakrishnan, 14 November 1939.
[5] Zetland to Linlithgow, 20 December 1939, Zetland papers, vol. 11.

By 1940, with the viceroy reiterating that the objective was dominion status and Indian opinion would be consulted with regard to the future constitution, it seemed to Radhakrishnan, always an optimist as regards British actions, that the question had narrowed itself to the way in which the future constitution was to be framed. The British, famous in his view for their pragmatic empiricism, should seek agreements with Gandhi and the Congress on matters relating to defence, the princes and British commerce.[6] Immediately after this speech he saw the viceroy and reported to Gandhi that Linlithgow was anxious to do everything he could (within his instructions) to straighten the political tangle. Radhakrishnan suggested that in purely internal matters such as revenue and public health Indians should be allowed to determine the future, while in matters such as defence and the princes and in foreign affairs there could be joint deliberations. In other words, Radhakrishnan suggested a dyarchic approach, with futher consideration after ten years. Linlithgow did not like the idea, moderate as it was, but promised to consider it; and Radhakrishnan pressed Gandhi to agree to it. Civil disobedience might very easily assume a communal character, and matters should not be allowed to drift.[7]

Radhakrishnan was too trusting of Linlithgow, for the viceroy, while talking sweetly to him, was assuring Zetland that he was not too keen to start talking about what would happen when British rule ceased, for that date was very remote. Nor was Gandhi prepared to qualify the demand made by the Congress, at its session at Ramgarh in the middle of March, for a sovereign constituent assembly. Civil disobedience was not certain; but there would be room for compromise only if the British renounced the decisive voice. Grieved by their unbending attitude, he would yield nothing on the fundamentals, no matter how weak one might feel: 'I ask you to be patient and firm.'[8] But Radhakrishnan was still hopeful and, passing on Gandhi's views to the viceroy, offered, if Linlithgow were in-

[6] Address to the Rotary Club of Delhi, 22 March 1940, *The Hindu*, 26 March 1940.

[7] Radhakrishnan to Gandhi, 29 March 1940.

[8] Gandhi to Radhakrishnan, 5 April 1940.

clined to accept his own scheme, to use his influence with the
Congress in favour of a settlement,[9] and gave publicity to his
proposals.[10] Maurice Gwyer, chief justice of India and vice-
chancellor of Delhi University, claimed to have independent
corroboration that Gandhi, whatever his stated position, might
be inclined to accept such a scheme.[11]

However, when the full details of the debate on India in
parliament came in, Radhakrishnan was forced to recognize
that the British were not serious about immediate self-government for India and, rather than channel the widespread
sympathy for Britain, preferred to lay emphasis on the communal problem, for which they themselves bore the main
responsibility. It was a confession of moral failure.[12] Radhakrishnan, from being a mediator, had fallen back in line with
the Congress: 'Your statement on the India debate is splendid.
Let me tell you that Gandhiji liked it very much. The Congress
case could not have been put better. You now see why Gandhiji
could not accept the formula you had suggested.'[13]

The situation rapidly deteriorated. The new government
under Churchill, ignoring offers of co-operation from the
Congress, were prepared for no imaginative offer such as
Radhakrishnan sought.[14] Nehru was arrested at the end of
October, while Gandhi thought of fasting unto death as a
protest against the adamant attitude of the British. In these
circumstances Radhakrishnan wrote again to Linlithgow,
pointing out the disastrous impact which such a fast, especially
if it ended tragically, would have, and suggesting a national—
not a Congress—government at the centre.[15] The viceroy's
response was contemptuous: 'As I write, I have just had a
somewhat characteristic letter from Sir S. Radhakrishnan,
whom you know . . . It is characteristic in its complete muddle-
headedness and failure to face upto the facts or to analyze the
situation and its difficulties, and the more interesting as it comes

[9] Radhakrishnan to Linlithgow, 8 April 1940.
[10] Statement to the press, 19 April 1940, *Education, Politics and War*, pp. 72–4.
[11] Sir Maurice Gwyer to Radhakrishnan, 24 April 1940.
[12] Statement to the press, 24 April 1940, *The Hindu*, 25 April 1940.
[13] Mahadev Desai, secretary to Gandhi, to Radhakrishnan, 28 April 1940.
[14] Speech at Calcutta, 18 September, *Civil and Military Gazette*, 19 September
1940.    [15] Radhakrishnan to Linlithgow, 4 November 1940.

from a man of Radhakrishnan's intellectual eminence.'[16] To Radhakrishnan himself he directed his secretary to send a formal acknowledgement, making obvious that he was unwilling to consider the proposal and discouraging further correspondence.

So Radhakrishnan, finding the government immovable, expounded the Indian case, as he saw it, in great detail. The British cause was manifestly superior to that of the Axis powers, for unfulfilled justice was better than a negation of justice. But British statesmen did not seem to realize sufficiently that new forces were at work which required a new outlook. Those in particular who were in charge of India policy had the traditional virtues, were 'immensely intelligent but highly insensitive'. They might win the war but they would lose the peace. They should give content to the noble phrases which they uttered and weld Britain and India together in a great democratic federation for mutual service and the service of the world.[17]

For Gandhi this was not good enough: 'Your language is all your own. You will however let me say that I miss the strength which I would expect from your pen or speech. The message of non-violence demands the utmost strength without sting behind it.'[18] Perhaps as a reaction to this, Radhakrishnan, in his speeches in the months that followed, did not deal with non-violence, but stated the nationalist position with even greater vigour. The government by now were ludicrously treating him as politically dangerous and forbade him from speaking at the university hall in Lahore unless he gave an undertaking to refrain from referring to political matters. This of course he refused to do and the meeting was shifted to another place.[19] In his speeches in 1941 he emphasized the shortcomings of a civilization which had made two world wars possible and called for the spread of the spiritual outlook for which India had always stood. But only a free India could give of her

[16] Linlithgow to Amery, 6 November 1940, Linlithgow papers, IOL MSS. EUR., F. 125, vol. 9.
[17] Convocation address at Patna University, 29 November 1940, *Education, Politics and War*, pp. 75–90.
[18] Gandhi to Radhakrishnan, 28 December 1940.
[19] *Civil and Military Gazette*, 28 February 1941.

best.[20] To stress the communal problem as the greatest obstacle to India's freedom was to accept the deficiency of British rule.[21] Speaking at Dhaka, a centre of Muslim communalism, and ignoring the warnings of a timid vice-chancellor who feared the anger of a British chancellor,[22] Radhakrishnan roundly, with chapter and verse, blamed the government for promoting communal differences among a generally harmonious people. It was therefore now Britain's duty to re-establish her good faith by implementing her many pledges. Indian opinion was on the side of the Allies, for they stood for unfulfilled law as against brute force, the whispers of conscience as against the law of the jungle. The time had come to convert this sympathy into whole-hearted support.[23]

## II

The government paid little heed to such warnings and advice even when they came from one who, while outside the bustle of politics, was regarded by even British non-official opinion in the country as 'perhaps the greatest intellectual force in India today'.[24] But soon Radhakrishnan had to consider more immediate problems than the condition of India and the future of the world. The University of Banaras, set up in 1917 as a nursery of Hindu culture, had by 1939 developed into the largest residential university in the country, with advanced courses both in the sciences and in the traditional classics. The respect which its founder and vice-chancellor, Madan Mohan Malaviya, commanded by his dedication and orthodox austerity had enabled him to collect considerable funds from Hindu princes and merchants so as to acquire an extensive site, construct numerous buildings and not only teach the basic subjects but introduce various disciplines not taught elsewhere; and all this was done without any grants for buildings or equipment from the state. Indeed, the grants from the governments of

[20] Speeches at Lahore, 26 February 1941, and Agra, 22 November 1941, *Education, Politics and War*, pp. 11–19 and 129–35, respectively.

[21] Statement at Calcutta, 24 April 1941, *Civil and Military Gazette*, 26 April 1941.

[22] Dr R. C. Majumdar to Radhakrishnan, 15 November 1941.

[23] Convocation address at Dhaka University, 25 November 1941, *Education, Politics and War*, pp. 136–51.

[24] *Civil and Military Gazette*, 28 February 1941.

India and the United Provinces to the university for its development amounted to a meagre three lakhs per year. But the
rapid expansion, along with administrative inadequacy, had
resulted in a debt of about Rs 2,000,000—in those times an
extremely high figure. Malaviya recognized that a younger and
more energetic vice-chancellor was required to deal with these
problems, and Radhakrishnan seemed to him his natural
successor—widely respected as a scholar and expositor of a
modern Hinduism and with a reputation of success in educational administration. Radhakrishnan had been associated for
some years with the Hindu University as an honorary professor
of philosophy but, with his dual appointments in Calcutta and
Oxford, he could not, even if he would, have considered taking
on the vice-chancellorship. The winter of 1939 he had planned
to spend at the University of Southern California. But the outbreak of war in Europe in September 1939 ruled out for the time
being prospects of leaving India, and Malaviya took advantage
of this to press Radhakrishnan again to assume administrative
responsibility at Banaras. Gandhi also having from the outset
been keen that he do so, Radhakrishnan rather reluctantly
agreed.[25]

Yet Radhakrishnan, happy at Calcutta, was unwilling to
give up his chair at that university and, at the start, served in
Banaras as a weekend vice-chancellor, travelling up on Friday
by the night train and returning to Calcutta on Monday
morning. Even this, given his flair for quick seizure of any issue
and for rapid decision and ability to delegate authority to the
right persons, helped to tone up the administration. N. V.
Raghavan, who had retired prematurely from official service
after serving as accountant-general because he would not
kowtow to British officers and who was known for his uncompromising integrity, was appointed to cleanse the financial management, while Radhakrishnan undertook extensive tours throughout the country to collect funds. This did not come naturally
to him. 'I see', wrote Gandhi, 'that in your deep and extensive
studies, the art of begging formed no part.'[26] Yet, within two
years of Radhakrishnan taking up the vice-chancellorship, a

[25] Mahatma Gandhi to Radhakrishnan, 23 August 1939.
[26] Mahatma Gandhi to Radhakrishnan, undated, but written sometime towards the end of 1939.

quarter of the debt was wiped off; and in addition donations were procured for specific purposes such as buildings and fellowships. All this demanded more than casual attention and Radhakrishnan found himself increasingly devoting more than a couple of days every week to the affairs of the university. So regretfully he decided, in the summer of 1941, to sever his connection with Calcutta and serve as a full-time vice-chancellor at Banaras. But, rather than receive a salary in that capacity, he accepted the offer of the Government of Baroda to establish a chair of Indian culture at the Hindu University and agreed to be its first holder. There was a certain strength to be derived from being an honorary vice-chancellor. Moreover, Radhakrishnan planned to be vice-chancellor only as long as the war lasted; thereafter he hoped to divide the year between Oxford and Banaras, as he had earlier done between Oxford and Calcutta.

Under Radhakrishnan's firm and continuous guidance the university steadied itself and even gathered momentum. He made it clear, by his talks to the students and his addresses at formal gatherings, that the Hinduism which the university should promote was rational and forward-looking, shorn of obscurantism and ritual. While the university had been set up in Banaras for, among other objectives, the promotion of Hindu culture and religion, Radhakrishnan gave this, in line with his general attitude, a wide and non-dogmatic definition. Religion was to him the promotion of spiritual values independent of doctrine; and a good Hindu, according to his understanding, respected all religions as much as his own. Even in 1938, a year before taking up the vice-chancellorship, in his address at the convocation at Banaras, he had pleaded for a chair of Islamic studies; and during his term of office he visited Hyderabad and secured a substantial donation from the Nizam's government. He set aside the obscurantist rules of the department of theology and admitted a girl to study the Vedas; and he gave, whenever he happened to be in Banaras, lectures on Sundays on the Gita. These popular discourses, stressing the fundamentals of religion transcending narrow creeds, drew large audiences, many going up even from Allahabad for the day to attend them.

A more bracing atmosphere could be sensed at Banaras

within months of Radhakrishnan's assumption of office. Sir
Maurice Gwyer had come to Banaras as Radhakrishnan's guest
to address the convocation, and on his return was effusive in his
praise: 'Your University excites my admiration and my envy
too! and how Delhi is ever to come near to the standards which
you have set I do not know.'[27] He liked the bond with Radhakrishnan of their common association with All Souls (of which
Radhakrishnan had been elected a Fellow in 1940) and suggested to Oxford University that Radhakrishnan be associated
with him to represent the university at the special convocation
at Shantiniketan in 1940 to award an honorary degree to
Tagore. These demonstrations of goodwill led Radhakrishnan
to advise the chancellor, the maharaja of Bikaner, to invite
Gwyer to head a committee, with educationists and financial
experts as members, to look into the working of the university
and suggest measures to improve both the academic and the
administrative sides, and ensure that the funds, received largely
as gifts, be spent well.

Such a smooth tenure of the vice-chancellorship lasted for
less than three years. Radhakrishnan had made no secret of his
sympathy with the Congress and resisted official efforts to
control opinion in the university. When the Government of the
United Provinces objected to some leaflets distributed among
the students, Radhakrishnan agreed that the government had a
tenable viewpoint. But university students were a part of the
general community and its goodwill would have to be won by
the government if anti-British propaganda was to lose all point.
Till then all that the university authorities could do would
perforce be only of a palliative character.[28] Radhakrishnan
also, while generally pleading for better sense and generosity on
the part of the British government, once, while extolling the
grandeur of Indian culture, lapsed (if press reports are to be
trusted) uncharacteristically into an unqualified censure of
Western civilization for having allowed its spirit to perish.
Even the *Indian Social Reformer*, the Bombay journal generally
friendly to him, expressed concern at such a sweeping judge-

[27] Sir Maurice Gwyer to Radhakrishnan, 24 December 1939.

[28] Panna Lal, adviser, UP government, to Radhakrishnan, 27 November 1939,
and Radhakrishnan's reply, 2 December 1939.

ment.[29] So the British community in India was not surprised by or appreciative of Radhakrishnan's invitation not to the viceroy or the governor but to Mahatma Gandhi to inaugurate the silver jubilee celebrations of the university in January 1942. This led to even the chancellor staying away while Nehru and other senior Congress leaders were present; and the whole occasion, in the words of the maharaja of Bikaner, had a 'distinct Congress colouring'.[30] All this doubtless piqued Gwyer. A few weeks after the silver jubilee celebrations of the Banaras University he surprisingly, and with no reason, took 'the strongest exception' to some innocuous remarks of Radhakrishnan, welcoming Gwyer's appointment as chairman of the expert committee and looking forward to an authoritative statement of the university's needs and friendly support of its demands:

I do resent very much the assumption that it is to act as an advocate for the University in its demands upon, I suppose, the Government of India . . . I am certainly not prepared, nor I am sure are my colleagues, to embark upon this considerable labour merely for the purpose of obtaining concessions for the University. Unless this is clearly understood, I could not continue to act as Chairman.[31]

This was hardly the language of a friend, either of Radhakrishnan or of the university.

### III

Throughout the early months of 1942 Radhakrishnan did what he could to prevent a head-on collision between the government and the Congress. He was one of the signatories, along with Sapru and Jayakar, to the appeal to Winston Churchill, then in Washington, to take some immediate step to change the atmosphere in India. This triggered the despatch of the Cripps mission, of which nothing came. Though critical of the Cripps

---

[29] *Indian Social Reformer*, 8 March 1941.

[30] To Lord Linlithgow, 24 August 1942, home dept file 3/60/43-Poll. I, National Archives of India (henceforth NAI).

[31] Radhakrishnan to Sir M. Gwyer, 6 March 1942, and Gwyer's reply, 13 March 1942.

proposals as likely to weaken the unity of the country, Radhakrishnan saw in them the saving grace that the British had at
last been educated to a perception of the truth that only a free
India could be an effective ally in fighting external aggression.[32]
But the lesson was soon unlearnt. After the return of Cripps to
London, even as Burma fell to the Japanese, their troops approached the eastern frontier of India and their aircraft bombed
coastal towns, Amery, the secretary of state, felt that nothing
could be of greater benefit to India than that the Congress
should disintegrate. The viceroy was engaged in making sure of
striking at the Congress at the right moment and Sir Maurice
Hallett, the governor of the United Provinces, urged that the
Congress could and should be got out of the way.[33] So it was
too much to hope for a response to the call of the Congress to
transfer power to the representatives of the people. But to the
last Radhakrishnan's optimism did not fail. The day the All-
India Congress Committee met in Bombay Radhakrishnan
appealed to the viceroy to form a coalition cabinet of the
Congress and the Muslim League with the commander-in-
chief in sole command of the military movements. But by the
time Linlithgow received this letter Gandhi and the members of
the Working Committee had already been arrested. 'Outdated!' was the viceroy's response to Radhakrishnan's proposals; and as for the arguments that the Congress attitude was
born of sheer despair and indignation at the way in which
India was being treated and that any popular upsurge and
danger to Gandhi's life would worsen the situation, Linlithgow
commented condescendingly that the difficulties were more
substantial than Radhakrishnan had suggested.[34]

Determined as the authorities in India were to have a show-
down with the Congress, they were unprepared for the scale of
the popular reactions to the arrests of the leaders in Bombay.
In the United Provinces Hallett had been expecting no more

[32] Speech at Kangri, 6 April 1942, *Civil and Military Gazette*, 8 April 1942;
speech at Banaras, 11 April 1942, *The Hindu*, 12 April 1942.

[33] Amery to Linlithgow, 28 May 1942; Linlithgow to Sir H. Twynam, 6 June
1942; and Sir M. Hallett to Linlithgow, 21 July 1942, *Transfer of Power*, vol. 2,
documents 95, 129 and 301.

[34] Radhakrishnan's letter to Linlithgow, 8 August 1942; Linlithgow's comment, 10 August 1942 and reply to Radhakrishnan, 15 August 1942, *Transfer of
Power*, vol. 2, documents 473 and 558.

than 'a somewhat fatuous attempt' at civil disobedience such
as had occurred on previous occasions—picketing, boycott and
possibly attempts at starting a no-rent campaign and to interfere with labour.[35] He was, therefore, startled by the outbreaks
of violence, interference with communications and recurrence
of dacoities. Culverts were destroyed by digging up the foundations and special spanners were used to remove the fishplates
and lift the railway lines.[36] Especially round Banaras and in the
eastern parts of the province, of strategic importance because of
the bottleneck of supply lines to the eastern war front, for a few
weeks the administration collapsed. There were special reasons
for this. The Congress, particularly its Seva Dal, was active in
this area and Nehru had toured it in the early months of 1942.
Economic distress was sharpened by the steep rise in prices and
the growing unemployment among the weavers of Banaras who
had no alternative avenue of occupation. These factors, strengthened by the prevalent feeling that the Axis powers were
doing better than the Allies, led in these districts to a popular
movement of a dimension not seen since 1857.[37]

It was certainly sufficient for Hallett to speak of a rebellion
and a carefully preconceived plan by the Congress with a secret
central direction.[38] Its nerve-centre he placed in the Banaras
Hindu University. Even the viceroy was constrained to admit
that Hallett was from the start painting a 'slightly more lurid
picture' than after all might prove to have been justified.[39] The
Congress might be accused of ultimate responsibility for the
disturbances but their organization by it could not be established. In Banaras and its environs local Congressmen seem to
have guided the activities at short notice. The students of the
university also played some role, although not as decisive a one
as Hallett believed.

In the circumstances Radhakrishnan, as vice-chancellor,

[35] Hallett to Linlithgow, 18 August 1942, Linlithgow papers, vol. 105.

[36] P. Woodruff, *The Men Who Ruled India*, vol. 2 (London 1954), pp. 310–11.

[37] C. Mitra, 'The Lion in Retreat: Eastern Uttar Pradesh in 1942' (cyclostyled
paper, Centre for Social Sciences, Calcutta); note of Cripps on interview with
Nehru, 30 March 1942, *Transfer of Power*, vol 1, document 449.

[38] Hallett to Linlithgow, 9 September 1942, Hallett Collection, IOL, MSS.
EUR. E. 251, no. 38.

[39] Linlithgow to Amery, 17 August 1942, *Transfer of Power*, vol. 2, document
577.

while not concealing his general support of the Congress, sought to dissuade students from indulging in violent activities even while he protected the university from the drastic measures which Hallett's government sought to impose. It was revealing of the blinkered vision of the government that they relied on a letter allegedly written by a communist student at the university, observing that Radhakrishnan was against the communists and secretly with the Congress though he did not show it openly; for Radhakrishnan, far from cloaking his attitude, wrote to the viceroy stating his views frankly and, at a public meeting at the university, deplored the arrests of the leaders of the Congress. If the students were greatly agitated, however much it was to be deplored, it was understandable; they could not be expected to be insensitive to the passion which the great idea of India's freedom evoked. The war had quickened the will to this objective. But, to prevent this excitement from moving out of control, he suspended teaching, closed the colleges for a month, directed the students to go home and arranged for special trains to be run for this purpose from Banaras. Considering that Radhakrishnan had refused to close the university in April after the Japanese bombing of some Indian towns, the step taken now was clearly against his first instincts and intended to help the government in maintaining the peace. But there had been a plan, agreed upon at a meeting on the university campus and not known to Radhakrishnan, for students to return to the villages and organize anti-government activity;[40] two members of the faculty went underground; and the closure of the university and dispersal of the students might have helped the spread of the movement. Hallett, caught napping by the violent reactions in the eastern districts of the province, saw the university as the base of operations. On 14 August the district magistrate, accompanied by police officers and with an armed force, came to the university and, after speaking to the vice-chancellor at the main gate, withdrew. Hallett's version of this incident was that the university had closed its gates even to the district magistrate and had declared itself 'Free India' and its training corps the 'Indian National Army'.[41] The vice-

[40] See Mitra.

[41] Radhakrishnan to Linlithgow, 22 August 1942; fortnightly report of the United Provinces government, 19 August 1942.

chancellor was said to have no control and the United Provinces government, after convincing the viceroy that the university was 'a hotbed of seditious activity', on the morning of
19 August, sent in troops, without a word to Radhakrishnan, to
occupy the campus.[42]

In this testing time Radhakrishnan did not slacken or yield
in any way. He advised the viceroy to release Gandhi as he was
the only person who could control the violence which had
erupted on such a large scale and to offer, even at this stage,
real autonomy in all matters except foreign affairs and the
conduct of the war.[43] He also wrote to Gandhi, in a letter which
was not forwarded by the Government of India, informing him
of the shape which the mass movement had taken and asking
him to halt it rather than undertake a fast in atonement: 'The
will to freedom is there, it is unbreakable and you alone can use
it to a higher purpose. I am voicing the deepest ideas of our
people and am speaking to you in the name of the conscience of
this great country.'[44] He calmed down the feelings of the
teachers and such students as remained on the campus, in-
flamed by stories that cows were being slaughtered and eaten
by soldiers in the university and that Malaviya had begun a
fast in protest, by securing an authoritative denial. But restrain-
ing the anger roused by the repressive policy of the government
was not a popular effort, and a leaflet was circulated contrast-
ing the unexcited attitude of Radhakrishnan with the seeming
ardour of Malaviya.[45]

What the students did not know was that at the same time
Radhakrishnan, with the authorization of the council of the
university, had protested to the viceroy against military occupation as being inconsistent with the dignity of the university
and had sought the withdrawal of the troops and police guards
as early as possible. Linlithgow was unwilling to promise this
and said he was quite satisfied that no action had been or would
be taken by the United Provinces government which was not

[42] Hallett's telegrams to viceroy, 15 and 16 August 1942, home dept, file
3/16/42-Poll. I, NAI; Linlithgow to Amery, 17 August 1942, *Transfer of Power*,
vol. 2, document 577.
[43] Radhakrishnan to Linlithgow, 22 August 1942.
[44] Radhakrishnan to Mahatma Gandhi, 23 August 1942, *Transfer of Power*,
vol. 2, document 614.      [45] 9 September 1942.

demanded or justified by the circumstances of the case and the nature of the situation.[46] But the viceroy and the governor soon found it difficult to maintain their position. To single out for arbitrary action an institution of an all-India character which enjoyed much public esteem and to take on as an opponent a vice-chancellor who had a unique standing in both Britain and India created problems for which neither Linlithgow nor Hallett had bargained. Radhakrishnan pressed persistently for the return of the campus to the university authorities; and he could not be ignored. Informed that the university could not reopen, as earlier planned, on 14 September, Radhakrishnan saw Hallett, and, when the governor hinted that he might depute an officer to assist in maintaining discipline in the university, threatened resignation—a possibility which the government were not anxious to consider. Radhakrishnan then lobbied in Delhi the Indian members of the viceroy's council, and put his case to Linlithgow. The behaviour of the students in Banaras was in no way worse than what was happening in other universities. The government should take action against those found guilty and do nothing incompatible with security; but this was very different to closing down a university on the basis of suspicions and deep-rooted prejudice:[47] 'There are some things which are against the very conception of a University, and which no University can adopt with self-respect.'[48] Radhakrishnan also had the advantage of friendly relations with William Finlay, the magistrate of Banaras, and Michael Nethersole, the senior official specially sent down from Lucknow to re-establish control over the disturbed districts. These two men had a contempt for those who issued orders from Delhi and Lucknow with little knowledge of the local scene;[49] and Nethersole in particular, a rough-hewn, hard-drinking administrator, had high respect for Radhakrishnan's scholarly distinction. On one occasion, when Hallett was seeking to adopt a firm line with Radhakrishnan, Nethersole, braced by

[46] Radhakrishnan's official letter to Linlithgow, 22 August 1942, and reply of Sir G. Laithwaite, private secretary to viceroy, 26 August 1942

[47] Records of Radhakrishnan's interviews with Hallett, 8 September 1942, and with Linlithgow, 11 September 1942.

[48] Radhakrishnan to Sir G. Laithwaite, 14 September 1942.

[49] Woodruff, pp. 310–11.

numerous lashings of whisky, suddenly interrupted, 'Your Excellency, you may be the Governor of the province, but can you ever hope to be a Fellow of the British Academy and of All Souls?' Hallett mumbled under his breath and quickly terminated the conference.

Radhakrishnan's influence prevailed and the government, setting aside the demand of the army for the conversion of the university buildings into a base hospital,[50] permitted the phased resumption of teaching from 26 October, on assurances that political activities of a subversive or dangerous character would be discouraged, proctors would be appointed and the tutorial system introduced.[51] But it was a decision reluctantly made, under the pressure of Radhakrishnan's personality. Hallett continued to distrust him. When Radhakrishnan criticized Winston Churchill for smugly claiming that the situation in India was satisfactory since there was a larger 'white' army in the country than at any time during the British connection and said that such words 'burn into the Indian soul deep resentment and bitterness',[52] Hallett complained to Linlithgow at what he thought was 'rather a stupid speech . . . There is no doubt that Sir Radhakrishnan wants to keep in with Congress, and if further trouble occurs, we may have trouble from the Banaras Hindu University.'[53] But Radhakrishnan's support of the Congress and particularly his loyalty to Gandhi, even though he was not a formal member of the party, was a matter of surprise only to the governor. Certainly the viceroy could not have been startled by Radhakrishnan's speeches, for he had been writing consistently to Linlithgow on these lines, the latest being his letter of 13 November, protesting against the government's refusal of permission to Rajagopalachari to meet Gandhi in prison. And then, as if to leave Hallett in no semblance of doubt as to his position, Radhakrishnan concluded his Kamala Lectures at Calcutta University in December 1942 with an unqualified tribute to Gandhi: 'He is not

[50] Home dept, file 3/60/43-Poll. I.

[51] Hallett to Radhakrishnan, 8 October 1942, and Radhakrishnan's reply, 12 October 1942.

[52] Address to the Banaras University convocation, 29 November 1942, *The Hindu*, 1 December 1942.

[53] Hallett to Linlithgow, 10 December 1942, Linlithgow papers, vol. 105.

today a free man; you may crucify the body of such a one but the light in him, which is from the divine flame of truth and love, cannot be put out.'[54]

Yet Hallett could not prevent Radhakrishnan and the university from functioning. His hope of the Intelligence Bureau helping him to complete a case against the university came to nothing. But then came Gandhi's fast in February 1943. Radhakrishnan again gave expression to his deep attachment to the Mahatma, whom he described as the symbol of national consciousness, reflecting in his suffering the humiliation of the country. The government should release him and seek his advice in establishing a national government. But he cautioned the students that a fast by Gandhi should not be the excuse for them to cause disturbances in the campus and thereby invite external intervention: 'Anyone who indulges in activities which will hurt the University is a traitor to the University and a traitor to the country.'[55] These strong words helped to curb the tension from mounting into disorder. But even before the fast ended, Radhakrishnan had to leave Banaras. A severe attack of enteric fever, which at one stage brought him close to death, forced his removal to Calcutta for medical care and then a long stay for convalescence in the south.[56] The university was reported to have gone completely out of hand, and an attempt was made to destroy an aircraft sent to the university for training purposes.[57] But Hallett was willing to let Nethersole deal with the situation rather than move in again; and Nethersole acted with circumspection.[58] 'I really do not know', he wrote to Radhakrishnan, 'what we shall do without you here . . . you are, if I may say so, an extremely difficult man to replace.'[59] He allowed the situation to quieten down and generally, in deference to Radhakrishnan even though he was away, acted in co-operation with the university authorities. It

[54] *Religion and Society* (London 1947), p. 238.
[55] Speech at Banaras, 12 February 1943, *The Hindu*, 15 February 1943.
[56] 'For a time', noted Radhakrishnan privately later, 'I felt that death had cried to me: "The game is done, I've won, I've won."'
[57] Fortnightly report of the UP govt, 5 March 1943; notes in the home dept, file 3/14/43-Poll. I.
[58] Hallett to Linlithgow, 9 March 1943, *Transfer of Power*, vol. 3, document 571.
[59] M. S. B. Nethersole, commissioner, Banaras division, to Radhakrishnan, 24 February 1943.

was primarily Nethersole's influence that led Hallett to advise
the viceroy to overrule the home department and pay the
annual central grant to the university just as the United Provinces government had paid their share.[60] Radhakrishnan also
secured the re-starting of the University Training Corps
twelve months after its disbandment in January 1943. The only
way in which the government could pander to their grouse
against the university was to decline to direct the maharaja of
Jodhpur to accept the chancellorship of the university: 'Let the
chickens roost.'[61] But this was too minor an issue to cause
Radhakrishnan worry. He persuaded the maharaja of Kashmir
to accept the office. Indeed, he was not even aware of the
government's role in this matter. Thereafter, for the remainder
of the war years, Radhakrishnan maintained levels of discipline among the students on which even the local authorities
were obliged to congratulate him.[62]

## IV

Throughout this long period of crisis Radhakrishnan's literary work had not suffered. He wrote and delivered the Kamala
Lectures at Calcutta on religion and the problems of social reconstruction. He also started on a translation of the Bhagavad
Gita with explanatory notes. Before the war his friend H. N.
Spalding had been keen on publishing English editions of the
spiritual classics of East and West as part of a programme of
inter-religious understanding; and Radhakrishnan had agreed
to provide an introduction and notes to Sir Edwin Arnold's
well-known translation in verse of the Gita. But now, when he
began the task, it seemed to him that it would be more worthwhile to prepare his own translation in modern prose.

The measure of stabilization in the affairs of the university
gave Radhakrishnan more time for this work, and he was
also able to give greater attention to more general issues. The

[60] Note of Home Secretary, 11 March 1943, home dept, file 3/60/43-Poll. I;
Hallett's telegram to Linlithgow, 19 March 1943, Rashtrapati Bhavan file, 196-
G/43.
[61] Linlithgow's note, 17 June 1943, Rashtrapati Bhavan file 196(2)-G/43.
[62] See, for example, commissioner, Banaras division, to Radhakrishnan, 31
January 1944.

end of the war was at last coming in sight, and in the new world
which would emerge Radhakrishnan had no doubt that fundamental changes in the structure and spirit of society would
be required. If empires and racial domination were to continue, the war would have been a criminal waste. India
remained the supreme test of British statesmanship and sincerity of purpose. The best answer to the Nazis was to practise the
ideals professed even before the war ended; for only a national
government could start thinking in terms of the educational
and industrial effort required to transform India. The Indian
people were not revolutionary by instinct and should not be
made so by necessity. But freedom for India was only part of
the problem. The deeper roots of the world crisis were moral
and spiritual. A new type of education, reverent to the eternal
values and responsive to the demands of an interdependent
world, was needed everywhere. The human brotherhood of the
future should be based on heart and mind and not on chains
and fear.[63]

It was the same concern for India as well as interest in the
coming post-War order that took Radhakrishnan to China for
two weeks in May 1944. An earlier invitation, in 1942, to visit
China to present a portrait of Tagore to the Chinese government could not be accepted because of the disturbances; and
now, when asked to lecture at Chinese universities, Radhakrishnan agreed. His first experience of air travel was from
Calcutta to Kunming, across the Himalayan hump, regarded
in those war years as the most dangerous journey in the world.
One flew at 16,000 to 20,000 feet, according to the weather, in
an unpressurized aircraft with oxygen available only for the
pilot and the king's messenger.[64] The planes flying immediately
before and after the one in which Radhakrishnan was a
passenger were both brought down by Japanese fighter aircraft.
Such a risky journey to lecture on Buddhism and religion at a
time when China was at war with Japan as well as moving towards civil war would seem unnecessary and foolhardy; but,

[63] See texts of Radhakrishnan's speeches delivered between December 1943 and
April 1944, *Education, Politics and War*, pp. 170–208.
[64] For a description of the flight, see E. R. Dodds, *Missing Persons* (Oxford
1977), p. 150.

though Radhakrishnan's addresses were well received, his visit had broader dimensions. He noted the inefficiency and corruption of the Kuomintang government; but he observed too the 'radiant spiritual power' which political distress had liberated among the ordinary people, particularly the young. It was important to Radhakrishnan that the new India which was also emerging should stretch out a friendly hand to the new China, irrespective of the government in that country. Nations were to be judged by the dreams in their hearts; and India and China had much the same dream.[65] But he also, in his own eyes, had a more specific mission. Since the visit of General and Madame Chiang Kai-shek to India in February 1942 the Government of India had censored correspondence between the Chinese and the leaders of the Congress; and Radhakrishnan, as the person outside prison best fitted to express the Congress viewpoint, was able to give the government at Chungking an authoritative account of developments in India since August 1942. He also saw in Chungking the correspondence between Chiang, Churchill and Roosevelt and the plans made by the British government in case Gandhi died during his fast in February 1943; and he informed Gandhi of this when they met, after Gandhi's release, in July 1944.[66] Radhakrishnan's visit to China was significant at many levels.

Radhakrishnan also, while not too happy with Gandhi's talks with Jinnah at which he conceded not the two-nation but the two-state theory, implored Gandhi not to undertake another fast. Suffering was the essence of service but not suffering which might incapacitate us from offering any service.[67] While he publicly stressed the urgency of political freedom for restoring the self-respect of the Indian people,[68] with Gandhi he took the line that British unwillingness to take any risks till the war with Japan was over was intelligible even if unjustified. Gandhi would not promise that he would not start a fast: 'the ultimate decision will be His not mine. I would have been untrue to

[65] For the lectures given by Radhakrishnan in China as well as his general impressions of that country, see his book, *India and China* (Bombay 1944).

[66] These documents are now available in the *Transfer of Power* volumes.

[67] Radhakrishnan to Gandhi, 1 November 1944.

[68] For example, speech at Banaras, 10 September 1944, *Madras Mail*, 11 September 1944; convocation address at Patna University, 30 November 1944.

friends if I had not shared with them the struggle through which I am passing.'[69] In fact, the crisis passed.

## V

Radhakrishnan was amongst those invited by Sapru in 1944 to serve on the committee which he formed, after consulting Gandhi, of non-party men to draft a constitution for a free India. Wavell did not think much of this 'somewhat decrepit committee', and, while recognizing Radhakrishnan's individual eminence, dismissed him as 'the academic type'.[70] But the report of the committee was useful in showing the extent of general support commanded by the Congress outside its own ranks. The committee stood for a united India. The concept of Pakistan as well as the claims of some princes not to accede were both unequivocally rejected. While endorsing this position, Radhakrishnan signed two minutes of dissent. The first, signed jointly with a few others, emphasized that the seats given to the Muslim and other minorities in the constitution-making body in excess of what their numbers demanded could only be on condition that the Muslims accepted joint electorates. In a further separate minute Radhakrishnan deplored the provision of weightages and proportions to religious communities in the central and state cabinets, and favoured the abolition of 'primitive political forms' which retarded the development of a spirit of common citizenship. He would have liked the committee to declare openly against the disruptionist policy of the Muslim League and not to mince words about communal electorates, for which the British government were directly responsible and which had led to the existing position. India should turn her back on all these retrograde trends and work for the speedy attainment of parliamentary democracy based on adult franchise.

Radhakrishnan's position in these years was thus very critical of the Muslim League. Following from this, he considered seriously a plan for training young persons to preach Hinduism at its best and, more explicitly than before, spoke of Hinduism

[69] Gandhi to Radhakrishnan, 6 November 1944.

[70] Wavell to Amery, 5 and 6 December 1944, *Transfer of Power*, vol. 5, documents 134 and 135.

as alone being capable of giving modern civilization a soul and
men and women a principle to live by.[71] Of the politicians out
of prison, he found himself more in sympathy (barring Gandhi)
with Shyama Prasad Mukherjee, even though the latter had
joined the Hindu Mahasabha, than with Rajagopalachari, who
was willing to sacrifice national interests in an effort to reach a
compromise with Jinnah. Of Jinnah himself Radhakrishnan at
this time saw very little. In 1926 he had travelled to Europe on
the same liner with Jinnah and his wife. With Jinnah he had
exchanged a few words, but Mrs Jinnah sought him out to discuss philosophy and mysticism. Radhakrishnan's recollection
was of long conversations frequently punctuated by Mrs Jinnah
lifting her skirt and plunging in a hypodermic syringe with the
bright exclamation, 'it's morphine'. It was years later, in the
early forties, that Radhakrishnan saw Jinnah again, in a chance
encounter on the train from Delhi to Bombay. 'Radhakrishnan', said Jinnah, 'you are one of my major enemies.' On
Radhakrishnan looking puzzled Jinnah added, 'Because you
have made Hinduism respectable.'

In June 1945 Radhakrishnan reminded the viceroy that the
British government, which could not be absolved of responsibility for the communal problem, had therefore an obligation
to do their utmost to build a free, united and democratic
India.[72] Soon after, when Wavell announced that the members
of the Working Committee would be released and a representative conference convened at Simla, Radhakrishnan wrote to
both Gandhi and Nehru urging a positive response. The
viceroy's omission of any reference, such as had found a prominent place in the Cripps proposals, to non-accession of any
unit was a point in his favour. The quick formation of a representative interim government would have many advantages
which would more than compensate for inadequacies on other
points. He disliked the parity between 'caste' Hindus and the
Muslims proposed by the viceroy but thought parity between
the Congress and the League to be no better; and he regretted
the omission of Shyama Prasad Mukherjee from among the
invitees to Simla. But he thought Wavell was earnest and

[71] Kamala Lectures at Calcutta, December 1942, printed as *Religion and Society*
(London 1947), p. 43.
[72] Radhakrishnan to Wavell, 8 June 1945.

13

honest and he was willing, therefore, if no settlement could be arrived on principles, to agree to names being proposed for the viceroy's consideration, leaving it to him to choose from them the members of the interim government. If such a government started functioning it might diminish communal antagonism: 'Politics is one long second-best.'[73]

Gandhi replied that what Radhakrishnan had written appealed much to him and he would not only remember but convey it to Nehru, whose own reply was more non-committal:

What you wrote of course deserves consideration. It is a difficult situation. Anyhow events are marching ahead and before long you will know more or less what has happened or is likely to happen. None of us, I can assure you, wants to adopt a purely negative attitude. Every effort will be made to find a way out of the tangle.[74]

During the Simla conference, on learning that the Muslim League was being intransigent, Radhakrishnan urged the viceroy not to give in to Jinnah and betray the large number of Muslims outside the League: 'The one great benefit that the British Government has conferred on India is the unity of the country. And it will be a tragedy, if at the time when they are transferring power to Indian hands, they do so at the expense of Indian unity.'[75] But Wavell, in his desire to bolster Jinnah, was in no mood to listen to such advice; and he allowed the conference to break down. Even Rajagopalachari could not exonerate the viceroy for his refusal to carry on without Jinnah's consent while rejecting his claim: 'Rejection without following it up with necessary consequence is tantamount to acquiescence, is it not?'[76]

In the pause that followed the failure of the Simla conference Radhakrishnan gave his attention mostly to the university. The end of the war had brought its own problems. The release of tension led to a slackening of discipline while local and provincial Congressmen brought pressure to bear on the vice-

[73] Radhakrishnan to Nehru, 15 June 1945, and to Gandhi (with copies to Nehru), 17 and 19 June 1945; statement to the press, 15 June 1945, *The Hindu*, 16 June 1945.

[74] Gandhi to Radhakrishnan (in Hindi), 21 June 1945, and Nehru to Radhakrishnan, 26 June 1945.

[75] Radhakrishnan to Sir E. Jenkins, private secretary to viceroy, 9 July 1945.

[76] Rajagopalachari (from Simla) to Radhakrishnan, 14 July 1945.

chancellor for a lowering of standards for admissions. But Radhakrishnan, with the support of Gandhi, insulated the university from post-War euphoria:[77] 'Very soon we will be in a position to rule and no one can rule well who does not know how to obey.'[78] On the administrative side the institution, despite the storms of previous years, was fairly stable. Radhakrishnan had, since he took charge in 1939, avoided deficit budgets even while raising the size of the budget from Rs 1,400,000 to Rs 3,000,000, reduced the debt, expanded to take in nearly 5000 students, and raised the salaries of teachers. But funds were still inadequate. Donations from the Indian states had dried up after the disturbances of 1942, for the princes were frightened of annoying the government; and Radhakrishnan, though he did not relish the role, had to travel round the country collecting what he could from businessmen. Though he collected over Rs 7,900,000 in eight years as against Rs 2,800,000 in the eight years before he became vice-chancellor, it was the help of the central government which was required; and they awaited the report of the Gwyer committee. When that report was released at the end of 1945 it was found to be mindless and even vengeful in its proposals for retrenchment. Gwyer suggested that departments such as theology, which he regarded as 'purely Hindu', should be paid for by the Hindu community and not by the government; nor should the central government finance at Banaras such academic activities as were also to be found in provincial universities. That some disciplines are of such a basic character that no university can function without them was an obvious axiom which the Gwyer committee ignored, just as it refused to recognize the fact that students at Banaras for these courses were drawn from all over India.

In all these matters Radhakrishnan kept Gandhi continually informed and secured his support for all measures taken. Nehru took a more detached position, for he did not wish to be involved in the politics of the university; but his personal relations with Radhakrishnan remained cordial. It would be unnecessary to say this but for a remark by E. M. Forster, who was present at Jaipur that autumn at the PEN conference when

[77] Radhakrishnan to Mahatma Gandhi, 3 August 1945, and Gandhi's reply, 6 August 1945.　　[78] Speech at Banaras, 7 August 1945.

both Nehru and Radhakrishnan spoke from the same platform, that they were 'not getting on at all well'.[79] Forster was normally a percipient observer, but it is difficult to believe that there was even a temporary coldness between Nehru and Radhakrishnan. During his imprisonment at Ahmednagar Nehru had read Radhakrishnan's *Indian Philosophy* carefully and, as *The Discovery of India* bears witness, had been influenced by it. Within ten days after the conference at Jaipur he wrote to Radhakrishnan requesting him to obtain signatures from non-party men to a petition seeking sympathetic treatment of prisoners belonging to the Indian National Army: 'The idea appealed to me and immediately I thought you would be the best person to give a lead in this matter.'[80] And at Jaipur itself Nehru, with his sensitive appreciation of thought and style, could not but have been moved by Radhakrishnan's address, carefully prepared but delivered in his usual manner without notes. Drawing widely on both European and Sanskrit literature, Radhakrishnan developed the thesis that the supreme aim of literature was, like that of philosophy and religion, to kindle the human spirit. It was the distillation of personal experience, linking the transcendent and the empirical, the universal and the individual.[81] 'It was a tricky subject, if not a difficult one, but never for a moment did his masterly exposition flag or wander ... His tones were precise, unhesitant and compelling and his performance an extraordinary feat of oratory and cerebration.'[82]

These close links of Radhakrishnan with Gandhi and Nehru were doubtless in the mind of Lord Pethick-Lawrence, the secretary of state for India, when he went up to Oxford to see Radhakrishnan on the eve of the departure to India of the Cabinet Mission. Radhakrishnan reported to Gandhi, after his talk with Pethick-Lawrence, that the British now seemed genuinely interested in a treaty between Britain and India on a basis of equality. His own concern was to make Pethick-

[79] To William Plomer, 21 October 1945, M. Lago and P. N. Furbank (eds.), *Selected Letters of E. M. Forster*, vol. II (London 1985), p. 214.

[80] Nehru to Radhakrishnan, 31 October 1945.

[81] 'Moral Values in Literature', *Proceedings of the First All-India Writers Conference 1945* (Bombay 1947), pp. 86–105.

[82] Professor A. S. Bokhari in the *Hindustan Times*, 4 November 1945.

Lawrence realize that Britain should leave India not only free
but united. Communal tension being the direct result of long-
term British policy, if the country were broken up it would be
Britain's responsibility as well as her acceptance of failure.
Pethick-Lawrence himself seems to have been surprised at
Radhakrishnan's general friendliness to Britain and judged him
a little to the right of the Congress party while sympathetic to
it.[83] This suggests that Pethick-Lawrence regarded the main
body of the Congress party as more radical than it was.

Radhakrishnan had thus become more than a figure on the
sidelines; and it is not surprising that when, later in the year,
the Constituent Assembly came into existence, the senior leaders
of the Congress unhesitatingly invited Radhakrishnan to be one
of the non-Congressmen who would be put up by the party for
election to the Assembly. His credentials were, apart from an
authoritative exposition of Indian thought which strengthened
the roots of nationalism, resistance to official pressure at
Banaras University during the war, outspoken adherence to
the viewpoint of the Congress when its leaders were in prison,
and access to important figures in British public life. Radhakrishnan hoped for a great deal from the Assembly. Elected by
the representatives of the people, it might succeed in holding the
country together and deal with the economic problems which
were at the heart of the matter: 'Nothing can stop India from
getting independence, not even ourselves . . . If we do not show
respect for one another, love of ideals, disciplined disinterestedness, we may get rid of the British but we will not get rid of our
slavery.'[84] But, as the attitude of Jinnah and the Muslim
League made the functioning of the Constituent Assembly as a
sovereign body for an undivided India impractical, Radhakrishnan became severely critical of the British government.
They had realized that they had to leave India but it was not
in human nature to surrender power easily. Playing off
Muslims against Hindus was unworthy of a great people: 'We
have been kept apart. It is our duty now to find each other.'
Everyone in India had the same economic and psychological
problems, hunger and poverty, disease and malnutrition, the

[83] Radhakrishnan to Mahatma Gandhi, 27 February 1946; Pethick-Lawrence
to Wavell, 1 March 1946, *Transfer of Power*, vol. 6, no. 488.
[84] Article in *The Leader* (Allahabad), supplement on the Constituent Assembly.

loss of human dignity, the slavery of the mind, the stunting of sensibility and the shame of subjection. Even the princes would have to realize that they were slaves. The people of India, whatever their religious diversity, were held together by a persistent and continuous way of life. 'Live and let live' was the spirit of the country and that should help the people to overcome the existing crisis.

Fiercely critical of the British role in setting Hindus and Muslims against each other, it was inconceivable to Radhakrishnan that India should be a Dominion. She had no sense of belonging to a Commonwealth that supported racist policies in South Africa. The British·connection had to end; whether it ended in friendship or in convulsions and agony depended on the way in which the British government handled the problem. Partition was unthinkable; but India should develop into a multinational state, with a strong central government seeking to satisfy the fundamental needs of the common man, safeguarding the liberty of the human spirit and giving adequate scope for the play of variations of the different cultures. India would then be not, as Attlee had suggested, the light of Asia but, 'nay, the light of the world, giving to its distracted mind an integral vision and to its bewildered will an upward direction'.[85]

The emphasis placed by Radhakrishnan on tolerance and patience as constituting the genius of India was generally appreciated as timely. 'It was a great, a magnificent speech. Though addressed to the Constituent Assembly, it was clearly a message to the world.'[86] These speeches made Nehru keen that Radhakrishnan should address the Asian Relations Conference. But the speeches of Radhakrishnan in the early months of the Constituent Assembly do not show him at his best. The uncharacteristic bitterness against British authority and the looseness of thinking such as his reference to a multinational state reflected the disturbed public mood in India during the winter of 1946 and early 1947, when the British seemed unwilling to take decisions and the country lurched towards civil war and anarchy. But the statement of the British government of 20 February 1947 appealed to him as putting them right with

[85] Speeches, 11 December 1946 and 20 January 1947, *Constituent Assembly Debates*, vol. 1, pp. 36–9, and vol. 2, pp. 269–74, respectively.
[86] *Indian Social Reformer*, 14 December 1946, on his speech of 11 December 1946.

# BANARAS 189

the world and removing the suspicions of even their most bitter
critics;[87] and, with the shape of the future becoming clear by
June, Radhakrishnan's interventions in the Assembly reverted
to the accustomed highmindedness. His blend of robust, old-
fashioned patriotism with a sense of responsibility to the rest of
mankind was never seen to better purpose than in his speech
on the national flag when it was adopted by the Assembly. His
still remains the best exposition of the symbolism of the Indian
tricolour. The white band at the centre he saw as representing
the sun's rays, the path of light, the light of truth, of transparent
simplicity. But one had to traverse this path to attain the goal
of truth; and so in its centre stood the wheel, Ashoka's wheel of
the law. Dharma, or righteousness, was not static. If India had
suffered in the recent past, it was due to resistance to change.
The saffron band on top denoted the spirit of renunciation.
Leaders, to be worthy of their responsibility, had, like Gandhi,
to be disinterested, dedicated spirits. The green strip at the
bottom indicated that our efforts to build a paradise had to be
here, on this green earth. The message of the flag as a whole
was, 'Be ever alert, be ever on the move, go forward, work for
a free, flexible, compassionate, decent, democratic society in
which Christians, Sikhs, Muslims, Hindus, Buddhists, will all
find a safe shelter.'[88]

By now Nehru had heard Radhakrishnan on diverse occasions and knew his skills as a public speaker. So, two days before the historic session of the Constituent Assembly on the
night of 14 August 1947, he requested Radhakrishnan to speak
after him that evening with the specific directive that, once he
was called upon to take the floor, he should not stop till the
stroke of midnight so that the Assembly could then proceed to
take the pledge. Radhakrishnan therefore had to deliver an
important address under conditions known only to Nehru and
himself—an oratorical time-bound relay race. The two speeches
of Nehru and Radhakrishnan, even when read later, show that
these men, with a sense of occasion, had matched their talents
to the hour.

Radhakrishnan first paid tribute, in contrast to his earlier
attitude, to the political sagacity and the courage of the British

[87] Radhakrishnan from Oxford to Pethick-Lawrence, 22 February 1947.
[88] 22 July 1947, *Constituent Assembly Debates*, vol. 4, pp. 745–6.

people. Then came a reference to the Indian methods of struggle 'under the leadership of one who will go down in history as perhaps the greatest man of our age', a striking contrast to 'so-called' great men—Washington, Cromwell, Lenin, Hitler and Mussolini. Sorrow, he went on, at partition clouded the rejoicing, and Indians were in an essential sense, though not entirely, responsible for it. At least now there should be self-examination and correction of national faults of character, of domestic despotism, of intolerance which had assumed different forms of obscurantism, of narrow-mindedness and of superstitious bigotry.

Anger at the division of India would lead nowhere; passion and wisdom never went together. Like most other Indians at that time, Radhakrishnan believed that partition was a superficial and temporary phenomenon. The body politic might be divided but the body historic would live on. Cultural ties and spiritual bonds which held the peoples of India and Pakistan together should be preserved so that the lost unity of the country could be recovered.

Radhakrishnan then turned to the responsibilities of freedom. The opportunities were great but, if power outstripped ability, evil days would follow. A free India would be judged by the way it served the common man. Standards of efficiency in administration as well as in the production and distribution of the necessary goods of life could only be raised and maintained if corruption in high places was destroyed and every trace of nepotism, love of power, profiteering and black-marketing rooted out.

Abroad Radhakrishnan hoped for much from Nehru, 'a world citizen who is essentially a humanist, who possesses a buoyant optimism and robust good sense in spite of the perversity of things and the hostility of human affairs'. Under his leadership India should use her new freedom for the welfare of mankind. She had always stood for a great ideal, for the concept of civilization as not something solid, external and mechanical but as an achievement of the spirit, the inward aspiration, the imaginative interpretation of the human life and the perception of the mystery of human existence.

Radhakrishnan, as was to be expected of a philosopher of religion, concluded with a call to his fellow-citizens at this moment of national self-congratulation to bear themselves humbly before God, brace themselves to the tasks confronting them and conduct themselves in a manner worthy of the ageless spirit of India. Intolerance had been the greatest enemy of progress and true freedom was the development of the tolerant attitude which saw in a fellow-being the face Divine. Human efforts alone would not take them far; and they should make themselves dependent on that other than themselves which made for righteousness. Humility followed from the unimportance of the individual and the supreme importance of the unfolding purpose which we are called upon to serve.[89] On this note Radhakrishnan ended his speech precisely at the appointed minute, enabling Nehru to administer the pledge to the house. It was an unparalleled combination of two masters, in very different ways, of the public art.

[89] *Constituent Assembly Debates*, vol. 5, pp. 6–9.

# Part Two

Part Two

# PRELUDE

The withdrawal of the British raj from India in August 1947 revised the context of Radhakrishnan's varied endeavours in thought and writing. Though since the mid twenties his interests and activities had spread over a wide range, he had not given up his resistance to Christian efforts to weaken the Hindu identity. The claim that Christianity embodied the final and absolute truth for all time was to him unacceptable. 'You Christians', he told a missionary friend at Calcutta, 'seem to us Hindus to be rather *ordinary* people, making very *extraordinary* claims!' When the friend replied that they made these claims not for themselves but for Christ, Radhakrishnan retorted, 'If your Christ has not succeeded in making *you* into better men and women, have we any reason to suppose that he would do more for *us*, if we became Christians?'[1] More modest and more logical was the teaching of Hinduism, that the divine immanence in every man and woman makes it possible for all to seek the truth in their own ways: 'The fact of Gandhi is a challenge to the exclusive claims of Christianity.'[2]

Orthodox Christian reaction to Radhakrishnan's persistent attempt to move away from the different religions to religion itself in its basic aspects, which were common to humanity, was naturally hostile. When the board of studies in English in Madras University proposed that *The Heart of Hindustan*, a collection of Radhakrishnan's articles including that on Christianity written in 1924, be prescribed for study by undergraduates, the missionaries attacked the article as a caricature of Christianity and an outrage against Christian feelings, and had the proposal turned down.[3] Edward Thompson, sympathetic to Indian nationalism, regarded Radhakrishnan's version of

[1] Quoted in E. C. Dewick, *The Christian Attitude to Other Religions* (Cambridge 1953), p. 178, n. 2.

[2] Radhakrishnan's foreword to S. K. George, *Gandhi's Challenge to Christianity* (London 1939).

[3] Minutes of the academic council of Madras University, August 1932.

Hinduism as being so broad and syncretic as to be almost mean-
ingless, and advised him not to be always so aggressively on the
defensive. 'As an Indian once remarked to me of him, "he
smells a missionary before one is even on the horizon." '⁴ To
those who believed that the Supreme Being had, once and for
all, revealed itself in a historic person and that truth was to be
found only by relating one's self to him, Radhakrishnan remained at best, in Clement Webb's words, 'homini, in quis alius,
bonae voluntatis'—a man of good will, but different.⁵ They
regarded even his interpretation of Hinduism as distinctive to
him with little links to actual fact and heavily influenced by his
knowledge of Christian scriptures. It has also been suggested
that Radhakrishnan, despite his great knowledge of the
Christian religion, did not understand it, but, with his brilliant
versatility of mind, utilized his scholarship to denigrate it and
exploited this to further his mis-statements and overstatements
of Hinduism: 'He is a master in casting around, in a dazzling
way, a great quantity of obvious half-truths . . . his brilliant but
all too superficial conceptual harmonizations, in contradiction
to obvious facts.'⁶

These, however, are the voices of a dwindling minority; and
a major confrontation with dogmatic Christianity, such as
Radhakrishnan had in the twenties felt called upon to undertake, daily becomes increasingly irrelevant. As Sir Alfred Ayer
has observed, 'the beliefs to which a Christian is supposed to
subscribe appear to me so outrageously improbable that I am
continually astonished that so many intelligent people are able
to accept them.'⁷ Whitehead considered Christian theology to
be one of the great disasters of the human race;⁸ and Dr Kenny
has said that if the Church has been so wrong in the past on so
many topics, as forward-looking clergy believe, then its claims
to impose beliefs and obedience on others in the form in which
they have traditionally been made are mere impudence.⁹ But

⁴ Edward Thompson's review of 'The Legacy of India' in The Observer
(London), 30 May 1937.

⁵ Journal of Theological Studies, October 1951.

⁶ H. Kraemer, Religion and the Christian Faith (London 1956), pp. 99–136.

⁷ The Listener, 10 May 1984.

⁸ Dialogues of Alfred North Whitehead as recorded by Lucien Price (Harvard 1964),
p. 171.

⁹ A. Kenny, A Path from Rome (London 1985).

in fact many Christian thinkers do not adhere strictly to dogma.
The universality of the mystical experience which Radhakrishnan stressed was readily accepted by Evelyn Underhill and
Dean Inge. More recently theologians like the Bishop of
Durham and Don Cupitt have discarded the points in Christian
doctrine which strain reason and are not of the essence. They
neither assert the inerrancy of the Bible nor claim that their
religion possesses a monopoly of truth. They would find little
with which to quarrel in Radhakrishnan's understanding that
the Logos doctrine is the basis of Christianity and Christ is not
to be equated with the historic Jesus. Christ is the spirit of the
Supreme, the Eternal Word, and the manifestation of this Word
in history is not limited to Jesus. To be a good Christian is not
the profession of an outward creed but the living of an inward
life.[10] And, as against the suggestion that Radhakrishnan himself was more of a Christian than he would perhaps be willing to
admit,[11] we have had Heard, Huxley and Isherwood pro-
claiming themselves to be Christian Vedantists while Iris
Murdoch has told us of having been at one time a Christian
Buddhist.[12]

So, with India free, the basic affirmation of belief in Christ
on the decline, a gradual awakening from, in Kant's phrase,
'dogmatic slumber' and an emerging world community, the
priorities in Radhakrishnan's intellectual objectives shifted. He
now set himself to help in the building of the spiritual quality of
life in India, the promotion of character and the establishment
of the prerequisites in all spheres of activity which could make
such development possible. In the wider world, he saw his task
as the reconciliation of mankind on the basis, which he had already sketched out in *Eastern Religions and Western Thought*, of the
common ground among all the religions of the world. Whether
we like it or not, we live in one world and require to be educated
to a common conception of human purpose and destiny. At the
end of the First World War he had begun (but not finished) an
article on 'the spiritual basis of internationalism'; at the end of
the Second World War, with the world faced with the urgent
choice between human unity and universal destruction, he was

[10] *Recovery of Faith* (London 1956), pp. 159–60, 185.
[11] Rev. W. S. Urquhart to Radhakrishnan, 19 November 1953.
[12] *The Listener*, 27 September 1984.

convinced that inter-religious understanding was the only enduring foundation for solidarity in the nuclear age. Religion, in the sense of knowledge of self and service to others, could alone destroy 'mental fascism' and group loyalties,[13] overcome particular denominations and lead humanity from the fact of one world to the truth of universal brotherhood. Although knit together by science and economics, the world still needed the pyschological cohesion which would make for tolerance and understanding. The binding unity of the human race could be achieved only by the universal aim of an inner oneness of spirit. To the fulfilment of this aspiration India could, if she had regained her own balance, make a signal contribution; for, as Radhakrishnan's contemporary, Ananda Coomaraswamy, had said, 'all that India can offer to the world proceeds from her philosophy.' So Radhakrishnan recast his cultural inheritance into a vision for his times. The prevailing theme of the remainder of his life was 'the religion of the spirit and the world's need'.

[13] Radhakrishnan's speech at the Indian Students Union, London, 9 March 1939, *Times of India*, 22 March 1939.

# 9

# THE UNIVERSITIES COMMISSION

With the end of the war Radhakrishnan was once again seized of his commitments abroad. Under the terms of the Spalding Chair he had to spend two terms every year at Oxford. Now a Fellow of All Souls, in December 1945 he moved into what was to become, as he described it, his 'second home', a set of rooms on the ground floor on the left side of the front quadrangle. Though uninterested in food and drink, he was dutifully present at gaudies and enjoyed the corporate friendship of the common room. He attended college meetings and intervened rarely but with good effect. Once his vote shifted the balance in the election of the Warden. On another occasion, when the older Fellows sought to get rid of a younger colleague on the ground of moral misconduct and secured the opinion of the Visitor, the Archbishop of Canterbury, in their favour, the younger Fellows trumped this by persuading Radhakrishnan to speak in favour of broadmindedness and carried the day.

Comparative religion had been made an optional subject in the theology schools and Radhakrishnan found, to his gratification, the study of eastern religions securing slow root in the academic system of the university. He was now more content than ever before at Oxford. He gave much time and attention to his lectures and pupils, guided the Group for the Study of Religions formed by students, acted as supervisor to a growing number of postgraduate research workers, planned an authoritative work on the philosophy of religion and continued with the editing of the major philosophical classics of India.

There was also the pull of the international scene. In 1945 the methods of warfare had suddenly become more devastating;

but the thinking and attitudes of governments and peoples had undergone no revision: 'The play goes on, only the actors change.' As in 1918, so now, the victorious Allies, driven by greed and confused by guile, were drifting to the precipice of an incalculable catastrophe. It seemed that it was not the Axis powers but the whole-world that had lost the War. The diagnosis which Radhakrishnan had offered in the thirties seemed more than ever true. Civilization had reached a stage when the world had to become one. The physical unity and the increasing interdependence required the transformation of ideas, loyalties and habit systems, the creation of a real community of purpose.

In his speeches in India and Britain immediately after the War and during his lecture tour of the United States in the spring of 1946, Radhakrishnan contended that in the crisis of spirit which the world was facing India had a special contribution to make. Hers was an unexhausted mission of bringing grace into human hearts and virtue into human relations; and now that she was on the verge of freedom, and consequently rid of political obsessions, she could with unbroken vigour contribute the precious element in her heritage which could make for the healing of nations. Western civilization was enlightened, rational and disciplined but a little deficient in humanity. A severely scientific culture of means without ends had to be supplemented by an emphasis on spiritual values. Perhaps the wisdom of India could help the world to rise, in Pascal's words, from the order of thought to the order of charity. Religion as revelation and dogma was unacceptable to the modern mind; but religion as spiritual experience, the enhancement of one's being, the felt awareness of a transcendent reality, might be the faith for which the post-War world was in search. It was not exclusive or an escape from life. Every authentic religious tradition demands social action. Realized souls worked on earth in the knowledge that only in the life of our fellow beings is our own life complete. Gandhi was one such enfranchised person and his weapon of love in place of force was of primary relevance to the world and not just to the Indian national movement.[1]

[1] 'India and the West', *Asia and the Americas* (New York), April 1946; 'The Voice of India in the Spiritual Crisis of Our Time', *Hibbert Journal*, July 1946; Radhakrishnan to Nehru, 1 September 1946; speech at the unveiling of the statue

If the United Nations were to become a real and relevant organization, it needed as its basis a world soul and culture. In achieving this Radhakrishnan believed that UNESCO had a vital role to play. His membership for eight years of the International Committee for Intellectual Co-operation made him the obvious choice as India's chief delegate to the new organization, and from 1945 to 1952 he ungrudgingly worked for UNESCO, at the general conferences and as member, and for a term as chairman, of the executive board. His British colleague on the board, Lord Redcliffe-Maud, has observed that as chairman he was just, never lost his temper and was respected by everybody but that he often retired into meditative silence (and occasionally sleep), and made no pretence to detailed mastery of the documents.[2] This impression was probably created by the low priority given by Radhakrishnan to the minutiae of administration with which UNESCO has tended increasingly to be flooded. This diverted attention from what to Radhakrishnan was the organization's main task, the re-education and rehabilitation of man in order to create a new world community: 'We are a priesthood of the spirit.' Certainly no one expressed better and more persistently in these early years the ideals of UNESCO and the philosophy which should inspire it. Jacques Maritain, a member of the French delegation in 1948, passed Radhakrishnan a note across the table: 'I have followed with the utmost interest all your interventions, as I think that you represent the very spirit of philosophy.' It was in recognition of his clear statements and amplifications of the ideals of UNESCO over the years that Radhakrishnan was elected president of the general conference in 1952 and invited six years later to open the new buildings in the Place de Fontenoy in Paris.

## II

These academic and other engagements, compelling long absences from India, led Radhakrishnan to take steps to divest

---

of Mahatma Gandhi, Karachi, 14 September 1946, *Hindustan Times*, 15 September 1946; speech at the first general conference of UNESCO, Paris, 20 November 1946, *Proceedings*, pp. 27–8; 'Indian Culture', Sorbonne lecture, Dec. 1946, *Reflections on Our Age* (London 1948), pp. 115–33.

[2] Lord Redcliffe-Maud, *Experiences of an Optimist* (London 1981), p. 139.

himself of the vice-chancellorship of Banaras University. He
offered the post, after the Liberal politician Pandit Kunzru declined, to Shyama Prasad Mukherjee.[3] The coming into office
of the Interim Government, with Nehru and Patel as leading
members, in September 1946 meant better days for the university. The new government ignored the Gwyer report and sanc-
tioned a substantial augmentation of the grant from public
funds; and Radhakrishnan could plan his departure from the
university with an easier mind. But when Malaviya died in
November 1946 Radhakrishnan felt obliged to stay on a while
longer and suggested to Mukherjee that he come as pro-vice-
chancellor and look after the day-to-day administration under
Radhakrishnan's guidance. Mahatma Gandhi approved of his
continuance: 'My congratulations on your decision. I had expected nothing less of you. You will be in charge as long as you
are needed there.'[4] Mukherjee, though he had served as vice-
chancellor of Calcutta University, was willing to accept the
lower post at Banaras as long as Radhakrishnan was the vice-
chancellor. Radhakrishnan mentioned this to Gandhi and
Nehru. Though neither of them liked Mukherjee's association
with the Hindu Mahasabha, Gandhi acquiesced in Radhakrishnan's proposal while Nehru took the line that the matter
was none of his concern.[5]

However, Govind Malaviya, the son of the founder, was
eager to have the job. Gandhi frowned publicly on the idea;[6] but
the Congress in the province as well as G. D. Birla and a few
other industrialists supported Govind Malaviya, primarily in
the belief that this had been his father's dying wish. He also
gained the backing of the 'eastern UP' group,[7] politicians from
Banaras and adjoining districts who resented Radhakrishnan's
efforts (in the recruitment of staff and admission of students) to
retain the all-India character of the university. When Govind
Malaviya formally put forward his candidature Mukherjee,

[3] Radhakrishnan to S. P. Mukherjee, 7 August 1946, and Mukherjee's reply,
12 August 1946.
[4] Mahatma Gandhi to Radhakrishnan, 17 December 1946.
[5] J. Nehru to Mahatma Gandhi, 30 January 1947, *Selected Works of Jawaharlal
Nehru* (second series), vol. 1 (Delhi 1984), pp. 110–12.
[6] Article in *Harijan*, 8 December 1946, *Collected Works of Mahatma Gandhi*,
vol. 86, pp. 147–8.
[7] A. B. Ray, *Students and Politics in India* (Delhi 1977), p. 8.

who had throughout made clear that he would serve only if chosen unanimously, withdrew. The court of the university, rather than endorse Malaviya's claim, in January 1947 postponed a decision till the end of the year; and Radhakrishnan selected a senior professor to act as pro-vice-chancellor.

Even this rebuff did not weaken Malaviya's ambition, while Radhakrishnan's plans, entailing long spells away from Banāras, made it essential that he have as his chief executive assistant a person commanding his full confidence. In addition to his work at Oxford and UNESCO, Radhakrishnan had agreed to spend three months in Australia in 1947 as the guest of the Australian National University, and a semester the next year at the University of Southern California. He also set afoot a proposal after August 1947 to convert the Hindu University into a national university and B. N. Rau, the constitutional adviser to the Government of India, drafted a bill for this purpose. This too, had it gone through, presumed an administration of the university which had the confidence of the country. But, at the meeting of the court in December, Radhakrishnan's nominee secured less votes than Malaviya and Radhakrishnan, reading this as a vote of no-confidence in himself, promptly resigned. The students, with whom he was popular, started an agitation to secure his retention and a few even began a hunger strike. Maulana Azad, minister for education at Delhi, after consulting Gandhi and Nehru, decided not to interfere.[8] Gandhi had already made clear his support of Radhakrishnan; Nehru had no wish to be involved in this matter and apply informal pressure; and there was no room for official intervention. But this silence was interpreted as support for Malaviya and consequently the attacks on Radhakrishnan intensified. He was criticized as an absentee vice-chancellor, indifferent to the university's interests and careless of funds. Birla wrote a hurtful letter: 'the world seems to be full of politics and we do not seem to be liking democracy in practice although we all pay lip sympathy to this.'[9] When, a few years later, Radhakrishnan returned to Delhi in high office, Birla reverted without difficulty to his posture of deference. But the end of 1947 was not a happy time for Radhakrishnan. As for the university, with Radha-

[8] Maulana Azad to Radhakrishnan, 7 January 1948.
[9] G. D. Birla to Radhakrishnan, 19 December 1947.

krishnan's departure it moved steadily downhill, and within two years the Government of India, apart from dropping the proposal for converting it into a national institution, had to appoint a general committee of enquiry.

## III

Radhakrishnan's edition of the Bhagavad Gita was published in the spring of 1948. It was a comprehensive work, with a long introductory essay, transliteration of the Sanskrit text in Roman script, and English translation and explanatory notes where necessary. The audience Radhakrishnan had in mind was not scholars or even Hindus but all who had the religious impulse and sought knowledge of a classic of what Aldous Huxley termed 'the perennial philosophy', common to East and West. Radhakrishnan, in his introduction and notes, emphasized that the Gita contained the natural elements of true religion as he saw it: the need for discipline and realization of God, submission to His will and active participation in the furtherance of the cosmic plan. The world is neither illusion nor the ultimate reality, God and the Absolute are linked, and the liberated person, having attained personal perfection, works without involvement. The Gita as Radhakrishnan interpreted it emphasized both the personal and the social sides of spiritual religion. Man has, by his free will, first to ascend to the world of spirit and then to descend to the world of creatures. The highest perfection is a combination of knowledge, devotion and work, not renunciation of action but action with renunciation of desire. We must carry out our duties with the spirit directed to God, with detachment from all interest in the things of the world and with no enmity towards anybody. The aim of religion is not just individual salvation but the establishment of a brotherhood upon earth.

To a few critics it seemed that Radhakrishnan read into the Gita what he sought and allowed the pulls of modernity and his own views to distort the original text. But rarely was the translation loose, and the analysis, presented with freshness and vigour and with the customary range of thought, provided assurance and guidance to large numbers, including very many who would not have regarded themselves as religious in the con-

ventional sense.[10] On the basis of advance orders, Allen and
Unwin printed, even at that time of paper shortage, 10,000
copies; and these were sold out within twelve months. The best-
known classic of Hinduism, translated by India's best-known
philosopher and provided with a forthright and authoritative
commentary that took no religious knowledge for granted—that
was 'a real event in the publishing world'.[11] Since then the book
has gone, in cloth, cardboard and paperback covers, into innumerable (including pirated) editions and been translated into
various languages. It still remains a bestseller and holds the field,
among the many English editions available, for clarity, force
and scholarship; 'masterpieces need to be edited by a master.'[12]

When Radhakrishnan saw Mahatma Gandhi in Delhi in
December 1947, he told Gandhi that he intended to dedicate
the book to him. Gandhi demurred, protesting that he was the
seeker and Radhakrishnan the teacher: 'Who am I? What is
my service? You are my Krishna, I am your Arjuna.'[13] By the
time the book was out, Gandhi was dead. Radhakrishnan,
hearing at Oxford the news of the murder, was prostrate with
grief for days. At the memorial meeting organized at All
Souls he and Gilbert Murray were the chief speakers. His was
understandably an emotional utterance; but mixed with the
shock and indignation of bereavement was a clear assessment
of the quality of Gandhi and his role in history. It was the life
of a man who brought his religious commitments to the service
of humanity, who fought a clear and successful battle for political freedom but died in the effort to rid India of the poisonous
atmosphere in which communal feeling grew. He was the
leading prophet of the moral and spiritual revolution without
which the world could not find peace. He had had the faith

[10] E.g. Valentine Ackland: 'I have had my copy of this matchless book since
1948, and I have been reading it ever since it came into my possession, with
always-increasing Veneration. Your Introduction and Notes—very much in the
same way as the text does—become clearer, and cast a sharper light with every
reading, and I feel so much gratitude to you for giving us this book . . .' To
S. Radhakrishnan, 3 August 1953.

[11] P. A. Sorokin in the *New York Times*, 17 October 1948.

[12] Sir Richard Livingstone to Radhakrishnan, 15 May 1948.

[13] Pyarelal, 'Gandhiji's Krishna', *The Radhakrishnan Number* (Madras 1962),
p. 55. In the Gita, Krishna is the avatar who expounds the philosophy to the
warrior Arjuna.

that the world was one in its deepest roots and highest aspiration. He represented the conscience of the future man.[14]

Radhakrishnan had planned to expand the Gandhi birthday volume (first published in 1939) for presentation on his eightieth birthday in October 1949. He now sadly set about editing it as a memorial volume. He amplified his own address at All Souls as an introduction to the new section and sought contributions, especially from those who had not seen their way to write for the first edition. Bernard Shaw again refused: 'People interested in Ghandi [sic] want to read what he wrote, not what his commonplace disciples are writing about him. I will not contribute.'[15] Rajagopalachari felt unable to philosophize over the tragedy of Gandhi's death or patiently weave tributes.[16] Nehru said he could not develop the mood for writing in cold blood: 'I am afraid I am temperamental as a writer and when the subject is Gandhi my hesitation is all the greater.'[17] So Radhakrishnan included passages from Nehru's speeches and writings, as he did extracts from the tributes paid by leaders from various parts of the world. He also had less difficulty than in 1939 in securing articles from British politicians, for Gandhi had by now become politically respectable and the manner of his death hastened general acceptance. But this in itself deprived the memorial volume of some of the tang and excitement of the collection published in 1939.

## IV

With the success of the Bhagavad Gita, Radhakrishnan settled down to a long-term programme of translating the Dhammapada, the Buddhist work, and the other two major works of the Hindu canon, the Upanishads and the Brahma Sutra. The lines on which he worked would be the same as for the Gita; providing detailed introductions and notes with references to parallels in other religious texts and modern literature. To him the editing of these texts was more than pedestrian translation. A religious classic was a contemporary of all ages and it was for the

[14] 'Mahatma Gandhi', Hibbert Journal, April 1948.
[15] G. B. Shaw to Radhakrishnan, 30 March 1948.
[16] C. Rajagopalachari to Radhakrishnan, 2 May 1948.
[17] J. Nehru to Radhakrishnan, 17 April 1948.

commentator in each generation to bring out, as he himself had sought to do even earlier in *Indian Philosophy*, the relevance of the work to the problems of his own time. Total identification with ancestral voices was a sure sign of cultural decadence.

This task of reinterpretation of large and major works appeared to require full attention and Radhakrishnan, while he retained for the time being his chair at Banaras, planned to spend much of the year at Oxford. He took his own future to lie mostly outside India. So he wrote to Nehru offering even to resign his membership of the constituent assembly.[18] But Nehru obviously had other ideas. An element in his non-intervention in Banaras affairs was a feeling that Radhakrishnan was wasting his talents in too narrow a sphere. He now asked Radhakrishnan to continue in the constituent assembly even while rebuking him mildly for extolling the discipline of the militant Hindu organization, the Rashtriya Swayamsevak Sangh.[19] On Gandhi's death Radhakrishnan, giving much general advice, offered to do whatever he could to assist the prime minister, and Nehru, passing over the advice, promptly took Radhakrishnan at his word to bring him back to India.[20] First he asked Radhakrishnan to be chairman of the board of editors set up by the ministry of education to bring out a comprehensive history of Eastern and Western philosophy; but this was only part-time work. Nehru obviously looked on Radhakrishnan as the most clear-headed authority on education in India. In 1938 he had appointed him chairman of the education subcommittee of the national planning committee. He now consulted him on senior appointments in the ministry of education and, in August 1948, asked him to take a year's leave from Oxford to head a commission to study the working of Indian universities in all its aspects with a view to recommending measures for their improvement.

Most of the ten members of the commission were of high distinction. From India there were Zakir Husain, at this time vice-chancellor of Aligarh University and later to be vice-

[18] Radhakrishnan to Nehru, 8 January 1948.
[19] Nehru to Radhakrishnan, 22 January 1948. For Radhakrishnan's speech at Rewa on the Rashtriya Swayamsevak Sangh, 29 December 1947, see report in *The Hindu*, 1 January 1948.
[20] Radhakrishnan to Nehru, 2 February 1948.

president and president of India; Laksmanaswami Mudaliar,
vice-chancellor of Madras University; and Meghnad Saha,
physicist and Fellow of the Royal Society. Radhakrishnan had
hoped too to have Birbal Sahni, also a Fellow of the Royal
Society, but he was unable to join. From the United States
came Arthur Morgan, the first president of the Tennessee
Valley Authority, and John Tigert, a former commissioner for
education and president of Florida University. Radhakrishnan
had been particularly keen on having his friend and colleague
at All Souls, G. D. H. Cole, who was himself willing but was
dissuaded by his doctor. His place was taken by James Duff,
vice-chancellor of Durham University.

This team of powerful calibre was dominated by the
chairman, who worked them hard. After the first formal
meeting in Delhi in December 1948 a questionnaire was drawn
up and sent to about 2900 individuals and institutions throughout the country. The commission then visited all the twenty-five
universities in various parts of India and granted interviews to
all who wished to meet them. Thereafter, towards the end of
April, the members moved to Simla and produced a long and
comprehensive report, with no minute of dissent, by the end of
August. This was a record in time made possible by Radhakrishnan's commanding influence.[21] Apart from drafting the two
chapters on the aims of education and religious instruction, he
kept a close eye on the rest; and the whole report bears the
impress of his ideas and style.[22]

The commission regarded as its chief task the elucidation of
the principles on which higher education should be recast to
meet the changing needs and conditions of a free country. This
was vast and indeed limitless ground; for higher education
could not be looked at in isolation and the commission had to
examine the policies of even education in schools, and assess
such problems as the reconstruction of villages. Apart from
providing for every type of education, literary and scientific,

[21] The Radhakrishnan commission functioned also with great economy of
expenditure. The Sadler commission, meeting soon after the First World War and
concerned only with Calcutta University, spent Rs 3.69 lakhs; the Radhakrishnan
commission, thirty years later, when the rupee was worth much less, covered the
whole country at a cost of Rs 1.58 lakhs.

[22] *Report of the University Education Commission*, vol. 1 (Delhi 1949).

technical and professional, the universities had to train men and women for leadership in a democracy, and—a favourite idea with Radhakrishnan—for citizenship in a world community. The preamble to the draft constitution offered 'the makings of a national faith, a national way of life which is essentially democratic and religious', and the commission believed that the purpose of educational, as of political and economic, institutions should be the furtherance of democracy through the realization of justice, liberty, equality and fraternity. This meant the development of the body, mind and spirit of every individual, work for social justice and cultivation of the art of human relationships.

It was to be expected that a commission headed by Radhakrishnan would place stress on imparting instruction in nondogmatic religion in ways compatible with a secular state. It was asserted that every student should be given spiritual training and encouraged to work out by free inquiry his or her own approach to religious matters. So it was suggested that all educational institutions should start work with a few minutes for silent meditation, that in the first year the lives of the great religious leaders be taught, in the second year some selections of a universalist character from the scriptures of the world be studied, and in the final year the central problems of the philosophy of religion be considered. The neutrality of the state would be preserved in the institutions funded by it so long as the best in all religions, and their basic unity, were presented.

While dwelling mostly on the broad uplands of general principle, the commission did not shirk the issues of particular concern to India. It recommended that the constitution list university education as a concurrent subject so that the central government could intervene to ensure national standards whenever the necessity arose, even though most universities were under the jurisdiction of the provincial governments. For the same purpose, and also to reinforce the autonomy of universities, it proposed the establishment of a University Grants Commission which would itself be autonomous and in charge of distribution of funds provided by the Government of India. It urged an enhancement of the salaries of teachers both to raise their social status and to improve their quality, and asked the government to provide the money required. Funds should also be given generously for research, and refresher courses encouraged.

The commission voiced the general disapproval of examinations and, as a concession to John Tigert, preferred objective tests such as were common in the United States. But it coupled this with an emphasis on the writing of essays and advocated warmly the introduction of the tutorial system. As for the thorny question of the medium of instruction, the commission favoured the replacement of English as early as practicable by an Indian language. Every student at a university should obviously know the regional language as well as the federal language (Hindi), which should be developed for the purpose of teaching; and higher education should be imparted through the regional language with the option to use Hindi for some or all subjects. But English should be taught even in schools so that every boy and girl would be able to assimilate knowledge in that language. There should be no hasty attempt to introduce these changes and English should continue as the medium of teaching till the federal and regional languages had been sufficiently developed to take its place.

What, however, the public was most curious to learn was the commission's view on the matter of admissions. This had become a burning issue with the decision of the Government of Madras to allocate admissions to colleges on the basis of caste. The commission, under its chairman's guidance, faced up to this and declared roundly that distribution of educational opportunity should be on the basis of merit. The refusal to make higher education equally available to all who were deserving was a denial, at least in part, of the conception of a university. The difficulties in implementing this principle created by an inegalitarian society Radhakrishnan would have set right by a lavish provision of scholarships so that the poor would not be disadvantaged. But aware of the inequities of Indian society, he wrote into the report a reservation for ten years of not more than a third of the total seats for the students from the scheduled castes and such communities as were declared by the government to be backward.

The report of the university education commission is one of the great state papers of independent India. The sound idealism and sweep of the proposals gained attention throughout the world, for there was nothing specifically Indian in the commission's outlook. Sir Richard Livingstone, for example, commended even to Christian countries the suggestions that religious instruction should start with religion in the concrete, in the study of those who have lived it and of the books in which the religious spirit is embodied, and then move on to the philosophical approach: 'Above all they are an attempt to attack the problem (as we have not yet attacked it) seriously and rationally; a refusal to treat the most important subject in the world as if it was indifferent; an insistence that it is the concern of all higher education.'[23] In India the prime minister, who was concerned about the fall in educational standards and the poor quality of many teachers,[24] commended the report to the chief ministers, particularly the proposal for divorcing official appointments from university examinations.[25] Had the report been implemented even in part, it would have poured higher education into a new mould, better suited to an independent nation. Although the vice-chancellor of Madras University, after signing the report as a member, was very critical of some of its recommendations, particularly that which stressed the necessity of admissions by merit, both the Central Advisory Board of Education and the Inter-University Board endorsed the report as a whole. Yet the universities generally, taking shelter behind the value of autonomy, were indifferent to the report. The political will to push through the required changes was lacking, and the report was buried, as Radhakrishnan later complained, with 'respectful inattention'. Political pressures and caste interests have seen to it that admission by merit is increasingly overshadowed by reservation of seats. The problem of medium of instruction has still to be settled. The recommendations on religious education were shelved, and have come unfairly under fire as giving expression to a belief in a universal religion, which is itself a dogma to Christians and Muslims and an unacceptable one.[26] It was nearly twenty years after the submission of the report that the first steps were taken

[23] Sir R. Livingstone, *Education and the Spirit of the Age* (Oxford 1952), p. 36.
[24] Speech at Delhi, 18 April 1949, *The Hindu*, 19 April 1949.
[25] 2 September 1949, J. Nehru, *Letters to Chief Ministers*, ed. G. Parthasarathi, vol. 1, 1947–1949 (Delhi 1985), p. 453.
[26] D. E. Smith, *India as a Secular State* (Princeton 1963), pp. 351–6.

to bring the salaries of teachers nearer in line with the status
that they should command in society. Despite the caution suggested by the commission, new universities have proliferated,
frequently to fit in with the wishes of politicians. The only
major and immediate result of the recommendations of the
Radhakrishnan commission was the establishment of the
University Grants Commission, with substantial benefits to the
autonomy and development of Indian universities.

## V

Amid this welter of work, Radhakrishnan learnt that a volume
of essays was being put together to be presented to him on his
sixtieth birthday in September 1948. As is usual with such
volumes, the birthday came and went, and the volume was
published only two years later.[27] The essays themselves, dealing
mostly with parallels and contrasts in Eastern and Western
philosophies, were of average quality. But this book was raised
above ordinary levels by the distinction and representative
character of the editors—Dean Inge and L. P. Jacks from
Britain, E. A. Burtt of Cornell University, and M. Hiriyanna
and P. T. Raju, two of the leading philosophers of India. Their
introductory note was easily the best piece in the volume. It
both paid tribute to Radhakrishnan's work in the past and
underlined the importance in the post-War world of his teaching that each of us should live in his or her own way as well as
learn from others. Heir of the Indian tradition and master of
Western learning, he had been an outstanding pioneer in the
emergence of a universal perspective. If people all over the
world had a better comprehension of each other's culture and
shared their experiences, 'it was largely due to Radhakrishnan's genius, understanding, energy and undiscouraged endeavour'. He had made possible the wider acceptance of a
philosophy of life, based on the achievements of science and the
aspirations of humanity, and guided by spiritual values.
Radhakrishnan would have been more than human if he had
not been gratified by recognition from such different quarters
of his service in the cause of philosophy and international
goodwill.

[27] *Radhakrishnan: Comparative Studies in Philosophy* (London 1950)

# THE MOSCOW EMBASSY

By the spring of 1949 the foreign policy of free India had begun to take distinctive shape. Relations with Britain had stabilized with the country's decision to remain a republic within the Commonwealth, and the United States, despite an unsympathetic posture on Kashmir, recognized the value of strengthening friendship with India. But a policy of not taking sides in the cold war, if it were to be positive, assumed good relations with the Soviet Union as well; and this had not been realized. Moscow was critical of the way in which power had been transferred in India, and was convinced, along the lines of Indian communist thinking, that the new government were tied closely to the Western powers. The Nehru regime was accused of suppressing progressive elements and supporting violent reaction; the police action in Hyderabad was thought to be an effort by the big bourgeoisie to assist the Nizam and the landlords against the masses; and India was considered to be still a colonial dependency though in a new and concealed form.[1] While Nehru ignored these criticisms and sought to be friendly, his efforts were not translated on the ground by his first ambassador, Vijayalakshmi Pandit. Finding the austere society of Moscow irksome she, with the approval of Bajpai, secretary-general in the ministry of external affairs, kept in far too close touch with the American embassy, thereby confirming Soviet prejudice.[2] In fact, within a few months of her arrival in

[1] S. M. Vakar, 'Class Essence of Gandhism' (1948); E. M. Zhukov, 'Sharpening of Crisis of the Colonial System after the Second World War' (1949); A. M. Dyakov, 'Crisis of British Rule in India and the New Stage in the Liberation Struggle of Her Peoples' (1949).

[2] Vijayalakshmi to G. S. Bajpai, 23 January 1948, and Bajpai's note, 5 February 1948, ministry of external affairs (henceforth MEA) file 1/NGO/49, vol. I.

Moscow, Vijayalakshmi, on her own admission, gave up even attempting to promote Indo-Soviet relations.[3] So Nehru decided on a change óf ambassadors. If the objective of India serving as a point of contact for both the power blocs made the Moscow embassy an important link in India's diplomatic representation, it had also turned out to be the weakest.

For this key, if not attractive, post, there were several aspirants. Rajagopalachari, the governor-general, sought it for his son-in-law, Devadas Gandhi, the Mahatma's son. Nehru, unable to think of anyone else, was prepared to accept the suggestion;[4] but Vijayalakshmi thought he would be a misfit in Moscow.[5] The ministry of external affairs would have liked the appointment of an official; and several politicians were eager to be considered. But then the prime minister, in one of his most imaginative decisions, suddenly turned to Radhakrishnan. A psychological approach to the Soviet mind was required. The Kremlin had to be convinced that the Government of India meant what they said and were genuinely in favour of peace. For that a person who was well known internationally but was not a politician, who held broad nationalist and humanist views, was outspoken on the necessity in India of social and economic change and was steeped in the Indian tradition but had a modern mind, seemed the best choice. So, on 16 April 1949, Nehru requested Radhakrishnan to take up the Moscow post.

Radhakrishnan's first reaction was to decline. The report of the Universities Commission was almost ready and he was hankering to get back to Oxford and the academic work which seemed to him far more important than any diplomatic business. But he gave no firm reply, offering to go to Moscow despite his own inclinations if the prime minister really thought it essential;[6] and Nehru insisted. He found it difficult to say what positive results Radhakrishnan might be able to achieve, for that depended on many factors outside one's control; but he could at least prevent the situation in the world from deteriorat-

[3] See memorandum of conversation of Loy Henderson, US ambassador in India, with Vijayalakshmi, 28 April 1949, department of state papers, Washington.

[4] See Nehru's letter to Vijayalakshmi, 19 February 1949, Nehru papers.

[5] Vijayalakshmi to Bajpai, 3 March 1949, Nehru papers.

[6] Radhakrishnan to Nehru, 26 April 1949.

ing and might well help in bettering it, and that in itself was a big thing: 'In spite of our many failings in India, the world is opening out to us and recognizing some quality in us. It is up to us to try our best to take advantage of this; for the future may well be affected by it, our own and that of the world.' So the question of the appointment to Moscow could not be treated as just that of any other.[7]

This really left Radhakrishnan no choice.[8] Every philosopher, as he wrote in a note intended only for himself, has at some stage to go into the cave to shape his thoughts, and for him the cave was the Moscow embassy. He had always taken an informed interest in public affairs and had never been a thinker cut off from the outside world. But his primary concerns had been scholarly. Even now, Nehru permitted him to accept the post only for one year in the first instance to see how it worked out and to spend a half of that year in Oxford—terms which in themselves showed how keen Nehru was to get him to Moscow. But it was obviously the first step in drawing Radhakrishnan out of the academic scene and into wider spheres of public activity. To those who regarded his philosophic work as unique and irreplaceable, this could seem a betrayal. Radhakrishnan himself, happy on his arrival in Oxford in 1936, had jotted: 'For me to become a political leader would be like planting a banyan tree in a porcelain vase.' Would the mission to Moscow prove the beginning of his submission to such bonsai treatment, the first step in the mutilation of his psyche? It hurt him to have to set aside the major work on the philosophy of religion on which he had been engaged since the end of the War. But he did not believe that he was falsifying himself and giving up to country what he had earlier thought was meant for mankind. Always a nationalist, he could not refuse to serve India in a post which the prime minister portrayed as relevant to the maintenance of peace in the world. He saw himself as not just the ambassador of India concerned with bilateral relations but as the spokesman, which he had always been, of humanity at large. Such public office would also provide greater opportunities to work, in the now shrinking world, for the fellowship of the spirit which to him was the sole hope of mankind. That

[7] Nehru to Radhakrishnan, 7 May 1949.
[8] Radhakrishnan to Nehru, 9 May 1949.

Nehru's pressing offer should come at this stage was to him one more decision in his life taken for him by a higher power: 'We have to do work which we are called upon to do and hope for the best.'[9] In addition, no doubt, he was not devoid of ambition or immune to worldly temptation. All men, as he recognized, are victims of their own earthliness.

The appointment, announced in July 1949, was seen as unusual and generally welcomed. At one of the farewell functions Nehru justified it at a high level: 'Radhakrishnan goes as the symbol of India.' He had a capacity to understand the Soviet Union and developments in the world and also to make others understand what India stood for.[10] Foreign nations should realize that India was not a mere carbon copy of the West and had her own ways of thought and action; despite modernization, the roots remained.[11] From the right Golwalkar, leader of the Rashtriya Swayamsevak Sangh, the Hindu militant group, expected great advantages from the influence in Moscow of 'one of the greatest exponents of the sound philosophical basis of our culture'.[12] From the other end of the political spectrum Hiren Mukherjee of the Communist Party rejoiced in prison when rumours first circulated of Nehru's choice:

How you would laugh when I tell you that it is a sort of illustration of dialectics that, beset in contradictions, the powers that be make a real good appointment, so unlike that of Mrs Pandit, whom by the way I met several times and liked a lot but could never allocate a respectable intellectual age! The minor poet who missed his vocation to be India's Prime Minister has made, I must say, some amends this time.[13]

Sarat Bose, elder brother of the better known Subhas Bose, congratulated the Government of India, of which he was otherwise very critical, on selecting a man with such intellectual gifts, intense patriotism and strong common sense.[14] Abroad,

[9] S. Radhakrishnan to P. C. Diwanji, 29 July 1949.

[10] Speech at Delhi, 24 August 1949, *National Herald*, 25 August 1949.

[11] Nehru to Vijayalakshmi, 24 August 1949, Nehru papers.

[12] M. S. Golwalkar's telegram to Radhakrishnan, 15 July 1949.

[13] Hiren Mukherjee from Presidency Jail, Calcutta, to Radhakrishnan, 16 May 1949. Letter seen and passed by censor.

[14] Statement of Sarat Chandra Bose, 13 July 1949, published in *The Hindu*, 14 July 1949.

the results of the despatch of an idealist philosopher to the capital of the communist world were awaited with curiosity, especially as India's relations with the Soviet Union could well develop into one of the nerve-centres of world politics. The Soviet authorities themselves realized that Nehru had something special in mind and answered the signal by wasting no time in accepting Radhakrishnan's appointment and arranging for his presentation of credentials.

Radhakrishnan had not visited the Soviet Union earlier. He had been, along with Motilal and Jawaharlal Nehru, invited in 1927 to witness the celebrations of the tenth anniversary of the October revolution, but had to decline because of his commitments in Calcutta. Then, in 1943, he had to stand down from the leadership of a goodwill delegation because of the crisis at Banaras University. But, already fairly well-informed, he now read systematically all he could find on conditions in the Soviet Union and whatever he thought of value on the current state of the world. He took as his chief objective the establishment to the Soviet authorities of India's bona fides, that she had not sold away her liberty of action to any bloc but was genuinely interested in raising the living standards of her people and furthering peace in the world through freedom for oppressed nationalities and justice for all. His task in Moscow would be one of reconciliation, of understanding Soviet policies and interpreting and making the Soviet authorities understand India's policies.[15] This was best done, as far as he personally was concerned, by friendliness, without acting in any way alien to his own nature, pandering to the Soviet system or compromising on principles. On one occasion, for example, he flew into Moscow, making no effort to hide from photographers the book he had been reading on the aircraft, *The God That Failed*, which was written by intellectuals such as Arthur Koestler and Stephen Spender, expressing disillusionment with communism. In the Kamala Lectures delivered during the War he had drawn a clear line between sympathy with Marxism as an instrument for social revolution and unacceptability of the Marxist philosophy of life, its atheism, its naturalistic view of man and

[15] Radhakrishnan to Nehru, 9 May 1949; speech on resignation of membership of the constituent assembly, 24 August 1949, *Constituent Assembly Debates*, vol. 9, p. 676.

its disregard of the sacredness of personality.[16] His commitment to democratic values and belief in the freedom and spontaneity of individual life it would be ludicrous even to attempt to conceal. In one of his last speeches before taking up his new post, he spoke of the two ways of overcoming political conflicts: a knock-out blow, the power solution, or trying to understand the opponent's position so as to further a settlement, the knowledge solution; and India had accepted the latter.[17] His own deeply religious feeling and his dedication to Gandhi, about whom he had recently edited a memorial volume, were well known. But for organized, dogmatic religion he had never had any use; and he could understand the Russian repudiation of a religion which they thought had brutalized and divided the people and championed vested interests.[18] Indeed, he had always held that the truly religious man could not but be a peaceful revolutionary, disturbing and upsetting the existing order, transforming it to fit into the pattern of his ideals and establishing without bloodshed a just and equitable social order.[19]

The Soviet authorities were clearly intrigued by Radhakrishnan. They did not relish his attachment to Oxford and his continued holding of the chair; but the absence from Moscow for half the year that this entailed they did not resent. Quite a few ambassadors to the Soviet Union spent considerable time at the sessions of the United Nations in New York; and the Soviet ambassador to India himself spent only the winters in Delhi. While in Moscow, Radhakrishnan, having ensured that his staff was wholly Indian, left the day-to-day work of the embassy to them. He was fortunate in being served by very able deputies, first Rajeshwar Dayal and then Yezdi Gundevia. In his general approach to the Soviet government on matters of policy he acted on Benjamin Franklin's formula for a diplomat: 'sleepless tact, immovable calmness and a patience that no folly, no provocation, no blunders can shake'. He did not strike postures but stated his position unambiguously and was willing

[16] *Religion and Society*, p. 25.
[17] 24 August 1949, *Constituent Assembly Debates*.
[18] Speech at Pune, 19 July 1949, *The Hindustan Times*, 21 July 1949.
[19] See his sermon, 'Revolution through Suffering', 8 June 1930, printed in *East and West in Religion* (London 1933), pp. 101–25.

to discuss matters. In his notes of the time he wrote down de Vigny's comment, 'for a diplomat the right motto is: Only silence is great, all else is weakness', and put a question mark beside it. Certainly he himself was not silent and, in his speeches during his years as ambassador, frequently reasserted his faith in democracy, his aversion to the suppression of dissent and his dislike of one-party rule and of insistence on conformity to the party line. He was on cordial terms with his colleagues in the diplomatic corps but was not particularly close to the British or American ambassador, or anyone else. He spent, as the Soviet administration undoubtedly learnt, most of the day in bed reading and writing, firmly concentrated and happily absorbed. It is said that the Moscow police at that time was suspicious of any ambassador who could not be located in an automobile, in a museum or at a performance of *Swan Lake*. But Radhakrishnan was rarely to be found even in these places. He was punctilious in attending the many parties and receptions which are an unavoidable part of a diplomat's life but, unmindful of protocol, departed well ahead of anyone else, including whoever happened to be the chief guest, for he was accustomed to retire early. His only relaxation was occasional attendance at the theatre and at ballet performances. None of his family being with him for any length of time throughout his years at Moscow, it was a solitary but well-organized and self-sufficient life. The Russians, probably puzzled, were undoubtedly impressed.

## II

Radhakrishnan's arrival in Moscow in September 1949 coincided with a new phase in the cold war. The nuclear explosion in the Soviet Union, announced by President Truman, and the imminence of the proclamation of a people's republic in China curtailed severely the preponderance of world power enjoyed by the United States. But the chilliness of the cold war did not abate. The atmosphere in Moscow remained one of secrecy and suspicion, with heavy propaganda against the United States, provoked largely, in Radhakrishnan's view, by American hostility; nor did India, 'a specially trusted gendarme at the service of the Anglo-American imperialist masters', escape

attention. In his statement, approved by Nehru,[20] at the ceremony of presenting credentials, Radhakrishnan, after speaking
of India's willingness to learn from the Soviet Union in her
search for the progress so necessary for the flowering of democracy and freedom, emphasized her independence in foreign
policy and commitment to peace. More significant was his
public speech in Paris a few days later. Attributing the shadow
of conflict that was creeping over the world to the fundamental
lack of confidence between the two blocs, he contended that
aggression was the other side of fear. Accommodation between
the two ways of life was not impossible; and all the blame was
not wholly on one side. Intolerance was not peculiar to
Russian communism, and Stalin's repeated statements about
the possibility of peaceful coexistence should not be summarily
brushed aside. The United States and the Soviet Union had
much common ground, and coexistence would bring about
mutual adjustments. What the world needed was a wider distribution of the British respect for the rule of law, the American
love of freedom and the Soviet commitment to racial brotherhood and community-mindedness. It would be worthwhile to
hold a meeting of six heads of government, two from Asia and
two from Europe to join those of the United States and the
Soviet Union, not to achieve political results but to dissipate
the blinding mist of misunderstanding and break through the
mounting wall of prejudice.[21]

This was a characteristic speech of Radhakrishnan. He did
not ignore the deficiencies of either the Soviet or the American
system; indeed he spelt them out, but he stressed that it was
neither a black-and-white nor a static situation, and urged that,
faced with the disasters which a military confrontation would
involve, the building of peace was more important than all
other problems. His proposal for a meeting of heads of govern-

[20] MEA file 1 (46)-PT/48, appendix, NAI

[21] Speech at the general conference of UNESCO, 20 September 1949. Curiously, five years earlier, Winston Churchill, in a note drafted in Moscow in
October 1944 but ultimately not sent to Stalin, had expressed similar sentiments:
'We have a feeling that, viewed from afar and on a grand scale, the differences
between our systems will tend to get smaller and the great common ground
which we share of making life richer and happier for the mass of the people
is growing every year.' M. Kitchen, 'Winston Churchill and the Soviet Union
during the Second World War', *The Historical Journal*, June 1987, p. 431.

ment was made on his own, without any consultation with Delhi. Radhakrishnan had a personal position in the world and he saw no reason to abandon it merely because he had been persuaded to serve as an ambassador. This created concern among the officials back home, but the prime minister was willing to accept whatever embarrassment such free-wheeling might cause in return for the greater advantage of having Radhakrishnan at Moscow. So Nehru allowed his high-powered envoy to function in his own way, and it was Nehru alone who mattered.

In the Soviet Union itself there was no reaction to this speech. Attention was engaged by Nehru's visit to the United States and his speeches there confirmed the impression that India was definitely on the side of the Western powers. There was some justification for this feeling. It was to Britain and the United States that India looked for support both politically and economically; and as far as the Eastern bloc was concerned, Nehru, thanks in part to Soviet antipathy, stressed mainly a possible strengthening of cultural relations.[22] But Radhakrishnan was unapologetic in his replies to the complaints of the Soviet foreign office. He asserted that India's policies both at home and abroad were based on certain definite convictions and she was working towards the realization of certain specific objectives—peace and the raising of the standards of living of the masses. Her connections with the Western powers had not diminished her independence, and on several issues, such as Kashmir, Hyderabad, Indonesi and South Africa, she found herself at variance with them. The government were keen on developing an economy which would be mainly socialist in character. They did not accept Marxism and Leninism; but if communists in India were being arrested, it was because of their resort to violent methods and not for their ideology. But the Soviet authorities do not seem to have been convinced, and showed their distrust, as was the way in Moscow, by declining any social contacts. Not that this worried the ambassador: 'I do not dislike Moscow as I like to be left alone and here I am left alone.'[23]

So Radhakrishnan lived through a severe winter, with the

[22] See S. Gopal, *Jawaharlal Nehru*, vol. II (London 1979), p. 57.
[23] Radhakrishnan to Nehru, 27 October 1949.

temperature dropping to thirty-five to forty degrees below zero. He never missed his walk round the block both in the morning and in the evening even though his nose was frost-bitten, and otherwise carried on with his writing and reading. The government in India did not expect any change in this uneventful existence. The prime minister thought that 'mental jujitsu' was required to deal with the communists, and there was, under the circumstances, very little basis for co-operation with the Soviet Union.[24] Bajpai said that India had 'blotted its copybook' in dealings with the Soviet Union.[25] He obviously had in mind Nehru's visit to the United States. So it was a startling surprise when, on 13 January 1950, Radhakrishnan was told by the foreign office, in response to his casual remark made earlier to Vyshinsky, the foreign minister, that he would like at some time to call on Stalin, that Stalin would receive him the next evening at nine p.m. Radhakrishnan's predecessor, Vija-yalakshmi Pandit, had not been seen at any time by Stalin; now, at the first opportunity, he was given an interview. Since Radhakrishnan's arrival in Moscow in September, Stalin had been first away and then busy with Mao and Zhou. As soon as serious talks with them were over, Stalin, after routine inter-views with the American and British ambassadors, was willing to receive the Indian envoy and, doubtless knowing Radha-krishnan's habits, set the interview at, for Stalin, the very early hour of nine. 'I would like', Stalin is reported to have said, 'to meet the ambassador who spends all his time in bed—writing.'

Radhakrishnan found, like others before him, that Stalin in person was less formidable than one's thought of him. The ambassador opened the interview, which lasted half an hour, by saying that he had not come to discuss any specific issues but to convey his government's and his own desire to do all that was possible to strengthen good relations between the two coun-tries; and Stalin replied that that was also their wish. He also expressed his approval when told of India's anxiety to improve the living conditions of her people and of her independent foreign policy and keenness to work closely with the Soviet

[24] Memorandum of Nehru's conversation with Warren Austin and others in New York, 19 October 1949, department of state papers.

[25] Report of Bajpai's conversation at dinner in the US embassy, 17 November 1949, department of state papers.

Union and People's China. Radhakrishnan then moved on to the general state of the world and appealed to Stalin to explore the possibility of a detente. He should take the lead in creating an atmosphere in which, without long-range abuse and inflammatory propaganda, specific problems could be discussed in a better spirit. When Stalin observed that this did not depend upon him alone, Radhakrishnan replied that it takes two to make a quarrel but one can stop it. This was blunt speaking, for to say that it takes two to make a quarrel ran counter to the Soviet line that it was the Western powers which were the warmongers. But Stalin made no comment, and Radhakrishnan's impression was that he was not unfriendly to the appeal. Stalin's own particular interest was in India's status in the Commonwealth; was she more or less independent than, for example, Canada, and did she have her own army and navy? Radhakrishnan gave the necessary explanations to show that India was independent in every sense of the term, whereafter Stalin inquired of India's relations with her neighbours, told Radhakrishnan, from his own experience, that it was not so easy to liquidate landlords, and wanted to know about India's problem of language.

Despite Radhakrishnan's clear exposition, Stalin and his officials could not fathom the seeming illogicality of a republic in the Commonwealth; and it was only the logic of facts which later convinced them of the independence of India's policies. But whatever their reservations, for the time being, on this matter, the interview with Stalin established, as it was clearly meant to do, their acceptance of the bona fides of India's ambassador. When Radhakrishnan modestly told Reuter's correspondent that his interview suggested that Stalin was becoming more accessible to envoys, the sentence was cut out by the censor.[26] The answer given to the Italian ambassador when, on hearing of Radhakrishnan's interview, he also sought one, was that Radhakrishnan had been received because of his 'eminence and moral authority', and this should not be regarded as a general precedent. Pavlov, the interpreter at the interview, sought out Radhakrishnan a few days later to tell him that Stalin had liked his frankness and that he hoped the

[26] A. J. Steiger, Reuter's correspondent in Moscow, to Radhakrishnan, 16 January 1950.

ambassador was as satisfied with his interview as he could see
they were: 'When others talk of peace they mean war, but we
know, Mr Ambassador, that when *you* talk of peace, you mean
peace.'[27] Pavlov also reported Stalin's remark: 'This man
speaks from a bleeding heart, not like an ordinary ambassador.'

Though the interview was primarily a personal recognition
of Radhakrishnan, it also indicated a more understanding
atmosphere and the prospect of a new relationship between
India and the Soviet Union. Radhakrishnan wished to capi-
talize on this by negotiating a treaty of friendship on the basis
of good-neighbourly relations and mutual respect. Coming after
India's recognition of People's China, it would give substance
to declarations of non-alignment and also perhaps reconcile
the Indian communists to the government. For once Bajpai was
in favour of a suggestion made by Radhakrishnan, and the
prime minister was willing to take 'some slight initiative' rather
carefully and mention it publicly even while going a little slow
to see how things shaped themselves. But the senior officials in
Delhi could not overcome their prejudice against communist
Russia and smothered the idea while claiming to consider the
model on which such a treaty of friendship should be cast.[28]

Yet, though no headway could be made on this proposal,
there was a considerable gain to consolidate. The interview
with Stalin was reflected in the new mood among Soviet
officials. In contrast to their earlier reluctance to be seen in the
Indian embassy, they turned up in considerable number,
headed by the foreign minister, Vyshinsky, at the reception on
26 January, celebrated by India as Republic Day. This thaw
enabled Radhakrishnan to raise with the Soviet leaders the
concerns uppermost in his mind about their policies and
practice. He told Vyshinsky, for example, that he did not approve of the Soviet boycott of the Security Council in protest
against the presence of the Kuomintang representative, asked
whether their joint-stock enterprises in Sinkiang would not
mean the economic penetration and ultimate domination of

[27] R. Dayal, counsellor at Moscow, to K. P. S. Menon, foreign secretary,
27 January 1950.
[28] Radhakrishnan to Nehru, 24 January 1950; notes of Bajpai and Nehru,
MEA file 42/2/NGO; Nehru to Radhakrishnan, 6 February and 5 March 1950;
S. Gopal, *Nehru*, vol. II, p. 64.

China, criticized their attitude to Tito's Yugoslavia, and deplored the suppression of individual freedom and the general atmosphere of suspicion in the Soviet Union. Vyshinsky gave replies, sometimes with vehemence, and contended that his country had not had a fair deal from others. In turn, he asked Radhakrishnan why his government were treating the communists so harshly. Radhakrishnan told him to use his influence with them to get them to desist from criminal activities. We do not advise them, said Vyshinsky, though we are interested in them; and the two smiled at each other, obviously in knowing and shared disbelief.[29] The whole unbuttoned discussion was conducted within the compass of Soviet acceptance of Radhakrishnan's unbiased and friendly attitude to the Soviet Union. It was the same rapport which enabled him to arrange for an Indonesian delegation a favourable reception and to secure recognition of the Sukarno government and support for Indonesia's admission to the United Nations.

Radhakrishnan's main anxiety, however, was about better relations between the great powers. He had gained the impression, when talking to Stalin, that the Soviet leader was keen on an understanding with the West and was not pessimistic about reaching it. That the Soviet Union was prepared to negotiate was underlined by the press in Moscow republishing at this time Stalin's earlier statements about the possibility of peaceful coexistence and the absolute necessity of settlements of disagreements. Radhakrishnan, in this context, took up again his suggestion for a meeting of six heads of government, including Nehru and Mao, and passed it on, via his friend H. N. Spalding, to Winston Churchill, then leader of the opposition, who after Yalta had thought that Anglo-Soviet friendship could be maintained as long as Stalin lasted[30] and had himself at this time spoken of the need for a conference at the highest level with the Soviet Union.[31] On the other hand, both the Labour govern-

[29] Record of Radhakrishnan's talk with Vyshinsky, 7 April 1950.

[30] B. Pimlott (ed.), *The Second World War Diary of Hugh Dalton 1940–1945* (London 1986), p. 836.

[31] Churchill's speech at Edinburgh, *The Times*, 15 February 1950; Radhakrishnan's interview in London, *News Review*, 16 February 1950; Radhakrishnan to H. N. Spalding, 18 February 1950; and to Nehru, 14 February 1950. For the reiteration of Stalin's statements in the Soviet press, see despatch in *The Times*, 21 February 1950.

ment in Britain and the Truman administration played down
the idea. But, as the weeks passed, Radhakrishnan felt a sense of
urgency. A race in stocking atom piles and conducting research
on the hydrogen bomb was going ahead dangerously, and in
such a tense atmosphere a war might well be thrust on mankind
without anybody willing it: 'The first war arose out of an incident in Serbia; the second war from Poland. It is just conceiv-
able that a third may break out with an incident in the East.'
Agreement with communism was not essential for an understanding with Russia. Stalin was getting old and would like to
see in his time a settlement so that his country was not left in a
state of insecurity. This was the opinion also of the correspondent in Moscow of the *New York Times*, who had written that
Stalin was prepared to go anywhere in Europe for discussions:
'If after that we hesitate the blame will be on our heads.'[32]
Radhakrishnan also raised with Vyshinsky, in the context of
Indochina, the possibility of a meeting of the six heads of
government and spoke of the advantage particularly as the
Security Council, in the absence of the Soviet Union and the
representation of China by the Kuomintang, was of little consequence. Vyshinsky said the Soviet Union would be agreeable,
though all depended on the situation then, and developments.[33]

The stage had now come when Radhakrishnan's efforts
required official backing, and Nehru, though interested, was
wary about making any specific move while the situation with
Pakistan was tense and wished to wait till after the meeting of
the foreign ministers of the United States, Britain and France,
scheduled to take place early in London.[34] But the informal
soundings continued. Radhakrishnan conveyed to Churchill
his fears that the British and American governments seemed to
grasp neither Stalin's interest in peace nor the weakness of
international communism; for Radhakrishnan believed that the
Soviet authorities anticipated that, after Stalin, China would
break away and Titoism would spread. Even within Russia
there was likely to be a loosening of regimentation and of the
techniques of a police state. But were war to come, apart from

[32] Radhakrishnan's cable to Spalding, 17 March 1950, and letter, 24 March
1950.
[33] Record of Radhakrishnan's talk with Vyshinsky, 7 April 1950.
[34] Radhakrishnan to Nehru, 21 April 1950, and Nehru's reply, 5 May 1950.

the disasters that it involved, even if Russia were defeated, communism would gain ground. Radhakrishnan went as far as to
suggest that, if he had Churchill's authority to proceed in the
matter, he would, with Nehru's approval, obtain Stalin's
written consent to a private conference to discuss outstanding
problems.[35]

Nothing could come of this as Churchill was still out of office
and would not commit himself. Radhakrishnan's public efforts,
therefore, centred on building up opinion against the continuance of the cold war with the danger of its developing into
hostilities. Opposing the efforts of the United States to convert
UNESCO into a political weapon in the crusade against communism, he demanded, not that UNESCO should not concern
itself with politics, for that did not seem possible, but that the
organization should commit itself to international understanding. For this purpose, People's China should be recognized
and the Soviet Union encouraged to join: 'Idiotic chatter of
national virtues and vices should be replaced by an emphasis
on the basic unity of mankind and on human rights.' While
over half the population of the world in Asia and Africa lived
below normal levels of subsistence, the other part was spending
its time, wealth and energy in preparing for a war which would
solve nothing but destroy a great deal, including democratic
ideas and ideals throughout the world. The closed mind and
the hatred of the heretic were not limited to any group, and
armed missionaries for one's own way of life were to be found
on both sides. Radhakrishnan rejected the Manichaean view of
world politics as a struggle of good versus evil. The cold war was
not a conflict between undiluted righteousness and unmiti-
gated crime. It was a clash not of ideologies but of rival powers
and diverted attention from the major issues of the world. If
opportunities were not provided to the poor and hungry peoples
to rehabilitate themselves, they would turn to 'the other pattern
of life' which offered a vision of human equality and brotherhood, promised deliverance from poverty and insecurity and
supported liberation movements. It was UNESCO's task to re-
educate man into a new sense of fellowship and social responsibility.[36] These interventions helped to stave off the crisis

[35] H. N. Spalding to Winston Churchill, 13 May 1950.
[36] Speeches at the UNESCO general conference, Florence, 24 and 30 May

precipitated by American policy and persuaded the director-
general, Torres Bodet, to withdraw his resignation.

'I am glad', wrote Nehru, after reading Radhakrishnan's
first speech at UNESCO, 'that someone can speak straight
about these matters.'[37] He alone in Delhi appreciated Radhakrishnan's success in Moscow and consequent influence there
and elsewhere. Bajpai wondered if a high-powered mission was
at all necessary in Moscow and was critical of what seemed to
him Radhakrishnan's frequent displays of woolliness and
naivety.[38] K. P. S. Menon, the foreign secretary, wrote to ask
what Radhakrishnan's plans were after his term of a year was
over. He added that the prime minister would not like him to
continue to combine his commitments at Oxford with the
embassy at Moscow.[39] But Nehru requested Radhakrishnan to
stay on for another year, which was likely to be 'critical from
every point of view', even if it meant Radhakrishnan's absence
for five months from his post. No one could perform miracles,
but it was something at least to hold the fort and generally to
ease the situation. 'I think you are performing a great service
there and it would be a great pity if you came away at this
critical juncture.'[40]

## III

The incident in the East which Radhakrishnan had foreseen as
a possible starting-point of the next war occurred just three
months after his prophetic observation. On 25 June 1950 fighting broke out in Korea. The Government of India accepted the
two resolutions of the Security Council deeming North Korea
an aggressor and asking all members of the United Nations to
render assistance to the organization and to South Korea. To
condemn aggression and support the United Nations did not

1950; BBC broadcast, 12 June 1950; 'Unesco and World Revolution', *New
Republic* (New York), 10 July 1950.
[37] To Radhakrishnan, 6 June 1950.
[38] R. Dayal to Radhakrishnan, 18 March 1950, reporting conversation with
Bajpai; cable of the US embassy in Delhi to state department on Bajpai's views,
3 July 1950, department of state papers.
[39] 16 March, 13 April and 8 May 1950.
[40] Nehru to Radhakrishnan, 8 April, 26 May and 6 June 1950.

seem to Nehru to weaken India's independent foreign policy; nor was he concerned about Soviet reactions. At this time the Soviet government, while they liked the ambassador, remained critical of his country. The prime minister was blamed for accusing communists of using terrorist methods when it was 'the reactionary rulers' who were doing so;[41] and Nehru in turn was concerned about Soviet expansionism, not only in the normal sense but also in encouraging internal trouble.[42] But Radhakrishnan objected that the resolutions of the Security Council were the decisions of one bloc, for the Soviet Union had been absent and Yugoslavia had voted against; and for India to support these resolutions was to persuade the United States that in a crisis India would be with them. Having kept out of the civil war in China and the fighting in Indochina, for India now to side with Syngman Rhee was an act likely to strengthen the interference of foreign powers in Asian affairs, It had also, to a certain degree, impaired India's moral authority in Asia and in international relations, and given ground for complaint that she was not quite honest about her non-alignment. On the second resolution, even Egypt had abstained. Something definite, like negotiations for a treaty of friendship, had to be initiated to regain lost ground not only with Soviet Russia but in the world: 'Am I only to mark time here and not do something positive for building up better relations with Soviet Russia and effectively contributing to peace?'[43]

Such criticism, supported independently by Krishna Menon from London, strengthened Nehru's resolve to limit India's commitment to resistance of aggression in Korea and not to be drawn in to backing United States policy on Taiwan. He had already directed Radhakrishnan to urge the Soviet government to use their authority to end the Korean conflict quickly and to resume their place in the Security Council.[44] But Zorin, one of the deputy foreign ministers whom Radhakrishnan saw, would not react and made clear that his government had been greatly surprised by India's support of the resolutions. Radhakrishnan

[41] Article in *New Times*, 23 June 1950.

[42] Nehru to chief ministers, 15 July 1950, J. Nehru, *Letters to Chief Ministers*, ed. G. Parthasarathi, vol. II, 1950–1952 (Delhi 1986), p. 141.

[43] Radhakrishnan to Nehru, 30 June and 4 July 1950.

[44] Nehru's telegram to Radhakrishnan, 30 June 1950.

contended that India's non-alignment was positive and dynamic; each question was decided on its merits and on this occasion their views happened to coincide with those of the United States. But Zorin was not convinced.[45] Bajpai felt that Radhakrishnan's attitude had not been strong enough, though the British embassy in Moscow, whom Radhakrishnan had consulted on his demarche, thought it too stiff and persuaded him to tone it down.[46]

As a preliminary to the return of the Soviet Union to the Security Council, India continued to press for the admission of People's China: 'All we can do in this present context of affairs is to go on trying. What the ultimate result will be lies with the Gods.'[47] At this point Radhakrishnan, in his personal capacity, wrote to Gromyko, then a deputy foreign minister, asking for his views on a formula whereby the United States would support the admission of People's China to the Security Council in return for such a fully representative Council supporting in Korea an immediate ceasefire, withdrawal of North Korean troops to the 38th parallel and mediation by the United Nations for the creation of a united and independent Korea. Radhakrishnan's reasoning was that this would satisfy those circles in the United States who regarded recognition of Communist China as appeasement; and he did not see how the Soviet Union, after its repeated declarations about non-interference in other states, could reject the second point of the formula.

'I am confident', concluded Radhakrishnan to Gromyko, 'that my government, if encouraged by you, will press for a settlement on these lines.'[48] His confidence was based on his feeling that he would be backed by Nehru, who felt, and in fact had again written, that his presence in Moscow was essential;[49] and this seemed a way of retrieving India's position in the Soviet Union. Bajpai disapproved of Radhakrishnan's action; the Soviet government would take notice only of official proposals and there was to him no possible chance of the United

[45] Radhakrishnan's telegram to Nehru, 1 July 1950, and letter, 3 July 1950, reporting conversation with Zorin.
[46] Cables of the US embassy in Moscow, 2 July 1950, and of the US embassy in Delhi, 3 July 1950, department of state papers.
[47] Nehru to Radhakrishnan, 8 July 1950.
[48] Radhakrishnan to A. Gromyko, 9 July 1950.
[49] Nehru to Radhakrishnan, 8 July 1950.

States agreeing to China's admission.[50] But in fact Gromyko, while declining to commit himself on Radhakrishnan's proposal, gave the British ambassador the impression that the Soviet government were seeking a means of escape, perhaps including a compensatory concession about the admission of China;[51] and Radhakrishnan's formula would have met this requirement.

The United States, however, to whom also Radhakrishnan had, through Admiral Kirk, then ambassador in Moscow, given the text of his formula, was inflexible. Radhakrishnan had expressed his concern about the dangers inherent in the Taiwan situation and urged recognition of People's China as a 'great and noble act by America as leader of the free world'. Acceptance of his formula would cast no doubt on the resolutions of the Security Council and on the military action of the United Nations in Korea, put the Soviet Union in the wrong and weaken the Sino-Soviet partnership. But the United States, having been told that Russia had not accepted the second part of the proposal, objected to any settlement which could be construed directly or indirectly as payment or reward to the aggressor in Korea.[52] The stress placed by Radhakrishnan on the recognition of People's China was attributed to an idealistic streak pervading his thinking when urgent problems arose; and the American and British ambassadors in Moscow, comparing notes, concluded that Radhakrishnan was 'vague and starry-eyed, rather professorial in manner and gave impression of not always paying close attention to what was being told him'.[53] In fact, Radhakrishnan was much shrewder than they suspected, and as the Russians realized; and the American envoy being unable to make any impression on him, the United States complained in Delhi at the linking up of China's admission with withdrawal of the North Koreans.[54] But meantime Nehru had taken the matter in his own hands and sent, on 13 July, similar

[50] G. S. Bajpai's note, 10 July 1950, Nehru papers.

[51] Quoted by Nehru in his message to Attlee, 11 July 1950, Nehru papers.

[52] Cables from the US embassy in Moscow, 8 and 10 July 1950, department of state papers; Radhakrishnan's telegram to Nehru, reporting conversation with Admiral Kirk, 12 July 1950; Dean Acheson, *Present at the Creation* (London 1969), pp. 419–20.

[53] Cables of the US embassy in Moscow, 13 and 14 July 1950, department of state papers.

[54] Bajpai's note after conversation with American ambassador, 14 July 1950, Nehru papers.

messages to Stalin and Acheson, the secretary of state, stressing
the need to admit People's China and bring back the Soviet
Union to the Security Council. Radhakrishnan's view, after
seeing Gromyko to hand over this message, was that neither
side was totally intransigent. This was in fact truer of the
Soviet Union than of the United States, and Nehru asked
Radhakrishnan not to pursue discussions with Kirk.[55]

The prime minister's appeal to the two great powers went
some way towards establishing Soviet confidence in the independent approach of the Government of India. But that they
were still not fully convinced is suggested by the censor's de-
letion of a sentence in a despatch from Moscow by Reuter's
correspondent that 'the Soviet press has been relatively non-
committal with respect to the Indian position, indicating that
Soviet views are still flexible and receptive towards Nehru on
the Korean problem.'[56] Radhakrishnan himself, gathering that
his offer of a formula—which seemed to him to lie within the
framework of Indian policy and aimed at giving it support—
had not been relished in Delhi, offered to relinquish his post.[57]
Nehru sent no reply; silence was one of his favourite weapons
when confronted with anything distasteful. But he discouraged
Radhakrishnan's suggestion that the prime minister incorporate
his two-point formula in a personal message to Stalin. Any such
move was unlikely to succeed in view of the insistence of the
Western powers that the Soviet Union return unconditionally
to the Security Council and of their refusal to agree to the
immediate admission of China.[58]

Radhakrishnan reluctantly gave way. As he wrote later to
Nehru, 'with great unwillingness I kept quiet'.[59] It was to him
a question of the egg and the hen: which should come first,
admission of China to the United Nations or withdrawal of
North Korean troops from South Korea. If the Soviet Union
could be committed to work for the second position, the United
States would have the satisfaction that the spirit of the Security
Council's resolutions had been achieved. But, realizing the

[55] Nehru's telegram to Radhakrishnan, 13 July 1950.
[56] A. J. Steiger to Radhakrishnan, 16 July 1950.
[57] Radhakrishnan to Nehru, 18 July 1950.
[58] Radhakrishnan's telegram to Nehru, 20 July 1950, and Nehru's reply,
21 July 1950.     [59] 11 August 1950.

resistance in Delhi to his diplomatic activity in Moscow, he proposed that Nehru send an envoy in whom he had full confidence to Moscow and Washington.[60] To this letter Nehru did reply: 'I wish you would not think that there is lack of confidence in your work, because that would not be true.' All that sometimes happened was a difference of opinion about some approach, because Delhi had to judge events from a variety of viewpoints and on the basis of information from many capitals, and (here Nehru was being disingenuous) final decisions were taken not by him or by his ministry but by the cabinet.[61]

Meantime, the situation had changed with the Soviet Union's return to the Security Council on 1 August. Radhakrishnan wanted the United States to utilize the occasion by agreeing to the entry of People's China into the United Nations. This would weaken Sino-Soviet ties and strengthen the position of the United States in Asia. He also pressed them to take advantage of the Soviet Union's return to the Security Council to recommence general negotiations for peaceful settlements. Bajpai in Delhi reacted cynically: 'I don't know which is greater, the Ambassador's faith in the essential goodness of human nature, or his naivety.'[62] The American embassy in Moscow also refused to give serious consideration to Radhakrishnan's proposals:

Like many genuine idealists, he was naïve enough to suggest that something might come of direct approach to Malik by the United States or one of its friends to the effect, 'My dear fellow, what are you chaps up to? You know you can't blackmail us, so let's get down to business.' Nurtured in the atmosphere of British power in India, which was flexible and compromising, he fails almost completely to understand the implacable and fanatical persistence of Soviet Communist power.[63]

So, with the United States adamant, the Security Council deadlocked and fierce fighting developing in Korea, there was hardly any scope for diplomatic manoeuvre. As early as 4 August, seven weeks before Zhou spoke to Panikkar on

[60] Radhakrishnan to Nehru, 25 July 1950.
[61] Nehru to Radhakrishnan, 10 August 1950.
[62] Prime minister's secretariat, file 18 (12)-47/PM, vol. II.
[63] Cable from the US embassy in Moscow, 1 August 1950, Truman papers, Harry S. Truman Library, Independence, Missouri.

21 September, Radhakrishnan warned Delhi that if the Americans attempted to move north of the 38th parallel, China or Russia might enter North Korea to deal with the situation: 'That will be a moment of great danger.'[64]

In September, meeting Vyshinsky before the latter's departure for New York, Radhakrishnan spoke of the possibility of a United Nations commission, comprising the Soviet Union, the United States, Britain, China, Indonesia and India, to administer Korea for three to six months, during which time elections could be held and a government for a united Korea established. Vyshinsky showed little interest, as the Soviet Union still seemed to be hoping for a military rather than a diplomatic solution.[65] But Radhakrishnan's initiative this time not only irritated the officials in Delhi but also made the deputy prime minister, Sardar Patel, uneasy, for a similar international commission had been suggested for Kashmir by Sir Owen Dixon and sharply rejected by India. 'Radhakrishnan is rather expansive at times', explained Nehru, 'and says a little more than he should. We had hinted this much to him previously and have done so again.' But Nehru was not much worried, for Russia was totally opposed to an international commission in Korea and could not therefore exploit the idea.[66] All that he told Radhakrishnan was that priority should be given to a resolution in the General Assembly for early elections in Korea under the auspices of the United Nations; and if the time did come for setting up a commission it should be predominantly Asian and non-aligned and not include the Soviet Union, the United States and Britain.[67] Radhakrishnan thought little of Nehru's proposal. A resolution at the General Assembly seemed a mere elaboration of the obvious, a waiting on events rather than controlling them. It was also unrealistic to try to convert the Korean problem into an Asian one when the United Nations was involved and American and British troops were engaged in the fighting.[68] But he recognized that the scene was now set in New York and dropped the matter.

[64] Radhakrishnan to Nehru, 4 August 1950.
[65] Radhakrishnan's telegram to Nehru, 9 September 1950.
[66] Vallabhbhai Patel to Nehru, 11 September 1950, and Nehru's reply, 12 September 1950, Nehru papers.
[67] Nehru's telegram to Radhakrishnan, 11 September 1950.
[68] Radhakrishnan to Nehru, 15 September 1950.

As for Nehru, the overall advantages of Radhakrishnan's presence in Moscow transcended the weaknesses in detail of his occasionally airy proposals, and he had no wish to precipitate a fresh offer of resignation by despatching the faintest semblance of a reprimand.

## IV

Right through the Korean crisis in the summer of 1950, Radhakrishnan had, despite the profusion of business, not broken the normal tenor of his way of life in Moscow. In addition to working on a translation of the Upanishads with an introduction and a commentary, he wrote the opening and concluding chapters for a volume on his philosophy to appear in the Library of Living Philosophers edited by Paul Schilpp, prepared the speeches to be delivered at UNESCO and at the School of Religion in London University, and wrote an essay for Sir James Marchant's collection, *What I Believe*. This would seem enough work to occupy all waking hours. But Radhakrishnan also had the daily business of the embassy to look after in the gap between Dayal's departure in the spring and Gundevia's arrival in the autumn; nor did he neglect his social commitments. He entertained regularly, marked attendance at official and diplomatic parties, visited a factory and a collective farm, and spent a morning at Moscow University. On that occasion, at a gathering of professors and students, he was asked by one of the audience to justify his belief in God. In return he inquired if they believed in truth, in beauty and in goodness. When they answered all three questions in the affirmative, he said that that comprised his definition of God. 'If', replied the Russians, 'you call this God, we believe in Him.'[69]

With the normally grim-faced and unsmiling members of the Soviet bureaucracy Radhakrishnan maintained cordial, informal relations, treating them all, from the ministers to the interpreters, as a bunch of intelligent and likeable, if misguided, students.[70] Though the ministry of commerce in India had no

[69] It was a definition which not only won over his listeners in Moscow but also appealed to Nehru. See R. N. Chowdhary, *Nehru in His Own Words* (Ahmedabad 1964), pp. 11–12.
[70] Y. D. Gundevia, *Outside the Archives* (Bombay 1984), p. 93. Gundevia gives a vivid account of Radhakrishnan's style of functioning in Moscow.

wish to develop trade with 'these damned Communists',[71]
Radhakrishnan on his own took up the matter and requested
the Soviet government to deal directly with India and not
through Western middlemen. Nehru supported him by issuing
a directive to one of the ministers concerned not to discriminate
against the Soviet Union for political reasons and to buy goods
from them if cheaper than those available elsewhere.[72] But the
officials showed no interest.

Departing from Moscow for the winter of 1950, Radhakrishnan's attention shifted to explaining Soviet policy and motives
to the outside world and stressing the danger of war breaking
out because the two sides were lacking in communication. To
provide contacts was one of the vital tasks of a non-aligned
nation and in attempting to do so Radhakrishnan, even while
he exercised considerable independence on points of detail,
acted in the confidence that he was in effect carrying out
Nehru's general policy. At Oxford Radhakrishnan happened to
meet, on various occasions at All Souls, Attlee, the prime minister, Halifax, by now the elder statesman of the Conservative
party and Douglas, the American ambassador. To all of them
he spoke of his conviction that Russia was anxious for peace and
it would be wrong to brush aside her conciliatory gestures as
propaganda moves. None of the major powers might be
anxious for war but some incident might occur that would
occasion war. To Attlee he criticized Britain's inconsistent
attitude on the question of admitting China to the United
Nations and asked him to test Russia's intentions by proposing
the abolition of the Cominform. He warned Douglas that by
trying to isolate China the United States was making her more
dependent on the Soviet Union. Douglas was for talks with
Russia but not hopeful of any immediate progress. Radhakrishnan said the United States should take Russia at her word
and press her, for example, for withdrawal of all foreign troops
from both West and East Germany. Without giving up their
own convictions, the Western powers should try to understand
other countries and reach agreement wherever possible. To
Nehru himself Radhakrishnan suggested that he should seek to
prevent American intervention in Indochina. While India did

[71] Ibid., p. 80.
[72] Nehru to K. M. Munshi, food minister, 8 August 1950, Nehru papers.

not want communism, other things, like French imperialism in Indochina, she wanted even less.[73]

As we can now see, most of these observations were not without justification, and Nehru saw the general value of Radhakrishnan functioning as an ambassador at large. At this time, both he and Radhakrishnan were of the view that the Americans were more bellicose than the Russians; and the American ambassador in Delhi thought that Nehru was systematically undermining American prestige and character by his public statements.[74] But the official perspective of Radhakrishnan's activity was different. According to the foreign secretary, he 'is simply amazing. He recently sent us a summary of his conversation with Attlee. The way in which he talks to the high and mighty would be regarded as cheek, if he was not a philosopher, and naive, since he is. However, his naïveté has paid us very good dividends.'[75] Evidence of these dividends was provided on Republic Day in January 1951 when, even in the absence of the ambassador, a large number of Soviet officials headed by Vyshinksky came to the reception at the Indian embassy as testimony of friendship: 'There was one person missing and missed —by everybody—and that was Ambassador Radhakrishnan who has made India's name what it is in Moscow today.'[76]

On Radhakrishnan's return to Moscow in March 1951, Nehru, finding the United States reluctant to provide unconditionally foodgrains to India, which was facing famine in parts of the country, asked him to negotiate on the basis of a Soviet offer to supply 50,000 tonnes of wheat. In return the Soviet Union wanted raw jute, a commodity which India did not possess in sufficient quantity. Radhakrishnan saw Zorin, told him it was not just a technical matter but involved political considerations, said that a nation like the Soviet Union should offer not 50,000 but 500,000 tonnes, and added that he was sure that Stalin would be willing to help India.[77] Two days

[73] Radhakrishnan from Oxford to Nehru, 15, 22 and 25 October 1950.

[74] Loy Henderson, American ambassador in Delhi, to department of state, 5 October 1950, Truman papers.

[75] K. P. S. Menon to Y. D. Gundevia in Moscow, 3 November 1950, MEA file 42/1/NGO–50, vol. 2.

[76] Y. D. Gundevia to K. P. S. Menon, 29 January 1951.

[77] Radhakrishnan's telegram and letter to Nehru, 26 March 1951; Gundevia, p. 91.

later, as Radhakrishnan had expected, Kumykin, the deputy minister of foreign trade, called the ambassador and made the official offer of 500,000 tonnes of wheat in return for raw jute, raw cotton fibre, shellac and rubber. Now the hard bargaining started. Gundevia has a delightful vignette of Radhakrishnan as a negotiator. Seeing Kumykin on one occasion doodling continuously, 'that's right, carry on, carry on', said Radhakrishnan. 'This, Mr Minister, is a sign of nervousness. You can't think correctly, if you don't draw these circles', he added with a chuckle. A very surprised Kumykin promptly put his pencil down. 'No, no', said Radhakrishnan, 'carry on, carry on. It will help you to come to the right decision.'[78]

The Government of India offered, in exchange for wheat, goods other than those sought by Russia, felt that the price quoted for wheat was high and preferred payment to barter. They also, probably distrustful of the enthusiasm of the embassy, wished to conduct further negotiations in Delhi. They were interested in the immediate dispatch of 50,000 tonnes but envisaged difficulties regarding shipping. Discussions in Delhi were slow, as the Russian side had to refer most points to Moscow; but on 10 May, even before the deal was concluded, *Pravda* announced that Soviet ships bearing 50,000 tonnes of wheat had sailed from Odessa for India, and a further consignment of 50,000 tonnes would be sent the next month. Even Novikov, the Soviet ambassador in Delhi, learnt of it only from the press. The decision had been taken in Moscow and, according to him, the entire credit for the transaction went to Radhakrishnan.[79]

This consignment of 100,000 tonnes seemed to the Government of India sufficient. The food minister, K. M. Munshi, was anti-Soviet, and preferred to receive foodgrains from the United States which was now, on hearing of the despatch of Soviet wheat, more forthcoming. The excuse given to the Soviet government was that Indian ports could not handle any more grain. Radhakrishnan wrote to Nehru that, even with the arrival of foodgrains from the United States, there was no harm in procuring an additional 400,000 tonnes from the

[78] Gundevia, p. 93.
[79] Y. D. Gundevia to K. P. S. Menon, 5 August 1951, recording conversation with Novikov.

Soviet Union and building up stocks. If this were refused the
Soviet government, who had done their utmost to be accom-
modating, might take it amiss.[80] Krishna Menon from London,
who had seen copies of the telegrams, had also cabled Nehru
that Radhakrishnan's hands should be strengthened and avoid-
ance of famine should have priority over prejudice.[81] It was
only during Radhakrishnan's term in Moscow that he and
Krishna Menon, in a long acquaintance of over fifty years,
saw eye to eye on certain issues. But Bajpai considered purely
political reasons irrelevant in this matter of procuring Soviet
wheat and gave greater weight to the reduction in dollar-
earning exports which might ensue from barter with the Soviet
Union. Perhaps his concern at Radhakrishnan's desire for
closer ties with Russia fuelled his criticism of Radhakrishnan's
intention to fly from Paris (where he had gone to attend the
general conference of UNESCO) to London to meet Herbert
Morrison, the British foreign secretary.[82]

I suggest that Ambassadors, whatever their personal eminence, should
be discouraged from visiting Ministers in London without our approval. The tendency to regard oneself as the saviour of the world
may be human but the capacity to succeed in this is rare. The proper
person to speak on foreign policy to British Ministers is our High
Commissioner in the United Kingdom.[83]

But Nehru, attaching more importance to political flair and
understanding of events than to niceties of diplomatic protocol,
took no action to dissuade Radhakrishnan.

Radhakrishnan had no illusions about the authoritarian
nature of Soviet society. He was only too conscious of the suppression of free thought and of the treatment of writers, in
Zhdanov's phrase, as 'ideological workers'. In his time in
Moscow Ilya Ehrenburg's novel *The Storm*, hailed when published in 1948 as the great work comparable to Tolstoy's *War
and Peace*, was banned as it spoke highly of Tito and the Yugo-
slav partisans.[84] He noted too the presence of the police every-

[80] Radhakrishnan to Nehru, 6 June 1951.
[81] Krishna Menon's telegrams to Nehru, 8 April, 30 April and 9 May 1951,
Nehru papers.
[82] Radhakrishnan to Nehru, 24 June 1951.
[83] Note of Bajpai, 5 July 1951, MEA file 42/6/NGO-51.
[84] 'Behind the Iron Curtain', *Times Literary Supplement*, 24 August 1951.

where. On one occasion, for example, driving out of Moscow, he was struck by the hard labour being done by women in road construction under the supervision of an armed soldier for each dozen or fifteen workers. But he was convinced that Stalin wanted to consolidate peace in the few years left to him and that the people were kindly and human. To an American critic who alleged that Radhakrishnan treated the communist rulers of the Soviet Union as if they were Quakers or 'non-dualistic Vedanta pacifists', he replied that to strive for a peaceful settlement was not to appease. What was of prime importance was that our actions should be governed by right principles. A third world war had to be prevented, if only because it would result in the triumph of communism. This was not the moment for fanaticism, and sharp distinctions between good and evil would be the sure road to disaster. Apparent opposites had to be reconciled and contained within a peaceful world order. Never in history had the universal in the soul of man burnt so dimly, and it was for philosophers to realize the human in all peoples of the world.

To resolve the cold war it was not necessary to adopt either the method of negation or that of mergence. To destroy Soviet Russia or to submit to it were not the only alternatives. Soviet rule had well-known weaknesses—the defiance of constitutional methods, the faith in the doctrine that the end justifies the means, the use of democratic liberties for attaining power and then their suppression, the cunning and cruelty in administration. There was much resentment of their dominance in eastern Europe. But if, despite all this, communism was a widespread force in the world, it was because the doctrine satisfied certain basic human needs. It spread among people who were alienated from capitalist society, were not held together by a bond of a shared moral principle, and found no meaning in or purpose to individual existence. The popularity of communism showed the need for a new type of society whose main concern was the welfare of all its people, for the transformation of the community so as to give it a new social vision. Fighting communism on the battlefields was to attack only the symptoms, not the disease. So long as democracy ceased to be a revolutionary force and compromised with its own foundations, it could not stop the spread of communism.

It was wishful thinking to imagine that because certain liberties were lacking in the Soviet Union, therefore all its people were disgruntled and ready to revolt at the first opportunity. Radhakrishnan himself believed, after two years in Moscow, that there was much to commend in the country. Living standards had risen, the distribution of food and opportunity was more equitable than before, literacy was widespread and intellectual interests were growing. Religion was tolerated and art was not decadent. The success of the Soviet ballet had a deeper meaning than aesthetic pleasure: 'The wordless beauties which are enacted before our eyes are the eternal protest of men and women of refined feeling against the glamour and falseness of so much tinsel that passes for life.' The children were full of spontaneous life and gaiety and their interests were served with care. Above all there was an atmosphere of hope. The eyes of Russia were turned towards the future, towards the possibilities of things. Not even the most hostile witness could affirm that any living Russian would prefer the return of the tsars.

Like all historic institutions, the Soviet system had elements of evil as well as of good, and Soviet society was neither a paradise of workers nor a hell on earth. Marxism being not dogmatic but creative, and conditions in Russia changing continuously, Radhakrishnan was hopeful that patience and restraint might lead to peaceful adjustments and approximations between the communist and non-communist worlds. The police state need not necessarily be enduring. Stalin himself had spoken of the primacy of the logic of facts. By providing Soviet Russia with a feeling of security the Western powers should encourage liberalization, even as the rulers of the communist countries should abolish the Cominform and demonstrate their commitment to coexistence. What was of importance was that the Soviet state was in flux and changing as the result of conflicting ideas and circumstances, intentions and realities; and if these peoples under communist rule were treated as human beings, with all the human failings, that would help them to improve the system under which they lived. The enemy of all men and women, wherever they might be, was the anonymous machine.[85] The sense of the impotence of the individual was

[85] The dissident Czech playwright Vaclav Havel is, in our own time, of the

not limited to any one country or ideology. A free and universal humanism was the goal of democracy, the task of human intelligence, the demand of Eastern religions and the postulate of Western science. It was the vision of the future.[86]

## V

In the latter half of 1951 there arose the specific issue of the peace treaty with Japan as drafted by the United States. Radhakrishnan feared that, apart from its other defects, it would obviously confirm Soviet fears of hostile encirclement; and what surprised him was not that Russia found it as unacceptable as India did but that Gromyko went to San Francisco. India preferred to stay away. As he told Vyshinsky, 'We are much too civilized to create scenes. Polite behaviour at international conferences would contribute to improvement of general relations.' But he pressed Vyshinsky to do more than merely condemn the United States. Soviet talk of peace was distrusted because it was not supported by deeds. If the Soviet Union accepted a settlement in Korea, concluded the Austrian peace treaty, worked for German unification by a free vote, reduced armaments not proportionately but to limits of self-defence—recognizing the extent of the land frontiers of the Soviet Union and the People's Democracies—and abolished the Cominform, then the United States might be persuaded to recognize People's China, withdraw from Taiwan, improve international trade and reduce armaments in the United States and the NATO countries.[87]

This was a grand design, mind-boggling in its scope. But Radhakrishnan did not, of course, expect it all to happen at

same view. He believes that the Soviet system and advanced Western society have in common a trend towards impersonal power and rule by mega-machines that escape human control: 'I believe the world is losing its human dimension.' *Times Literary Supplement*, 23 January 1987.

[86] Radhakrishnan's reply to the criticisms of Professor F. S. C. Northrop of Yale University, written in May 1951 and published as part of his 'Reply to Critics' in P. Schilpp (ed.), *The Philosophy of Sarvepalli Radhakrishnan* (New York 1952), pp. 829–37.

[87] Radhakrishnan's telegram to Nehru, 25 August 1951, reporting conversation with Vyshinsky.

once. His purpose was to make the Soviet authorities move out of the ruts of suspicion, plan constructive policies and prove the genuineness of their advocacy of coexistence. He even suggested that Stalin announce publicly that coexistence implied non-interference in other countries.[88] Coexistence was the application in international relations of the Hindu concept of respect for all human beings. Whether it be the Russians or anyone else, it was our duty not to assume that they were monsters of iniquity or total embodiments of sin, but to help them realize the divinity latent in them.[89] So too all religions deserved our respect; and in a sense Marxist communism was a religion, 'a Christian heresy', as Radhakrishnan once termed it.[90] In the same spirit Radhakrishnan wished governments and public opinion in the West to abandon frozen postures of expectation of a world war. One should not always distrust Moscow and doubt its sincerity. Greece, the blockade of Berlin, Yugoslavia and Korea were all indications that the Russian bark did not lead to a bite; and the danger to the world was more from American defence than from Soviet aggression. Magnanimous behaviour could be the best strategy as well as the highest statesmanship.

At the non-official level Radhakrishnan encouraged the Society of Friends in Britain to build contacts in the Soviet Union and helped the Quaker mission of peace and goodwill on its visit to that country. He told them that Stalin was an old man who wanted peace for his country, and it was unfortunate that Britain had abdicated her leadership and, along with the United States, failed to respond in a more forthcoming way to what he believed was a genuine change of climate in the Soviet Union. The mission got the same impression and on its return pleaded for sympathy, tolerance and understanding.[91] Through Kathleen Lonsdale, a member of the mission, he came in touch with Dorothy Hodgkin and other scientists in Oxford, and

[88] Radhakrishnan to Gromyko, 11 July 1951.

[89] See Radhakrishnan's later speech at Hyderabad, 13 January, *Madras Mail*, 13 January 1953.

[90] Discussion with Bertrand Russell on 'Europe and Asia and the Modern World', recorded by the BBC, 28 October 1952.

[91] Report of the Friends Mission to Russia in July 1951, *The Friend*, 14 September 1951; P. Cadbury, *A Personal Diary of the Quaker Mission to Russia* (for private circulation).

stressed the need for them to be in close touch with their professional colleagues in the Soviet Union. 'Knowing Dr Radhakrishnan', Dorothy Hodgkin wrote many years later, 'made a great difference to my life.'[92]

Another occasion for Radhakrishnan to place his views before the Western public was provided by the invitation of the Carnegie Endowment to write a companion piece for the famous article written by William James many years earlier in 1910, 'The Moral Equivalent of War'. Emphasizing that war had now become total and would end with neither side being the victor, Radhakrishnan expressed his surprise that plans were still being made for war and justified as necessary to destroy communism. The moral equivalent of war in our age was the non-violence of Gandhi, resisting evil without hating the evil-doer, and giving up the claim to infallibility. The courage, sacrifice and suffering associated with war should be directed to building a free society and removing hunger and poverty. The United States was distinguished in matters of mind and spirit, but several of her leaders had developed a distorted perspective which sometimes appeared to be a betrayal of her soul. In the Soviet Union freedom had been forfeited; but those who attacked freedom in the name of freedom were no less dangerous than those who attacked it in the name of the state. American policy was inspired not so much by ideology as by opposition to the Soviet Union. All these trends in the United States showed that she was suffering defeat from within and had little to defend or offer the world. The Soviet government had to be condemned for its suppression of political freedom, its large standing army and its domination by force of Eastern Europe. But Radhakrishnan said he had found the Russian people no different from others; and especially their young men and women were friendly, cheerful and pleasant. They were proud of their country and its achievements, were aware of the gross shortcomings of the Soviet system but believed that these were transitional. They wished to live in peace with others and did not complain of conditions in their country because they feared that it was being encircled. Soviet Russia was neither as black as some in the West believed nor as white

[92] To G. Parthasarathi, 8 June 1985. I thank Mr Parthasarathi for letting me see this letter.

as *Pravda* painted it. If the rest of the world were friendlier, conditions could well improve.

This was the fullest statement that Radhakrishnan had as yet made of his attitude to the cold war, and was intended to appeal to the best instincts of American liberalism. His whole background of personal religion, social commitment and acceptance of democratic values gave assurance that his effort was not propaganda. But the Carnegie Endowment, not surprisingly given that Dulles was chairman of its board, did not publish the article and, even after Radhakrishnan toned it down, filed it in its archives.[93] Perhaps this was the best testimony of all that Radhakrishnan deplored in current developments in the United States. But if Radhakrishnan was denied this chance to convey his anxiety directly to the American public, Bishop Bell of Chichester, with whom he was in close contact, passed on his views to Bishop Sherrill, chairman of the National Council of Churches in the United States, who promised to keep Truman, Acheson and Dulles informed. Like Radhakrishnan Bishop Bell was keen on a new approach to the Soviet Union and gave Radhakrishnan's views a tangible form by proposing a four-power conference with an Indian chairman.[94] Bell had had independent corroboration of Radhakrishnan's feeling that the Soviet Union was now keen on an understanding with the Western powers, and he pressed this view on Eden, the foreign secretary in the Conservative government which had just assumed office.[95]

## VI

Alongside, Radhakrishnan went ahead in his given task of explaining India's policy and furthering good relations with the Soviet Union. Stalin had still grave doubts about Nehru's government. In his talks with senior leaders of the Communist Party of India who visited Moscow secretly in the early months

[93] See J. E. Johnson, president of the Carnegie Endowment for International Peace, to Radhakrishnan, 12 October 1951. The essay has since been published in *Mainstream* (Delhi, 25th anniversary number, 1987).

[94] Bishop G. Bell to Bishop H. K. Sherrill, 21 August 1951 (copy to Radhakrishnan).

[95] Bishop Bell to Radhakrishnan, 31 October 1951.

of 1951, he advised them to convert their party into a mass party so that popular discontent could be transformed into a popular movement which could utilize non-parliamentary methods. To him Nehru's foreign policy was still essentially that of British imperialism, and such acts as the recognition of China, denunciation of atomic weapons and opposition to branding China as an aggressor in Korea resulted from the rivalry between Britain and the United States combined with mass pressure. But he thought that the Nehru government, while lacking a mass base, was not a puppet government which would fall easily; and he advised the Indian communists against theoretical rigidity, one-sidedness and a priori arguments on the basis solely of economic analysis. They should be more aware that the reality was complex.[96] It was in the same mood of flexible willingness to respond that the Soviet government viewed Radhakrishnan's efforts at promoting bilateral confidence.

One problem of special interest to India, more important than the attitude to the Japanese treaty and even the need for foodgrains, and which Radhakrishnan introduced into Indo-Soviet relations with far-reaching long-term consequences, was Kashmir. The Soviet Union had not shown much interest in it and indeed did not even seem to comprehend it fully. The invitation to Liaquat Ali Khan in 1949 to visit the Soviet Union was not proof of an acceptance of Pakistan's policies but part of a general intention to show dislike of Nehru's attitudes. There is no evidence to confirm either Vijayalakshmi's suggestion that the invitation might be linked with Soviet interest in Kashmir or her impression that Russia was becoming increasingly interested in the problem from an 'unhealthy' point of view.[97] The first major Soviet article on the subject was published in 1950, and its argument, that the predominantly Muslim peasants in the area were exploited by Hindu landlords and therefore subjected to the double yoke of national discrimination and feudal oppression,[98] made clear that official Indian efforts to explain the case had not succeeded. Perhaps

---

[96] Stalin's question–answer session; 'The Tactical Line', April 1951; Statement of Policy, November 1951, M. Sen (ed.), *Documents of the History of the Communist Party of India 1951–1956* (Delhi 1977), pp. 31–43.

[97] Dean Acheson's memorandum of conversation with Vijayalakshmi, 29 June 1949, department of state papers.

[98] R. B. Remnek, *Soviet Policy towards India* (Delhi 1975), p. 124.

offended by the failure of the Government of India to take up
an informal offer of help in 1948 by Novikov, the Soviet ambassador in Delhi, the Soviet Union took no interest whenever
Kashmir was discussed in the Security Council. In September
1950, when Novikov applied in the routine manner for a visa
to return to India, Radhakrishnan sent a reply that the visa
would be granted on one condition. On the puzzled foreign
office inquiring what the condition was, Radhakrishnan said the
visa would be granted if Novikov came to lunch at the embassy.
Novikov accepted the invitation, as did Gromyko and his wife.
Radhakrishnan tried to explain the Indian position on Kashmir. Gromyko said he had met Sheikh Abdullah in New York,
had a favourable impression of him and asked if he was a
Hindu.

In the early months of 1951 the Kashmir issue again came
up before the Security Council, and the United States and Britain introduced a resolution which was wholly unacceptable
to India. Passing through London Radhakrishnan spoke to
Zarubin, the Soviet ambassador, and gained the impression
that Soviet Russia might veto the resolution.[99] In fact, the
Soviet representative on the Council remained silent: 'To be
quite frank this attitude of silent aloofness has not been very
pleasing.'[100] Radhakrishnan thought that the Soviet government expected to be asked explicitly for their support; and this
the Government of India had not done. The fact was that
Nehru was in two minds. He would have liked Soviet support
on Kashmir, but was also concerned that such support would
worsen the Kashmir issue by making it part of the conflict between the great powers. He was also probably wary that a
request for Soviet support might encourage Moscow to seek
India's commitment to the Soviet position in other matters.
Dependence on the Soviet veto in the Security Council on such
a vital matter to India as Kashmir would place a heavy tilt on
non-alignment. In the event, as the years passed, American
policy left India no option.

Radhakrishnan saw, much earlier than most people in the
ministry of external affairs, that this anti-Indian trend in the
outlook of the state department would not change; and he,

[99] Radhakrishnan to Nehru, from London airport, 8 March 1951.
[100] Note of Nehru, 31 March 1951, Nehru papers; and telegram to Radhakrishnan, 1 April 1951.

17

therefore, despite Nehru's ambivalence and feeling that 'we can hardly ask Moscow to do anything', took the initiative. Novikov, when he again came to lunch at the embassy in 1951 in quest of a visa, was told that the Soviet Union should take a more positive attitude in the Security Council when the Kashmir issue next came up.[101] Then, calling on Vyshinsky before his departure for Oxford, Radhakrishnan directly confronted the minister with the Soviet Union's failure to support India on Kashmir. On Vyshinsky mumbling that they had not been asked, Radhakrishnan replied that he was now doing so and drew Vyshinsky's attention to a point that had risen earlier in Radhakrishnan's discussions with Novikov, that the Soviet Union should be concerned about the future of Kashmir, if only because it was to her a borderland.[102] The response to this intervention by Radhakrishnan came a few months later, in January 1952, when the Soviet representative on the Security Council for the first time spoke on Kashmir, supported India fully and used the veto in her favour. Nehru's immediate response was one of embarrassment, and Bajpai assured the American ambassador in Delhi that the Government of India were as much surprised as the United States government must have been at the Soviet charges of interference by the Western powers in Kashmir.[103] But the Soviet intervention was a turning-point in India's relations with the Soviet Union, with deep significance to her connections with Britain and the United States and of consequence to India's general role in the world. From Moscow Radhakrishnan had given a decisive and enduring shift to Indian foreign policy.

## VII

As Radhakrishnan's second year in Moscow was drawing to its end, Nehru requested him to continue for another year on the same terms of spending six months at Oxford. Three years in Moscow was somewhat hard, but Radhakrishnan assured

[101] Y. D. Gundevia to K. P. S. Menon, 5 August 1951, recording Radhakrishnan's conversation with Novikov.

[102] Gundevia, *Outside the Archives*, pp. 95–8.

[103] Gopal, *Jawaharlal Nehru*, vol. II, p. 116; report of the US charge d'affaires in Delhi to dept of state on conversations with Bajpai, 18 and 19 January 1952, *Foreign Relations of the United States 1952–1954*, vol. XI (Washington 1983), pp. 1173–4.

Nehru that he was willing to serve not where it would be most comfortable but where he would be most useful 'to a much harassed Prime Minister'.[104] At the end of that third year Radhakrishnan planned to return to Oxford and combine the professorship, if possible, with a nominated place in the upper house of parliament, odd jobs such as chairmanships of commissions and participation in international conferences as India's representative.[105] This was, for a man of his standing, no high ambition; but even before the third year in Moscow was over, once again, as so often in his life, destiny took a hand.

In the spring of 1952, after the general elections in which the Congress won an overall majority, elections were to be held under the new constitution for the offices of president and vice-president of India. Rajendra Prasad, who had taken over as president in January 1950, obviously expected to continue in office; but Radhakrishnan's name began silently but rapidly to gather momentum. The leading exponent of Hinduism who had been a spectacular success as ambassador in Moscow, he had become the involuntary hero of both the right and the left wings of political opinion as well as of progressive sections within the Congress party itself. Indeed, Nehru himself was thought to favour Radhakrishnan as against Prasad. But when Megh-nad Saha, the distinguished physicist, wrote to Nehru proposing Radhakrishnan, the prime minister found that the majority in the party was strongly in favour of the continuance of Prasad. Nehru wished to avoid an election for the high office, for although, with the Congress controlling so much of the vote, any candidate sponsored by that party was bound to win, it would be embarrassing if a rival of Radhakrishnan's stature secured a heavy poll in his favour; and Radhakrishnan himself was clearly not uninterested. He wrote to Nehru from Oxford, on his way back from India to Moscow after an operation for appendicitis, that he had informed Saha that he would allow his name to be put forward if for any reason Prasad was not a candidate;[106] and he followed this up two weeks later from Moscow thanking Nehru, on the basis of a newspaper report,

[104] Radhakrishnan to Nehru, 17 July 1951, Nehru to Radhakrishnan, 30 July 1951, and Radhakrishnan to Nehru, 17 August 1951.

[105] See his letter to Nehru, 17 July 1951.

[106] Saha to Radhakrishnan, 12 February 1952, and Radhakrishnan to Nehru, 6 March 1952.

for sounding opinion in the Congress about him and agreeing to serve if the suggestion found general acceptance.[107] The compromise that Nehru worked out was to offer Radhakrishnan the vice-presidentship. Senior Congressmen like Pattabhi Sitaramayya, a former president of the party, and B. G. Kher, the retiring chief minister of Bombay, had their eye on this post; while Rajagopalachari recommended the Speaker, Mavalankar.[108] But Nehru's proposal was strongly supported in the working committee by Azad, who always preferred Prasad to Radhakrishnan. Party ties mattered much to Azad and he never fully comprehended the reasons which caused Nehru to attach such importance to Radhakrishnan's non-political contributions to India's cause. Now, to ensure that Radhakrishnan did not in any way endanger Prasad's continuance, Azad wrote to Radhakrishnan in Moscow urging him to accept the vice-presidentship and even claimed to be the author of the proposal.[109]

However, Azad need not have worried. Radhakrishnan, though disappointed by the decision, was too decent to press his claims for the highest office. He gave his assent to the Congress sponsoring his name for the vice-presidentship and, with the election a foregone conclusion, started his round of farewells in Moscow in the first week of April 1952, within two months of his return from Oxford and India. The Soviet government never gave such 'a cordial and grandiose' farewell to any foreign envoy leaving their country.[110] Vyshinsky hosted a lunch in his honour and Stalin saw him at short notice—the first interview granted by him to an ambassador for over two years. It also provided Radhakrishnan with the unique distinction of being the only ambassador to be received by Stalin at both the start and the end of his term in Moscow.

From both Stalin and Vyshinsky Radhakrishnan did not conceal that there was much in the Soviet Union of which he did not approve. He even spoke to Vyshinsky of the labour camps and of the report that about 15,000,000 to 20,000,000

[107] Radhakrishnan to Nehru, 20 March 1952.
[108] Sri Prakasa, governor of Madras, to Nehru, 11 March 1952, Nehru papers.
[109] Maulana Azad to Radhakrishnan, 27 March 1952.
[110] *Paris Presse*, 7 April 1952; 'Moscow Fuss for Indian', *Newcastle Morning Herald* (Australia), 9 April 1952.

prisoners worked in them. Vyshinsky denied this, adding, 'The ambassador loves our people but hates our government.'[111] In both conversations Radhakrishnan also emphasized that while India and the Soviet Union had some common ideals, India was committed to peaceful and democratic methods in attaining those objectives and would not deviate from this. This was mentioned in Reuter's message from Moscow and was not deleted by the censor.[112] But Stalin was sceptical of any peaceful advance to socialism by easing the landlords out of their estates: 'When a Russian peasant sees a wolf, he knows how to deal with it. Liquidate, Mr Ambassador!' he said, thrice bringing his hand down like a chopper on the table. Radhakrishnan, as reported by Gundevia who was present, was visibly revolted.[113] He ended this part of the interview by saying that India would continue to use peaceful methods to get rid of all exploiters and, if she succeeded, it would be a great lesson for other nations.

Radhakrishnan then turned to foreign policy, explained India's independent stance and asked Stalin whether, to prove his sincerity about peaceful coexistence, he would be willing to abolish the Cominform just as earlier the Soviet Union had dissolved the Comintern. Stalin avoided a direct answer, saying this was of no importance and was a matter which concerned other countries as well. On Germany, as the Soviet government objected to a United Nations commission as bound to be pro-American, Radhakrishnan suggested a neutral commission to see if conditions for a fair election existed. Stalin thought this was a matter only for the four occupying powers, but seemed prepared for negotiations among them.

On bilateral issues, the question was raised of the unfriendly despatches being sent by the *Tass* correspondent in Delhi and which were being carried by Soviet newspapers and broadcast by Moscow Radio. The Government of India had been complaining of this for some time. Stalin now turned to Vyshinsky and ordered that the correspondent be withdrawn. 'Both you and Mr Nehru', said Stalin to Radhakrishnan, 'are

[111] Y. D. Gundevia to K. P. S. Menon, 7 April 1952, recording Radhakrishnan's talk with Vyshinsky; Lionel Curtis to Lt Col. Nugent Head, 16 April 1952, reporting conversation with Radhakrishnan, Curtis papers.
[112] 4 April 1952.   [113] *Outside the Archives*, p. 109.

persons whom we do not consider as our enemies. This will continue to be our policy and you can count on our help.' At the conclusion of the interview, Stalin came round the table to shake hands with Radhakrishnan, who patted him on the cheek, wished him well, hoped that he would prove as great a man of peace as he was of war and told him of the emperor Ashoka and his change of heart at Kalinga: 'Will that happen to you?' Radhakrishnan then reminded Stalin of Christ's saying— What shall it avail a man if he gain the whole world and lose his own soul?—and Stalin was visibly moved as he replied, 'I too was in a theological seminary for some time and miracles may happen.'[114]

The interview had been intended as a token of the Soviet government's new goodwill towards India as well as of personal esteem for Radhakrishnan. Later in the year, the public orator at Oxford, presenting Radhakrishnan for the honorary degree of Doctor of Civil Laws, summed up his standing in the world: 'Although there are many persons whose abilities and sincerity have enjoyed a high reputation either among the Russians or among the rest of the world, it is doubtful whether anyone else has been equally well thought of by both.' Pavlov, who had acted as interpreter, reported later to Radhakrishnan that Stalin had remarked after the interview, 'He is the only man who treats me not as a monster but as a human being.'

The interview made front-page news in all newspapers of the world and 'the jaw-breaker name' of Sarvepalli Radhakrishnan was in all the headlines.[115] Coming immediately after the Soviet offer of talks between the four Powers on a German peace treaty, it was thought that Stalin might have put forward fresh suggestions in a way flattering to India and acceptable to the United States in that it seemed to bypass China.[116] Radhakrishnan denied that he had been given any specific proposals or that India had been asked to act as a mediator;[117] and Bajpai as usual, in his talks with the American ambassador,

[114] Record of Radhakrishnan's interview with Stalin, 5 April 1952; Radhakrishnan to D. K. Joshi, 12 October 1966.
[115] Newsweek (New York), 21 April 1952.
[116] Walter O'Hearn in the Montreal Daily Star, 8 April 1952.
[117] Interviews at London, 9 and 12 April 1952, The Hindu, 10 and 13 April 1952, respectively.

played down the interview as having been largely a token of goodwill.[118] But Radhakrishnan had got the impression that there was no problem then dividing the world that could not be settled by discussion and negotiation. Stalin was suspicious of the Western powers but desired peace. So long as the United States was so determinedly hostile, the Soviet Union would not relax its grip on eastern Europe and would try to bring Tito into line. But Stalin did seem to want to reach a *modus vivendi* with the West and his one preoccupation was to keep out of war. So Radhakrishnan thought it would be unwise to bang the door against every approach and give up the task of keeping the peace as impossible. Every effort should be made to get the top people together.[119]

This raised the hopes of many in the Western world. Bishop Bell, for example, urged the British government to take it seriously:

I know Professor Radhakrishnan personally. I had various conversations as well as correspondence with him last summer and autumn. He is no sentimentalist; he is a philosopher and a statesman. When he sees Mr Molotov and Marshal Stalin, he is well aware of the burning issues that divide the world. Is it not possible that an Ambassador from India should understand the East and the West better than they understand one another? Should not a voice from India be heard with respect? I know of no man more concerned than he about the danger to the world if an heroic effort is not made to end the present strain.[120]

A few Americans like Averell Harriman were of the same view as Radhakrishnan, 'that with the Soviets much can be accomplished by honest, friendly, unsentimental negotiation and nothing at all by hostile rhetoric, warlike threats or efforts to persuade their leaders of our infinite capacity for kindness.'[121] But on the chief policy-makers in the United States Radha-

[118] Memorandum of conversations between Chester Bowles and Bajpai, Chester Bowles papers, Yale University Library; see also Robert Trumbull in *New York Times*, 13 April 1952.

[119] *The Times*, 7 April 1952; 'India Hatching Moscow Peace-Egg', *Buenos Aires Herald*, 7 April 1952; *New York Herald Tribune*, 12 April 1952; Nehru to chief ministers, 15 April 1952, on Radhakrishnan's report on his conversation with Stalin, J. Nehru, *Letters to Chief Ministers*, vol. II, 1950–1952, pp. 582–3; R. H. S. Crossman, *The Backbench Diaries* (London 1981), pp. 172–3.

[120] *Parliamentary Debates* (House of Lords), vol. 176, no. 50, 9 April 1952.

[121] J. K. Galbraith, *A View from the Stands* (London 1987), p. 342.

krishnan could hope to make no impression. They were committed to a crusade against Soviet Russia at the cost of the permanent division of Europe.[122]

Specifically, Radhakrishnan believed that some progress could be made on the problem of Germany. The Soviet government were so concerned about the rearming of West Germany that in March 1952 they had offered reunification in return for the withdrawal of all foreign troops and neutral status; and Radhakrishnan thought it possible that they would consider elections in Germany and the conclusion with an all-German government of a treaty providing for neutralization and disarmament for ten years. Radhakrishnan mentioned this to Henry Usborne, a Labour member of parliament then on a visit to the Soviet Union, and Usborne passed on the message to Selwyn Lloyd, the minister of state in the foreign office, as well as to Attlee. Lloyd thought there could be something in it but took no action, perhaps because the British ambassador in Moscow, very rigid in his views, brushed the suggestion aside. Churchill might have been more responsive and even in Washington some believed they could 'smell something cooking'.[123] Even if it were only an olive branch in a mailed fist, it had to be considered carefully and counter-proposals made.[124] But the foreign office in London would not even consider it; nor was the leadership of the Labour party more understanding. Attlee's comment to Usborne was, 'I know Radhakrishnan; he is a nice man, but he isn't experienced. He may have got this wrong.' A fortnight later Attlee told Usborne that he had checked the story and there was nothing in it.[125] But Radhakrishnan, for all his lack of long years of diplomatic service, had a better insight into the mind of the Soviet politbureau than most others at this time. For it is now thought that a powerful section of the Soviet leadership was then in favour of a settlement of the German issue on broadly the lines formulated by Radhakrishnan.[126] The failure to respond was the 'missed

[122] For their views, see W. Isaacson and E. Thomas, *The Wise Men: Architects of the American Century* (London 1986).

[123] Report in the *Continental Daily Mail* (Paris), 9 April 1952.

[124] Hanson Baldwin in the *New York Times*, 11 April 1952.

[125] See H. Usborne's letter in *The Observer* (London), 4 February 1962.

[126] I. Deutscher, 'Will Russia Abandon East Germany', *The Observer* (London), 28 January 1962.

chance' of the post-War years, ending perhaps for ever the
possibility of a united Germany.[127] *Tass* officially denied on
23 April that Stalin had suggested to Radhakrishnan a four-
powers meeting; and by July the Soviet government seem to
have given up hopes of a conference of the four occupying
powers unifying Germany by agreement.[128]

Despite his striving, therefore, Radhakrishnan's term at Moscow had not resulted in any substantial improvement in the
official relations between the two sides in the cold war. He had
conveyed to the British and American authorities the desire of
the Soviet government for peace, just as he had minced no
words in telling the rulers at Moscow, from Stalin downwards,
the reasons for the deep suspicion in the West of Soviet policies.
This was most important in itself and explains the value of his
presence in Moscow. 'A hard-boiled Scot said, "The departure
of Radhakrishnan at this juncture may spell international disaster"—these were the exact words. I wondered why.'[129] But
the governments of the Western powers were in no mood to act
on Radhakrishnan's suggestions. More rewarding to him was
the impact of his understanding of the Soviet mood on intellectual and academic circles in Europe and America. Even
more spectacular was the change he had wrought in the relations between his own country and the Soviet Union; and this
was accepted on almost every side. The Soviet administration
have always recognized his crucial role in initiating Indo-
Soviet understanding; and so did Nehru. He was more than
satisfied with the results of what had started as 'rather an
interesting experiment'.[130] No Indian mission abroad had had,
according to the prime minister, to face a more delicate task,
and Radhakrishnan had carried it out 'with marked success.
Our relations with the USSR during this period and today bear
witness to this fact.'[131] His successor at Moscow wrote over two
years later that the embassy was still reaping the rich dividends

[127] See Neal Ascherson in *The Observer* (London), 26 January 1986, on R.
Steininger's book, *A Missed Chance.*
[128] R. H. S. Crossman's report of a conversation with Pietro Nenni, the Italian
socialist leader, who saw Stalin in July 1952, *New Statesman*, 1 September 1952.
[129] Professor D. P. Mukherji, after a visit to Moscow, to Nehru, 29 April 1952,
Nehru papers.
[130] Nehru to Vijayalakshmi, 24 August 1949, Nehru papers.
[131] Nehru to Radhakrishnan, 18 April 1952.

of Radhakrishnan's tenure.[132] Public opinion, of both the left and the right, was agreed on his achievement. Only in the rarefied atmosphere of the ministry of external affairs did doubts linger: 'There is little to do, however, in Moscow. Russians are unconfiding and no Ambassador—we have had two eminent non-officials so far—has influenced them in any way.'[133]

[132] K. P. S. Menon, ambassador in Moscow, to Radhakrishnan, 13 August 1954.

[133] Note of G. S. Bajpai, 13 March 1952, Nehru papers.

# VICE-PRESIDENT

Radhakrishnan had had some hesitations about accepting the vice-presidentship, an office which, under the constitution, entailed no more than presiding over the Rajya Sabha, the upper house of parliament, and discharging the functions of the president when that post was vacant or the president was ill or absent. It did not seem to him worthwhile to give up the chair at Oxford and his work outside India for such a limited role. But Nehru assured him that he hoped to develop conventions which would expand the role of the vice-president, particularly on the political and diplomatic sides.[1] It was also the general belief that Radhakrishnan, with his wide concerns and intellectual energy, would not allow himself to be caged in an honorific office.[2] He frequently asserted that he was no more than a member of the government on the decorative side. Citing once the description given by Pythagoras of those who went to the Olympic games, a few to gain laurels, some to do business and the many simply to look and watch, Radhakrishnan said he belonged to the third category. The government had sent him to Moscow to watch and report, and had then recalled him lest he develop an attachment to diplomacy. Now as vice-president he sat and watched the administration and as the chairman of the Rajya Sabha he sat and watched parliament. The role of a detached spectator was especially suited to a student of

[1] Radhakrishnan to Nehru, 30 March, and Nehru's reply, 8 April 1952.

[2] Cf.: 'If Dr Radhakrishnan confines himself merely to his statutory duty the expectations raised all over the country by his unanimous election to the Vice-President's office will not be fulfilled. Whatever the intentions of the Constitution-makers might have been, the people expect that his mature wisdom and varied experience will be fully utilized by the Government for the benefit of the country.' Editorial in *Amrita Bazar Patrika* (Calcutta), 11 May 1952.

philosophy.[3] But few took such disclaimers seriously.

The prime minister's efforts to give Radhakrishnan a formal place in the conduct of foreign policy and request him to help the president in maintaining contacts with the diplomatic corps were frustrated by the president himself;[4] but Nehru was able to provide Radhakrishnan with the requisite status and amenities to exercise influence on the domestic scene. State governments were informed that the vice-president should be treated on a par with the prime minister when he travelled outside Delhi and he was given the same right as the president and the prime minister to utilize the VIP squadron of the Indian Air Force. So, when the Rajya Sabha was not in session, Radhakrishnan moved around India, speaking frequently. Lord Casey tells the story of Radhakrishnan's reply to a minister who complained about having been misreported in the press. 'It's your own fault', said Radhakrishnan, adding:

You make a different speech every time. Why don't you do as I do— I make the same speech every time, with only minor variations—and all the newspapermen know it almost by heart and so I get reported correctly. I talk about loving your fellow man, honesty and hard work being the only practicable policy, charity to the afflicted etc. All quite true and you can't say it too often.[5]

The light-hearted modesty cloaked the fact that throughout these years Radhakrishnan lifted every public issue 'to the sphere where conscience sits' in language that drove itself into the minds of his audiences. Whatever the topic, he could relate it immediately to a network of general principles and take it out of dull factuality into a glow of significance. Wilder Penfield, after hearing Radhakrishnan's concluding remarks at a convocation of Delhi University, remarked on his way home: 'I would be prepared to give up the honorary degree if I could get in return the text of Dr Radhakrishnan's speech.'[6]

    [3] Speech at Jai Hind College, Bombay, 26 August 1952, Saraswati (Jai Hind College magazine), March 1953.

    [4] Nehru's note, 19 April 1952, Nehru papers; V. Chowdhary, President and the Indian Constitution (Delhi 1985), pp. 44–8.

    [5] Diary entry, 7 October 1955; T. B. Millar (ed.), Australian Foreign Minister. The Diaries of R. G. Casey 1951–60 (London 1972), p. 220.

    [6] Escott Reid, Canadian high commissioner in Delhi, to Radhakrishnan, 3 May 1957.

Radhakrishnan's main purpose was to draw attention to what he regarded as the essentials of Indian culture and the need to vivify them in the contemporary context: 'India today must take the risk of her own character.'[7] The spiritual values which were a part of her living tradition demanded social progress and the advance of the Indian people into the modern age: 'The fact that his reputation in the West is as an Orientalist has not prevented him from appearing in the ordinary day-to-day affairs of the East as a keen Occidentalist.'[8] Even before going to Moscow Radhakrishnan had spoken in public about the urgency of major economic and social change,[9] and from Russia he continued to press these views on the leaders in Delhi. Unless bold and radical measures replaced the halting and compromising steps which were being taken to raise the lot of the common man, India would go under. If a social revolution were achieved without destroying the soul of the people and it could be shown that in India liberty, economic equity and social justice could be combined, the battle against communism would have been won. Nehru could do it and without him the country would drift to extreme reaction or complete anarchy; but even he would have to act quickly: 'History is on the march and if we are hesitant we will be thrust aside.' Radhakrishnan even suggested that Nehru abandon 'the show of a united Congress' and place himself at the head of progressive forces.[10]

Nehru replied that he shared Radhakrishnan's concern about the dissatisfaction in the country with the half-heartedness about carrying out basic economic and social reforms. There were many difficulties in the way and problems could not be considered in isolation: 'But I entirely agree with you that our pace has been very slow and we have to quicken the historic process.'[11] Radhakrishnan then warned that if Nehru did not act speedily enough the regime as a whole might be swept aside: 'The country has still faith in your leadership but it feels that

[7] *East and West* (London 1955), p. 43.

[8] Andrew Schonfield, 'Problems of Under-Employment: This Day and Age', BBC, The Third Programme, 12 March 1957.

[9] Speeches at Baroda, 14 July 1949, and at Delhi, 16 August 1949, *The Mail* (Madras), 16 July and 17 August 1949, respectively.

[10] Radhakrishnan to Rajendra Prasad, 16 January 1950, and to Nehru, 25 July 1950, 11 August 1950, 15 October 1950 and 1 June 1951.

[11] Nehru to Radhakrishnan, 13 June 1951.

you are a good man of integrity and vision fallen among conservatives and undesirables.'[12] Nehru did not reply to this letter,
probably regarding the forecast as too gloomy and the estimate
of himself as too severe; but he could expect, with Radhakrishnan by his side as vice-president, his own efforts to push
the country forward to be strengthened. His assessment of
Radhakrishnan, as possessing a modern mind which was yet
anchored in the Indian heritage, suggests this. No one appeared
to him to have to a greater extent than Radhakrishnan both
the experience and wisdom of the kind accumulated in India
over the centuries as well as the capacity to interpret such
wisdom in new environments and to meet the demands of a
changing situation.[13]

Nehru's description of Radhakrishnan was strikingly borne
out by the latter's speech at the inauguration of the International Conference on Planned Parenthood at Bombay later
in the year. To counter Gandhians and Roman Catholics who
preached abstinence as the sole means of family planning,
Radhakrishnan argued that even abstinence was a form of
interference with nature and so there could be no logical objection to other forms of interference. Human intelligence was a
divine gift to be utilized in furtherance of individual happiness and social development. Frequent childbirth should be
avoided, being a form of cruelty to women, and contraception
was justified if used for reasons of health. Birth control was no
worse than so much else which had made civilization possible.[14]
This speech was adjudged the most remarkable feature of the
conference,[15] for Radhakrishnan 'embodies perhaps more than
any other person the spirit of the new India'.[16] Radhakrishnan's
acceptance of the advantages in certain situations of birth control could have eased the way for the government to speed up
its programmes in this sphere—had there been the necessary
will.

For twelve years, from 1952 till Nehru's death in 1964, he

[12] Radhakrishnan to Nehru, 15 January 1952.
[13] Nehru's speech in the Rajya Sabha, 16 May 1952.
[14] Speech of 24 November 1952, reprinted in *Eugenics Review* (London), January
1953.
[15] 'Notes of the Quarter', ibid.
[16] Mildred Gilman, 'Margaret Sanger Back from India', *Nation* (New York),
21 February 1953.

and Radhakrishnan were thrown closely together, and their association, based till now on an appreciation of each other's achievement, blossomed into a warm mutual attachment. They were opposite in provenance, the outworks of their lives were different and their temperaments dissimilar. But there was also much to unite them. They were virtually of the same age and fired with the same ambitions for their people and humanity. Their hopes for transforming the texture of Indian society and their keen sense of India's international duty were sustained by shared principles and a common ethical concern. Nehru relied on Radhakrishnan's understanding of the times in which they lived and of the broad forces at work, recognized in him a reassuring presence who imparted a touch of high-mindedness to the government, and consulted him on big issues as well as small. There was not, of course, complete agreement on all matters, and, in particular, Nehru knew that Radhakrishnan was critical of some of his personal likes. It has even been suggested that Nehru only sought Radhakrishnan's opinion on matters where he was confident of Radhakrishnan's support.[17] Certainly, Nehru did not always act, particularly when individuals were involved, on Radhakrishnan's advice. But this did not affect the unbroken confidence, for the prime minister knew that the advice was always given with detachment.

The relationship, nurtured by affinity of aspiration and trust, gradually spread beyond the region of public affairs. Neither by nature gave more than a limited part of himself to any one person. But they took pleasure in each other's intellectual vitality, grace of mind and verbal skills, and relished being themselves despite high office. With each other they were relaxed and not solemn; and their conversation was spiced with gossip. They were the two most life-enhancing persons in Delhi and were aware of this; in this respect they justifiably did not regard anyone else in the capital as their equal. In many ways they complemented each other. Nehru, for example, had a better-trained eye for art and ear for music; Radhakrishnan's appreciation went no higher than *No, No, Nanette* and *My Fair Lady*, musical comedies of which he was fond, and his obligatory presence at concerts of Western classical music was always a

[17] T. T. Krishnamachari to the author, 14 December 1968.

burden. But he was more deft than Nehru in small talk, and at
official dinners, while Nehru mostly sat silent, Radhakrishnan
sparkled pleasantly. But both had an unerring appreciation of
quality and took a keen interest in all that was happening
around them.

It is cold in the high mountains, and personal relations at the
top of any kind of politics are rarely consistently cordial. But,
despite what rumour-mongers said on occasion, during the
dozen years of the close association between Nehru and
Radhakrishnan there was no tension or rivalry between them.
Nor was there need for them to work on what developed into a
natural, unimpeded friendship. In the last months of Nehru's
life they even moved on from matters of state and personal
exchanges to philosophical and spiritual problems. The firm
affection lasted till the end.

## II

About the necessity of rapid economic and social change,
Radhakrishnan continued as vice-president to be as outspoken
as ever before. He deplored the pampered living and confused
thinking which had taken the place of idealism and tenacity of
purpose and warned the Congress party in particular against
complacency. It no longer enjoyed the same confidence and
affection among the people as it had done before independence
and should not slacken in carrying through the 'unfinished
revolution' in social and economic affairs: 'Hurry up, otherwise
it will be too late.' Slowness of evolution was the cause of all
revolutions.[18] This speech to Congressmen caused a stir, and on
being told by Azad that at an informal meeting of senior
Congress leaders Nehru had remained silent when Radhakrishnan's speech had been criticized, Radhakrishnan offered to
resign when Nehru called on him the next morning. Nehru said
no one had criticized Radhakrishnan in his presence, and there
the matter ended.

Radhakrishnan was also of service to the prime minister in

[18] Interview on Radio Zurich, reported in *The Hindu*, 23 May 1952; speech at
Bombay, 27 August 1952, *Indian Nation* (Patna), 29 August 1952; speech to Congress workers at Calcutta, 4 September 1952, *Statesman* and *Mail* (Madras),
5 September 1952.

internal politics. In July and August 1952 he visited Kashmir twice to talk to Sheikh Abdullah, who trusted him as secular-minded, and conveyed to the prime minister Abdullah's fears and hopes. He also tried to get the prime minister and Shyama Prasad Mukherjee, with whom Radhakrishnan had greater influence than anyone else, to talk about their differences; Mukherjee was willing, but Nehru declined for he had been led to believe that this would smack of appeasement. So events moved on to personal tragedy, with Mukherjee's arrest and sudden death in Srinagar at a time when both Nehru and Radhakrishnan were out of India. Feeling rose high, especially in Bengal, but Radhakrishnan was able to get at least one step taken to defuse the situation. Nehru, caught between the outraged emotion of a section of opinion among the Hindus and the drift towards secession of Abdullah and his supporters, remarked with some bitterness to Radhakrishnan, 'Indians are not civilized, whatever you may say.' Radhakrishnan advised him, as a conciliatory gesture, himself to move the adjournment of the house and pay a tribute to Mukherjee rather than leave any such action, as the cabinet and the Congress parliamentary party favoured, to the decision of the presiding officer; and Nehru complied.[19]

In the south, an agitation for a separate province developed in the Andhra districts. As one interested for many years in this problem, Radhakrishnan suggested to Nehru, who had announced that the government were willing to form an Andhra province out of the 'undisputed' Telugu-speaking areas, to omit the qualifying word in his statement made a week later, thus settling with a verbal amendment the long bickerings between the coastal districts on the one hand and the districts in Rayalaseema and in the old state of Hyderabad on the other. In fact, when Nehru was prepared to say in the Lok Sabha only that some steps might be taken fairly soon which might lead to more formal steps later for the creation of an Andhra state, Radhakrishnan said the same day that he had been authorized to inform the Rajya Sabha that the prime minister had taken steps in regard to the formation of an Andhra pro-

[19] Record of conversation of Nehru and Radhakrishnan, 30 July 1953; Radhakrishnan to Nehru, 2 August 1953; and Nehru's speech in the Lok Sabha, 3 August 1953.

18

vince out of the Telugu areas.[20] No one questioned the chairman's authority to make such a clear statement on an administrative matter on behalf of the government when the prime minister himself was vaguer. In unstated acknowledgement of Radhakrishnan's major contribution to a solution of the problem, Nehru insisted that Radhakrishnan, in his words 'the greatest of the Andhras', should accompany him to Kurnool for the inauguration of the new state.

Nehru's utilization of Radhakrishnan in domestic matters generally was as a sounding-board and source of disinterested advice. On education he regarded Radhakrishnan as the greatest authority in India, but none of Radhakrishnan's suggestions at the level of policy could be carried out because of Azad's obduracy as minister. Radhakrishnan could also have been of active help in dealing with problems concerning students for he had a natural sympathy with the young, speaking to them without effort and without condescension. But even here unimaginative authority frequently came in the way. In Uttar Pradesh, for example, Munshi, as governor, served also as chancellor of the universities in the state, and his needless interventions offended the students and led to trouble in Lucknow and Allahabad. Nehru requested Radhakrishnan to speak somewhere on this subject and Radhakrishnan offered to go to Uttar Pradesh and address the students. Nehru thought this a good idea: 'He speaks frankly and strongly to the students. But because his approach is essentially friendly, what he says goes down.'[21] Govind Ballabh Pant, the chief minister, thought it would be appropriate to invite Radhakrishnan to address the convocation of Lucknow University, but nothing came of this, probably because of the resistance of Munshi.

Of the Sahitya Akademi (the National Academy of Letters), set up in 1954, Nehru was the first chairman, but left all decisions to be taken by Radhakrishnan, who was the vice-chairman. Nehru also sought Radhakrishnan's opinion on matters of personnel in the government and administration. Radhakrishnan pressed him to take the socialists into his cabinet—an effort which proved infructuous; but Nehru, knowing that Radhakrishnan wished him not to surround

[20] 16 December 1952.
[21] Nehru to G. B. Pant, 10 November 1953, Nehru papers.

himself only with conservatives, requested Radhakrishnan to persuade Azad to cease from standing in the way of the appointment of Krishna Menon to the cabinet. Radhakrishnan was not convinced of Menon's financial integrity; nor did he overestimate his own influence with Azad. But when Nehru said to him, with tears in his eyes, that to question his (Nehru's) affirmation of Menon's probity was to regard Nehru either as a fool for not discerning that Menon was a crook or as a crook himself who supported another crook, Radhakrishnan broached the matter with Azad. As he expected, he carried no conviction, and it was only two years later that Azad gave way.

More effective in 1954 was Radhakrishnan's intervention to prevent the resignation of the finance minister, C. D. Deshmukh. Relations between the prime minister and his colleague had so deteriorated that Deshmukh wrote sharp, wounding letters while Nehru had begun to regard Deshmukh as not a financier but a banker with a closed and narrow mind. But Radhakrishnan, who had a high opinion of Deshmukh's intellect and public-spiritedness, advised him to be less rigid even while he persuaded Nehru not to let Deshmukh go. So this personal crisis was surmounted, at least for a while. In similar fashion, the next year, when the commerce minister, T. T. Krishnamachari, resigned in a huff, Radhakrishnan told Krishnamachari not to be hasty and gained him time to return to his post.

Radhakrishnan also wished the prime minister to take into the cabinet M. C. Chagla, a liberal and secular-minded judge of the Bombay high court:

It is essential that you should relieve yourself, to some extent, of the burden you are carrying. Prime Ministership and Foreign Ministership are enough for any one man. You must be able to get two or three good men of integrity and progressive outlook to help you in the Cabinet. That should not be impossible.[22]

Not impossible, perhaps; but certainly difficult. Chagla came into the cabinet only in 1963.

However, Radhakrishnan did not compromise his office by open intervention in political affairs. When the executive committee of the Congress parliamentary party requested him, at

[22] Radhakrishnan from New York to Nehru, 29 October 1954.

the height of the troubles over the formation of linguistic provinces, to arbitrate, along with Azad, in the settlement of
border disputes between the various provinces, he unhesitatingly declined.[23]

### III

Presiding over the sessions of the Rajya Sabha was the aspect of
the vice-presidentship which had attracted Radhakrishnan the
least: 'This sitting for six hours a day in the chair for two
months at a time will give me headache.'[24] In fact, except on
important occasions, he reduced his presence to the first two
hours, looking after the question hour and the zero hour which
followed, when the opposition usually raised various issues in
the hope of embarrassing the government. The long hours of
debate which followed he left to the deputy chairman to re-
gulate. Even this, however, was a strain; and he tried once in
1955 to persuade the government to amend the constitution so
as to dissociate the vice-presidentship from the chairmanship of
the Rajya Sabha. Though Nehru was willing, the effort came
to naught. Failing to rid himself of this task, Radhakrishnan
performed it scrupulously. He took pride later in the fact that
during his ten years as the chairman he had hardly missed the
crucial period at the beginning of the day at any sitting of the
house. He attended even when running high temperature and,
on one occasion, when he had to preside over an important
meeting in Bombay, he flew from Delhi in the late afternoon
and flew back in the early hours of the morning the next day.

However much he disliked the job, Radhakrishnan was a
great success as chairman. 'I belong', he told the house on the
very first day, 'to no party and that means I belong to every
party in the House.'[25] He was coolly impartial between the
government and the opposition and established his credentials
in the very first week by securing the release from preventive
detention of a communist who had been elected to the Rajya
Sabha. Soon it was taken for granted that no favours would be
shown to the government and the ruling party and that the

[23] Secretary of the Congress parliamentary party to Radhakrishnan, 31 July
1956, and Radhakrishnan's reply of the same date.
[24] To his son from Moscow, 28 March 1952.      [25] 16 May 1952.

rights of every member would be protected against improper interference even by the official whips. The chairman did not hesitate when need arose to rebuke even the prime minister or expunge his remarks when they transgressed propriety, and with grace and style and humour established high standards of fair and reasonable decision.

As the first chairman of the newly assembled Rajya Sabha, Radhakrishnan took pains to build up conventions for its proper functioning. He chose a member from the opposition to serve on the panel of vice-chairmen, in contrast to the Lok Sabha, where all the members of the corresponding panel were chosen from the ruling party. To confirm the position of the Rajya Sabha as a deliberative body indispensable for parliamentary democracy in India, he at times went beyond the silent role of a presiding officer. For example, he requested a communist member to rise superior to his passions,[26] directed members when debating sensitive issues such as Kashmir or preventive detention to exercise restraint and not to lose themselves in wrangling,[27] and even, as in the case of the Special Marriage Act, gave the lead in the debate.[28] But what made his imposition of discipline easily acceptable was the coating of wit and humour. Once, when the problem of unemployment was being discussed and the opposition complained that the concerned minister was not present in the house, Radhakrishnan ruled that it was sufficient that a minister, whatever his portfolio, was present for the whole lot of ministers were responsible for unemployment.[29]

Radhakrishnan was jealous of the rights of the Rajya Sabha and ensured that it was represented in the public accounts, the estimates, joint and select committees and in all parliamentary delegations. But he was also careful to see that the two houses did not clash and enjoined on the members of his house the need to work in collaboration with the other wing of parliament. On the one occasion when the two houses got to cross purposes with each other, Radhakrishnan and Nehru, working together, steered parliament into calmer waters, and the problem never rose again in their time.[30]

[26] 26 May 1952.     [27] 5 and 9 August 1952.
[28] 8 July 1952.      [29] 11 September 1953.
[30] 1 May 1953.

## IV

When in Delhi Radhakrishnan spent at least three hours every day meeting people. Indians from all walks of life, be they resident in Delhi or passing through the capital, came to him with their personal problems or for counsel on general issues. Knowing his influence with Nehru, supplicants from ministers downwards often made their way to his door seeking his support. To diplomats and visitors from abroad he was a great draw; for the greatest living philosopher 'east of Bertrand Russell', the man whom Justice Douglas described as 'one of the greatest scholars of all time', was a sprightly and lucid conversationalist, elaborating on India's hopes and efforts, commenting on the state of the world and speaking on problems of philosophy and religion, all with unmatched erudition spiced with wit.[31] To Zhou en-lai he spoke, with a touch of mischief, of the merits of the Commonwealth and the delights of an Oxford senior common room: 'The last subject is said to have confused the Chinese Prime Minister.'[32] Lester Pearson, while thinking Radhakrishnan somewhat garrulous, was taken by his application to diplomacy of Jowett's definition of logic as being neither an art nor a science but a dodge. 'We may not, I fear', wrote Pearson on his return to Ottawa,

have been sufficiently appreciative of Indian classical music, but I sincerely appreciated to the full your wisdom and wit during the talk we had together. Among other things, I received a new definition of diplomacy which I cherish and will, I warn you, not fail to use; but not without suitable acknowledgements to Dr. Jowitt [sic] and yourself.[33]

Also, representing as vice-president the Government of India, Radhakrishnan attended all receptions at foreign embassies on national days and was present at official banquets hosted by the president or the prime minister. These were perforce tedious affairs, though even here Radhakrishnan managed to

[31] Douglas was quoted by Mrs Graham Hall, wife of an official of the US embassy in Delhi, to Radhakrishnan, 1 May 1955.

[32] The Times (London), 3 July 1954.

[33] L. B. Pearson to Radhakrishnan, 9 November 1955; Escott Reid, Envoy to Nehru (Delhi 1981), p. 92.

liven up his corner.[34] All this added up to a full day's work of a
normal person; yet Radhakrishnan seemed to have enough
time for his solitary, creative life. His translation of the Upanishads, with a long interpretative introduction and full notes,
was published in 1953. Though completed in the spare hours
of public life, it measured up, in analysis and range of reference,
to the best of Radhakrishnan's professional writing and drew
from a Christian theologian the recognition that since the
classic commentators of the thirteenth century 'we have not
had anyone in the intervening centuries equal to this great
Indian philosopher in depth of insight, profundity of scholarship, ease of illuminating exposition.'[35]

In 1955 two works of Radhakrishnan were published,
*Recovery of Faith*, a volume in the World Perspectives series
edited by Ruth Nanda Anshen, and *East and West*, based on the
Beatty Memorial Lectures delivered at McGill University in
October 1954. Both these books were really long essays, restat-
ing with vigour and a breath of prophecy what were by now
well-known positions of Radhakrishnan and supported by a
vast spread of scholarship and apposite quotations drawn from
recent writings. He was convinced that, despite all the successes
of science, humanity still thirsted for that which religion alone
could give. The fundamental need of the world, far deeper
than any social, political or economic readjustment, was a
spiritual reawakening, a recovery of a faith which would assert
the power of spirit. But no religion based on dogma or historic
events could fill this role; what was needed was spiritual,
creative religion free of doctrine, in accordance with the scientific temper of the age and in sympathy with its social aspirations. Such a religion, being not exclusive or intolerant but
universal, would also foster the unity of the world. The future
of religion was bound up not with the acceptance of one religion by all but with the recognition that all the major religions
had a common foundation—a Transcendent Supreme, the
freedom of the individual as the manifestation of the Supreme
and the unity of mankind as the goal of history. East and West
were not two historical or geographical concepts but two

[34] Escott Reid, pp. 201–2.
[35] David. G. Moses, president of the Indian Christian Council, quoted in *Time*
(New York), 15 October 1956.

movements of the human spirit, two possibilities which every person in every age carried within oneself. Now when the world was converging into one society, it had become more important than ever to bring closer the two impulses in mutual understanding at the highest level.

## V

Returning after an unbelievably successful tenure as ambassador in Moscow, lack of an official role in the making of foreign policy in Delhi could not reduce in public estimation the influence which Radhakrishnan was bound to exercise. While Nehru took steps to endow the vice-presidentship with a status which matched Radhakrishnan's personal position, abroad his eminence had never shone brighter. Oxford bade him farewell by bestowing its two highest honours, an honorary doctorate of civil laws and an honorary fellowship at All Souls: 'What an extraordinary career you have had! An Indian professor becoming an international figure. I am proud to know you. Don't give up Oxford. It is yours. You always belong to it.'[36] That summer also saw the publication in New York of a massive volume on Radhakrishnan's thought in the 'Library of Living Philosophers' series, setting one more stamp of recognition on his philosophical work.

Much was, therefore, now expected in the outside world of Radhakrishnan and his partnership with Nehru. Illustrative of average opinion in the West was the comment of the *Denver Post* that

next to Premier Nehru—perhaps even ahead of him—he is India's most distinguished citizen. Certainly no other Indian is so well qualified to help Nehru steer the course midway between the Soviets and the West... Western statesmen know that the new Vice-President has consistently opposed any policy that would swing India into the Soviet orbit. As he sits now at Nehru's right hand, Radhakrishnan will be watched from both sides to see whether his Moscow assignment has brought any amendment of his views.[37]

[36] Douglas Veale, registrar of Oxford University, in conversation with Radhakrishnan, 1 November 1952. The remarks were recorded by Radhakrishnan that evening.
[37] Editorial, 'A Veep in India', 13 May 1952.

But those who knew him better were more confident that his efforts to understand developments in the Soviet Union indicated tolerance and consideration rather than partisanship. Even though, for example, he had never spoken in favour of Israel, the World Jewish Congress, on the basis of the reports from UNESCO of Radhakrishnan's general outlook, welcomed his election;[38] and the Government of Israel invited him to visit their country.[39] But it was his old friend Gilbert Murray who stated most clearly why so many thought that his occupancy of the vice-presidentship of India might well be a position of world-wide importance:

The reconciliation of Asia and Europe, or of the 'Christian' and Non-Christian civilizations, seems to me the most critical problem, I would even say the most challenging ordeal, now facing the civilized world. The conflict between UN and Communism is very serious, but can, I think, be faced by a united body of law-abiding nations; but if there were a further permanent conflict of a revolutionary kind between continents or between colours, I should begin to despair. There is perhaps no one in the world who has an understanding equal to yours of what is loosely called 'Eastern' and 'Western' thought. . . . It is a great comfort, and always present to my mind, that you and Pundit Nehru occupy such authoritative positions in this great enterprise.[40]

Yet Radhakrishnan's entry as vice-president into international politics was not propitious. In one of his first speeches he was reported as having accused the Western powers of following Hitler's policy of trying to crush Russia.[41] There was immediately loud criticism in India and abroad. Louis Fischer, on a visit to India, described the statement as prejudiced and harmful to India and suggested that Radhakrishnan would have been better advised to compare Hitlerism with Soviet imperialism;[42] the International Latex Corporation placed a large statement in the *New York Times* criticizing Radhakrishnan for so badly misreading the history of his own day; and newspapers

[38] A. Steinburg, head of the cultural department of the World Jewish Congress, to Radhakrishnan, 9 May 1952.

[39] Message of Israel's envoy in Moscow, 10 April 1952.

[40] Gilbert Murray to Radhakrishnan, 20 November 1952.

[41] Speech at Bombay, 27 August 1952, *Times of India*, 28 August 1952.

[42] Statements, 29 August 1952, *Indian Express*, 30 August 1952 and 4 September 1952, *Amrita Bazar Patrika*, 6 September 1952.

across the United States commented severely. Nehru himself
was concerned. While the vice-president did not speak for the
government, his views were supposed to be in general line with
official policy; and what Radhakrishnan was reported to have
said, though not incorrect, was only part of the truth. So he
wrote to Radhakrishnan that, as his words had needlessly led
to anger and queries on whether India had given up non-
alignment, he might explain and amplify his statement.[43]
Even this, however, was not required, for All India Radio had
recorded the speech and was able to place beyond doubt that
Radhakrishnan had said no more than that some people complained that Hitler's policy was being followed.[44]

This should have ended the controversy. Nehru for one was
fully satisfied, there being nothing in the full report of the
speech with which he did not agree: 'But people are over-
sensitive nowadays and imagine things.'[45] Criticism continued
to simmer in India,[46] while in the West, despite Radhakrishnan's explicit clarification,[47] the feeling lurked that he was inclined to regard the Western powers as more likely than the
Soviet Union to provoke a war. To Radhakrishnan, who
regarded his business as peace and the promotion of understanding between the two blocs,[48] this failure to comprehend
his basic attitudes was naturally worrying. Far from being
sympathetic to communism, his criticism of the Western democracies was that by such policies as racialism, colonialism
and blind preparation for war they were facilitating the spread
of communism in the world. The answer to communism was
democracy in action. But the inability of the West to discern

[43] Nehru's note to foreign secretary, 31 August 1952, Nehru papers; Nehru to
Radhakrishnan, 31 August 1952.

[44] Text of speech as released by All India Radio, 5 September 1952, *The Hindu*,
6 September 1952.

[45] Nehru to Radhakrishnan, 1 September 1952.

[46] E.g. 'India in the World', *Indian Social Reformer* (Bombay), 5 September 1952;
'A Philosopher's Folly', *Thought* (a right-wing journal of Delhi), 6 September 1952.
It was even insinuated in *Harijan*, a journal started and edited by Gandhi, that
Radhakrishnan favoured birth control because he now accepted, under com-
munist influence, that the end justified the means. See editorial of 20 December
1952.

[47] Interview in *New York Times*, 7 September 1952.

[48] Interview on Radio Zurich, *The Hindu*, 23 May 1952; speech at Calcutta,
2 September 1952, *The Hindu*, 3 September 1952.

that such a position was not pro-Soviet betrayed a short-sightedness which weakened the force of the non-aligned endeavours of Nehru and himself.

The prime minister, knowing that Radhakrishnan was persuasive in personal encounters, was keen that as vice-president he should travel almost as much abroad as in India. So he now suggested that he go to Egypt, where Farouk had just been displaced by an army coup, and combine a visit to some European capitals with the leadership of the Indian delegation at the general conference of UNESCO in Paris; 'With his broad outlook and his general understanding both of the position in India and the world situation, his visit should prove helpful.'[49] It was made clear that Radhakrishnan was travelling informally and on no specific 'peace' mission;[50] and the prime minister himself gave him no specific mandate and did not go beyond requesting him to explain India's positions on Korea and Kashmir whenever opportunity offered. But, given Nehru's confidence and esteem and Radhakrishnan's own standing in the world and particularly in the Soviet Union, it was generally thought that while Nehru minded the store at home, Radhakrishnan was being sent abroad as the best salesman of India's policies.

On this tour Radhakrishnan set the tone for his approach to statesmen in other countries during the next fifteen years, first as vice-president and then as president. In public speeches he stated his views and commitments in forthright terms. A world war was not inevitable and it was therefore essential not merely to talk about peace but to foster the necessary conditions for peace. Both the Western democracies and the communist states would have to remove their shortcomings; indeed, interaction might bring about mutual modifications and make the world a true home for humanity. In private interviews he gave advice, however unpalatable, which he expected to be received without resentment as coming not from a high Indian dignitary but from a philosopher and seeker of peace whose parish was the world. In Cairo, where General Neguib was seeking to govern amidst unsettled conditions, Radhakrishnan, while applauding the lack of violence in changing the regime and

[49] Nehru's note to foreign secretary, 12 August 1952, Nehru papers.
[50] *The Times* (London), 25 September 1952.

assuring the military rulers of India's goodwill, warned against the violence to which the dispossessed landlords and others might be driven, the ambitions of politicians and the corrupting influence of power: 'Remember one thing, General. Today you and your associates are men of integrity and restraint. But you are all-powerful. Power is intoxicating. If you see that it does not go to your heads, it will be to your country's and your own good. Otherwise both will suffer.'[51] These were bold words, of a kind which heads of autocratic governments are not accustomed to hear; but Neguib, far from showing displeasure, was visibly moved. That too had been Stalin's attitude; and whomever Radhakrishnan thus spoke to in the coming years, the reaction was to be the same.

At Rome the foreign office suspected Radhakrishnan, possibly on the basis of his Bombay speech, as being sympathetic to communism, and opposed suggestions of his being elected president of the coming general conference of UNESCO. But then he met the prime minister, De Gaspari, and the talk resulted in the prime minister issuing instructions to the Italian delegation to back Radhakrishnan's name.[52] In Bonn his meeting with President Heuss marked the beginning of a personal friendship which grew stronger with the years. Visiting West Berlin, Radhakrishnan received a secret message from President Pieck inviting him in his personal capacity to the eastern sector. Radhakrishnan went and Pieck pleaded for India's recognition of East Germany. On Radhakrishnan saying that this could only be considered when the division of Germany seemed permanent, Pieck spoke of their genuine desire for German unity. Radhakrishnan's response was that, as there seemed to be little chance of a four-power agreement, East and West Germany should improve bilateral relations or suggest a commission of neutral countries in which both sides had confidence.[53]

[51] Telegram of K. M. Panikkar, Indian ambassador in Cairo, to prime minister, 27 September 1952; K. M. Panikkar, An Autobiography (English translation, Madras 1977), pp. 247–8.

[52] Indian ambassador in Rome to foreign secretary (undated); G. Scarpa, member of the Italian delegation, to Radhakrishnan, 10 November 1952.

[53] Telegram of Indian ambassador in Bonn to prime minister, 8 October 1952; N. B. Menon, 'Relations with the GDR: Dr Radhakrishnan's Secret Visit' (Delhi, October 1981, unpublished paper).

The prime minister was very pleased with the results of this tour: 'He is a very fine ambassador of India.'[54] Nehru was therefore unwilling to let Radhakrishnan's name be put forward, as acceptable to both the blocs, for the succession to Trygve Lie as secretary-general of the United Nations. When both the United States and the Soviet Union persisted and sent word to Delhi that they would like Radhakrishnan to accept the office, Nehru left the decision to Radhakrishnan who, after a night's deliberation, turned it down. The prime minister's comment was that he was both glad and sorry.[55]

Radhakrishnan's warm references in the Rajya Sabha to Stalin on the latter's death in March 1953, and his call at the Soviet embassy, where the ambassador introduced him as 'the man who had patted Stalin on the back', kept alive in right-wing circles the suspicion that he was sympathetic to communism. But there was no reason to fail to see, especially after his outspoken utterances in the early months of 1953, that Radhakrishnan was, while friendly to the Russian people, firmly anti-communist. He urged the rapid introduction of economic and social reforms to meet the communist threat to the country, but advised his audiences, even if they disapproved of Soviet methods, not to regard the Soviet government and people as 'monsters of inequity or complete embodiments of sin'.[56] On their part, the Soviet government should abolish the Cominform as testimony of their desire for peaceful co-existence.[57]

This suggestion, coincidental with President Eisenhower's challenge to the Soviet Union to take practical steps towards peace and believed to have Nehru's support, though, in fact, Radhakrishnan had made it on his own, naturally gained

[54] Letter to chief ministers, 2 October 1952, J. Nehru, *Letters to Chief Ministers*, ed. G. Parthasarathi, vol. III, 1952–1954 (Delhi 1987), p. 118.

[55] *Times of India*, 15 November 1952; record of conversation of G. S. Bajpai, governor of Bombay, with Radhakrishnan, 24 November 1952; record of conversations of Nehru and Radhakrishnan, 11 and 12 March 1953; report of interview of C. Manshardt of the US embassy in Delhi with Radhakrishnan, 12 March 1953.

[56] Speeches at Bangalore, 1 January 1953, *The Hindu*, 3 January 1953, and at Hyderabad, 13 January 1953, *The Mail*, 13 January 1953.

[57] Speech at Delhi, 16 April 1953, S. Radhakrishnan, *Occasional Speeches and Writings 1952–1959* (Delhi 1960), p. 401.

world-wide attention.[58] It was regarded as the beginning of a fresh effort by India on the international scene, even seeming to fit into what Pakistan had for some time suspected, an attempt by Nehru and Radhakrishnan to create a third bloc with India as leader.[59] The United States government welcomed the proposal, Dulles repeating it the day after Radhakrishnan had suggested it and endorsing it on his visit to Delhi in May.[60]

That Radhakrishnan had suggested a step which was acceptable to Dulles created unwittingly the right atmosphere for a tour of the United States: 'We want to be loved.'[61] Nehru encouraged Radhakrishnan to undertake the journey, although this meant Radhakrishnan's absence from Delhi at the time of the visit of Dulles, leading to allegations that Radhakrishnan, Nehru's 'principal un-American adviser', had been deliberately sent away.[62] Radhakrishnan spent five weeks in the United States (with a week in Canada half-way through), travelling from coast to coast and speaking at a dozen universities. The theme of his addresses was the necessity of giving the world unity—which had been created by mechanical devices—an enduring base in a religion of the spirit. Such true religion, transcending narrow doctrine and stressing the irreplaceable worth of every individual, irrespective of circumstance and ideology, would also affirm world peace. If we crusaded for the divine in ourselves and not against the demon in others we were bound to see our twin brother in the heart of our enemy. The world, having been made one, required to be educated to a universal acceptance of spiritual values and a common conception of human purpose and destiny: 'What we want today is not the American way or the Russian way, but the human way.' With faith, forbearance and flexibility, the world could be made a better place. The United States, in particular, could obstruct the spread of communism more by showing by deeds its belief in democracy rather than by supporting privilege and reaction abroad and preparing for war.

In Washington Radhakrishnan explained India's policies to

[58] Despatch from Delhi, 17 April 1953, *New York Times*, 18 April 1953.
[59] Despatch from Delhi, 26 January, *Dawn* (Karachi), 29 January 1953.
[60] *Hindustan Times*, 23 May 1953.
[61] Paul Hoffman to Radhakrishnan at Delhi, 23 April 1953.
[62] *Blitz* (Bombay), 23 May 1953.

Dulles and the officials of the state department; but with Eisenhower he moved on to other issues and stressed that the United States should work more positively for peace. 'I wish', said Eisenhower, 'that I could talk with you every day'; but he added that there were 'extremists' in the country who had to be taken into account.[63] This was a reference to McCarthy, whose anti-communist campaign was at this time at its height. Radhakrishnan saw for himself enough evidence of its disastrous effects in the universities and he touched upon this problem in some of his speeches. At a private alumni luncheon in Oberlin, for example, he referred to the duty of universities to stand as sentinels and speak out with conviction and simplicity for the great ideals for which the United States stood. The heart of the country was sound and its conscience was clear; but this should manifest itself in daily activities.[64]

Yet Radhakrishnan could not restrict expression of his anxiety to private utterance. He had the previous year presided over the general conference of UNESCO and he was now officially informed that Alva Myrdal, at this time a senior official of the organization, had been harassed on a visit to the United States because of alleged links of a member of her family with the Communist party. With this incident in mind, Radhakrishnan, speaking at UNESCO in Paris on his way home, condemned publicly the pressures being applied by member states for conformity with their domestic policies. The most dangerous of the enemies of human rights were 'the deluded, unconscious enemies who suppress liberty in the belief that they are safeguarding it'.[65] If the press in the United States had not been happy with his references to the need to seek friendship with the communist countries and had played down his visit, his forthright speech in Paris was not cast in words likely to secure the sympathy of the broad mass of American opinion. Only a few sensitive individuals could sense that he was 'a great transition figure', with a highly developed spiritual sense and an equally developed social sense, showing the way to a

[63] Indian ambassador's record of Radhakrishnan's discussions with Eisenhower, 21 May 1953.

[64] 8 June 1953.

[65] *New York Herald Tribune* and *The Hindu*, 2 July 1953.

new age.[66] To many others, especially those outside the universities, he seemed out of tune with the real currents of the time and unappreciative of the interests of the United States. A broadcast by him on United Nations Day, analysing the appeal of communism to unprivileged peoples while expressing his own distaste for it and asking for understanding so as to give a chance to communist societies to democratize themselves,[67] was reported by the *New York Times* as anti-American sentiments voiced by 'an exemplar of Indian thought' and drew a sharp rejoinder from the paper.[68] Radhakrishnan was told that the United States did not intend to accept his advice, which appeared to imply passive submission to an evil system and endurance of centuries of tyranny and darkness while waiting for communism to turn democratic and restore freedom.

Such coolness towards Radhakrishnan's approach was symbolic of the general state of relations between India and the United States at this time. The American offer of military assistance to Pakistan had alienated Nehru: 'I don't want any Americans outside America and anywhere near my borders.'[69] George Allen, the American ambassador, hinted to Radhakrishnan that if emphasis were placed on the danger to India of arming Pakistan rather than, as Nehru was wont to do, on India's dislike of the cold war being brought to South Asia, then there would be greater understanding in Washington of India's position. But such understanding was too remote a possibility. Dulles, despite his visit to Delhi, had no comprehension of India's role and views, and told American officials on that occasion that the way to handle Indians was to 'make them come to you'. India's need for foreign assistance was so great that they could not do without the United States: 'Leave them alone for a while and the Indians will come crawling to us on their bellies.'[70] This insensitivity, and total ignorance of

[66] Nancy Wilson Ross, 'Talks with India's Vice-President', *Atlantic Monthly*, October 1953.

[67] Broadcast on United Nations Day, 24 October 1953, *Occasional Speeches and Writings 1952–1959*, pp. 1–5.

[68] Despatch from Delhi, 25 October 1953, *New York Times*, 26 October 1953, and editorial, 'An Answer to India', *New York Times*, 27 October 1953.

[69] Nehru's remark to Radhakrishnan, 6 March 1954.

[70] Recollections of Chester Bowles ten years later, 3 and 10 September 1963, Chester Bowles papers.

the area, were powerfully reinforced by an obsessive anti-communism.[71] It is unlikely that Allen even passed on to Washington Radhakrishnan's suggestion that the United States postpone by a year the grant to Pakistan of military assistance so as to give a chance for a settlement on Kashmir.[72]

The formation by treaty of the South East Asia Treaty Organization in September 1954 was a further blow to the acceptance of any community of interest between India and the United States. But Radhakrishnan was not easily defeated and he broke journey in Washington on his way to the general conference of UNESCO at Montevideo in November. Having learnt that the ivory gavel used in the Senate since 1789 had begun to come apart and that a search was being made for a piece of ivory large enough from which a similar gavel could be carved, Radhakrishnan took one of appropriate size with him as a gift from the Rajya Sabha and was invited to address the Senate on the occasion of its presentation. Radhakrishnan spoke of India's goodwill towards the United States, made no mention of current differences but courageously reiterated his own approach to the basic issue of relations between the United States and the Soviet Union: 'No society is static; no law is unchanging; and no constitution is permanent. Given time and patience, radical changes may happen both in human nature and in systems of society which reflect human nature.'[73] At least one member in the audience was impressed. John

[71] A conversation between Dulles and Walter Lippmann soon after the establishment of the South East Asia Treaty Organization in September 1954 is worth noting:

'Foster', he asked, 'what do you think you are going to accomplish with that thing? You've got mostly Europeans, plus Pakistan, which is nowhere near South East Asia.'

'Look, Walter ... I've got to get some real fighting men into the south of Asia. The only Asians who can really fight are the Pakistanis. That's why we need them in the alliance. We could never get along without the Gurkhas ...'

'But, Foster, the Gurkhas aren't Pakistanis, they're Indians.'

'Well, they may not be Pakistanis, but they're Moslems.'

'No, I'm afraid they're not Moslems, either, they're Hindus.'

'No matter', Dulles replied, and proceeded to lecture for half an hour on how SEATO would stem communism in Asia.

R. Steel, *Walter Lippmann and the American Century* (New York 1980), p. 504.
[72] Escott Reid, *Envoy to Nehru*, pp. 123, 124–5.
[73] *Congressional Record* (Senate), 17 November 1954.

19

Kennedy, listening as a young Congressman from the gallery, went home and made a note of this sentence; and he repeated it to Radhakrishnan in the White House nearly ten years later.[74]

Radhakrishnan also, while talking mostly in general terms to Eisenhower, Nixon and Dulles, suggested that the United States might use her influence with Portugal in securing the transfer of Goa to India. Nixon thought that something could be done, as Portugal was economically in a bad way and heavily dependent on the United States. In fact, nothing happened. Yet Dulles thought the visit of Radhakrishnan might be utilized to improve relations (which could not have been worse) with Nehru. So he advised Eisenhower to write a personal letter to Nehru, mentioning the instinctive fellowship between the Rajya Sabha and the Senate which Radhakrishnan's visit symbolized, and speaking of the common ground on which the two countries could work out mutual problems and minimize differences. Nehru replied in the same terms with a specific support of Radhakrishnan's views: 'He is not only our Vice-President but, if I may say so, one of our wise men who is greatly respected by all sections of the people here.'[75] Relations between the two countries had been helped to turn the corner.

With the governments of the other Western powers, Radhakrishnan was at this time on the best of terms. He was always a success with royalty. In Belgium King Bauduoin, his father King Leopold, and Elizabeth the Queen Mother, and in the Netherlands Queen Juliana, were among those interested in his philosophy of religion. In West Germany, on the initiative of President Heuss, he was elected to the exclusive order of Pour Le Merite. In Britain, of course, his contacts continued to be close. When the foreign secretary, Anthony Eden, visited Delhi in April 1955 and addressed the members of parliament, Radhakrishnan, in his presidential remarks, summed up in

[74] Radhakrishnan to J. McEwen, minister for trade, Australia, 29 November 1965.
[75] Note of Dulles to Eisenhower, 30 November 1954, Eisenhower to Nehru, 30 November 1954, and Nehru to Eisenhower, 13 December 1954, *Foreign Relations of the United States*, 1952–1954, vol. XI, pt 2 (Washington 1983), pp. 1786–7 and 1794–5.

three paragraphs the state of relations between the two countries. History is not what we remember but what we choose to
remember; and India remembered the positive aspects of
British rule and 'elected to forget' the rest. Re-entering the
stream of world history, India had preferred to remain in the
Commonwealth because it meant complete independence and
informal association, sharing of ideals though not of allegiance,
of purposes though not of loyalties, common decisions leading to
better understanding and not binding decisions restricting
independence.[76] This analysis in a single sentence has been
frequently quoted as the clearest and most precise statement of
the principles of the Commonwealth;[77] but at the time too this
short speech made a deep impression, not least on the main
speaker:

This time the task [of addressing the members of the Indian parlia-
ment] was made more formidable by a beautifully phrased introduction from India's Vice-President, Mr Radhakrishnan. Few Englishmen could match his eloquence. I certainly could not and felt rather
like a little boy stumbling across a ploughed field after a leveret has
shown its swift, light paces.[78]

This year Radhakrishnan's only visit abroad was to Nepal
as India's chief representative at the king's coronation. He had
been approached to participate, in his personal capacity, in the
celebrations at San Francisco of the tenth anniversary of the
United Nations. While Nehru thought that 'Dr Radhakrishnan's personality is likely to be a dominating figure at such a
function', he did not feel it appropriate that Radhakrishnan
should be involved in a political session concerning mostly
foreign ministers.[79] Rather, he thought Radhakrishnan's services could be better utilized at home in guiding a committee
which would make a factual and objective survey of the consequences of a nuclear war. Since 1953 Bertrand Russell had
been urging that India should undertake such a detailed investigation as a means of spreading sanity between 'the two

[76] 3 March 1955, *Occasional Speeches and Writings 1952–1959*, pp. 14–15.
[77] For example, the editorial 'Crisis in the Commonwealth', in the *Toronto
Evening Telegram*, 2 May 1960.
[78] Anthony Eden, *Full Circle* (London 1960), p. 222.
[79] Nehru's note to secretary-general, 13 April 1955, and Nehru to Radhakrishnan, 17 May 1955.

lunacies' who both believed in a military solution of international problems;[80] and though Nehru had been at first reluctant,[81] he had been talked round in London in February 1955 by Russell as well as by an all-party group in the House of Commons.[82] By compelling people to face the facts and appealing not to any lofty idealism but merely to self-preservation, India might be able to strengthen the forces for peace; certainly the chance should not be missed. Radhakrishnan was willing to help;[83] but Homi Bhabha, the leading nuclear scientist in India, reported, after consulting Blackett and Oliphant, that there was as yet insufficient data for an assessment of the effects of nuclear weapons;[84] and scientists in the United States preferred a commission set up by the United Nations.[85] So the Indian commission did not come into being.

This permitted Radhakrishnan to undertake, in the summer of 1956, on the eve of the Suez and Hungarian crises, a long journey, first to the Soviet Union and East Europe and then to East Africa. While contending in the West that the Soviet regime should be given a chance to improve, he had not faltered in condemning the 'religion of communism' for suppressing the human spirit: 'In communism there is little of the pursuit of truth, no passion for individual integrity and spiritual perfection, no faith in the inwardness of human life.'[86] But he hoped that with Khruschev there would be a change. Encouraged by the abolition of the Cominform, which he had suggested two years earlier, Radhakrishnan believed that Stalin's successors, responding to 'a sense of anticipatory uneasiness' in the Soviet Union, were attempting, within the limitations of circumstance, an improvement in the protection of individual rights and the provision of impartial justice.[87] So,

[80] B. Russell, 'India Can Save the World'.

[81] Nehru to B. G. Kher, high commissioner in London, 5 November 1953, Nehru papers.

[82] Hilary Marquand to Nehru, 11 February 1955, Nehru papers.

[83] Nehru to Radhakrishnan, 22 February 1955, and Radhakrishnan's reply, 23 February 1955.

[84] H. J. Bhabha to Nehru, 8 March 1955, Nehru papers.

[85] Letter of the Federation of American Scientists, 6 March 1955, *The Hindu*, 7 March 1955.

[86] *Recovery of Faith* (New York 1955), p. 68.

[87] Ibid., p. 61.

when Bulganin and Khruschev visited India in the winter of 1955, Radhakrishnan expressed the hope publicly in their presence that the people of the Soviet Union would be given opportunities 'to develop the graces of mind and the virtues of spirit without which life is not worth living'.[88] The same notes, of the need for peace in the world and for liberty at home, were struck in all his speeches and live broadcasts in the communist countries. As the world had become smaller, people everywhere had become inter-responsible and should develop larger minds and work for love and life and not hate and destruction. This was as true for the United States as for the Soviet Union: 'Love is vain if we do not treat other human beings as brothers; it is empty if we do not adopt an attitude of patience, sympathy and understanding when dealing with problems which seem to separate us. Love is bound to win.'[89] But more significant at this time were Radhakrishnan's references to internal conditions in the Soviet Union. He asserted that governments should respect the sacredness of the human personality, distinguish between the mechanics of living and the art of living, and promote the free mind and a democratic society: 'I dare say that liberties of the mind, which are as important for healthy human lives as comforts for the body, will follow.' Material progress unchecked by the higher values of mind and spirit would bring its own revenges, resulting in inner disquiet and impoverishment. Radhakrishnan even made bold to plead for true religion, which was rational and ethical, and to argue that any system which suppressed the individual conscience was un-Marxist.[90]

No one had ever before spoken out in such a way in Moscow and other communist capitals and cities; and Radhakrishnan's speeches elicited much comment in diplomatic circles. After his address at Charles University in Prague, the British ambassador described it to Radhakrishnan as 'an event in world history'; and dissident elements in Czechoslovakia rejoiced.[91] Charles

[88] Speech on the occasion of the visit of Bulganin and Khruschev to parliament, 21 November 1955, *Occasional Speeches and Writings 1952–1959*, p. 22.

[89] Radhakrishnan to President Eisenhower, 1 January 1956.

[90] For Radhakrishnan's speeches and broadcasts in the Soviet Union and Eastern Europe in 1956, see *Occasional Speeches and Writings 1952–1959*, pp. 25–44 and 195–203.

[91] Sir Robert Bruce Lockhart, *Giants Cast Long Shadows* (London 1960), pp. 169–70.

Bohlen, the American ambassador in Moscow, reported home that while Radhakrishnan was speaking at the Kremlin 'Khruschev and Bulganin had a hang-dog look but Molotov had a smile on his face.'[92] In fact, except in Bucharest, where Radhakrishnan had the feeling that some in the audience did not like his views, elsewhere the communist leaders took it well. No attempt was made to delete reports of parts of his speeches and what was said on one occasion in the American press to be censorship was explained to him by his Soviet hosts as being no more than a failure to follow Radhakrishnan's rapid extempore performance. Certainly it was not sought to prevent him from speaking direct to the public; and some of his sharpest utterances were in the broadcasts. It is, of course, possible, as the Indian ambassador believed, that the people of the Soviet Union had been so heavily indoctrinated that Radhakrishnan's arguments made no dent.[93] But the leaders themselves were not indifferent. Khruschev told Radhakrishnan that he had listened to him on the radio in Moscow and, asked what he thought of the broadcast, replied that it was 'quite good'—an unenthusiastic but not reproving comment. Radhakrishnan then stressed that the future of the world depended on a proper recognition of moral values and the worth of the individual and said that he hoped to see the Soviet Union transformed into a welfare state. To this Khruschev replied, 'come back in three years and you will see the change. We had first to look after our safety. Now having achieved it, we shall devote ourselves to the welfare of the people.'

It was not just that the atmosphere was less unfavourable than it had been for a long time for public expression of such sentiments, but also that only Radhakrishnan, with his philosophical standing, known friendliness for the Soviet people and reputation for fearless criticism of the inadequacies of American policies and for firm commitment to peace, could be true to himself and yet not cause offence. The audacity, for example, while speaking over Kiev Radio, to quote Bukharin by name— 'We might have a two-party system, but one of the parties would be in office and the other in prison'—could not be hoped

---

[92] C. Manshardt of the US embassy in Delhi, in conversation with Radhakrishnan, 6 August 1956.

[93] K. P. S. Menon, *The Flying Troika* (Bombay 1963), pp. 154–6.

to be emulated with impunity by others. But, far from resenting Radhakrishnan's speeches, the Soviet government arranged for him to be elected an honorary professor of Moscow University, a distinction which gave Radhakrishnan far more pleasure than any decoration. He was now emeritus professor at Calcutta and Oxford and honorary professor at Banaras and Moscow—an unprecedented expanse of academic recognition testifying to the wide acceptance of his scholarship.

## VI

Towards the end of 1956 Radhakrishnan set off on a trip to the east which would have taken him to Indonesia, Japan and China; but he had to terminate it midway because of a sudden deterioration in the health of his wife. Repeated childbirths and the early years of accumulating hardships had worn down her health; and she was handicapped too by poor eyesight which had not been improved by an operation in Oxford in 1937. An operation on the other eye in Delhi in 1953 was a little more successful; but even so, thereafter she hardly left her home in Madras. Her blood pressure was consistently high and in October 1956 she suffered a major heart attack. Radhakrishnan, then in Tokyo, flew back immediately and spent the next few weeks between Delhi and Madras. Assured by the doctor of her progress, he was in Delhi when informed early in the morning of 26 November that her heart had stopped suddenly. He came back for the cremation that afternoon and supervised the performance of elaborate rituals for the next fortnight—not that he believed in them but because that was what she would have wanted. To those present it was clear that he was devastated by grief, even at one time sobbing like a child. 'The end of a long chapter', was his remark as he returned from the funeral. Doubtless he lived through again in his mind the years when she had supported him and recollected his need for her love at later times even though he had not rejected self-indulgence elsewhere. The black misery that enveloped him on her death was no assumed posture.

Sivakamu had not been educated in the conventional sense. But she was proficient in Telugu and, while in Calcutta, engaged a tutor to teach her to read and write English. Percep-

tive, lively and courageous, she easily held her own with those
who could claim to have gone through school and college. Even
more, she was a woman of character, veined with fire. She who
had once sunk her existence in that of her husband, later, when
lacerated by his non-marital wanderings, pretended to be
independent of him and gain satisfaction in motherhood. She
was too proud to let the public know how much she had been
hurt, especially by his mistress from the forties, a hard, bitchy
woman of jarring and aggressive gracelessness who was determined to flaunt to the world her place in Radhakrishnan's life.
To Sivakamu her marriage seemed, if not broken, certainly
fractured; the human relationship was now a half-lie even if
she would not allow it to become merely a social habit. But
total devotion to him was still the bedrock of her existence,
weathering all his wounding actions; and the sudden fits of rage
which marked her last years were in fact explosions of posses-
siveness and expressions of unspoken pain. It has been asked
recently about three wives of great men whether, given a
second chance, they would have married the same husbands.[94]
In Sivakamu's case there is no doubt about the answer. Being
the wife of the greatest creative intellect of his generation in
India had not been easy; but she would not have had her lot
cast otherwise.

# VII

Of the very large number, from India and all other parts of
the world, who condoled with Radhakrishnan, the two who
sensed most the intensity of his sorrow were, curiously, his
friends in public life, Rajagopalachari and Nehru. 'The part-
ing', wrote Rajagopalachari, 'that overtakes loyal Hindu
couples at some age or other is a sorrow of its own kind not to
be matched by any other calamity.'[95] Nehru fussed, sent two
messages of sympathy, one warm and personal and the other on
behalf of the Government of India, and directed Vijayalakshmi
Pandit in London and Krishna Menon in New York also to
send messages. Deputizing for Radhakrishnan as chairman of a
seminar which was part of the Buddha Jayanti celebrations, of

[94] Edna Healey, *Wives of Fame* (London 1986).
[95] Rajagopalachari to Radhakrishnan, 26 November 1956.

whose organizing committee Radhakrishnan was president, Nehru gave the audience a glimpse of his view of Radhakrishnan. He, said Nehru, had been the right person to preside, 'not only because of his scholarship but because his own life is witness to many of the things that we talk about here'.[96] Then, to help Radhakrishnan to immerse himself in work, Nehru asked the Kashmir government to invite Radhakrishnan to inaugurate the newly-built Banihal tunnel linking Jammu with Srinagar. Radhakrishnan dejectedly picked up the threads of official life again. But soon his · attention, as that of most politically-minded persons in Delhi, was centred on the presidential elections due in the summer of 1957.

In January 1955 Rajendra Prasad, on his own initiative, had written to the prime minister that, though his term as president had still two years to run, he would like to retire as he had completed five years in office. As Nehru did not respond, a few months later he reiterated his proposal; and this time the prime minister told him that he should stay on till the end of his elected term.[97] Perhaps Nehru was concerned that relinquishment of office by the president in mid term would be endowed with political overtones; but the episode led him to take for granted that Prasad would not seek a second term in 1957. Certainly he did not conceal his expectation and desire that Radhakrishnan would succeed Prasad, whom he had found stuffy and slow-going, in Bagehot's phrase a 'consecrated obstruction'. But Azad favoured a further term for Prasad, if only to keep out Radhakrishnan. It was a sign of Radhakrishnan's political innocence that he believed that his secular attitude would prevail over all other factors with noncommunal Muslims in India. But Azad was motivated by more personal considerations. His long service to the Congress and resistance to the Muslim League earned him a place in the cabinet of free India; but he was a symbol and not an administrator and his preference for the education portfolio became a national disaster. If India has still a long way to go in achieving even the minimum standards and objectives in education,

[96] Speech at Buddha Jayanti seminar, Delhi, 29 November 1956, All India Radio tapes.
[97] R. Prasad to Nehru, 6 February 1955; Nehru to Pant, 24 June 1955. Nehru papers.

a considerable part of the responsibility lies with Azad who, with his henchmen, stifled substantial development for eleven years. Nehru, for wider political reasons, put up with this; but Radhakrishnan was less patient with Azad's lack of commitment and grip. Azad wrote complaining that Radhakrishnan's criticisms of official handling of problems of higher education were getting known, but Radhakrishnan held his ground.[98] He also expressed publicly his displeasure at the ministry of education not caring to be represented in the Rajya Sabha when questions concerning it came up, and reminded Azad that he should at least occasionally be present in the Rajya Sabha, obliging Azad to plead ill-health and even offer to resign.[99] To Radhakrishnan these were incidents which would be of no consequence to men of stature, but they obviously festered in Azad's memory and now influenced his stance.

Even towards the end of 1956, Azad spoke to Prasad without Nehru's knowledge and asked him if he would agree to continue as president if requested. Prasad replied that this was for Azad 'and other friends' to decide, and Azad said he would speak to Nehru.[100] This set off in December, at a time when the prime minister was away in Washington, a concerted chorus in the press that it had been practically decided to invite Prasad to continue in office and that he had agreed. The prime minister on his return expressed to the cabinet his distress at this campaign and asserted that he had given no thought to the matter of the presidentship.[101] Nehru's view soon became public but it could not smother discussion; and the rival claims of Prasad and Radhakrishnan were continuously debated by leading commentators and writers of editorials.

[98] Azad to Radhakrishnan, 31 July 1953, and Radhakrishnan's reply of the same date.

[99] Comment in the Rajya Sabha, 30 July 1952, *The Hindu*, 1 August 1952; Radhakrishnan to Azad, 15 September 1953, and Azad's reply, 16 September 1953; Azad to Radhakrishnan, 16 March 1955, and Radhakrishnan's reply of the same date. Nehru also was concerned at Azad's neglect of his duties in parliament: 'If the Education Ministry could have closer contacts with MP's it would help.' Note to ministry of education, 11 April 1956, Nehru papers.

[100] G. Darbar, *Portrait of a President* (Delhi 1974), p. 154; Durga Das, *India from Curzon to Nehru and After* (London 1969), pp. 333–4.

[101] Nehru's note to the cabinet, 29 December 1956, Nehru papers.

For Radhakrishnan it was contended that he had served with distinction as vice-president for five years, was highly respected in all parts of the world, and, belonging to no party, was more acceptable than Prasad outside the Congress. There was also strength in the argument that the second president of India should be from the non-Hindi belt and the selection of Radhakrishnan, who came from the south, would consolidate the forces of integration. But opposition to Radhakrishnan developed within the Congress, particularly when it became common knowledge that Prasad was disinclined to leave Rashtrapati Bhavan. It was brought up against Radhakrishnan that he had taken no active part in the nationalist movement, had not joined the Congress at any stage and did not wear khadi. Few Congressmen could appreciate, as did Nehru, that Radhakrishnan's work of scholarship was a contribution of higher quality to national self-respect than the activities of many politicians; and indeed the elements ranged against Nehru within the party gave vent to their feelings by campaigning against Radhakrishnan. As for the point about regional representation, the chief ministers of southern India hastened to point out that they would rather have Prasad than one from their own part of the country who happened to be born a Brahmin.[102]

On 23 March 1957 Nehru discussed with Prasad for the first time the matter of the presidentship and speaking, as he said, not as prime minister but an old colleague, urged the need for healthy convention. Prasad heard him out in silence and made no commitment.[103] A signature campaign was then started among members of parliament in support of Prasad. The decision lay with the Congress parliamentary board, which met frequently for this purpose, after the general elections, in the last week of March 1957. Of the six members, only Nehru and, surprisingly, Morarji Desai, who liked Radhakrishnan as a person, were for Prasad stepping down; and when Prasad asked Desai for advice, he was told that having offered to resign in 1955 he should not now hang on.[104] Jagjivan Ram was

[102] For the attitude, for example, of K. Kamaraj, chief minister of Tamil Nadu, see *The Mail* (Madras), 6 May 1957.

[103] Record of Radhakrishnan's conversations with Prasad and later with Nehru, 23 March 1957.

[104] Record of Desai's conversation with Radhakrishnan, 20 March 1957.

for Prasad but not assertive, while Pant and U. N. Dhebar, the president of the Congress, were willing to accept any decision. Much depended, therefore, on Azad; and Azad made sure of Pant, Dhebar and Ram by contending that if Prasad wished to continue they should not set him aside in favour of one who was virtually an outsider.[105] Nehru spoke out against the same persons continuing in places of high responsibility,[106] but finding himself in a minority of one (Desai being too ill to attend) at the meeting on 31 March of the parliamentary board, accepted defeat. 'What weight', as he ruefully commented when they reached the next item, 'do I carry with the Parliamentary Board?'[107]

It was also decided at that meeting to request Radhakrishnan to continue as vice-president for a second term; and Nehru wrote an apologetic personal letter:

You know my views on the subject. Many of my colleagues broadly agreed with them, but they felt that in the circumstances as now existing and taking into consideration various factors, it would be difficult and unwise to lay stress on the convention we would like to develop. And so, they felt that in the wider interests of the country, in the balance, they should agree to the President standing again for election. If a year or more ago we had been wise enough to lay down this convention, it would have been easy now. But personal equations have arisen now and have an important influence. Whatever we decide leads to difficulties. We have to choose the path of lesser difficulty and more cohesion.[108]

To Radhakrishnan this was a blow. He was tired of being minor royalty, with the added tedium of presiding over the Rajya Sabha, and was looking forward to winding up his career with five years as head of state. So, within an hour, he replied to Nehru declining to serve again as vice-president. While claiming not to question the wisdom of the decision to re-elect Prasad, he brushed aside Nehru's explanations: 'The pretexts of party pressures and importunities of friends admit

[105] For a detailed account of Azad's attitude, see I. Malhotra, 'Heads of State or Figureheads?', *Illustrated Weekly of India*, 10 June 1973.

[106] Speech at meeting of Congress parliamentary party, 29 March 1957, tape M-23/C (II), NMML.

[107] Shriman Narayan, *Memoirs* (Bombay 1971), pp. 211–12.

[108] Nehru to Radhakrishnan, 1 April 1957.

of no answer and carry no conviction.' As for himself, he would step down from the vice-presidentship and thereby help to set up the convention that posts of honour should not be held for more than one term. Removal of the unfortunate impression that men in high places do not voluntarily retire was in the larger interests of a young democracy: 'Please understand that if I were anxious for the higher office, I would continue as Vice-President, bide my time and take my chance. That I do not wish to do so should satisfy you and your colleagues that I am not keen on power or patronage.'[109]

This letter would seem to have slammed the door; but the parliamentary board was determined not to let Radhakrishnan go, if only because it would show up Prasad in such a poor light. Pant called on Radhakrishnan to plead that he should continue in the national interest, Nehru said that it would be 'ruinous' if he left and his departure would hurt the government both within the country and abroad, and Dhebar added his voice to the rest. Indira Gandhi wrote to say that her father was deeply distressed: 'I can't tell you how much today's news has upset me—it seems to be the worst possible thing that could happen to us just at this stage. You have been, if you will excuse the impertinence, the star exhibit of the Republic of India; Delhi without you is unimaginable.'[110]

Radhakrishnan was unshaken by these emotional assaults: 'The decision is not pleasant to me but at some stage or other one has to take one's stand on principles . . . This one term convention will have to start somewhere. Why not I start it?'[111] But the next morning his defences were weakened by Morarji Desai, who had been throughout Radhakrishnan's ally and who took another tack. His line was that Radhakrishnan would appear petty in seeming to have walked off in a huff because he had been denied the higher office; his duty was to stay and not leave Nehru surrounded wholly by sycophants.[112] This was followed up by Azad, posing as Radhakrishnan's supporter: 'Public opinion will be hostile to you if you leave. The Prime Minister came here from your place weeping. I am your friend.

[109] Radhakrishnan to Nehru, 1 April 1957.
[110] Indira Gandhi to Radhakrishnan, 2 April 1957.
[111] Radhakrishnan to Indira Gandhi, 2 April 1957.
[112] Record of Radhakrishnan's conversation with Desai, 3 April 1957.

You should not go now.'[113] Radhakrishnan could not see through such dissembling and <u>agreed to accept a second term, knowing that he himself had stated the arguments against it most vigorously and he now stood, in a sense, self-condemned.</u>

Why did Radhakrishnan go back on a clearly affirmed decision to retire? He rationalized it by the assertions that he should not seem to be petty-minded and he could not refuse help to Nehru who expressed his happiness and gratitude at the decision.[114] Perhaps there was, too, a subconscious desire for office; it could not have been pleasant to contemplate joining the long line of extinct volcanoes in Madras. To Rajagopalachari's snide congratulations on Radhakrishnan's re-election—'So you are at the old place again: we must go on doing whatever we can wherever we are—as you have often told people!'[115]—Radhakrishnan replied hinting that he would not stay for the whole term of five years. 'If I am satisfied that I am of some service in my present post', he wrote, 'I would not have hesitated to accept it for another term. I do not feel that I am doing anything very useful.'[116] He was more forthright to his old friend Doraiswami: 'I wished to avoid unpleasantness at the time, but after some time I may quietly fade out.'[117] In 1959 he offered to retire from the vice-presidentship, which seemed to him an office of no significance and utility, to show the people that offices of dignity should not be held for as long as possible. But nothing came of this and, in fact, he continued for the full term.

## VIII

<u>The common setback in the choice of the president in 1957 drew Nehru and Radhakrishnan even closer together.</u> The prime minister said he had never since 1947 been as depressed as he was now. Though the Congress had gained an overall majority in the general elections the forces of caste and communalism had become stronger; and, as Radhakrishnan

---

[113] Record of Radhakrishnan's conversation with Azad, 3 April 1957.
[114] Nehru to Radhakrishnan, 3 April 1957.
[115] C. Rajagopalachari to Radhakrishnan, 30 April 1957.
[116] Radhakrishnan to Rajagopalachari, 1 May 1957.
[117] To T. K. Doraiswami, 4 May 1957.

pointed out to Nehru, not one of his colleagues in the cabinet shared his views on these subjects. Knowing the prime minister's concern, Radhakrishnan, in his first speech after his re-election as vice-president, spoke of the demoralization in the country. The caste spirit, communal passions, personal ambitions and the craze for power had been prominent in the elections: 'We seem to be victims of too many small loyalties.' This needed hard thinking and self-examination as well as dynamic, vigorous, courageous, imaginative leadership. If that were not provided in the next five years, the position would be worse.[118]

Strong words, intended to strengthen Nehru's hands against his reactionary colleagues and a lethargic party; yet one provincial newspaper at least read in it criticism of, and even a conspiracy against, the prime minister.[119] Nehru, when his attention was drawn to this by Radhakrishnan, brushed it aside with the remark that he had liked the speech.[120] Indeed the two men were working at this time in close concert. Radhakrishnan regarded Nehru as the greatest single influence in the world for peace and all his own efforts were intended at a different level to support Nehru's policies. Internally too he was convinced that Nehru alone stood between the country and chaos: 'My only complaint is that you are not sufficiently strong to get your ideas through. You are so democratic in your spirit and so tender in your dealings with men that sometimes wrong things happen.' So he asked Nehru not to give up, as some suggested, the headship of the government; and Nehru in his reply, without, as was his way, touching on the point made by Radhakrishnan, said he had given up even his tentative ideas of withdrawing for a while and would hold on.[121] On his part, Nehru took an opportunity, later in the year, to pay a long tribute to

a person who has somehow or other the amazing ability to keep his feet on the ground and head in the clouds and join them together. This is a tremendous thing. Never to lose grip of reality, never to lose grip of the fundamentals of life that have made life great in the past in

[118] Speech in the Rajya Sabha, 13 May 1957.
[119] *Deccan Herald* (Bangalore), 18 May 1957.
[120] Radhakrishnan to Nehru, 24 May 1957, and Nehru's reply of the same date.
[121] Radhakrishnan to Nehru, 26 May 1957, and Nehru's reply of the same date.

our country and elsewhere. At the same time he is an ancient sage and
a very modern philosopher which is really a very remarkable achievement.

Radhakrishnan, perhaps more than any politician or anyone
else, could help in troubled and disturbing times:

and so, whenever he speaks, he speaks not only to the audience's
requirements but to a vast audience all over the country and sometimes beyond the country too; because his words are words of national
importance and also of international importance. Because they carry
with them something, that spirit of universality which affects everybody wherever he may be. Therefore whether he goes to China or the
United States of America, his words count for the people there, even
though they might be looking in different directions. His words and
wisdom bring them nearer to each other and join them.[122]

It was a perceptive assessment from a near and authoritative
quarter of Radhakrishnan's approach, efforts and impact.

Foremost in Nehru's mind when making this speech was
Radhakrishnan's trip the month before to China. Scheduled to
visit China in 1956, Radhakrishnan had had to cancel it because of the sudden deterioration in his wife's health. In May
1957, a week after Radhakrishnan's re-election as vice-
president, the prime minister suggested that the idea be taken
up again.[123] Radhakrishnan agreed to go, halting on the way in
all the states of Indochina, and also going on from China to
Mongolia for two days. On his arrival in Cambodia, the little
finger of his right hand was caught in the door of the car and
suffered a multiple fracture. Bleeding profusely, Radhakrishnan
drove through cheering crowds, and made light of the injury—
'I have today shed my blood for Cambodia!'—and personally
intervened with Prince Sihanouk to prevent the dismissal of the
officer responsible. In severe pain throughout the rest of the
tour, he who normally winced even at an injection carried on
smilingly and impressed all his audiences, even perhaps more
than by his words, with the calm of the philosopher.

In Hanoi Radhakrishnan, as was by now his set habit in

[122] Nehru's inaugural address at the All India Writers Conference, Baroda,
26 October 1957, All India Radio tapes.
[123] Nehru's note to secretary-general and foreign secretary, 22 May 1957,
Nehru papers.

communist countries, laid stress on individual freedom and the advantages of a democratic system. As for the unification of Vietnam, it should be accomplished fairly; nothing was settled unless it was settled right. Ho Chi Minh treated him with great personal deference, set aside protocol to receive him at the airport and said, in response to Radhakrishnan's advice not to alienate the people of South Vietnam, that he was prepared to retire and efface himself if that would facilitate a solution of the Vietnam problem. In contrast, in South Vietnam, on the way back from China, the reception was correct but muffled; and Radhakrishnan's warnings against the spread of personal corruption and excessive reliance on foreign assistance were received in silence.

The visit to China itself Radhakrishnan could not have timed better. After Mao's famous speech on contradictions, accepting, among other things, that people's minds could not be coerced, there had been a surge of complaint and criticism; and the reaction against 'monsters and serpents' had set in. The Chinese authorities could have had no doubts as to the line Radhakrishnan would adopt. Apart from his addresses in the Soviet Union and North Vietnam, he had, in a foreword to a sympathetic account of the communist regime in China, hoped that free elections would be introduced;[124] and in welcoming Madam Soong Ching Ling to Delhi he had suggested that China had become a powerful nation because of the qualities of restraint, humaneness and brotherly co-operation.[125] The implication was clear. But the prospect of unpalatable advice did not deter his Chinese hosts from extending to Radhakrishnan courtesies which were more than normal. Mao himself returned to Beijing after an absence of some months (which had given rise to many rumours) to be able to meet Radhakrishnan, the rest of the leadership listened to all his speeches in the capital and, because of the injury to his finger, a senior surgeon and a nurse were deputed to accompany him on his tour to other parts of the country.

Radhakrishnan responded with a transparent goodwill and friendliness which conveyed themselves to his audience; and he also warmly congratulated the Chinese government on their

[124] Foreword to Peter Townsend, *China Phoenix* (London 1955).
[125] 17 December 1955, *Occasional Speeches and Writings 1952–1959*, pp. 22–5.

achievements and deplored the absence of People's China from
the United Nations. All this was greatly appreciated; but then
came Radhakrishnan's refusal to compromise on principles.
At Beijing airport he asked the Chinese, on the lines of his
speech in Delhi, not to forget the lessons of moderation and
humanism which had come down to them for over four
thousand years and to seek assent by the practice of virtue and
righteousness. At Mao's banquet, pointing out that the history
of the Chinese people had been marked by freedom from
dogmatism, he turned to Mao and, acclaiming him for looking
on Marxism not as a rigid creed but as a dynamic faith, said
he had no doubt that 'under your leadership socialism will
become democratic and humanistic'. To the National People's
Congress he gave an elaborate analysis of democracy as a faith
and a vision, as a political arrangement, as a social and economic
technique and as an international approach. A rally in Beijing
was reminded that the greatness of nations, as of individuals,
consisted not in physical strength or material wealth but in the
possession of humanity and gentleness. In a broadcast he
described spontaneous conformity and not enforced obedience
as the binding principle of a democratic society in which both
China and India believed; and, as he had done in the Soviet
Union, here too he was not afraid of speaking of man's need
for a creative religion.

In his private talks with Mao, no immediate problems were
raised; but there were some remarks of significance. Mao, when
discussing prospects in the two countries of reducing expenditure on defence, said that for them it was not just the questions
of Taiwan and Indochina; 'we have to watch Japan too.'
China was not worried much about Korea or Vietnam, but
she was definitely concerned about the possibility of Japan
building up her military might with the backing of the United
States. China felt about Japan as the Soviet Union felt about
West Germany. When Radhakrishnan said that if India and
China stood together it would be a lesson to the rest of the
world, Mao's reply, even then, in September 1957, was
guarded and conditional: 'If India and China stood together
for a score of years, no one will ever be able to pull us apart,
but I am aware that there are some forces which are constantly trying to separate us.' During the general discussion

Radhakrishnan asked Mao if he believed in coexistence. Mao replied that he did. Then Radhakrishnan asked if coexistence meant only with those with whom one agreed or also with those with whom one disagreed; coexistence meant converting in a friendly way the one who disagreed and not suppressing him. Mao had no adequate reply.[126] Then, while saying goodbye to Mao, Radhakrishnan patted him on the cheek. Mao appreciated the gesture; but the others round him were visibly taken aback. Noticing this, Radhakrishnan remarked, 'don't worry; I have done the same to Stalin—and to the Pope.'[127]

How much effect, if any, did Radhakrishnan's speeches and observations have? Hsinhua, the Chinese news agency, tended to report only those passages which suited the Chinese authorities. *China Today* later printed the speeches more fully;[128] but this journal is intended primarily for circulation abroad. The only direct reaction was that of Mao, who, at Radhakrishnan's banquet for him, remarked privately that it was necessary for the people to be allowed 'to let off steam' by criticizing the bureaucracy and drew Radhakrishnan's attention to the large wall-newspapers in universities, offices and factories. The other Chinese leaders said nothing at all and Chinese policy showed no sign of any impact of Radhakrishnan's visit. But both Radhakrishnan and Nehru thought that the attempt to speak to the Chinese of the qualities of human conscience and compassion had been worthwhile.

Nehru also wanted Radhakrishnan to visit the United States again;[129] and this Radhakrishnan did in the spring of 1958. In Washington he met Eisenhower and Dulles. The briefing note provided to the president by the department of state is a revealing and sad commentary on the department's knowledge of the outside world: 'Dignified and reserved in manner, Dr Radhakrishnan is a brilliant and epigrammatic conversationalist and an accomplished public speaker and linguist. He speaks English, French, Hindustani, Tamil and Bengali.'[130] Of

---

[126] Record of Radhakrishnan's conversations with Mao, 18 September 1957; Nehru's note, 2 October 1957, Nehru papers.

[127] K. Natwar Singh, who was present, to the author.

[128] No. 18 of 1957.

[129] Nehru's note to foreign secretary, 18 July 1957, Nehru papers.

[130] Note for the president, 25 February 1958, department of state papers.

these languages Radhakrishnan spoke only English and Tamil;
the only other language which he spoke was his mother-tongue,
Telugu, and that is not mentioned in this list. The stress laid
by Eisenhower and Dulles, as well as by the senators and congressmen whom Radhakrishnan met, was on the need for
better relations between India and Pakistan. Radhakrishnan
agreed that it was essential for the two countries to live in
friendship and develop common policies even in defence; but,
thanks to American military assistance to Pakistan, India had
had to increase her own expenditure on defence. The passing
reference to the desirability of a common policy on defence led
to a newspaper report that Radhakrishnan had said that if
Pakistan were attacked by the Soviet Union, India would help
Pakistan. The Soviet embassy obtained a disclaimer of this
from the prime minister.[131]

Radhakrishnan's main concern, in his talks with officials
as well as in his public addresses, was to strengthen the prospects of peace by seeking understanding and drawing the attention of people in the United States to the better side of the
Soviet Union. The crisis which faced the world was a moral
and spiritual one, caused by narrow exclusiveness: 'A bad
citizen is all right because he belongs to our state; a good alien
cannot be all right because he doesn't.' But he who despised the
faiths of other peoples in fact despised his own. If, in spite of
great material abundance and intellectual power, peace was still
in peril, it was due to a persistent cussedness in human nature,
a moral blindness, a spiritual affliction. As he put it more
sharply on a visit to Sri Lanka a few weeks earlier, the tiger and
the ape in man are easily tamed, but not so the donkey in him.
What was needed was the inner development of the person as a
spiritually, morally and socially creative being. We must see
the human family as one and look upon even our enemies as
people like ourselves: 'The spirit of God transcends man-made
curtains.' At Salt Lake City, asked to speak after the singing of
the negro spiritual, 'Were you there when they crucified our
Lord?', Radhakrishnan, taking that as the text, gave the
answer in the affirmative, for the Lord was being crucified
every day on the cross of power, domination, national idolatry

[131] Nehru's note on conversation with Soviet chargé d'affaires, 19 April 1958,
Nehru papers.

and racial arrogance. To convert the opponent, we must not always speak of his shortcomings but present to him his own higher and nobler side.[132]

## IX

His missions abroad, with their standing ovations, and the hope that his words might have some influence, formed only a part of the task. Within India there was a lack of a deep moral earnestness and a sense of integrity, leading to what was to Radhakrishnan a crisis of character.[133] But his exhortations appeared to make no impact on either the government or the people. Nehru was a close friend, and nothing could weaken Radhakrishnan's affection, even devotion. But the prime minister seemed unable or unwilling to act on his intentions to better society or even to tone up the administration:

You are so good and kind and people take advantage of your great qualities. I have no doubt that you will impress on the A.I.C.C. the need for extreme vigilance. When you speak about the socialist pattern of society they say 'yes' to you and go their own way. Policy statements made by some of our ministers do not seem to support our ideals.[134]

Nehru replied that he would bear in mind what Radhakrishnan had written.[135] In support of Nehru, Radhakrishnan continued to speak out in strong terms for personal rectitude in public life and against dishonesty and corruption: 'My words were uttered not out of anger but out of sorrow, out of anguish of the heart. It was a call for self-examination and improvement in our general behaviour.'[136] But his audiences in India seemed content to admire his oratory and forget the substance of his speeches, while critics abroad picked up stray sentences to

[132] Interview in *Ceylon Daily News*, 4 February 1958; speech at Harvard University, 25 March 1958, *Christian Science Monitor*, 26 March 1958; Gabriel Silver Lecture, Columbia University, 8 April 1958, *Occasional Speeches and Writings 1952–1959*, pp. 76–88.

[133] Speech at Bombay, 15 June 1957, *Occasional Speeches and Writings 1952–1959*, pp. 368–71.

[134] Radhakrishnan to Nehru, 22 October 1958.

[135] Nehru to Radhakrishnan, 22 October 1958.

[136] Radhakrishnan to Nehru, 7 December 1958.

belabour India.[137] The 'turbaned, lean and saintly' vice-president was heard with respect but his advice not taken.[138] 'The longer I was in office I felt that the less I counted.'[139]

So Radhakrishnan set off, probably not too unwillingly, on his travels again, this time to Paris for the opening of the new buildings of UNESCO and to West Germany as the guest of President Heuss. In Paris he spoke with his usual eloquence of the need for a commonwealth of intellect and spirit to subdue the innate malignity in human minds and of UNESCO's responsibility in this matter: 'Vous avez fait entrer la vie dans cette série de discours inauguratifs et vous l'avez fait de la manière la plus valable comme la plus fondamentale. J'ai été (égoïstement) très fier de l'Inde.'[140] But it was in his major philosophical address at Bonn University that Radhakrishnan was seen at his very best. After touching on the contribution of German scholarship to Indian studies and his own indebtedness to German idealism, Radhakrishnan rapidly surveyed current developments in European philosophy to prove his own argument that metaphysical ideas are founded on a basic awareness which cannot be established by scientific measurement or rational logic. But experience was not limited to sense experience nor had verification to be direct. The cosmic process was ordered and progressive; a spiritual presence greater than man was posited by science and the end of man was to place himself in harmony with this presence. Truth exists by its own majesty and its language is silence; but hard metaphysical thinking gives to religious thought dignity and strength, articulates ultimate presuppositions about the world and restores spiritual wholeness to men and women:[141]

The clarity and the conviction with which the Vice-President presented his thesis to the audience held everyone spellbound. The stream of perfectly formed sentences and the rapidity with which they were rained on the listeners had an almost hypnotic effect. A tension was created which was only broken when the speaker had finished ex-

[137] E.g. *Morning News* (Karachi), 2 December 1958.
[138] Cyril Dunn, 'Indian Notebook', *The Observer* (London), 2 November 1958.
[139] Jotting of Radhakrishnan, written sometime in 1958.
[140] 'Le Corbusier' to Radhakrishnan, 4 November 1958.
[141] 'The Metaphysical Quest', 17 November 1958, *Occasional Speeches and Writings 1952–1959*, pp. 385–99.

pounding his theme. No one who heard it is likely to forget it in a hurry.[142]

The German response was echoed the next day at Mainz, when the university conferred an honorary degree on 'a model of humanity and an outstanding scholar . . . a messenger of things divine and human . . .' Radhakrishnan was always a welcome visitor in Germany. He returned in 1959 for the conference of the International PEN (of which he was one of the vice-presidents) and received the Goethe plaquette from the city of Frankfurt. Two years later he came back to receive the Peace Prize of the World Book Fair.

There were invitations also from other countries where, whatever the state of official relations with India, Radhakrishnan was an acceptable personality. Yigal Allon, an old student of Radhakrishnan at Oxford, was keen that he should visit Israel; and Radhakrishnan did not dismiss the idea out of hand.[143] But an invitation to the golden jubilee celebrations of the University of Natal was courteously declined. The Government of India were in two minds as to whether Radhakrishnan should attend. While officials in the ministry of external affairs and one or two members of the cabinet thought that Radhakrishnan should not go, some others thought that a visit by Radhakrishnan to South Africa would produce a powerful impression and by increasing India's prestige indirectly help the Indian cause. But as the invitation was to Radhakrishnan in his personal capacity and not as vice-president and the Indian community felt strongly that he should not accept, Radhakrishnan turned down the invitation.[144]

He did, however, undertake the long journey to Hawaii to attend an East–West Philosophers' Conference and such was the impact of his scholarship, social vision and universal outlook that a businessman of Chinese origin, who was in the

[142] B. F. H. B. Tyabji, Indian ambassador in West Germany, to foreign secretary, 24 November 1958.

[143] Y. Allon to Radhakrishnan, 25 June 1959, and Radhakrishnan's reply, 31 July 1959.

[144] Vice-chancellor of Natal University to Radhakrishnan, 10 March 1959; Nehru to Radhakrishnan, 25 March 1959; president of South African Indian Congress to Radhakrishnan, 6 May 1959; statement of Radhakrishnan, 21 October 1959, *The Times* (London), 22 October 1959.

audience, volunteered to provide the funds for the next session of the conference.[145] The same recognition of his pre-eminence in the world as a scholar of comparative philosophy and religion took him the next year to Harvard for the dedication of the new Center for the Study of World Religions. In the course of an hour Radhakrishnan outlined the common responses to the one reality in all religions and stressed the imperative of developing ecumenical persons in a world which had become a neighbourhood. If the spiritual dimension of life were recovered, it would reveal that all men and women were one in fellowship.[146]

Within India there was the established routine—working steadily on the translating and editing of the Brahma Sutra, presiding over the Rajya Sabha, speeches in various parts of the country calling for higher levels of thought and conduct, channelling information to the prime minister. The looming crisis in the summer of 1959 was the agitation against the communist government in the state of Kerala. At the very last minute the ministry sought to avert dismissal by offering to hold elections the next year; Radhakrishnan conveyed this message to Nehru but by then it was too late.[147] His own regular talks with the prime minister, even if they had little bearing on day-to-day decisions or even on long-term policy, were a relief to him from the frustration and intellectual drabness around, as they perhaps were too for the prime minister: 'Now I'm just back from half an hour with Pandit Nehru—how tired and sad he seems! It is tragic: but what a good thing you are there to cheer him up and stimulate him.'[148]

On the developing problem with China he stood squarely behind the prime minister and when Zhou en-lai, in an effort to suggest that Radhakrishnan was less determined than Nehru, invited him in 1959—within two days of an incident when several Indian soldiers were killed—to visit Beijing, Radhakrishnan politely declined. The next year, when Zhou visited Delhi, Radhakrishnan outlined India's position with knowledge

[145] Professor C. A. Moore of the University of Hawaii to Radhakrishnan, 17 August 1959.

[146] *Fellowship of the Spirit* (Harvard University Press 1961).

[147] Radhakrishnan from Madras to Nehru, 28 July 1959, reporting his talk with the minister for law in Kerala.

[148] Sir Julian Huxley to Radhakrishnan, 20 February 1959.

and courteous clarity. But if on China prime minister and vice-president saw eye to eye, on Goa Radhakrishnan made no secret of his dislike of military action. He tugged the British high commissioner by the sleeve at a test match: 'Can't you do something about this nonsense?'[149] In fact the Western powers did nothing to forestall Indian action; but even so Radhakrishnan was candid to Nehru. The action, he told the prime minister, was a mistake which distressed him; and Nehru confessed that he thought and felt the same.

In the flow of foreign visitors to Radhakrishnan's residence there was no ebb. Mortimer Wheeler found him merry and reminiscent of Russell,[150] while Sybil Thorndike put him in the company of Gandhi, Schweitzer and Gilbert Murray, men whose personalities seem stronger and more vivid because unhampered by self—'almost a transparency they convey, these enlightened ones'.[151] The climax was the arrival of President Eisenhower in December 1959. Friendly and well-intentioned, yet it would seem that Eisenhower, while admiring Radhakrishnan's eloquence,[152] grasped very little of what was discussed. 'He said he does not think that all of the Indians are as peaceful as some of the governmental leaders. Some of these, such as Radhakrishnan and Rao,[153] are such high-caste Hindus, with such a professed love of peace, as to consider themselves already part of the Divinity.'[154]

A more rewarding encounter was with John D. Rockefeller IIIrd. With him Radhakrishnan raised the possibility of an institution in Delhi similar to the International House in Tokyo, where men and women of scholarship and interest in culture, from both India and abroad, could meet in pleasant surroundings. Rockefeller showed much interest and Radhakrishnan set up a committee to plan the details at the Indian

[149] Lord Gore-Booth, *With Great Truth and Respect* (London 1974), p. 283.

[150] J. Hawkes, *Mortimer Wheeler* (London 1982), p. 330.

[151] Sybil Thorndike in *Gilbert Murray: An Unfinished Autobiography* (London 1960), pp. 157–8.

[152] D. D. Eisenhower, *Waging Peace* (London 1961), p. 501; M. C. Chagla, *Roses in December* (Bombay 1973), p. 266.

[153] V. K. R. V. Rao, at this time vice-chancellor of Delhi University.

[154] Memorandum of Eisenhower's conference at Washington with representatives of Congress, 3 February 1960, Eisenhower papers, Dwight D. Eisenhower Library, Abilene, Kansas state.

end.[155] He also recruited the support of the prime minister who personally selected a site adjoining Lodi Gardens and directed the government to donate it. The Rockefeller Foundation provided the greater part of the funds required for construction; the Crown Prince of Japan laid the foundation stone in November 1960; and Radhakrishnan opened the building in January 1962. The India International Centre, an architectural showpiece, is also now an integral part of the social and cultural landscape of Delhi.

## X

Nehru, caught on the wrong foot in the election for the presidentship in 1957, was now more wary and began, even two years ahead, to clear the way for Radhakrishnan's succession. In the summer of 1960, when Prasad went for two weeks on an official visit to the Soviet Union, the prime minister, citing the possible need for emergency measures in case of a general strike as the reason, had Radhakrishnan formally sworn in to discharge the duties of the president. But Prasad had clearly not given up hopes of a third term even after twelve years in office; and he was encouraged in this by conservative members of the Congress party. Relations between the president and the prime minister took a steep dive. Prasad, aware and resentful of Nehru's hints to the British government that the queen should not for the time being invite the president on a state visit to Britain,[156] raised in public the question of the president's powers and wondered whether he was to be regarded as a constitutional figurehead. Nehru did not react openly to this; but he obtained the authority of the cabinet to inform the president that a third term was out of the question. Then, when a bill was introduced in the Rajya Sabha by a member of the opposition limiting the tenure of the presidentship to two terms, Nehru secured its withdrawal by stating that such a limitation was best achieved by a 'clear and strict' convention.[157]

Even before this, Prasad, accepting what—with Azad and

[155] John D. Rockefeller IIIrd to Radhakrishnan, 28 February 1958.

[156] Nehru to Vijayalakshmi, high commissioner in London, 26 March and 27 June 1959, Nehru papers.

[157] Rajya Sabha proceedings, 18 August 1961.

Pant no longer on the scene—seemed inevitable, had announced that his desire to retire from office had been generally
known for some time.[158] But it was thought that, even if he had
to go, he would have preferred someone other than Radhakrishnan to succeed him. This too he could not prevent, if only
because his own health deteriorated rapidly from the summer
of 1961, and Radhakrishnan virtually officiated as president
twelve months before he was formally elected.

Deputizing for the president meant that Radhakrishnan had
less time for presiding over the Rajya Sabha. He had never
really enjoyed this but, over the years, in a small house where
he came to know personally all the members, his detached
benignity and natural assumption of the role of a teacher were
appreciated on all sides. No presiding officer relied less on the
rules of procedure and debate; and when tempers rose the
chairman restored order with a smile: 'that's enough, Mr A,
now sit down.' Always the member accepted the reprimand
with surprising meekness.[159] Bhupesh Gupta, the leader in later
years of the Communist party in the house and, that being the
largest party after the Congress, the leader of the opposition,
had in fact been Radhakrishnan's pupil at Calcutta. Sharp-
tongued and well-stocked with facts, Gupta was a formidable
parliamentarian; yet he accepted with good humour Radhakrishnan's admonitions as if still in a classroom and, as Radhakrishnan described it, was co-operative 'though co-operative
with an effort'. The triangular exchanges between Radhakrishnan, Nehru and Gupta often enlivened, with their wit
and good nature, otherwise dreary proceedings. Gupta now
asked the Congress party to choose as the next vice-president
someone cast on the same lines as Radhakrishnan, with

that tolerance which has been shown here, that wisdom, that knowledge, that high humour and that great intelligence we have been ex-
periencing . . . In our view the Vice-President should be a non-party
man, a neutral man, who has no touch with the party, who is held in
high esteem by all sections in the country, who is above party considerations, who evokes a certain measure of confidence and brings
dignity and lustre to this great office . . . Now, we project ourselves to

[158] Communiqué from Rashtrapati Bhavan, 18 June 1961.
[159] B. Shiva Rao, 'Radhakrishnan as President', in K. I. Dutt (ed.), *Sarvepalli
Radhakrishnan* (Delhi 1966), pp. 72–3.

the world at large in some ways through the Vice-President. Therefore, it is important in seeing that the personality is of such a stature that he brings credit and dignity to the country. As it is, he is doing it today . . . We know this House has its own dignity. But then for the creation of that prestige and dignity the present Vice-President has played an important role.[160]

[160] Rajya Sabha proceedings, 12 December 1961.

# 12

# PRESIDENT

In May 1962 Radhakrishnan was elected president by an overwhelming majority. He was the official Congress candidate; the other major political parties decided not to oppose him and most of them directed their members to vote for him. Two individuals, eager for publicity rather than hopeful of success, ensured that it was not a unanimous election; and there was stray resentment in the ranks of the Congress at what was felt to be Nehru's acceptance of a cuckoo in their nest. But on the whole Radhakrishnan came as near as was possible to election by national consensus. Nearly thirty years earlier, at a farewell function in Madras in 1936 on the eve of Radhakrishnan's departure for Oxford, Richard Littlehailes, the vice-chancellor of Madras University, indulging in what then seemed an absurd flight of the imagination, had suggested that Radhakrishnan might attain such high office. Radhakrishnan, he said, 'had raised himself step by step. When would he reach the summit of the Mount Everest of his career? Would he aspire to higher things in this life and emulate such a man as Woodrow Wilson who was at one time a professor, and ended up as President of the United States of America?' Littlehailes said he would look forward to Radhakrishnan 'taking a similar place somewhere'.[1] That prophecy had now unbelievably become reality.

As president, Radhakrishnan appeared almost too good to be true. Patrician and patriarchal, endowed with a noble face and trim figure, he dressed with dignity, carried himself with distinction, and performed the ceremonial duties of his office with the proper measure of gravitas. But he was always more than an ornamental figurehead. An important figure in his

[1] 31 March 1936, *The Hindu*, 1 April 1936.

own right, with a world-wide reputation as a philosopher, he was well-liked in all countries. 'It might', wrote *The Times*, 'almost have been thought a reflection on India had a man of Dr Radhakrishnan's attainments not ended his years in public life with a period of service as India's President.'[2] Men as far apart as Allon of Israel and Albert Schweitzer from Lamberene joined the routine chorus of congratulations; and Rudolf Bojanovsky of Munich composed a Eurasian Cantata in his honour. In India he was acceptable to all sections of public opinion and on cordial terms of easy understanding with the prime minister. Radhakrishnan was not, therefore, obsessed, as his predecessor, Prasad, had been, with the powers and prerogatives of the president as laid down by the constitution and which, as Rajagopalachari reminded him, in practice added up to nothing.[3] For ten years as vice-president he had spoken out freely on major issues without getting involved in the daily political fray; and he intended to continue to do this but with even higher authority. Without violating the constitution and keeping well above party politics, he opened out new horizons for the presidentship. The prime minister was concerned with government; it was for the president to draw attention to values. Contemplative and disinterested, he set before the people a vision of humanity and civilization as well as the possible ways towards its achievement. It was the president's duty to interpret the world, as it was the prime minister's task to change it. Nehru was among the few who recognized and appreciated this casting of roles. Apart from their regular meetings on Monday mornings, president and prime minister kept in continuous touch. Nehru approved of Radhakrishnan's forthrightness in public speech and, in private, sought his advice on matters important as well as minor. Also, Radhakrishnan had only to mention a matter for Nehru to send him all the papers on the subject. For the first time the office of president became more than marginal; nor has it ever again attained such healthy significance.

Radhakrishnan's tenure began under cloudless skies. The British Academy, of which he had been a Fellow since 1939, now elected him an Honorary Fellow, and the Government of

[2] 'A Philosopher for President', leader in *The Times*, 16 April 1962.
[3] *Swarajya*, 19 May 1962.

India, on the request of the National Federation of Teachers, declared that his birthday, 5 September, would be celebrated every year as Teacher's Day. Radhakrishnan himself dutifully sent his draft speech to be made after taking the oath of office to the prime minister for approval, who returned it—'As usual, it is excellent'—with a very minor addition.[4] But it soon became clear that there was now a positive personality in Rashtrapati Bhavan. When the first case came to him for the exercise of the prerogative of mercy, Radhakrishnan proposed the abolition of capital punishment. Nehru's own inclination was also in favour, retaining the death sentence only for cases of treason or brutal murders of children, and he asked the home minister to consult the state governments:[5] 'Whatever we may do, I feel sure that we must limit capital punishment very severely to special cases which are peculiarly bad.'[6] Radhakrishnan and Nehru were unable to have their way, but throughout his five years in office Radhakrishnan rarely rejected a petition for mercy.

His next step, which appealed to the community of scholars to which he belonged, was to transfer the vast pile of buildings which had been constructed by the British as the viceroy's residence in Simla and had hardly been used since Mountbatten's departure, to the ministry of education to house an Institute of Advanced Study, which Radhakrishnan fondly hoped would develop on the lines of Princeton or All Souls. He also initiated the process of throwing open the gates of the president's palace in Delhi twice a week to whosoever might wish to present petitions or voice grievances; and these plaints were promptly passed on to the authorities concerned with a request for report on action taken. For Radhakrishnan, who as vice-president had been thought to be the most accessible person in Delhi, this was a natural step to take. Some wondered how the prime minister would view this encouragement of direct contact between the president and the public; but Nehru's reaction was good-humoured. He knew that this

[4] Radhakrishnan to Nehru, 7 May 1962, and Nehru's reply of the same date.
[5] Radhakrishnan to Nehru, 21 May 1962, Nehru to Radhakrishnan, 22 May 1962, Radhakrishnan to Nehru, 23 May 1962, and Nehru to Radhakrishnan, 25 May 1962.
[6] Nehru to L. B. Shastri, 22 May 1962, Nehru papers.

gesture of goodwill had no political overtones. That anyone from any part of India and from any level of society could, if able to get to Delhi, approach the president and seek redress or a grant from his discretionary fund was in itself—and Nehru knew this too—a support to democracy and unity.[7] But Radhakrishnan's successors have not continued this practice of public interviews.

Officially, in these early months, there was little to do. Radhakrishnan continued his practice of travelling round the country and speaking on general issues. He happened to be in Calcutta on 1 July, the day the chief minister, Bidhan Roy, died, and, finding the governor incapable of dealing with any serious problem, virtually took charge. He directed her to swear in the most senior member of the cabinet to function as chief minister and asked the latter to convene as soon as possible a meeting of the party in the legislature to choose the permanent leader. Thus was established the proper democratic procedure in case of a sudden vacancy in the headship of the government. In accordance with established practice he moved to Hyderabad for a few weeks in the summer in the cause of integration of the country and had the prime minister as his personal guest for two days. Nehru approved without change the text of Radhakrishnan's broadcast on the eve of Independence Day. It was in Radhakrishnan's normal vein, drawing explicitly on human and spiritual values. He wanted the people to strive to remove poverty and build a better society in the context of a new spiritual ethos: 'We have faith in the future of man.' His nature had changed so often and would change again. He was always becoming something different and often better. He had now to take a great leap forward in conscious-

---

[7] 'I am now a citizen of the Indian Republic. We have a President called Radhakrishnan. He read a huge lot of books, and wrote some too. When we chose him for President I think he was afraid that he knew more about books than people. So he thought of a plan. Every week, or perhaps oftener, he gives a public audience. And anyone who wants, including girls no older than you, can come and visit him. Some of them just want to see and hear him. But others want him to put a wrong right. Perhaps a policeman hit a woman's son, or a government officer dismissed a man who had worked hard. The President can't always put things right. But at least he knows what a lot of ordinary people think unfair; and he will try to get this altered.' J. B. S. Haldane to Marion Potten, 1 June 1962. Haldane sent a copy of this letter to Radhakrishnan.

ness. Individuals, nations and civilizations were a part of this
tremendous process of becoming sensitized, refined and
noble.[8]

The close bonds between Radhakrishnan and Nehru also
stretched to include Nehru's daughter. Since meeting her at
Oxford in 1937 Radhakrishnan had developed an affectionate
concern for Indira Gandhi, and she seemed to appreciate this
and respond as warmly. 'You have, of course', she wrote to him
on the occasion of his receiving the decoration of Bharat Ratna,
'been widely recognized as a true "ratna" of Bharat for many
years. But it is just as well to make it official. You have set a
high standard for other "ratnas" to follow—if they deserve the
title as truly as you do, India will always hold her head high.'[9]
Three years later, even though she was by now immersed in
Congress party politics, Radhakrishnan, to draw her out into
the wider world, nominated her a member of the court of
Delhi University. Her attendance was irregular but she agreed
twelve months later to re-nomination. Her father urged her to
do so; also 'it is difficult to say "no" to you.'[10] In the same
strain, thanking Radhakrishnan for a birthday gift the next
year, she added, 'actually I should thank you for so much more
but it is difficult to put into words and would perhaps be
impertinent too. I don't see much of you but just the thought
that you are there is a sense of comfort and pleasure.'[11] Then,
in 1960, after her term as president of the Congress was over,
Radhakrishnan selected her as India's candidate for membership of the executive board of UNESCO. Here again, after her
election, her attendance was erratic; so now Radhakrishnan
suggested that she take on a regular job in India. Her reply is
worth quoting at some length: 'The other day when I was with
you, you said something about my future. I was rather taken
aback—almost struck dumb—for a moment— . . . Your kindness and thoughtfulness is the only nice thing that has happened

[8] 'A Nobler Freedom', *President Radhakrishnan's Speeches and Writings 1962–1964*
(Delhi 1965), pp. 65–7. *The Christian Science Monitor* reprinted the broadcast in full
(26 September 1962) as a noble utterance in contrast to the speeches of communist leaders and the great majority of Independence Day addresses in the
United States, and as an indication of what India could contribute to world
society.

[9] Indira Gandhi to Radhakrishnan, 15 August 1954.

[10] Ibid., 28 June 1958.      [11] 20 November 1959.

to me in a long time.' But she wondered if she were suited to the plans Radhakrishnan had for her for she claimed to be completely devoid of personal ambition and to be uninterested in an official position: 'I have been close enough to the sources of power to be aware of the price that power must exact. In terms of human values, it is a price I cannot afford to pay.' All she wanted, she said, was to live quietly, write, have a few friends, earn enough to support her sons and build a small house and take part unobtrusively in activities connected with education and welfare: 'In the meantime, it is good to have you as Head of the State and to be able to unburden myself!'[12] Radhakrishnan had not expected this gush of response to a casual suggestion and replied in friendly but general terms: 'You have great qualities and I am at liberty to have my dreams of your future.'[13]

## II

All such matters, however, were swept aside by Chinese aggression on a large scale on both the western and the eastern sectors of India's northern boundary. Although the Chinese had come down the Thagla ridge in the east on 8 September, followed a few days later by an exchange of fire, the crisis had not yet developed to such an extent as to necessitate the cancellation of Nehru's visit to Sri Lanka early in October; and on his return the prime minister could give attention to such matters as the Bertrand Russell Peace Foundation and seek the president's advice as to whether he should agree to be a sponsor.[14] But then, on 20 October, Chinese armies began to move deep into both Ladakh and what was then the North East Frontier Agency. Radhakrishnan had no hesitancy about his role in this new situation. He would give full support to the prime minister and, with events shifting from day to day, his rapidly moving mind, which could reach and grasp intuitively what others followed very slowly if at all, could be an asset. That Radhakrishnan had no high opinion of Krishna Menon

[12] Indira Gandhi to Radhakrishnan, 17 August 1962.
[13] Radhakrishnan to Indira Gandhi, 17 August 1962.
[14] Nehru to Radhakrishnan, 16 October 1962, and Radhakrishnan's reply, 17 October 1962.

as defence minister was made evident when he directed Menon to bring the three chiefs of staff with him to explain the situation to the conference of governors then meeting in Delhi.[15] He also suggested to Nehru on the 23rd afternoon that Menon should be moved from the defence ministry. When the prime minister argued that Menon was the only person who knew anything about defence, Radhakrishnan replied that, whatever Menon's ability, the country had no confidence in him. Certainly Menon did his utmost to justify this lack of confidence. He told the press that there was no limit to the Chinese advance,[16] confused India's friends abroad by referring to the reverses in an almost exultant tone,[17] and, on the eve of the fall of Towang, set off for Bombay to deliver irrelevant speeches. The American ambassador, Professor Galbraith, informed Radhakrishnan, whom he had never seen 'so tough and angry', that the United States was willing to supply any equipment that might be needed but had yet received no request for military assistance.[18] This tied in with what General B. M. Kaul, the chief of the general staff and a protégé of Menon, told the president on 28 October, that Menon still insisted that no approach should be made to the Western countries. Nehru defended Menon to Radhakrishnan by describing Galbraith's statement as only partially true; a list was being prepared of the equipment required and this would be presented when ready to the United States and other countries.[19] But to Menon himself Nehru pointed out that there was no explanation for India's unreadiness and that he entirely agreed with Radhakrishnan that they should now secure what was needed from wherever they could. The immediate need was great and they should rather overdo than underdo things.[20] Lunching with the president on 28 October the prime minister remarked repeatedly, 'yes, we have failed'.

The crisis strengthened the nation's confidence in Nehru

[15] Radhakrishnan to Krishna Menon, 22 and 23 October 1962.

[16] Times of India and Indian Express, 22 October 1962.

[17] Despatch of G. H. Jansen from Beirut, The Statesman, 25 October 1962.

[18] J. K. Galbraith, Ambassador's Journal (London 1969), p. 438; Radhakrishnan to Nehru, 27 October 1962.

[19] Nehru to Radhakrishnan, 27 October 1962.

[20] Nehru to Krishna Menon, 27 and 28 October 1962, Nehru papers.

even while the howl of condemnation of Menon in the national press intensified. Nehru responded on 31 October with a half-measure. He took charge of defence with Menon continuing in the cabinet as minister for defence production. Radhakrishnan hinted that he regarded this step as inadequate: 'Let us see how it works.'[21] Menon himself made the prime minister's position no easier by asserting that nothing had changed, for he was still in the cabinet and still sitting in the defence ministry.[22] Radhakrishnan drew the prime minister's attention to this: 'Whatever the facts may be, it is unnecessary to state them in this blunt manner.'[23] The prime minister sought to explain it away as perhaps a casual statement which did not give the right impression; he was dealing with defence directly and Menon had but a limited responsibility in regard to production.[24] But Menon's wilful contrariness helped to keep alive the demand for his total removal from government. The parties in opposition clamoured for it; there was strong support for it in the Congress itself; all the chief ministers, who had come to Delhi, excepting Bakshi Ghulam Mahommed of Kashmir—who supported Menon—and Kairon of the Punjab —who expressed no opinion—recommended it; and many colleagues of Menon in the cabinet favoured his departure.[25] Then Indira Gandhi saw Radhakrishnan and asked him to save her father from himself. So, when Nehru saw the president on 7 November with two letters from Menon, pleading his innocence but offering to resign, Radhakrishnan advised Nehru to advise the president to accept the resignation.[26] That evening Nehru informed the Congress parliamentary party that he was accepting the resignation; but thereafter, instead of formally recommending acceptance to the president, wrote a letter which requires quotation in full.

[21] Radhakrishnan to Nehru, 31 October 1962.
[22] At Tezpur, 1 November 1962, *Times of India*, 2 November 1962.
[23] To Nehru, 2 November 1962.
[24] Nehru to Radhakrishnan, 2 November 1962.
[25] Y. B. Chavan in conversation with Radhakrishnan, 17 November 1962; T. V. Kunhi Krishnan, *Chavan and the Troubled Decade* (Bombay 1971), p. 77; C. Subramaniam, 'My Days with Chavan', *Bharatiya Vidya Bhavan Journal*, 1 May 1985.
[26] A slightly garbled account of this conversation can be found in S. Dwivedy, *Quest for Socialism* (Delhi 1984), pp. 262-3.

7 November 1962

My dear President,

I enclose copies of two letters I have received from Shri Krishna Menon offering his resignation from Government. I have already shown you these letters.

I propose to write to him accepting his resignation after I learn your wishes in the matter. These wishes have been conveyed to me orally by you already. But I would be grateful if you would kindly repeat them in writing.

Yours affectionately,
Jawaharlal.

In other words, Nehru wished to leave the responsibility for the final decision to the president, with perhaps a subconscious hope for at least delay in, if not abandonment of, Menon's departure. Certainly the recognized procedure of the president acting on the advice of the prime minister was reversed. Radhakrishnan in his reply did not communicate his wishes but took a firm decision: 'As you said, in the circumstances, for the sake of national unity we have to accept Shri Krishna Menon's resignation with regret. On hearing from you a formal announcement will issue from the Rashtrapati Bhavan.'[27] The carefully drafted sentences maintained constitutional propriety by asserting that it was the prime minister who had suggested acceptance; but the door was firmly closed on any possibility of reconsideration.

After the dislodgement of Menon, Radhakrishnan, with the prime minister's approval, set off on a visit to the battle-front in the eastern sector. He met the generals in command, went to the forward areas, and talked to the troops in retreat after the first round of Chinese attacks. He saw for himself the lack of training and proper clothes and equipment. As president he regarded himself as above government and party and the spokesman of public feeling; and he now publicly acknowledged the 'credulity and negligence' of the government which had brought matters to this pass.[28] Such outspokenness by the head of state in India was unprecedented; but Radhakrishnan's position was also unique. A philosopher with a moral

[27] Radhakrishnan to Nehru, 8 November 1962.
[28] Speech at Tezpur, 8 November 1962, *The Hindu*, 10 November 1962.

authority which high office could not circumscribe, he had, even as vice-president, adopted a non-aligned style within India; and he knew that Nehru had always appreciated this. Only a few months before the prime minister had written that Radhakrishnan had served India in many capacities but 'above all, he is a great teacher from whom all of us have learnt much and will continue to learn.'[29]

Radhakrishnan had been assured by the generals that the Chinese would be able to advance no further; but on 14 November their troops were on the move again and caused panic in the Indian command. He was involved in the decision to replace the chief of the army staff and backed the prime minister solidly in sustaining Indian morale and securing international support.[30] Talking to a group of American senators he was 'in high form'. Without minimizing India's past mistakes, he stressed China's deceit and perfidy and said that if India went down, so would all of Asia. So it was in the interests of the United States to support India. Asked about the rumour that the Chinese had taken General Kaul prisoner his comment was, 'it is, unfortunately, untrue'. Synchronizing with Nehru's appeals to President Kennedy for air support, Radhakrishnan brought home to the senators the need to protect important cities, vital installations and supply centres.[31] A few days later, speaking to a large supply mission from Washington, he elaborated the principles for which India was fighting and the moral as well as strategic consequences which would follow if she were defeated: 'It was admirably designed for the purpose; you could have heard a pin drop during the proceedings.'[32] But it was no longer an immediate crisis, for the Chinese had on 21 November declared a unilateral cease-fire.

## III

The president and the prime minister, therefore, had during these critical weeks functioned closely together; and Nehru knew that even if the president had taken, or helped to take,

---

[29] *The Radhakrishnan Number* (Madras 1962).

[30] See General J. N. Chaudhuri, *An Autobiography* (Delhi 1978), pp. 173–4.

[31] Note of secretary to the president, 20 November 1962; Galbraith, *Ambassador's Journal*, pp. 487 and 489.    [32] Galbraith, p. 495.

unwelcome decisions and had spoken out on occasions with
candour, everything had been done or said in the prime minister's interests as well as that of the nation. That leaders of the
opposition utilized passages in Radhakrishnan's speeches to
belabour the government did not worry Nehru. But the situation was fertile ground for mischief-makers. Rajagopalachari
was the first to utilize the opportunity. He recommended that
the constitution be revised so that, instead of the president
acting on the advice of his ministers, the prime minister and the
cabinet should act on the advice of the president.[33] This, of
course, was precisely what had happened in the matter of
Menon's resignation, and Rajagopalachari would have been
aware of rumours to this effect in the press;[34] but to propose an
amendment of the constitution on these lines was bound to
embarrass Radhakrishnan and sour, if that were possible, his
relations with Nehru. The expected reactions to Rajagopalachari's references to Radhakrishnan came from left-wing
circles still nursing the wound of Menon's departure. They
chose as their spokesman Bhupesh Gupta, a leading member of
the Communist party, even though he was on close personal
terms with Radhakrishnan. Gupta wrote to Nehru protesting
against certain bantering remarks of Radhakrishnan which
Gupta described as constituting interference by the president in
the making of policy.[35] Nehru did not even bother to reply to
Gupta; but when a Congressman made similar allegations
Nehru rejected the interpretation and warned him that it
would be very improper for him to criticize or say anything
about the president.[36]

The press abroad also took an interest in the possibility of
building up the president as against the prime minister. It was
suggested that with India in crisis and the prime minister for
the first time in indifferent health, Radhakrishnan would
continue to play a decisive part, and that this was all to the
good, for he was politically shrewder and more balanced:[37]
'Behind the gentle philosopher there stands, one suspects, a

[33] Speech at Madras, 8 December 1962, *The Hindu*, 10 December 1962.
[34] E.g. F. Moraes, 'The President's Role', *Indian Express*, 12 November 1962.
[35] Bhupesh Gupta to Nehru, 26 December 1962, Nehru papers.
[36] Nehru to A. M. Tariq, 26 December 1962, Nehru papers.
[37] *The Economist Foreign Report*, 29 November 1962.

figure of political acumen and personal force.'[38] Then the
Intelligence Bureau reported that at a secret session of the
Swatantra party in February 1963 Rajagopalachari and
others had decided to launch an offensive against Nehru for
permitting China to humiliate India, and Rajagopalachari was
said to have added that in his talks with Radhakrishnan and
some important Congressmen he had found general support
against Nehru's policies and ideology. Rightly not believing
what was said of Radhakrishnan, Nehru promptly sent the
report to him. Radhakrishnan in turn showed it to Rajagopalachari whose denial was emotionally emphatic: 'The whole
story is a diabolical fabrication. I can assure you that from A to
Z it is a fabrication . . . You should disabuse the P.M. of any
notion that there is even an iota of truth in the story . . . it is all
a tissue of falsehood. We are living in the midst of dangerous
liars and fabricators.'[39]

Far from thinking of weakening the prime minister, Radhakrishnan had to deal with a problem of his own. The small
socialist group insisted that, at the opening of parliament, he
read the address first in Hindi and not in English and, when he
declined to do so, walked out after a noisy demonstration. The
prime minister dealt with this affront to the president by
having the offending members formally reprimanded by
parliament—the first time such a step had been taken since
1947. Obviously nothing could shake the close relationship between Nehru and Radhakrishnan. The prime minister, seeking
to maintain the course of non-alignment while securing assistance from all sources and resisting attempts by the United
States and Britain to extract concessions to Pakistan on Kashmir, encouraged visits by Radhakrishnan abroad to improve
India's image and strengthen India's policy. The president
first went to Afghanistan, with which country relations were
already friendly, and then to Iran. The situation here was more
tricky, for cordiality could not be bought at the cost of approval
of the Shah's dictatorship. Radhakrishnan was suited to handle
such a problem: 'From the moment we saw his wise and kindly
face coming out of the aircraft in Teheran to the time I waved

[38] Selig S. Harrison, 'The Passing of the Nehru Era', *New Republic*, 8 December
1962.
[39] Rajagopalachari to Radhakrishnan, 27 April 1963.

farewell to him at Zahidan it was pure joy.'[40] He was seen not
as a mere head of state but as a 'striking father figure',[41] a man
of wisdom, 'one of the great prophets'.[42] With transparent goodwill he spoke in public of the need for Iran and all countries to
move towards democratic government and honest administration if they wished to avoid revolution.[43] In private he was
even more specific. Patting the Shah on the back in his by now
well-known informal way he remarked, 'I say, Shah, you need
a little more democracy here.' The Shah showed neither surprise at the approach nor resentment at the advice even though
he had no intention of acting upon it. Only our president, said
Nehru, could have got away with it.[44]

Of even more importance to India were Radhakrishnan's
visits the next month to the United States and Britain. Thanks
to Chinese aggression the previous year, India's relations with
these countries had never been closer. President Kennedy, as a
gesture of respect for Radhakrishnan, set aside protocol and
authorized for the first time the landing of the helicopter bearing the visiting dignitary on the lawns of the White House.
Mrs Kennedy, who had had an enthusiastic reception the
previous year in India, appeared for the first time in months at
an official function and arranged, after the banquet, for the
most lavish production yet seen in the White House of the first
act of Mozart's *The Magic Flute*. There was from the start a
personal warmth in the attitude of the Kennedys to Radhakrishnan. They took him up to the family quarters to meet their
children and, in all his speeches, Kennedy spoke with grace of
Radhakrishnan the philosopher as much as the president. In
his welcoming remarks he mentioned that when he had expressed his regret at the drizzle, Radhakrishnan had replied,
'we cannot always control events, but we can always control
our attitude towards events.' Nor was a touch of humour lacking: 'today the President made an outstanding speech at the

[40] M. R. A. Baig, *In Different Saddles* (Bombay 1967), p. 347. Baig was Indian
ambassador in Teheran at this time.

[41] Prime minister of Iran, 22 May 1963, *Times of India*, 23 May 1963.

[42] A former prime minister to Baig, in Baig, p. 347.

[43] Speeches at the Shah's banquet, 16 May 1963, and at the civic reception in
Teheran, 18 May 1963.

[44] Speech at conference in Delhi of heads of mission in South East Asia, 29 May
1963.

World Food Congress without notes. He rode through the parade today, with tremendous cheers, without waving. He lunched today without meat. We have learned a series of valuable lessons.'

This easy friendship also covered their private discussions. With no fixed agenda, as was appropriate for talks between a head of government and a constitutional head of state, Kennedy and Radhakrishnan ranged from India's problems to the general condition of the world. Kennedy told Radhakrishnan of Nehru's visit the year before, when he had felt that he had been unable to rouse the prime minister's interest, and Radhakrishnan explained that Nehru was essentially a lonely man with a deep sense of responsibility. Kennedy then mentioned that when he had asked Indira Gandhi what she thought of Krishna Menon, she had replied that she had great admiration for his intellectual powers and this view was shared by many in India. Kennedy, who had a deep suspicion of Menon, had obviously been surprised at her remark. Radhakrishnan did not comment on this, making clear that, whatever his own opinion of Menon, he would not talk of him to foreign governments. Kennedy then suddenly sat up and asked, 'Is there any chance of your becoming the prime minister of your country?' Radhakrishnan quickly disabused him of any such hope.

On India Kennedy said repeatedly that it was important not only in itself but for Asia and the world that India should prosper and he committed the United States to assistance both in the struggle against China and in the furtherance of economic and social development. The joint communiqué after their talks spoke of the 'mutual defensive concern' of the two countries against Chinese aggression and Kennedy told Radhakrishnan that their aid in training, equipment and radar facilities would be such as to make China realize that any further attack on India would be likely to involve the United States. Radhakrishnan, without going into details, said that American assistance should be such as would help India to build herself up; and Kennedy agreed. A few weeks later he told the National Security Council that Radhakrishnan had not asked for any economic or military assistance but had created such an atmosphere of prestige for India and such a climate of understanding of her hopes and aspirations that the United

States would feel ashamed if she did not assist India.

There was, however, the problem of Pakistan, creating resistance both in the department of state and in Congress to any plan of full support for India. Kennedy said that if they were pressing India hard on Kashmir it was only because they did not want to add to the tensions in the area or bring to a crisis their own relations with Pakistan. It was not for the purpose, in Kennedy's phrase, of 'maintaining the umbilical cord'; but public opinion attached importance to it. Radhakrishnan replied that though the sessions between the ministers of India and Pakistan had led to no results, India would not freeze the situation but would continue to seek a solution.

Kennedy also talked about the issue of the banning of nuclear tests which was then under consideration and Radhakrishnan encouraged him to take a positive stand in a matter where the stakes were so high. A few days later, while Radhakrishnan was still in the United States, Kennedy delivered the address which opened the way to the conclusion of an agreement on the partial banning of nuclear tests. On civil rights, which at that time was a burning issue in the United States, Radhakrishnan told Kennedy that, as Lincoln had liberated the blacks from slavery, it was his duty to rid them of humiliation. To Radhakrishnan's invitation to visit India, Kennedy replied that he planned to do so in his second term. 'If', Mrs Kennedy said to Radhakrishnan, 'you are as clever as they say you are, we will be in India soon.'

Radhakrishnan also took trouble to get his views across to influential members of Congress and to the press corps in Washington, and to the public generally during his hopping tour for ten days across the country. He spoke of the importance of non-alignment to the world and of India's commitment to democracy, freedom and the peaceful solution of international disputes. While dwelling on India's need to strengthen her defensive forces against China and dispelling suggestions that this was for menacing or attacking Pakistan, he set these urgent issues in the wider context of the importance of the awakening of an international spirit and of promoting the concept of humanity above all nations. That he was 'a man who walks with serenity amidst the alarms and excursions of our temporary problems' made all the more impressive his expositions of India's aspirations, achievements and requirements.[45]

The coverage of Radhakrishnan's speeches and broadcasts in the American press was not extensive mainly because hardly any of them were from a written text. But the leading newspapers commented on his visit, often in terms which were embarrassing to him. It was harmless enough for the *Washington Post* to say that he was 'thrice welcome', as a statesman, a philosopher and a friend;[46] but the same journal had carried a despatch two days earlier asserting that Radhakrishnan was a man to watch for his influence had never been greater and the decline in Nehru's standing never more painfully apparent. Radhakrishnan, it was suggested, was feeling his way towards a more meaningful role and the exercise of what was fast becoming a veto power without collision with the prime minister: 'Nehru listens to Radhakrishnan as to few others because he accepts him as an intellectual equal and as a kindred spirit on basic policy issues.'[47] *The New York Times*, while agreeing that Radhakrishnan was emerging as a key personality on the Indian political scene, drew a sharper picture of confrontation with the prime minister and suggested that with Nehru's leadership of the Congress and government declining, 'the center of gravity has begun to shift to the President with his residual control in time of emergency over the military and the bureaucracy.'[48] These analyses might have ensured that Radhakrishnan would be listened to with extreme care in Washington; and it was even felt that his success, by 'quiet and rational eloquence', in winning official and public support for India's cause, though rousing adverse criticism in Pakistan and China,[49] would strengthen his hand on his return to India. 'He should return home to new eminence in Indian political prestige, together with a comforting sense of mission accomplished. He is truly an impressive Chief of State.'[50] In fact, Radha-

[45] President of the Washington press association, 5 June 1963.

[46] 3 June 1963.

[47] S. S. Harrison, 'India's President: A Man to Watch', *Washington Post*, 1 June 1963.

[48] 9 June 1963.

[49] E.g. *Morning News* (Dhaka), 9 June 1963, Z. A. Bhutto, foreign minister of Pakistan in Karachi, 22 June 1963, *The Times* (London), 24 June 1963, *People's Daily* (Beijing), 15 June 1963.

[50] *Washington Daily News*, 12 June 1963.

krishnan had carried conviction with the American public not because of his seemingly increasing authority but as 'a man of extraordinary goodness' who was also a very distinguished scholar.[51] But recognition of this in India was distracted by the expressions of editorial opinion in the United States. Left-wing opinion denounced *The New York Times* for fomenting an anti-Nehru conspiracy,[52] while Rajagopalachari congratulated it on being a shrewd observer.[53]

Unlike in the United States, the government in Britain was in no mood to discuss public affairs; and Radhakrishnan had to compete for the headlines with Christine Keeler. So the visit became mostly an exercise in public relations. As this was the first time that a Commonwealth head of state was being received, a special programme extending over twelve days was arranged with a mixture of state occasions and informal functions. Radhakrishnan was, of course, no stranger in Britain and the press was enthusiastic in its welcome to this 'tremendous chap'.[54] They saw in him 'in some ways almost an Englishman', at home in Oxford and All Souls, but also a symbol of the new India, one of the great philosophers of the century and a philosophical middleman between East and West: 'No living head of State in the world approaches his intellectual distinction.' A man of peace wise in his time and seeking to promote amity in the world, he was yet an idealist with his feet on the ground, an optimist who knew very well that the worst could happen.[55]

Such expectations on such an unprecedented visit would have made most persons quail, but Radhakrishnan carried it off by being throughout his normal self. He set the tone at Victoria Station by greeting the queen by clasping her hand between both of his, and by this 'warmer, more meaningful salutation than the limp European handshake'[56] he 'superimposed the quiet dignity of his personality on a regal and

[51] *Link* (Delhi), 23 June 1963.

[52] *Patriot* (Delhi), 12 June 1963.

[53] *Swarajya*, 22 June 1963.

[54] Sir Percival Griffiths in the BBC Home Service News, 11 June 1963.

[55] *Sheffield Telegraph, Northern Echo* (Darlington), *Daily Herald*, 12 June 1963; *Yorkshire Post*, 13 June 1963; *Daily Telegraph*, 15 June 1963; *Coventry Evening Telegraph*, 19 June 1963.

[56] William Hickey in *Daily Express*, 13 June 1963.

colourful scene.'[57] Then, ignoring protocol, he broke off from the royal party to exchange greetings with a group of Indians who had gathered to receive him: 'It was a graceful and eloquent moment.'[58] After the state drive to Buckingham Palace, the queen made him an honorary member of the Order of Merit. 'I can think', she told him, 'of no one who deserves it more.' This not being a title, he could accept it; and his prime minister had already approved.

With the queen Radhakrishnan was soon, as became clear to observers, on cordial terms:

It is apparent, even though Dr Radhakrishnan has been in this country for so little time, that a real and personal rapport has sprung up between the Queen and her distinguished guest; when the two of them catch each other's eye, as has been happening often these past two days, there is a friendly warmth which communicates itself to the beholders.[59]

Here again it was Radhakrishnan's unaffected approach which was probably responsible. Invited for lunch at Windsor Castle, he found that the queen planned to take him to Ascot in the afternoon. 'Hullo', said Radhakrishnan, 'I see you are dressed for the races', and the queen, though perhaps startled, appeared to like this informality. But for the first time Radhakrishnan was concerned. He had never in his life been to the race-course and asked his high commissioner what he was expected to do. Would we have to bet, which he hated? Assured that he need do no more than continue to chat lightly, he relaxed and enjoyed the outing.[60]

With the public too 'Dr Rad', as he was soon termed,[61] was a great success. In his speeches he stressed India's appreciation of British goodwill since 1947, and touched on her immediate needs; but he gave most attention to the fundamentals of living, the call of religion and the necessity of world understanding. His earnestness and courage roused even hard-headed businessmen in Manchester to give him a standing ovation such as none could recall in living memory; but there was more to his

[57] *The Guardian*, 13 June 1963.        [58] *Yorkshire Post*, 13 June 1963.
[59] Patrick Keatley in *The Guardian*, 14 June 1963.
[60] M. C. Chagla, *Roses in December*, p. 318.
[61] *Evening News*, 13 June 1963.

speeches than eloquent appeal.[62] The discerning knew that Radhakrishnan had a shrewd sense of political possibility, and, as *The Guardian* pointed out, Kennedy and Khruschev were now getting round to the view of the cold war which Radhakrishnan had expressed many years before as ambassador in Moscow.[63] But he was also capable of descending from lofty heights and turning from general issues to immediate circumstances. For example, to a staid audience of British men and women who had lived in India before 1947 he spoke, without once mentioning Profumo, of the need for politicians to behave and not to tell lies and then ended the 'hilariously funny' performance by suddenly veering away to suggest that he had only India in mind.[64] With the press 'he seemed to forget his Presidential status to become the professor on an informal occasion, teaching, yet not in the least holding forth. In fact, he showed a new technique in dealing with the press, but one which only a few people would be capable of imitating.'[65] When a child approached him solemnly with a garland he took it and put it round the child's neck, spent a night at All Souls and acted virtually as a host to his party, took time off at Manchester to visit a bookshop, and in London called without notice on his publisher, Sir Stanley Unwin. The outriders had to be informed midway to somewhere else to take a different route and, on reaching Museum Street, Radhakrishnan walked up the stairs to Sir Stanley's office on the first floor. 'Mr President', remonstrated a surprised Sir Stanley, 'why didn't you inform me? I would have made proper arrangements.' Radhakrishnan replied, 'Never mind the arrangements. I have come to find out how my books are selling.'[66]

Unqualified then was the triumph in Britain of Radhakrishnan, 'who bends protocol as he likes, taking the stiffness out of the most formal occasions by his spontaneity and warm personality, and conquering all he meets with a charm that owes nothing to artifice'.[67] The combination of 'innate dignity

[62] *Manchester Evening Chronicle*, 18 June 1963.

[63] 24 June 1963.

[64] Taya Zinkin, 'Tweedle Smith and Tweedle Singh', *Opinion* (Bombay), 25 June 1963.

[65] *Eastern Daily Press* (Norwich), 13 June 1963.

[66] M. C. Chagla, *Roses in December*, p. 321.

[67] James Cowley in *The Statesman* (Delhi), 16 June 1963.

with total absence of pomposity'[68] had made receiving him in Britain 'a joy of a kind seldom experienced on state occasions'.[69] Nehru, who was away in Kashmir on the day Radhakrishnan returned to Delhi, wrote of his pleasure at 'the great success' of the tours,[70] while Rajagopalachari, who had been pleading since the Chinese aggression for better relations with the Western powers, expressed his appreciation in terms one does not normally associate with so cool-headed a person:

The splendour of your performance in America was great. It is dazzling in England, truly greater for here in Britain your heart goes out with your brain to acknowledge God's ways as the best for His creatures. I tender my most respectful, my most affectionate congratulations. You have done a miracle, the miracle that was the need of the hour.[71]

Ordinary readers in India did not have to depend solely on accounts in the newspapers of this impact but could see it for themselves in the film made of the visit. Though the film provided much colour and spectacle, it 'speaks volumes for the President that against this kaleidoscopic richness, where there is so much to please and to distract the eye from the human participants, his stellar quality shines through with megaton force.'[72]

Certainly the prime minister regarded these visits of Radhakrishnan to the United States and Britain, which had been 'so memorable and inspiring', as of great advantage to India.[73] He was therefore surprised and sorry that the Communist party criticized some of Radhakrishnan's speeches as inconsistent with India's ideals and traditions.[74] This was not only constitutionally improper but wrong in substance, for Radhakrishnan had not said anything which was not in keeping with India's policies. Nehru raised the matter in cabinet and it was decided that the resolution of the Communist party should be

[68] Nicholas Carroll in *Sunday Times*, 23 June 1963.

[69] *Sunday Telegraph*, 16 June 1963.

[70] Nehru to Radhakrishnan, 17 June 1963.

[71] Rajagopalachari to Radhakrishnan in London, 15 June 1963.

[72] *The Statesman* (Delhi).

[73] Nehru to K. Iswara Dutt, 4 July 1963, Nehru papers.

[74] Resolution of the Communist Party of India, 29 June 1963, *New Age* (Delhi), 7 July 1963.

dealt with by an informal rejoinder rather than an official reply.[75] So the prime minister first spoke about it to the Congress parliamentary party: 'First of all, our President is well aware, as far as I know—and I know him fairly well—of our foreign policy, apart from the fact that he knows well what should or should not be said on such occasions and in foreign countries.' Moreover, there were 'perhaps very few men who could make such an impact on the common people and the big and the small as he has done during this tour.'[76] Then, first in the Rajya Sabha and later in the Lok Sabha, Nehru affirmed his approval of Radhakrishnan's speeches abroad and paid tribute to the 'astounding success' of the tour, 'a remarkable event from every point of view'.[77]

The resolution of the Communist party, though directed against Radhakrishnan, was really a riposte to the comments in the American and British press about Radhakrishnan's increasing influence and his substantial role in the fall of Krishna Menon. Radhakrishnan knew this and, on his return, explicitly reiterated that in both the United States and Britain he had drawn repeated attention to the prime minister's leadership in consolidating the country and modernizing it.[78] Then, to counter the consistent drip of Rajagopalachari's writings urging that Nehru and Radhakrishnan exchange places, he informed a Swatantra delegation that his only desire was to help and support the prime minister and the government in the service of the people.[79] Nehru himself did not believe that Radhakrishnan fostered any political ambition. That his appreciation of the president's foreign tours was no surface gesture was demonstrated by his request to Radhakrishnan to undertake that winter a visit to Nepal, where the king was almost paranoic in his dislike of India. Radhakrishnan went, spoke of the 'calm connections' and the subconscious structure of kinship linking the two peoples and, as was his wont when in autocratic states, emphasized the importance of wise

[75] Nehru to Radhakrishnan, 4 July 1963.
[76] Nehru (in Hindi) at the Congress parliamentary party, 29 August 1963, tape M 71 C (I and II), NMML.
[77] Rajya Sabha proceedings, 2 September 1963, and Lok Sabha proceedings, 17 September 1963.
[78] The Statesman, 25 June 1963.
[79] At Hyderabad, 31 July 1963, The Hindu, 1 August 1963.

leadership, honest administration and a democratic bias to development. Even if it be too much too claim that during this visit fences were successfully mended and three years of unease ended,[80] it can be said that Radhakrishnan helped a turn in relations for the better.

Till now, therefore, not even the semblance of a cloud cast a shadow between the president and the prime minister. Nehru regretted the departure of Menon but he did not doubt Radhakrishnan's good intent in the matter. The story that whenever Radhakrishnan had raised the topic of Menon, Nehru had cut short the interview has in it no basis of truth.[81] In fact, on the occasions when they discussed Menon, Nehru had defended him at some length. But now, in the latter half of 1963, there was fresh opportunity for trouble-makers. With cataract developing on both eyes, Radhakrishnan's reading and writing were limited; and he spent more time than before talking to visitors. With some of those he thought he could trust he jokingly wove fantasies as to how it might be worthwhile, after Nehru, for the president to take charge temporarily of the government, set things right in policy and administration and then step aside for a democratically chosen prime minister.[82] This was not meant seriously and Radhakrishnan was confident that faith in his integrity was too well entrenched for his conversational excursions to be misunderstood. But Delhi at this time was a hothouse of rumour and gossip, and the atmosphere was charged with personal attacks on the prime minister and accusations of corruption against cabinet ministers and chief ministers. So Radhakrishnan's 'loose talk' gained circulation.[83] Nehru himself knew Radhakrishnan too well to attach importance to reports of Radhakrishnan's remarks if they reached him. The same could not be said of his daughter, and, even in May, Mountbatten, on a visit to India, cautioned Radhakrishnan to beware lest Indira Gandhi poison her father's mind against him.[84]

[80] As, for example, in the article 'Himalayan Tito', *The Economist*, 23 November 1963.

[81] M. Masani, *Against the Tide* (Delhi 1981), p. 261.

[82] Chester Bowles, *Promises to Keep* (Indian edition 1972), p. 496. Bowles succeeded Galbraith as the US ambassador in Delhi in the summer of 1963.

[83] M. Chalapathi Rau, *Jawaharlal Nehru* (Delhi 1973), p. 401.

[84] Record of Mountbatten's conversation with Radhakrishnan, 2 May 1963.

## IV

Any, even remote, possibility of discord between Radhakrishnan and Nehru was swept aside by the stroke which
Nehru suffered in January 1964. He gradually recovered from
the affliction but quietly came to terms with approaching
death. He now saw Radhakrishnan more frequently than
before, not just to talk about public matters but to listen to the
philosopher on his own subject. Nehru was by this time a
reverent agnostic, without religious faith but with a religious
feeling; 'I am not exactly a religious person, although I agree
with much that religions have to say.'[85] He now provided an
attentive audience to Radhakrishnan, who himself, after a
botched operation for the removal of cataract on his right eye,
reduced his travels within India and postponed foreign trips.
In the last months of Nehru's life the president and the prime
minister were in the closest interpersonal harmony.

On 23 May the home secretary called on the secretary to the
president and told him that the prime minister was not well
and the president should give consideration to what should be
done in case there was a vacancy in the office of prime minister.
Informed of this, Radhakrishnan, with no precedents to
follow, decided that he would act as he had advised in Calcutta
in 1962 on the death of Bidhan Roy, and swear in the second
man in the cabinet as prime minister to carry on the administration till the party could meet and elect a prime minister.
This was necessary because there was no provision in the
constitution for the executive to function without a prime
minister. The only person to whom Radhakrishnan spoke of

---

C. L. Datta, aide-de-camp to Rajendra Prasad and to Radhakrishnan in his first
year as president, wrote some years later a book of the 'what the butler saw'
genre, alleging that Radhakrishnan, coached by Rajagopalachari, hoped to dis-
place Nehru in November 1962 and, the next year, conspired with Kamaraj, the
chief minister of Madras, to oust Nehru (*With Two Presidents*, Delhi 1970). The
charges now appear outrageous. There was no question of Nehru leaving office
after the Chinese aggression and the Kamaraj plan was Nehru's own skilled
manoeuvre to get rid of some unwanted colleagues. But it is surprising that anyone
was taken in by Datta's charges even at the time of publication. Yet the book was
in the headlines for a few days and Radhakrishnan, by then in retirement, felt it
necessary to issue a statement describing the book as a tissue of lies.
[85] To J. Cook, 7 April 1964, Nehru papers.

his intention was Lal Bahadur Shastri, who had left the cabinet the previous year under the Kamaraj plan but had been brought back by Nehru after he had been incapacitated in January 1964. It was tacitly understood by Nehru and Radhakrishnan that Shastri was the best person to succeed Nehru; and the allotment to Shastri of work in the ministries of external affairs and atomic energy, which were held by Nehru, was a clear indication of this. Now, when Radhakrishnan told Shastri as to how he planned to act when the necessity arose, Shastri agreed.

On the morning of 27 May Indira Gandhi telephoned Radhakrishnan to tell him that 'Father is not at all well.' Radhakrishnan went to the prime minister's house and found that Nehru was unconscious and, according to the doctors, very gravely ill. Radhakrishnan returned home and was informed by the cabinet secretary at 1.50 p.m. that Nehru had passed away. Though expected, it was to Radhakrishnan a severe blow. The years in Delhi together had converted their shared approaches on most issues into a strong personal bond, and public life without Nehru lost to Radhakrishnan much of its attraction. In his broadcasts and speeches at this time can be discerned a strong sense of personal loss and deprivation. After Nehru's death, Radhakrishnan for the rest of his term was politically a lonely person. But, on hearing the news, he, despite the grief, immediately fulfilled the demands of his office. He went back to the prime minister's house and told Gulzarilal Nanda, the most senior member of the cabinet, that he would swear him in as prime minister at 2.30 p.m. Thereafter the cabinet secretary informed the president that the emergency committee of the cabinet had met that morning and decided that, as Nehru had become unable to function, Nanda should be sworn in as prime minister. But Radhakrishnan had already informed Nanda of his own decision to the same effect after Nehru's death.

Nanda came at 4.30 p.m. and was sworn in. Radhakrishnan told him that, though this could not be mentioned in the official communiqué, he was only prime minister till the party had elected a leader. The home secretary was asked to explain this to the press; and Nanda too mentioned this in his broadcast to the people that night. Radhakrishnan carefully kept aloof from the manoeuvring for the election to the succession and did not meet either of the chief contenders, Shastri and Morarji Desai, till after the election was over. But he saw the chief of the army staff on the morning of 28 May and, to kill rumours of a possible coup, received his renewal of the pledge of loyalty. Radhakrishnan also granted an interview to Kamaraj, now president of the Congress, who told him that Nanda had wished the election to be postponed by two months. This the president did not encourage. The election was held, Shastri was chosen leader, and Radhakrishnan accepted Nanda's resignation and administered to Shastri the oath of office as prime minister. Shastri requested the president to persuade Morarji Desai, the defeated candidate, to join the cabinet, but Radhakrishnan declined to interfere. Shastri also asked Radhakrishnan if Krishna Menon could be taken into the cabinet. Radhakrishnan pointed out informally the drawbacks of such a step and Shastri did not pursue the matter.[86]

Radhakrishnan's actions at this unprecedented time, when he had no prime minister to advise him and had to take decisions on his own, made constitutional history and gave the lie, if that were needed, to all insinuations that he was interested in the exercise of political power. The studied correctness of his posture throughout these days was testimony of the highest integrity. Chester Bowles, who had been one of the few with whom in the previous year Radhakrishnan had bantered about exercising his powers, now saw what 'a very, very great man' he was. 'How easily and logically he could have introduced President's rule; yet not an hour passed when India did not have an elected chief of state.'[87] But there were now fresh problems. Radhakrishnan liked and respected Shastri, but obviously had little in common with him. Shastri was essentially a party organizer, diffident about succeeding Nehru, soon stricken by a heart attack and yet to carry all sections of his own party with him. Desai stayed out of the cabinet. Indira Gandhi also at first declined to join but then changed

---

[86] Radhakrishnan's memorandum on the death of Pandit Jawaharlal Nehru and the assumption of office of prime minister by Shri Lal Bahadur Shastri, 15 June 1964; M. Brecher, *Succession in India* (Oxford 1966), pp. 34–5, 42.

[87] Diary entry of Chester Bowles, 12 July 1964, Bowles papers. When Bowles speaks of chief of state, he in fact has in mind head of government.

her mind because she said she wished to close the door on suggestions that she had refused her co-operation. Shastri appointed her minister for information and broadcasting; but their relations were never more than correct. It was known that she would have preferred Nanda to continue as prime minister, and now, within the cabinet and the party, she became the standard-bearer of the Nehru tradition. It was mainly to keep her out of the ministry of external affairs that Shastri assigned it to Swaran Singh, a limited politician who had nothing to say for himself except that he had nothing to say.

In these circumstances everyone—ministers, dissidents, members of opposition parties—turned to the president for guidance and decision. He had become 'a much-loved elder uncle who understands all of one's problems'.[88] In the quiet of his bedroom the nation's leaders used to gather to ask his counsel.[89] Even Shastri and Indira Gandhi complained to him of each other. Radhakrishnan did what he could without transgressing his constitutional limitations and forwarded all letters, memoranda and records of discussions to the prime minister with his own suggestions. But sometimes there crept into his sentences the tone of a stern headmaster admonishing a rather dull student. For example, when the vice-president, Zakir Husain, complained that the government were mishandling a rich legacy from a citizen of the United States for the study of Urdu poetry, Radhakrishnan passed this on to the prime minister with the remarks, 'By such bungling we are losing goodwill and financial support for worthwhile projects. The matter should be investigated and set right, if possible, even at this late stage.'[90] The texts of his major addresses he sent to Shastri for approval; but in his speeches round the country he spoke out freely and severely. The intrigues in Delhi at the time of Shastri's election had, he said, made him sick and feel more and more that the common person in India had greater basic honesty and better manners than the politicians.[91]

[88] S. Sabavala, 'Philosopher Guides India', *Christian Science Monitor*, 15 October 1964.

[89] Associated Press special report, *Rome Daily American*, 20 January 1965.

[90] Radhakrishnan's note to Shastri, 17 July 1964.

[91] Speech at Pondicherry, 12 July 1964, *The Hindu*, 14 July 1964.

Radhakrishnan's main effort at this time, however, was in the field of foreign policy. It was here that he could help India most, not only because, with the death of Nehru, he was the last of the pioneers of non-alignment still in office; his own standing and his personal philosophy based on the dignity and autonomy of man made him universally acceptable: 'Such a man can be a stranger nowhere.'[92] Even as he landed in Delhi on his return from Washington and London in the summer of 1963, the Soviet government announced that he had accepted their invitation to visit their country; but Radhakrishnan's problem with his eyes and Nehru's illness obliged him to defer going out of India till September 1964.

This visit to the Soviet Union was obviously of crucial importance for the balance of India's policies in the context of Chinese expansionism. Two hours before Radhakrishnan reached Moscow an agreement on Soviet military assistance to India was signed; so he did not need to concern himself with these details. What the Soviet leaders wished to hear from him, whom they regarded as an old friend, was that there had been no change in India's commitments to non-alignment and socialism; and this assurance Radhakrishnan could give. The Soviet government in turn pledged themselves, in the joint communiqué issued at the end of the visit, to the position that states should refrain from the use of force in the solution of territorial and border disputes and should pay due regard to historically formed boundaries. During their talks Khruschev said the Soviet government were as concerned as the Government of India about China, where chauvinistic tendencies were developing powerfully and silencing socialism and Marxist-Leninist philosophy. Mao had evidently lost his wits and argued on the basis of China's vast and increasing population; but it did not follow that the larger the nation the wiser it was. This was the philosophy of a fool. Mao would go the way of Stalin, for the people could not be deceived; they could only be frightened. The 'Chinese disease' could be compared with cholera; like cholera it would pass and mankind would survive it. Khruschev added that he would like to see India attain normal relations with Pakistan and China and India should

---

[92] 'Visitor from India', *Irish Independent* (Dublin), 21 September 1964.

not, in Gromyko's phrase, 'over-wait' for negotiations. One could not change one's neighbours as one changed one's shoes if they became too tight. Radhakrishnan replied that India's attitude towards both these countries was not rigid and in favour of peaceful settlements.[93]

From the Soviet Union Radhakrishnan went for a few days to Eire to pay in person the tribute of India to the legendary figure of de Valera and, in passing, to correct if possible the ambiguous attitude which the Irish government had for years adopted on the question of Kashmir. In this he was successful. The prime minister of Eire acknowledged after their talks that he now understood that Kashmir was more than a legal or a territorial issue and hoped that it would be settled by bilateral discussions.

So Radhakrishnan could claim modestly on his return that in both countries 'we got on well, I thought.'[94] His achievement in Moscow and the reception 'beyond all expectations'[95] which he had received in all parts of the Soviet Union were appreciated by all sections of opinion in India barring that on the extreme right. Only Rajagopalachari, who had been so ecstatic about Radhakrishnan's efforts in Washington and London, now regretted that he had gone to the Soviet Union as the agent of the Congress government and danced to its dictates.[96] But the success of Radhakrishnan's visit was primarily personal and grounded on a deep and cordial understanding with Khruschev. As James Cameron described it, their names formed the new way of spelling Russo-Indian relations.[97] Khruschev had gone as far as he could to give India his support, and Radhakrishnan had made sure of this. To convince him that his work had not been undone by the overthrow of Khruschev four weeks later, the Soviet government directed a senior official to break journey in Delhi on his way

[93] Record of Radhakrishnan's talks with Khruschev, 11, 12 and 18 September 1964.

[94] Interview at Delhi airport, 27 September 1964, *Indian Express*, 28 September 1964.

[95] T. N. Kaul, Indian ambassador in Moscow, to foreign secretary, 28 September 1964.

[96] Speech at Tiruchirapalli, 26 September 1964, *Indian Express*, 27 September 1964.

[97] In the *Sun* (London), 18 September 1964.

to East Asia to explain to the president that nothing had changed in Indo-Soviet relations.[98]

Not quite an aspect of foreign policy was Radhakrishnan's trip to Bombay later that year to receive Pope Paul VI. At that time a pope's travels abroad were not the routine matter they have become today; and Pope Paul did not visit Delhi as he was coming to India not as the head of state but, in his words, as 'a pilgrim' to attend the International Eucharistic Congress. Yet Radhakrishnan, along with Zakir Husain and Shastri, went to Bombay to receive the pope, if only to establish that secularism in India did not mean indifference to religion but respect for all religions. 'I feel', he told Pope Paul, 'that ultimately at the top all people will work together and beckon to each other as one common family of God.'[99] The pope voiced similar sentiments, cited Hindu texts and claimed to share 'moral citizenship' with India. Radhakrishnan hoped that this exchange would reduce narrow Hindu bigotry and help to draw together persons of all religions.

Bigotry of another kind, however, soon after demanded attention in the new year. Radhakrishnan, in his message for Republic Day, listed national shortcomings and urged disciplined behaviour and hard and honest work on both government and people.[100] This text he had not been able to show before delivery to the prime minister, who was out of Delhi; and Shastri complained to a few colleagues of 'a somewhat critical note' in some of the president's remarks.[101] Radhakrishnan explained that the points he had raised were not new and had been mentioned by him to Shastri even earlier: 'My anxiety is to help you to do the right things.'[102] The same anxiety showed itself in the crisis which now developed over the question of language. On 26 January 1965, fifteen years after the promulgation of the constitution, Hindi became the official language of the union; and doubts arose as to whether

[98] Note of foreign secretary on Radhakrishnan's talk with I. G. Ignatov, first deputy chairman of the Presidium of the Supreme Soviet of the USSR, 7 November 1964.

[99] Report in *Western Mail* (Cardiff), 4 December 1964.

[100] 'A Testing Time', 25 January 1965. *President Radhakrishnan's Speeches and Writings 1964–1967* (Delhi 1969), pp. 33–6.

[101] L. B. Shastri to Radhakrishnan, 26 January 1965.

[102] Radhakrishnan to Shastri, 26 January 1965.

the Shastri government would abide by Nehru's assurance that English would continue as an associate official language as long as the non-Hindi-speaking people required it. This uncertainty led to widespread and violent agitation in southern India in support of the demand for a statutory endorsement of the commitment made by Nehru. Radhakrishnan suggested to Shastri that, in a broadcast he was scheduled to give, he should be 'precise and unambiguous' about this: 'Forgive me for writing this letter to you.'[103] But, as Shastri gave no undertaking to initiate a legal affirmation, two leading members of his government, who were from the south, resigned. Shastri took the resignations to the president who advised Shastri not to press him to accept them, but instead to conciliate opinion in southern India. Shastri took back the resignations but came again to say that the cabinet was unwilling to make any commitment in law. This time Radhakrishnan bluntly told the prime minister that he was developing a 'pro-Hindi' image and leaving it to Indira Gandhi, who had flown down to visit the riot-stricken areas in the south, to appear as the only national leader: 'You will lead the country to ruin and disintegration.'[104]

Meanwhile, violent demonstrations continued in the south. Few knew of Radhakrishnan's advice to the prime minister; and resentment at his continuance in office in Delhi showed itself in the burning down of his ancestral house in Tirutani, which he had a few years earlier donated to the Tamil Nadu government, along with a financial endowment, for the establishment of a library and cultural centre. While publicly condemning such violence, Radhakrishnan added that the rulers should ask themselves whether they had done all they could to avert such unhealthy developments. Political wisdom consisted in anticipating and, if necessary, forestalling events.[105] The criticism was thinly veiled but was not immediately grasped by Nanda, the minister for home affairs, who continued to assert that no more need be done and drove Radha-

[103] Radhakrishnan to Shastri, 11 February 1965.
[104] Record of Radhakrishnan's two interviews with Shastri, 13 February 1965.
[105] Speech at Delhi, 14 February 1965, *President Radhakrishnan's Speeches and Writings 1964–1967*, pp. 36–8.

krishnan to a sharp and explicit rebuke.[106] Shastri was more sensitive and included in the president's address to parliament a paragraph drafted for him by Radhakrishnan, categorically reaffirming Nehru's assurances and asking parliament to consider the whole policy in all its aspects—in other words, whether these assurances could be incorporated in a statute.[107] The crisis receded.

## V

The address itself Radhakrishnan found difficulty in reading because of his defective vision and soon after went to London for an operation for the removal of cataract on the left eye. On his way back he was met at Moscow airport by Mikoyan, who encouraged an Indian move to promote the prospects of a settlement in Vietnam. With his eyesight much improved and looking and acting 'like a new man confident, affirmative and incisive' Radhakrishnan took the initiative.[108] On the occasion of the presentation of credentials by the high commissioner of Tanzania, he suggested that the non-aligned countries should think on some such lines as cessation of hostilities in both parts of Vietnam, policing of boundaries by an Afro-Asian force, and maintenance of the existing boundaries so long as the people desired it.[109]

The ministry of external affairs, although it had not been consulted, took over the proposal as being in line with its own thinking and circulated it to the governments of non-aligned countries. One advantage of the proposal, in the ministry's view, was that it was likely to embarrass China, which promptly accused Radhakrishnan of trying to find a way out for the United States.[110] The North Vietnam government were more moderate in their reaction and it was clarified to them that cessation of hostilities implied not merely the stopping of the bombing of North Vietnam but withdrawal of American troops from South Vietnam, and that the aim of the proposals

[106] G. L. Nanda to Radhakrishnan, 15 February 1965, and Radhakrishnan's reply, 16 February 1965.
[107] President's address to parliament, 17 February 1965.
[108] Telegram of Bowles to state department, 27 April 1965, department of state papers.     [109] 24 April 1965.     [110] Hsinhua, 27 April 1965.

was to facilitate the unification of Vietnam in accordance with the Geneva agreements. The Soviet Union reserved comment and the United States reacted favourably without committing themselves. Their ambassador in Delhi urged that support be announced as that might open the door to negotiations.[111] The department of state preferred to wait for the proposals to be elaborated in greater detail and for some reaction secured from Moscow; but, despite considerable support among the non-aligned countries and encouragement from U Thant, the secretary-general of the United Nations, the Government of India took no further step. Even so, when informed that the prime minister would like to know, before leaving for Canada, whether the United States would like India to press ahead with the proposal,[112] it was authoritatively stated in Washington that the idea of an Afro-Asian peace force was warmly welcomed.[113] The Canadian government too gave full support to Radhakrishnan's proposal; but Shastri decided to omit any mention of it in the communiqué. The prime minister and his advisers had, in fact, by now become unenthusiastic about Radhakrishnan's proposal.[114] Not daring to tell him this, they continued to provide clarifications, such as that an Afro-Asian force would police the cease-fire on the boundaries, which meant not only the borders but also the sea coast of South Vietnam, and suitable points in the interior. But the proposal itself was smothered.

Soon there was trouble nearer home. Skirmishing with Pakistan in the Rann of Kutch was controlled from developing into large-scale fighting; and, to strengthen his prime minister's hand against bellicose elements, Radhakrishnan asserted that it was essential to come to terms with China and Pakistan with honour and dignity so that some of the vast amount being spent on arms could be diverted to internal development.[115] Sheikh Abdullah welcomed this call as did Jaya-

[111] Telegram of Chester Bowles to state department, 4 May 1965, department of state papers.

[112] Telegram of Bowles to state department, 6 June 1965, reporting conversation with secretary to prime minister, department of state papers.

[113] *The Times*, 14 June 1965.

[114] Indian high commissioner in Ottawa to foreign secretary, 15 June 1965.

[115] Speech at Mettur, 2 July 1965, *President Radhakrishnan's Speeches and Writings 1964–1967*, p. 457.

prakash Narayan and the Communist party.[116] Radhakrishnan
was perhaps ahead of the government; but any hope that
they would be needled by the president into rethinking
foreign policy was scotched by Pakistan. President Ayub
Khan, even while agreeing with Radhakrishnan that both
countries should 'demilitarize' their minds,[117] sent about three
thousand guerrilla infiltrators into Kashmir. The Indian
government accepted the challenge and retaliated across the
cease-fire line. This was with Radhakrishnan's full approval.
When attacked one has to defend oneself and sometimes attack
becomes the best form of defence.[118]

The fighting spread with Pakistan troops crossing the international boundary south of Kashmir on 1 September. The
security council called for a cease-fire and, in pursuance of this,
U Thant flew to Rawalpindi and Delhi. On 11 September,
staying as Radhakrishnan's guest, U Thant conveyed to
Radhakrishnan the greetings of Zulfiqar Bhutto, once his
student at Oxford and now foreign minister of Pakistan. Radhakrishnan was much moved, repeated that India had the friend-
liest feelings for the people of Pakistan, but stated India's
position in the current crisis in the firmest terms. There was no
question of India agreeing to Pakistan's demand for a plebiscite. But he advised Shastri to accept the recommendation
of the United Nations for a cease-fire. All the assumptions of
the Pakistan government—that India would not fight, that
Kashmir would revolt and that communal disturbances would
break out in India—had been proved wrong, and this had
upset them. Indian troops were in Pakistan and acceptance of
a cease-fire would provide a favourable position on the ground
and set India right with the world. The resolution provided for
the ending of infiltration for which Ayub and Bhutto, in their
talks with U Thant, had virtually accepted responsibility; but
the resolution did not concern itself with long-term solutions
of the Kashmir problem.

[116] Sheikh Abdullah's letter to Radhakrishnan, 9 July 1965; Jayaprakash
Narayan's speech at Calcutta, 10 July 1965, Statesman, 11 July 1965; editorial in
New Age, 18 July 1965.

[117] Report on presentation of credentials of Indian high commissioner in
Pakistan, 6 August 1965.

[118] Speech and broadcast in Srinagar, 26 August 1965, President Radhakrishnan's
Speeches and Writings, pp. 47-8.

The Soviet chargé d'affaires and Chester Bowles, the American ambassador, also saw the president the day before. The Soviet envoy was asked to curtail Indonesia's supplies of military aid to Pakistan and informed that if U Thant's efforts failed, India would accept the offer of the Soviet government to mediate. To Bowles Radhakrishnan spoke of India's desire to live in friendship with Pakistan, her reliance on American assistance in case China intervened, and her hope that the United States would use her influence with Turkey and Iran to cut down their despatch of strategic material to Pakistan.[119] Bowles would seem to have required little convincing that India should be supported: 'Pakistan is in bed with China and India is standing up to her.'[120] As Indian forces continued to demolish the American tanks being employed by Pakistan, Radhakrishnan's advocacy of a cease-fire came under increasingly heavy pressure, and Bowles hoped that his position would hold.[121]

That evening Radhakrishnan broadcast a 'gentle sermon' to the nation.[122] Ayub, he said, had announced that Pakistan was at war with India; but India did not regard herself as at war with Pakistan and confined her attention to military targets. This conflict had been forced on her but her people should not and could not forget their traditions, ideals and history. The government would give the fullest consideration to U Thant's suggestions; but Pakistani infiltrators as well as troops should be withdrawn and the United Nations should ensure that these acts of aggression were not repeated. India was fighting not for a piece of territory but for fundamental principles. It was not her desire to hurt Pakistan in order to save India: 'We do not believe in any unbridgeable chasms. There are more things which bind us together than keep us apart.'[123]

U Thant wrote later that he had been disappointed by this broadcast, which was not what he had expected from a philo-

[119] U Thant, *View from the U.N.* (London 1977), p. 405; Radhakrishnan's note on talks with Soviet envoy and American ambassador, 10 September 1965, and with U Thant, 11 September 1965; Radhakrishnan's note to prime minister, 11 September 1965.

[120] Chester Bowles to department of state, 21 February 1965, Bowles papers.

[121] Ibid., 10 September 1965.

[122] S. Sabavala in *Christian Science Monitor*, 14 September 1965.

[123] *President Radhakrishnan's Speeches and Writings*, pp. 49–51.

sopher.[124] It is difficult to see what greater spirit of friendliness breaking through the clouds of war he could have wished for. Radhakrishnan's was 'the authentic voice of India',[125] interpreted in Pakistan as that of the leading 'dove'.[126] Even more, Radhakrishnan was at this time very much the head of state and the guide of his people. He kept in close touch with the chiefs of staff and, when they complained to him of lack of vital intelligence, he called for and received a detailed report from the government to find out for himself if the charge were justified. In his broadcast he congratulated the Muslims in India on their unshaken loyalty, thanked the Sikh leader Sant Fateh Singh for postponing his fast on a local issue, and later advised the government to avert his self-immolation.[127] In a grave crisis, Radhakrishnan helped to hold the people together, supported the government's policies, assisted in their proper implementation, and did not allow the larger vision to be forgotten. Above all was clear his uncompromising sense of humanity.

With the cease-fire on 23 September, Radhakrishnan broadcast again calling on Indians not to be short-sighted but to look far ahead. China and Pakistan were India's neighbours and should be persuaded to become good and friendly neighbours. This might seem difficult but was not impossible.[128] He then travelled abroad to secure support for India's actions. With Britain cool and even unfriendly, opinion in eastern Europe and Africa had become of added importance. At Brioni, after talks with Radhakrishnan, Tito backed India strongly against both Pakistan and China. He described Kashmir as an internal problem of India and condemned China's aggressive policy of interference. In Prague the Czech government, while avoiding attribution of responsibility for the latest crisis, reaffirmed support for India and promised whatever military assistance might be sought by her. Rumania, preoccupied with weakening Soviet influence, seemed more

---

[124] *View from the U.N.*, p. 407.

[125] 'India's Voice', editorial in *Patriot* (Delhi), 13 September 1965.

[126] P. Preston in *The Guardian*, 13 September 1965.

[127] L. P. Singh, 'The President We Need', *Indian Express*, 21 June 1987. Singh was home secretary in 1965.

[128] 25 September 1965, *President Radhakrishnan's Speeches and Writings*, pp. 52–5.

interested in mediating between India and China. Radhakrishnan being known to favour an honourable settlement if it
were possible, Chinese diplomats went out of their way to meet
him in all the capitals he visited, and in Bucharest the government, without being officially explicit, sought to give the
impression that if India wished to negotiate they themselves
could be of help.[129] But Radhakrishnan stated clearly that it
was for the Chinese government to take the first step, as suggested by six non-aligned countries, by giving up some of the
territory occupied by them in 1962, and the Rumanian
government went no further: 'They never offered, we never
accepted.'[130]

Radhakrishnan next visited Ethiopia, for Haile Selassie was
at this time an influential figure in African politics; and on his
way to Addis Ababa he met Nasser at the airport in Cairo.
While reaffirming his commitment to India, Nasser felt that
India's case was not being sufficiently explained in the Arab
and Islamic countries. No such inadequacy could have been
felt in Ethiopia after Radhakrishnan's visit. Haile Selassie
publicly stated his view that the principle of self-determination
applied only to colonial territories and not to parts of sovereign nations; and he later saw to it that the Organization of
African Unity did not give a hearing to Pakistan's complaint.

Back in Delhi, Radhakrishnan had much to do, keeping in
touch with every section of public opinion and helping the
government from the outside. Sheikh Abdullah's plea from
detention was passed on to Shastri and Sant Fateh Singh was
reminded that he should not embarrass the government as the
crisis with Pakistan was not yet over. Rajagopalachari wrote to
Radhakrishnan daily, and sometimes twice a day, about the
suppression of some of his articles under the Defence of
India rules; and Radhakrishnan persuaded the home minister
to withdraw the ban. 'This is to thank you for everything',
wrote Rajagopalachari. 'It is wonderful that you have kept
your affection for me warm through thick and thin.'[131] But

[129] J. A. Lukas in *New York Times*, 18 October 1965, and R. Knox in *Daily
Telegraph* (London), 19 October 1965.

[130] Radhakrishnan on his return at Delhi airport, 14 October 1965, *Times of
India*, 15 October 1965.

[131] Rajagopalachari to Radhakrishnan, 30 December 1965.

Radhakrishnan had more to worry about than the personal problems of distinguished individuals or the demands of internal politics. There were continuous violations by Pakistan of the cease-fire line and trouble fomented by infiltrators even in Srinagar. The Soviet ambassador saw Radhakrishnan with a message from Kosygin and Mikoyan, reporting that the United States was pressing the Soviet Union to make India agree to either a plebiscite or an independent Kashmir; and they thought the best arrangement would be for the prime ministers of India and Pakistan to meet outside the United Nations.[132] Radhakrishnan forwarded this message to the prime minister who, exasperated by the lack of understanding of India's position in the security council, was prepared for India even leaving the United Nations.[133] So the scene was set for India and Pakistan to meet under the auspices of the Soviet Union. The Soviet ambassador again saw the president to inform him that the United States was urging Ayub Khan to be tough at the meetings at Tashkent and ask for an arbitration commission consisting of the president of the International Court of Justice, the secretary-general of the United Nations and the president of the World Bank—a composition loaded heavily against India and obviously unacceptable to her. Radhakrishnan's formula was a no-war declaration, disengagement of troops, evacuation from occupied areas in India and Pakistan, and the acceptance of the cease-fire line with rectifications as the international boundary.[134] Along with this he also urged his own government and people to settle domestic issues within Kashmir to the satisfaction of the citizens of Kashmir and never to forget the overall approach of friendliness to Pakistan:[135] 'President Radhakrishnan is very anxious to reemphasize the Gandhi–Ashoka tradition.'[136] It was because of this approach that Jayaprakash Narayan declared that 'I

[132] Record of Radhakrishnan's interview with Soviet ambassador, 19 October 1965.
[133] Record of Shastri's conversation with Radhakrishnan, 26 October 1965.
[134] Record of Radhakrishnan's interview with Soviet ambassador, 27 December 1965.
[135] Speeches at conference of governors in Delhi, 17 November 1965, and at Bangalore, 6 December 1965, *Speeches and Writings*, pp. 56–7 and 189 respectively; speech at Bangalore, 9 December 1965, *The Statesman*, 16 December 1965.
[136] Barbara Ward from New Delhi to J. Valenti, special assistant to President

344 RADHAKRISHNAN: A BIOGRAPHY

consider it a matter of great good fortune for this country and a divine boon that we are privileged to have at this juncture such a wise, courageous and humane President as Dr Radhakrishnan . . .'[137]

Radhakrishnan was not happy about the Tashkent declaration. It seemed that, after the losses in human life during the fighting, no more had been secured by Shastri than a declaration of good intent. Pakistan had not been obliged to settle the Kashmir problem by recognizing the cease-fire line as an international boundary, and the line itself had not been improved by allotting to India the mountain passes which she had captured. Nor had Pakistan given binding assurances that she would not again send armed infiltrators into Kashmir. All that the two sides had done was to reaffirm their obligations under the United Nations charter not to use force and to settle disputes through peaceful means. But discussion of the merits of the Tashkent declaration did not last long. At 2.15 a.m. on 11 January 1966 Radhakrishnan was woken up to be told that Shastri had died at Tashkent of a massive heart attack about ten minutes before. He immediately sent for Nanda, the most senior member of the cabinet, and administered to him the oath of office as prime minister on the understanding that, as in 1964, this was only till the Congress parliamentary party met and elected a leader. Radhakrishnan's reading of the constitution was that there should never be a vacancy in the office of prime minister, with the corollary that the president should never exercise executive authority. This once more left no room for talk of his own personal ambition.

Only two other members of the cabinet, Indira Gandhi and the finance minister, were present at the swearing in of Nanda. A few hours later, at 8.15 a.m., Indira Gandhi came back to see the president. She said Nanda had got in touch with her, told her that he had some support and wished to know if

Johnson, 2 December 1965, Lyndon Johnson papers, Lyndon B. Johnson Library, University of Texas at Austin.

[137] Convocation address at Mysore University, 29 November 1965.

she herself were a candidate. 'When your father was prime minister', replied Radhakrishnan, 'I was against your being appointed a minister. Thereafter I was for your joining the cabinet. Now I am for your being prime minister. We will all help you.' Finding her diffident, he advised her, 'Keep quiet, don't say yes or no.'

Clearly there were four in the field—Nanda, Morarji Desai, Indira Gandhi and Yashwantrao Chavan, the chief minister of Maharashtra who had come to Delhi as defence minister in 1962 after Menon's resignation. Radhakrishnan regarded Nanda as too limited; Desai he liked personally but thought him too rigid and narrow; and Chavan in his view had not made good in Delhi and provided the classic case of over-promotion. Indira Gandhi he was fond of both for herself and as her father's daughter. He thought little of her intellectual abilities, and this was an opinion which was generally shared. For example, after Nehru's death Zakir Husain, the vice-president, had described Indira Gandhi as a woman of poor mind and no experience whom all of them should assist and Radhakrishnan should treat as his daughter.[138] But as minister in Shastri's cabinet Indira Gandhi had grown in stature, and her prompt visit to south India at the time of the disturbances on the language issue showed political imagination.[139]

So Indira Gandhi was Radhakrishnan's choice and he worked for her silently behind the scenes without compromising the dignity of his office. He was surprised when Krishna Menon called on him to urge Nanda's claims but was relieved to find that Kamaraj, the president of the Congress, was not interested in the post and was inclined to favour Mrs Gandhi. That evening Radhakrishnan sent for her, told her that she could not count on Menon and left-wing support, but that

[138] Record of Radhakrishnan's conversation with Zakir Husain, 6 August 1964.

[139] It is worth mention that one shrewd observer had noted even then the significance of her action. 'There was a time when any reference to her as the likely future Prime Minister was interpreted in many circles as emanating from those who might be trying to flatter her. But today, thanks to the pathetic ineptitude of Shri Shastri if not incompetence, and the demonstration of adherence to national values on her part, Shrimati Indira Gandhi's name is being seriously talked about in the capital as worthy of being the Prime Minister of the country.' Nikhil Chakravarty in *Mainstream* (Delhi), 20 February 1965.

Kamaraj was friendly and suggested that she quietly build up her position.

The next day, 12 January, a 'mood of negative consensus' was developing in the working committee in favour of Nanda, with Desai determined to contest.[140] On the 13th, hearing that Mrs Gandhi's response to enquiries as to her own attitude was to say that it was for the party to decide, Radhakrishnan sent word to her that it was time for her to let her candidature be informally known. She acted on this advice, but more effective than the canvassing of her own committed supporters was that of Kamaraj, who had by now become a personal friend of Radhakrishnan and did not, when need arose, hesitate to say that the president, while taking no interest in what was a party matter, had advised that they choose 'the most broad-minded person'—and everyone knew who, in contrast to Desai, he had in mind. 'You told me', Kamaraj said later to Radhakrishnan, 'that she was the best and I worked on those lines.'[141] Rajagopalachari, it may be added, was for Nanda remaining as prime minister, at least for a year.[142]

On 15 January eight chief ministers declared their support for Mrs Gandhi and, though the poll was to be four days later, the battle was as good as won. Mrs Gandhi at once called on Radhakrishnan. 'Thank you for your help', she said, to which he replied, 'Don't be formal.' They then moved on to discuss the composition of her cabinet. Krishna Menon had asked Radhakrishnan to secure for him the portfolio of external affairs; Radhakrishnan passed on this request but Mrs Gandhi would not agree. She wished to shift Nanda from the home ministry. Radhakrishnan suggested that he be made minister without portfolio and leader of the Lok Sabha with the second position in the cabinet, deputizing for the prime minister whenever required. But Nanda rejected the formula and retained the home ministry. Committed to take the former leader of the Socialist party, Asoka Mehta, whom Kamaraj disliked, she secured his consent by also appointing Jagjivan Ram, whom Kamaraj wanted and whom Radhakrishnan re-

[140] M. Brecher, *Succession in India*, p. 198.

[141] Record of conversation, 19 January 1966. (Translation from Tamil.)

[142] Rajagopalachari to Vijayalakshmi Pandit, 19 January 1966. Vijayalakshmi sent a copy of this letter to the president.

garded as under heavy clouds of charges of corruption. Radhakrishnan felt so strongly about Ram's inclusion that he seriously considered resignation. 'My worry is', wrote Indira Gandhi to him the day after she had taken office as prime minister,

that I have caused you displeasure by being unable to follow your advice in one matter, even though I fully realize the correctness of your view. Please do not think that I am one of those who believes in balancing at all costs or willing to do anything for a position. By nature and training I cannot tolerate what is wrong or unjust. I do not want to say more about this, but please have patience and confidence in me. I think I can, with time, change many such matters and shall certainly try hard to do so as quickly and efficiently as possible.[143]

## VII

The president's attitude to his new prime minister was affectionate, supportive—and non-serious. A comment of his in these early months, which gained wide circulation and was said to have been disliked by Indira Gandhi, was that now one could at least be sure of seeing a pretty face every morning in the newspapers. Reading in *The Times* of her election to an honorary fellowship of Somerville College at Oxford he congratulated her in a teasing way, seeming to mind that she had not mentioned it to him. 'I am angry, very angry, you are numb and dumb! Why did you not tell me all this yesterday morning?' Indira Gandhi took this seriously and sent a handwritten letter of explanation: 'How can you be angry with me? I simply did not remember ... I am most unhappy and upset at your anger. You know how very much I value and depend on your friendship and goodwill.' So Radhakrishnan had to write again: 'All that I mean was it would have given me greater joy if I had heard it from you than read it in cold print. I am not angry!'[144]

Having helped to secure Mrs Gandhi the office of prime minister, Radhakrishnan set out to train her to function adequately. She had the background—'brought up in an environ-

---

[143] Indira Gandhi to Radhakrishnan, 25 January 1966.
[144] Radhakrishnan to Indira Gandhi, her reply and his second letter, all on 18 March 1966.

ment of exalted idealism'[145]—and she seemed willing to learn. It was this which Radhakrishnan commended in these early months of her tenure. 'You are', he wrote to her on the eve of her first visit abroad as prime minister, 'sincere and earnest and they will have their return.'[146] Two months later, declining to write a foreword to a book about her, he added, 'I know the young lady is showing political maturity, high sense of duty and is keenly responsive to public opinion.'[147] Nor did he think that the prime minister would take amiss his efforts at coaching her. His standing in India was unrivalled. A poll taken in the four major cities of India soon after Shastri's death showed him to be the Indian who was most admired.[148] Members of the Congress party as well as leaders of the opposition turned to him for advice or redress and he did not hesitate to state his views. Michael Scott kept him informed of his discussions with the prime minister on the Naga problem.[149] He received deputations which listed grievances against the central and state governments and was reported to have remarked of one matter, 'The whole thing is fishy.'[150] He also told Mrs Gandhi what he thought should be done. Fateh Singh wanted him to help on the Punjab issue and Radhakrishnan advised the prime minister not to postpone a settlement. She agreed and decided soon to bisect the Punjab.[151] For the nomination of members to the Rajya Sabha, Radhakrishnan insisted that the prime minister abide by the convention set up in her father's time that those who could secure election should not be considered.[152]

Radhakrishnan also continued to speak out as before in his role as the keeper of the public conscience. He condemned the disorderly behaviour of some legislators which set a bad ex-

[145] Radhakrishnan's broadcast to the nation, 25 January 1966, *President Radhakrishnan's Speeches and Writings* (second series), p. 65.

[146] Radhakrishnan to Indira Gandhi, 22 March 1966.

[147] Radhakrishnan to K. A. Abbas, 14 May 1966.

[148] 'The Structure of Urban Public Opinion', a survey conducted by the Indian Institute of Public Opinion (New Delhi) in January–February 1966. Radhakrishnan polled 16 per cent of the vote, Indira Gandhi 7 per cent, Kamaraj 6 per cent and Rajagopalachari 3 per cent.

[149] M. Scott to Radhakrishnan, 16 February 1966.

[150] M. Limaye, MP, at Pune, on 10 April 1966, *Deccan Chronicle*, 11 April 1966.

[151] Radhakrishnan to Mrs Gandhi, 22 February 1966, and her reply, 24 February 1966.    [152] Radhakrishnan to Mrs Gandhi, 26 March 1966.

ample to the youth of the country and wished that political parties would select as candidates persons with faith, good sense and moral responsibility. He then criticized the economic mismanagement which led to a chronic dependence on other countries for food. When this became a regular habit, 'we lose our guts, we lose our self-respect and we lose all faith.'[153] He deplored the 'violence in the air', and a few days later he described the orgy of destruction in various parts of the country as essentially a discourtesy to the human spirit.[154] In July he denounced the lack of honesty and integrity which had brought India to a moral crisis.[155]

These speeches were widely reported and discussed. 'Apart from being constitutionally well-positioned to administer this rebuke, President Radhakrishnan is personally well-equipped to do so. He is the embodiment of poise and serenity.'[156] The prime minister herself made no comment and Radhakrishnan assumed that, like Nehru, she approved of the president asserting a national position above the bustle of party politics. Her own first year as prime minister was not distinguished. She had hardly any understanding of economics: 'When economic matters come up in cabinet, I'm not *au fait*. I have to ask what's going on.' Radhakrishnan said in her defence that at least she was not afraid to ask;[157] but unfortunately her right-wing advisers came up with the wrong answer and in June 1966 she approved the devaluation of the rupee. Conservatives such as Rajagopalachari were delighted: 'I have come really to admire Mrs Indira Gandhi.'[158] Correspondingly, radical opinion was infuriated,[159] and Aruna Asaf Ali told Radhakrishnan that they would prefer even Morarji Desai as prime minister.[160] Immediately more serious for Mrs Gandhi was Kamaraj's dislike of the measure. At her request

[153] Speech after unveiling a statue of G. B. Pant, New Delhi, 8 March 1966, *President Radhakrishnan's Speeches and Writings* (second series), pp. 399–401.

[154] Speech at Delhi, 17 March 1966, ibid., pp. 479–81.

[155] Speeches at Ludhiana, 2 July 1966, and Mysore, 26 July 1966, ibid., pp. 217–23.

[156] 'Ariel' (Frank Moraes), in *Sunday Standard*, 13 March 1966.

[157] Bruce Page, 'The Woman Who May Lead 480 Million People', *Sunday Times* (London), 16 January 1966.

[158] Rajagopalachari to Radhakrishnan, 7 June 1966.

[159] See, e.g., editorial, 'Betrayal of Mandate', *Mainstream*, 11 June 1966.

[160] Record of interview with Radhakrishnan, 12 June 1966.

Radhakrishnan spoke to Kamaraj, asked him to be more understanding of Mrs Gandhi's difficulties and, to prevent the
development of a rift, suggested to the prime minister that
she offer Kamaraj the deputy prime ministership. She offered
him instead the home ministry—'as you advised, I did it'—
but Kamaraj made no response.[161]

The prime minister, therefore, found herself criticized vehe-
mently both within the party and outside; and Radhakrishnan
advised her not to take it too much to heart: 'You should keep
well and everything else will shape well. Do not brood on
what other people say. Much of it may be imagination.'[162] But
it was generally known that the decision to devalue had been
taken under pressure from the United States; and Mrs Gandhi
was obviously not yet fully at home in foreign affairs.

From the start of her prime ministership foreign governments had looked to the president for counsel. Radhakrishnan's
interest was now once more centred in Vietnam. He told both
the Soviet ambassador and Vice-President Humphrey that the
Geneva conference should be reconvened to pave the way for
the withdrawal of United States troops and a unified Vietnam
under Ho Chi Minh's leadership.[163] The idea of the Geneva
conference meeting again appealed to both of them; but, as
nothing happened, Radhakrishnan suggested to Mrs Gandhi
that, when she met President Johnson in Washington, she
should urge him to terminate immediately and unconditionally the bombing of North Vietnam as a preliminary to the
reconvening of the Geneva conference. This was a matter on
which the Government of India could take the initiative.[164] He
put the same idea to the American ambassador in Delhi.[165]
Mrs Gandhi responded by making, on the eve of her departure,
a public appeal to the United States to cease aerial bombing
and calling for a meeting of the Geneva conference. Radhakrishnan would have preferred the matter to be broached in
private talks with heads of government and the cessation of

[161] Record of Radhakrishnan's talks with the prime minister, 16 June, 22 June
and 4 August 1966, and with Kamaraj, 6 and 21 July 1966.
[162] Radhakrishnan to Indira Gandhi, 22 June 1966.
[163] Record of Radhakrishnan's interviews with Soviet ambassador, 15 February
1966, and H. Humphrey, vice-president of the USA, 16 February 1966.
[164] Radhakrishnan to Mrs Gandhi, 5 July 1966.
[165] Record of Radhakrishnan's interview with Chester Bowles, 6 July 1966.

bombing made an essential preliminary to the meeting of the Geneva conference, where other matters like the withdrawal of all foreign troops could be considered. As it was, there was no hope of a favourable reply from the Soviet Union and the Vietminh to Mrs Gandhi's broadcast appeal, which was slanted in favour of the United States; but Radhakrishnan, with loyalty to his prime minister, commended it as at least an attempt to suggest ways of reducing the tension.[166]

Radhakrishnan repeated this in his broadcast on the eve of Independence day. Any step that thwarted the possibility of expansion of the conflict was worthwhile. The longing for peace represented the deepest feelings of the world and there was no chance for understanding if it were assumed that every offer from the other side was fiendish and machiavellian. Applying this axiom to India's own problems, Radhakrishnan advocated what had by now become for him a vital and urgent matter, an effort to improve relations with Pakistan and China: 'Nothing should be avoided because it is thought impossible. The only relevant question is, "Does it require to be done?" Then we must try and do it.'[167] Coming within a week of an assertion by the foreign minister that there was no basis for talks with China, Radhakrishnan's statement was seen as advice to the government and therefore welcomed not just by communist spokesmen but by independent opinion.[168] But the main concern of the broadcast was the deterioration of conditions within India. Radhakrishnan deplored the growing strength of the agitational approach, wanted better quality in members of the legislatures, and hinted that the government lacked the honesty and firmness to deal energetically with corruption: 'We are not willing or able to take action against anti-social elements.' Measures for austerity were being taken but these should start at the top for the large majority of the people were already leading austere lives by necessity.

The plain speaking on internal problems also drew wide

[166] Speech at Kottayam, 27 July 1966, *President Radhakrishnan's Speeches and Writings 1964-1967*, pp. 357-60.

[167] Broadcast on 14 August 1966, ibid., pp. 72-5.

[168] E. M. S. Namboodripad in Calicut, 21 August 1966, *The Hindu*, 22 August 1966; editorial in *People's Democracy*, 21 August 1966; editorials in *Times of India*, 16 August 1966, and *The Tribune*, 17 August 1966.

comment and some Congressmen complained to Mrs Gandhi about Radhakrishnan's criticisms. What they did not know was that he had shown her the text before recording and she had approved it. She probably did not recognize its import, her mind at this time being engaged by charges of financial irregularities against a few of her leading ministers. This was tided over, partly because the criticism was mainly in parliament and Mrs Gandhi was indifferent to that body. She told the president, citing an Urdu couplet, that she went there as she went to a bazaar but not as a buyer.[169] Much worse was the violent agitation against cow slaughter in the streets of Delhi, leading to the resignation of the home minister. The prime minister seemed to have little control of the cabinet or the party and even the glitter of the visit of Tito and Nasser just a few days before could not counter the decline of public confidence in themselves and the government: 'They applauded glumly when their President, Dr Radhakrishnan, used his gift for the immaculate phrase in a disheartening way. In one of his welcoming speeches at the airport he said, "we seem to be in the position of the Greek chorus which could foresee the tragedy but was powerless to prevent it." '[170]

## VIII

In the second half of 1966 Radhakrishnan was generally in a relaxed mood. He continued, though at an easier pace than before, his round of speaking engagements in various parts of the country and assisted in the preparation of a documentary film of his life: 'The fine, chiselled, scholarly face of the President in his young days ripens with maturity to the turbaned face we know and love so well. In cinematic terms an ideal face, a sedate, stately screen presence.'[171] He also completed a short book stating once again the case for a religion not circumscribed by narrow belief to fulfil the yearning of the individual and lay the base for a human community: 'We are on the threshold of a new age of spirit.'[172] Though it was the last year of his term of office he gave no thought to what had

[169] 11 August 1966.  [170] Cyril Dunn in The Scotsman, 25 October 1966.
[171] Film critic of The Statesman, 4 September 1966.
[172] Religion in a Changing World (London 1967).

already begun to interest some others—the possibility of his re-election. The first report in the press said that the government were likely to sponsor his candidature again;[173] and a member of the Congress parliamentary board called on him to say that if he had no objection the board would say that they would like to re-elect him.[174] Non-Congress opinion was not far behind. Hiren Mukherjee, the Communist member of parliament, described Radhakrishnan as the only rallying point in the country. True that he was getting on in years; but what was the use of young persons like the prime minister?[175] A few days later Jayaprakash Narayan, by this time far removed from the communists in other matters, voiced similar sentiments: 'Yours is the only sane voice in the country.'[176] To cap it all, in a poll taken in the four metropolitan cities in October, 21 per cent voted him 'the most admired person' in the world, with Indira Gandhi coming next with 9 per cent; and 76 per cent favoured him for the office of president of India.[177]

There gathered, then, an inevitability about Radhakrishnan's re-election—if he agreed to stand. Before he gave a firm answer, on 4 December, while watching a private showing of a Telugu film, he suddenly felt the fingers of his right hand go numb; and a little later he also had some difficulty with his speech. The prime minister and the vice-president were informed. But within two days the condition stabilized and improvement began with hand and speech therapy; and within a week he started attending to official business. He had wanted to go on leave and request Zakir Husain to act as president but Indira Gandhi requested him not to precipitate matters.[178] The same advice had been given by L. P. Singh, the home secretary, when Radhakrishnan sent for him to discuss the fasts undertaken by the Sikh leader Fateh Singh (for redress of certain grievances in Punjab), and by the orthodox Hindu

[173] *The Tribune*, 15 June 1966.

[174] S. K. Patil's interview with Radhakrishnan, 15 June 1966.

[175] N. Chakravarty's report to Radhakrishnan of H. Mukherjee's remarks, 15 August 1966.

[176] Jayaprakash Narayan in conversation with Radhakrishnan, 23 August 1966.

[177] 'The Structure of Metropolitan Public Opinion', The Indian Institute of Public Opinion (New Delhi, October 1966).

[178] Indira Gandhi's interview with Radhakrishnan, 29 December 1966.

monk the Shankaracharya of Puri (as a protest against cow slaughter). Radhakrishnan, while making personal appeals to both to terminate their fasts, conveyed to the government through the home secretary his sense of the danger inherent in the situation.[179] Fateh Singh was willing to accept the president's arbitration but the cabinet, in view of his indisposition, authorized the prime minister to settle the dispute; and the Shankaracharya also was persuaded to accept the president's advice.

The prime minister's reluctance to let Radhakrishnan go on leave was thought by him to give the lie to rumours that had been reaching him that she was keen on the election of Zakir Husain as president. It is possible that she felt more at ease with Husain than with Radhakrishnan, who must sometimes have given her the impression of a pedagogue addressing a pupil. But their personal relations were still unalloyed. The latest testimony of this was a letter to the president from a former secretary of Nehru making personal charges against Mrs Gandhi. Radhakrishnan passed it on to her with the advice not to let it depress her, asked her to discuss it with him[180], and, when she came and her eyes filled with tears, told her the best way to handle the matter.

Although Radhakrishnan's recovery was rapid, he regarded this first sign of failing health as an indication that he should retire. 'I have a right', he told the prime minister early in the new year, 'to declare my innings closed.' The doctors assured him that he would be able to participate in the public ceremonies associated with Republic day; but he asked the vicepresident to take the parade on 26 January and be the chief guest at the beating of retreat on 29 January. The excuse he gave was that his right hand was still in a splint and he did not wish to go to the parade 'with all this luggage'. He felt also that his hand was still not strong enough; he was, he said, like Bob Hope, who had said to a pretty lady, 'my fingers can grip but cannot let go.' But the real reason for his asking Zakir Husain to take his place on these occasions was to prepare the Indian public for a Muslim head of state.

[179] Radhakrishnan's interview with L. P. Singh, 25 December 1966; L. P. Singh, 'The President We Need', *Indian Express*, 17 June 1987.
[180] Radhakrishnan to Indira Gandhi, 30 December 1966.

PRESIDENT                                          355

The broadcast to the nation, however, Radhakrishnan decided to make himself. He spoke of the need for a national outlook, a vision of equality and a commitment to democratic
behaviour. The growing incidence of violent agitation and the
strengthening of sectional interests and regional pressures had
raised in many minds doubts about the stability of a united,
democratic India. To counter this, positive efforts were
required; the government should show that violence was not
the only means of securing change, should take steps to check
the dishonesty that was creeping into every side of public life,
and should investigate all charges of corruption. Describing
the past year as the worst since independence, Radhakrishnan
recognized that of the human failures which it had seen, the
government was not free; 'even after making allowance for all
the difficulties of the situation, we cannot forgive widespread
incompetence and the gross mismanagement of our resources.'
Regarding the world in general, Radhakrishnan spoke of the
barbaric nature of nuclear warfare and of the urgent necessity
of a moral awakening, a complete change of spirit. He then
wound up on a valedictory note. After recalling the pursuit
of wisdom which had been the main inspiration of his life, his
efforts to apply ethical considerations even in public activities,
and his good relations with his predecessor, his three prime
ministers and the representatives of all parties, he thanked the
people for their affection and goodwill and expressed his best
hopes for the future.[181]

This 'magnificent' broadcast was on the lines which Radhakrishnan's audience had grown to expect from him over the
years;[182] but the criticisms of all, including the government,
had never been as severe: 'He defined his Government's
record in terms I have never before in my experience heard
used by a Head of State. He remains in office, and nobody
seems to find it strange.'[183] But this was not, as James Cameron
assumed, due to disenchanted apathy, but because Radhakrishnan had accustomed the Indian public to his speaking in

[181] Broadcast to the nation, 25 January 1967, *President Radhakrishnan's Speeches
and Writings 1964–1967*, pp. 84–7.

[182] Editorial in *The Guardian*, 4 February 1967.

[183] James Cameron's despatch from Delhi, *Evening Standard* (London), 24
February 1967.

such forthright terms. But the timing of the broadcast was sensitive. The general elections were only a few weeks away, and the parties in opposition made full use of the text to denounce Mrs Gandhi's administration. The prime minister was naturally annoyed with the president but what made her angrier was that she had no cause to remonstrate. For Radhakrishnan had shown her the text of the broadcast during one of her regular weekly calls in January and Mrs Gandhi had flipped the pages and nodded her approval. Had Radhakrishnan sent her the text she would no doubt have read it carefully and consulted her advisers and perhaps suggested some changes; but she was not the quickest of readers and obviously did not absorb what had been shown to her.

Radhakrishnan was still determined to retire: 'Left to myself, I wish to get out of the present office.'[184] But the president is elected by an electoral college of all the elected members of the two houses of parliament and of the state assemblies, and the results of the elections in February 1967 suggested that a candidate sponsored by the Congress was not well assured of success. In these circumstances, the demand spread that Radhakrishnan be put up again by the Congress, for he, of all the possible candidates, was most acceptable to the parties of the opposition. The setbacks suffered by the Congress in the elections and the weakening of the dominance of Indian politics by one party enhanced the role of a non-party president: 'The range of the President's constitutional powers have never been put to the test. Yet if ever there was the occasion it is now and if ever there was the man he is here. Dr Radhakrishnan can be depended upon to rise to the occasion.'[185] Indeed, in the press there was a wide variety of support for Radhakrishnan's continuance in office.[186] As for the politicians, Rajagopalachari wanted him to agree to re-election[187] and the Jan Sangh expressed the same view publicly.[188] In the Congress the leading

[184] Radhakrishnan to Rajagopalachari, 3 February 1967.

[185] F. Moraes, 'The Silent Revolution', *Indian Express*, 27 February 1967.

[186] *Amrita Bazar Patrika* (Calcutta), 25 February 1967, *Hindustan Standard* (Calcutta), 27 February 1967, *The Mail* (Madras), 27 February 1967, *National Herald* (Lucknow), 2 March 1967.

[187] To Radhakrishnan, 6 February 1967, and at interview in Delhi, 14 March 1967; press conference at Delhi, 18 March 1967, *The Statesman*, 19 March 1967.

[188] *Hindustan Times*, 4 March 1967.

voice in this regard was that of Kamaraj, the president, though
his influence had been much drained by his own defeat in the
elections to the assembly in Madras. He spoke about it to
Radhakrishnan, who was non-committal.[189] He had recovered
well enough for his health not to be an objection and he waited
to see how the situation would develop. But by the end of the
first week of March it was thought there would be near unanimity on a second term for Radhakrishnan, as the only
person acceptable to both the Congress and the opposition.[190]

The bandwagon, then, was rolling for Radhakrishnan; but it
was reckoning without the prime minister. Upset by his broadcast on 25 January, Indira Gandhi was annoyed further by
Radhakrishnan permitting the opposition in Rajasthan, which
had not been invited by the governor to form a ministry, to
parade their number before him in Delhi in the presence of the
home minister, so as to establish beyond question that they
formed a majority in the assembly.[191] But it would be unfair to
suggest that Mrs Gandhi was swayed only by personal animus
against Radhakrishnan, that 'he shows up the mediocrity of
present-day leadership which seems only too willing to see him
retire.'[192] Believing that Radhakrishnan was determined to
depart, she had probably committed herself to Zakir Husain;
she now, in the new circumstances after the elections, inquired
if he would agree to a second term as vice-president and was
given a firm refusal. She was not so keen on retaining Radhakrishnan as to consider withdrawing her support to Husain's
candidature. Indeed, she relished this situation as Radhakrishnan was seen as Kamaraj's nominee and Mrs Gandhi's
relations with Kamaraj had deteriorated to the extent that she
was spoiling for a fight with him. Support for Husain had also
the advantages that she could depict it as a blow for secularism
while securing for herself a compliant president.

All this is understandable; but where Mrs Gandhi lapsed was
that she never discussed the matter directly with Radhakrishnan, even though she was seeing him regularly throughout

[189] 4 March 1967.
[190] Despatch from Delhi, *The Hindu*, 7 March 1967, *The Mail*, 8 March 1967,
*The Pioneer* (Lucknow), 8 March 1967.
[191] *The Statesman*, 16 March 1967.
[192] Sharokh Sabavala in *Christian Science Monitor*, 28 January 1967.

this period. He told both Kamaraj and Mrs Gandhi that he was prepared to continue as president only if it became necessary in the national interest.[193] Kamaraj replied that he thought it was necessary; Mrs Gandhi said nothing at all. She had also, according to Kamaraj, said nothing in the working committee when he had expressed himself in favour of Radhakrishnan. Such unbroken silence increased Radhakrishnan's belief that, in the context of their past relations and the continuous personal interest he had shown in her, if she now wanted him to step down she would have told him so and the decision could be taken with dignity on all sides. So he was deeply hurt when he later learnt that her silence to him on the subject was accompanied by vigorous campaigning for Zakir Husain. But personal gratitude and general broadmindedness are not virtues to be expected of insecure prime ministers.

Meanwhile, the support for Radhakrishnan gathered in volume. The Congress seemed to be committed to him.[194] Dinesh Singh, a young Congressman known to be close to the prime minister, called on Radhakrishnan to press him to continue;[195] and the next day M. C. Chagla, a member of the cabinet and a secular-minded Muslim, urged him not to expose Zakir Husain to an election for, even if Husain won, it would strengthen communal feeling in the country with disastrous consequences. The regional party that had won the election in Madras publicly stated their confidence in Radhakrishnan[196] and Rajagopalachari reiterated his position.[197] Left-wing opinion expressed itself in his favour,[198] and so did Fateh Singh. Radhakrishnan himself let matters drift: 'There is pressure on me to continue. I do not know what I will do.'[199]

Had the Congress at this time announced its choice of Radhakrishnan for a second term, all parties and groups in the opposition would have probably also given their assent. The

[193] Interview with Kamaraj, 22 March 1967, and with Mrs Gandhi, 24 March 1967.

[194] *Indian Express*, 23 March 1967.

[195] 28 March 1967. What Radhakrishnan did not know was that outside Rashtrapati Bhavan Dinesh Singh was lobbying for Zakir Husain.

[196] *Indian Express*, 24 March 1967.

[197] *Swarajya*, 25 March 1967.

[198] 'The President', editorial in *The Patriot* (Delhi), 25 March 1967.

[199] Radhakrishnan to A. R. Wadia, 26 March 1967.

re-election of Radhakrishnan appeared almost certain.[200] But
the differences between Kamaraj and Mrs Gandhi precluded a
quick decision and provided stray political elements with scope
for intrigue. The prime minister got in touch with Minoo
Masani, a member of the Swatantra party who was taking a
line different to that of his leader Rajagopalachari, and talked
to him (being at this time most at home with reactionaries) of
the possibility of the government and the opposition finding a
consensus candidate—implying clearly that she was looking
beyond Radhakrishnan and expecting Masani to lobby for
Zakir Husain. This tactic of using the opposition to settle differences within her own party was one which Mrs Gandhi was to
employ often in her career. Masani, while helping to break up
the consensus in the opposition in favour of Radhakrishnan,
sought to outwit Mrs Gandhi by not leaving the field to Zakir
Husain. Seven parties in the opposition suddenly came up with
the name of the chief justice of India without securing his
consent. Masani acted without the support of his party[201]
while other parties, assuming that the chief justice would not
agree, saw no more in this than a gimmick to embarrass the
Congress.[202]

At last the Congress parliamentary board met on 5 April.
Four members followed Mrs Gandhi and two went with
Kamaraj; and the final decision was left to be taken by the
prime minister and the president of the party. This was the
point at which Radhakrishnan should have announced that he
had no interest in the presidentship. With the Congress leadership publicly divided and the opposition coaxed into declaring
support for someone else, instant withdrawal by Radhakrishnan
would have defeated rumours that he was hankering for a job.
He himself was all set to do this but allowed his judgement to be
weakened by his personal affection for Kamaraj, who pleaded
that he be given a few more days. His reasoning was that the
warning given to the prime minister by the chief ministers of
Uttar Pradesh and Madhya Pradesh that they could not

[200] I. Malhotra in *The Guardian*, 4 April 1967.

[201] See C. C. Desai to M. Masani, 4 April 1967. Desai sent a copy of this letter
to Radhakrishnan.

[202] B. Madhok (of the Jan Sangh), in conversation with Radhakrishnan,
8 April 1967.

24

guarantee a solid Congress vote for Zakir Husain might make
her more cautious; and it was thought even by others that the
Congress would finally opt for Radhakrishnan.[203] He would
hold the Congress together and split the opposition while
Husain would divide the Congress and unite the opposition.
But all this did not make Radhakrishnan happier. 'In your
conflict', he told Kamaraj in Tamil, 'I am being sacrificed. I
have never been elected except by unanimity. I don't want this
job and want to issue a statement saying so.' But unfortunately
Kamaraj prevailed. Radhakrishnan allowed his prestige to be
tarnished in the eyes of some, at the very end of a dazzling
career stretching for over sixty years, because of his commitment to a friend.

Finally, on 9 April, Radhakrishnan, after ringing Kamaraj to
inform him that he had waited long enough, announced his decision not to allow his name to go forward; and this came within
minutes of the chief justice's consent to be a candidate, though
the two decisions had nothing to do with each other. In his statement Radhakrishnan did not fail to draw attention to the shortcomings on all sides—the failure of the Congress to decide
quickly and openly, the petty politics of some members of the
opposition and the suspected horse-trading by which the prime
minister was reported to be willing to support the chief justice
for the vice-presidentship if Husain were assured of the presidentship: 'Recent developments in connection with the two
highest offices in the country have made me most unhappy and
strengthened my resolve to retire.'[204] The statement made very
clear that 'he is not just old, he is fed up.'[205]

Once he had announced his decision not to allow his name to
be considered, Radhakrishnan was again the picture of tran-
quillity and, while others were engaged in the presidential
elections, he went through his last weeks in office with serene
detachment. He conducted investitures and pinned medals and
decorations on innumerable chests as if to demonstrate that
physical weakness was no longer a problem. He gave sittings
to Derek Hill for the portrait which now hangs in the hall at

[203] See reports in *Indian Express* and *Patriot*, 7 April 1967.
[204] Radhakrishnan's statement to the press, 9 April 1967.
[205] 'Guiding Hand for India', leader in *The Times*, 17 April 1967.

All Souls.[206] Bertrand Russell's gesture in sending him a signed copy of the first volume of his autobiography, which was to be published in Britain that summer, served as a reminder that his standing in the world had nothing to do with his office. There was no diminution of vigour or dilution of substance in his last addresses as president and his farewell broadcast was in line with the speeches he had made right from his youth, with its stress on the need for vision, tolerance and understanding, and its call for civilized conduct in human affairs in both India and the world. 'As a student', wrote a member of the audience at one of these final occasions,

I had heard you thirty years ago, and your speech had left on my mind an indelible impression. When I heard you today again I wondered what was more incredible—the superlative content or the strong lovely voice serving as a vehicle for your impeccable accent. May I have the impertinence to say that few men in any age could have served their country so well as you have served India.[207]

In his five years as the country's president, Radhakrishnan, without transgressing the letter or the spirit of the constitution, set healthy precedents and built for the office a role in confirming national purpose and unity. The people learned to look to him as the impartial guardian of the public interest, befriending and advising the government but also capable if need be of standing apart from it. Of his prime ministers, only Nehru welcomed an approach which led to a basically personal and, to this day, unique achievement.

---

[206] 'A most remarkable man of integrity, simplicity and dignity as well as learning. He seemed to me to be a mixture of Gandhi and Berenson, and I loved the sittings with him in Lutyens' great viceregal building in Delhi. Swallows nesting in his room flew in and out and all pomp and ceremony were absent.' Grey Gowrie, Derek Hill: An Appreciation (London 1987), p. 142.
[207] N. A. Palkhivala to Radhakrishnan, 12 April 1967.

# 13

# A LIFE AT MANY LEVELS

Radhakrishnan's departure from Delhi had dignity and personal quality. All who met him during those days became aware of an inner peace, born of a satisfying sense of fulfilment, the feeling that he had done what he had set out to do in various fields many years before. In retirement he was determined, the freedom of silence being now his prerogative, to make no public appearances. Rather than becoming tiresome by airing his views irresponsibly on all subjects, he would cultivate the private graces and spend his time reading and writing on philosophical subjects. He planned a major work on the Gospel according to St John but was diverted from this by the request of the Gandhi Foundation to edit a volume on Gandhi to mark the centenary of his birth. Radhakrishnan collected a wide variety of articles and *Gandhi: 100 Years* was published as scheduled in 1969. His own introductory essay, which proved to be his last piece of sustained writing, affirmed that his basic ideas had not altered over the years: 'Man is still evolving.'

Despite himself, however, Radhakrishnan found that enforced leisure and inconsequential living did not come easily to him. For someone who, like Auden, had always assumed that when he reached a crossroads the traffic-lights would turn green, the return to Madras in May 1967 was instinct with sadness. He missed the drug of public life and the hurt look in his eyes showed that he found it hard to reconcile retirement with belief in his invincible luck. When a long and variegated career passes its climax and one is no longer in the thick of things, reflective activity cannot fully replace the inquisitive enjoyment of life. Though surrounded by the affection of his family, a future away from the centres of great events appeared joyless. He was lonely in mind and spirit as he had himself

earlier defined it: 'to be lonely is to be depressed, to be frustrated, to have nothing which can occupy our mind or our
attention.'[1] Politics had become a part of his being and he now
felt the tedium such as is known only to those who have once
lived on the pinnacles of life. A succession of grey hours took
the place of years of public recognition and acclaim. His feeling
at this time partly reflected what he had written many years
before: 'The best fruits which we can pluck from the tree of
life turn to ashes in our mouth.'[2] His vitality ran low and he was
reduced to muscle-and-bone thinness covered by a wafer-like
skin. Only two functions broke this boredom. The Bharatiya
Vidya Bhavan, an institution for the promotion of Indian
culture, held a short ceremony at Radhakrishnan's residence to
present him with their highest award; and then, on 10 September 1968, Zakir Husain, in his capacity as president of the
Sahitya Akademi, called on him to confer the fellowship of the
Akademi.

'Articulation', said Radhakrishnan on that occasion, 'is our
precious possession. It was the beginning of things human.'
Ten days later his own articulation was affected and speech
became slurred when he suffered a stroke. At the start he was
aware of his condition and felt deeply the dishonour of his illness and his inability to co-ordinate thought and speech. Thereafter a succession of minor strokes punctuated a slow descent
spread over seven years. In this evening, in Larkin's words,
which lights no lamps, with both co-ordination of speech and
thought and memory affected before his body gave way, with
three sons-in-law and his few friends in Madras—Rajagopalachari, T. T. Krishnamachari, Mohan Kumaramangalam—
all departing before him, he himself was heartsick and in a
hurry to be gone. In September 1973 he slipped and broke his
hip; and thereafter he was bedridden and began patently to
break up. 'Ringed in by emptiness', with neither the will to live
nor the ability to die, he lingered on with the shadow of death
over him, existing but ceasing to be himself, slowly losing his
mental faculties and moving in and out of a nursing home with
a succession of complaints. His hold of reality gradually relaxed

[1] Speech, 13 December 1965, *President Radhakrishnan's Speeches and Writings*
(second series), p. 146.
[2] *Indian Philosophy*, vol. 2, p. 613.

and in his last weeks there was a look in his eyes of withdrawal beyond recall. Just then was announced the award to him of the Templeton prize for Progress in Religion. It is difficult to know whether he grasped this fact; and his family, knowing what he would have liked, transferred the prize money to Oxford University as a bequest. Finally, in the early hours of 17 April 1975, Radhakrishnan drifted out of the harbour on a silent tide.

> The curtain of your life was drawn
> Sometime between despair and dawn.
>
> —Peter Porter

## II

The sad winter of these empty years cannot cast a backward shadow on all that had gone before. In death he looked unconquered and fulfilled, the work accomplished and all the travail smoothed out; and there was appropriate justice in this. In an unbroken career of smooth ascendancy, progressing straight and upward seemingly without strain, he had crowded so much but within a unity. It is difficult to think of any side of his life which was apparently incomplete. His achievements in various fields have a touch of inevitability that robs them of the power to surprise. Every stage except the last in a long span of eighty-six years makes perfect sense. The last of his writings is implicit in the first and his final public actions in tune with the beginnings.

If, over the years, Radhakrishnan moved on and up as though by natural processes, missed no turning, always took the right road and did not need to resort to any winding stair, he attributed it all to the bounty of God. He shared Winston Churchill's feeling: 'over me beat invisible wings'. He had a personal sense of providence and, with the certainty that his life was a carefully planned script written by a power above, did not believe in conscious choices. 'The way of my life', he wrote sometime in the fifties in one of his private jottings, 'does not follow my desires or plans. He who has built me up all these years, amidst pleasures and pains so that He may make use of me He will guide me and use me in the service not of my country but of the world.' At about the same time he wrote to a close friend who had suffered a double bereavement:

I have had my share of sorrow and suffering in the world but go through life in a spirit of utter surrender. Look at the way in which I travel all alone from China to Mexico. I am protected by the grace of the Divine and the prayers of my friends. When there is nothing more to be done by me on earth, I will pass out, with no grievance but with an utter thanksgiving, for all that life has meant for me in joy and sorrow, in triumph and in defeat.[3]

This strong sense of design and purpose in his life required of him only, with the Supreme as his only guide, to do what came his way with a mental attitude of renunciation and to be compassionate to his fellow-beings: 'If we are careful and considerate, we will be protected. My life is not a bad example of the value of faith and kindness.'[4] Certainly throughout a long life he had never been guilty of a mean deed; and it is unlikely that he ever had a mean thought.

## III

The sense of being always surrounded by the Divine Presence gave Radhakrishnan an untroubled sense of wholeness. This belief in God marched with a belief in himself and he was confident from his earliest years that he was singled out for great achievement. Even the poverty of the early years seemed to him by divine appointment and he noted sometime in 1946 a statement of Mencius:

when Heaven intends to call a man to a great mission, it always first hardens his ambition, belabours his muscles and bones, starves his body, denies him the necessities of life and frustrates what he sets out to do so that his ambition may be kindled and his character be strengthened and he may learn to do what he could not do before.

He never talked about these lean years in later days except for a casual, oblique remark to his son, 'Your mother suffered a great deal at the start.' But his own experience may have helped to create his compulsive generosity to the less fortunate and there was always an added emphasis in his voice when he spoke of poverty being good for the soul only when it was voluntary.

[3] 21 November 1950.
[4] To his son from Moscow, 28 March 1952.

Drawn by accident into philosophy, Radhakrishnan by his confidence, concentration and strong convictions made himself into a great philosopher. From the crackling brilliance of the *Ethics of the Vedanta* to the autumnal grace of *Religion in a Changing World* written nearly sixty years later, his thought and writing developed with a steady and consistent assurance. His oeuvre has an inevitability of direction and singleness of purpose and is informed by a common spirit and set of concerns. To him, as to Russell, philosophy was an effort to find the meaning of life; and like Russell he had analytical skill, could engage in constructive thought and communicate with ease. Russell's prose was more crystalline; but Radhakrishnan made up for this with forceful and untentative writing for he had the advantage of an intense and powerful vision of the world. In this he was, among contemporary philosophers, nearer to Maritain, and asserted that to pursue genuine philosophy it was not necessary to forsake religion; but, unlike Maritain, he did not attach importance to divine revelation and therefore regarded philosophy as autonomous and not a mere handmaid of theology.

A philosopher, like any other thinker, is influenced by his environment. Radhakrishnan's early writings are set in the context of British rule in India, with Christianity appearing as an alien ideological force making unreasonable demands and many scholars writing off the thought of India as having nothing positive to contribute to the world. In reaction, Radhakrishnan's creative impulse was inspired by the passion of Indianness. His study of Indian philosophy served as a cultural therapy. Finding his country trapped in Western paradigms of thought, he turned the bars into gates by interpreting Indian thought in Western terms and showing that it was as imbued with reason and logic as any intellectual system anywhere. In this sense he restored India to Indians and helped them to recover their mental self-esteem. But he also made clear to them that their long and rich tradition had been arrested and required innovation and further evolution. While he elucidated Hinduism at its highest levels and renewed its dignity, he stressed that it had to cast off much that was corrupt and abhorrent. All seekers of truth were breakers of tradition, which was an attempt to fossilize truth:

If our ancients had a virtue it was courage, and if we have a fault it is timidity. We have lost today the many-sided adventurousness and resilience necessary to face new tasks and reorient our system of thought and practice. There is such a thing as degeneration of accepted ideas. Many of them are kept going artificially even after life has left them.[5]

As this suggests, Radhakrishnan was an adventurous philosopher. Tagore once remarked that he was one of the few Indian scholars the springs of whose mind had not been crushed by the load of scholarship. In the late twenties he was in the full flood of his talent and creative energy and, in his 'breakthrough' piece, *An Idealist View of Life*, he set forth his constructive metaphysic. His mind was soaked in Western thought; he once observed that if asked to mention the books which had most influenced him he would list the Bible, the works of Shakespeare and the writings of Kant.[6] But such deep familiarity with European intellectual traditions had not divested him of his own cultural identity and he now synthesized Eastern and Western idealism. The Advaita Vedanta was expounded in terms of the reason and science of his own day. Relying on a formidable breadth of reading, and expressing thought that was at one with deep intuitive insight, he set forth a structure which encompassed all forms of life and established relationships between the contingent and the universal. He provided for an awareness more profound than factual knowledge and in a tone of impassioned conviction urged the individual, held back by scientific rationalism, to step out into the fullness of experience.

At the same time, Radhakrishnan developed the discipline of comparative religion with a view to bringing to the forefront the moral values and spiritual insights common to all organized religions. He harmonized seeming opposites; and some critics have alleged that the parallels are at times too facile.[7] But he is best known for the bridges which he built between East and West in the realm of spiritual values and ultimate concepts. It has been said of him that—

[5] Speech at Madras, 31 March 1936, *The Statesman*, 2 April 1936.
[6] Speech at Madras, 14 January 1953, *The Mail* (Madras), 15 January 1953.
[7] For example, 'Between East and West', *Times Literary Supplement*, 20 February 1953.

no one has so delved into the spirit, thought and ideals of Eastern and Western minds as to reach a level at which both can meet with appreciation and understanding ... Professor Radhakrishnan will be remembered as the man who made possible, by his own eagerness, a shared understanding between East and West.[8]

To Western readers he interpreted the philosophy of India in a way which could be understood fully by them: 'Only an authority who has been brought up in that intricate citadel of the soul, and afterwards trained in the less complex patterns of the West could achieve such an exposition.'[9] His own people he taught to understand and appreciate the speculative and scientific thought of the Western world. They should not suffer from the narrowness of vision which comes from the hardening of the mind. The only faith that a modern, cultivated person could have was faith in a truth arrived at by reason.

To have helped Indians to hold up their heads, to have made Indian philosophy an integral part of the world's culture and to have shown the real ways in which East and West could respond to each other—these were solid achievements. 'Whatever', Radhakrishnan noted privately in 1941, 'may have been my youthful ambitions, no other career would have given me, as I draw towards the end of my life's work, greater satisfaction than that to which circumstances, rather than deliberate choice, ultimately led me.' But Radhakrishnan's work was as yet far from over. From the search for mutual understanding between followers of different religions and cultural traditions, he had, even in 1936, moved on to plead for the emergence of a new civilization based on the unity of mankind and common truths of the spirit; and after the war, with a free India in a world being drawn even closer by technology, the focus of Radhakrishnan's thought and activity shifted to the strengthening of understanding in mind and heart. Towards this end, his supreme purpose now was to restore a sense of spiritual values to the millions of religiously displaced persons in all parts of the world by reclaiming such men and women not to any church or creed but to the truth that underlies all religions. The essence of religion was the deepening of one's own awareness and compassion for the suffering world. The unity of humanity could be

---

[8] *Times Literary Supplement*, 10 August 1951.
[9] Gerald Heard in *New York Times Book Review*, 10 August 1952.

achieved only by producing a new type of human being who was totally dedicated to the spirit of brotherhood. True religion should bring about such a transformation and change of outlook. It went beyond traditional belief, metaphysical speculation and ritualistic piety to an insight into reality and expressed itself in a remaking of the individual and the practice of love— in Schweitzer's words, 'inward men with an active ethic'. Radhakrishnan's own fullness of insight and richness of public character, taken with his unique acceptance as a thinker everywhere, provided the best testimony for such a religion. 'A religion', he had written, 'ceases to be a universal faith if it does not make universal men.' He was himself recognized as such a universal man.[10] The area of his influence was immense, extending far beyond philosophers to all types of persons to whom he provided not only a philosophy and spiritual understanding but new ways of thought and life. 'When', Arnold Toynbee wrote to him, 'I preach the virtues of mutual understanding and appreciation in Western countries and meet rather determined opposition there, I take comfort in remembering that my point is one that you, too, have at heart.'[11] Such psychological resistance in Western minds has, since the years when Toynbee wrote, diminished with the erosion of Christianity, and the climate has become more propitious to the catholicity and enlightened reasonableness of Radhakrishnan's thought.

## IV

Once he had embarked on philosophical and religious studies, those formed the core of Radhakrishnan's life. But from the start he sought to engage such studies in the political and social developments of the contemporary context. A philosopher could not be coldly distant from everyday life and was as much concerned with current realities as with remote abstractions. While many great philosophers—Plato, Spinoza, Locke, Russell—have concerned themselves with public as well as philosophical problems, what differentiates Radhakrishnan's position is that his primary interest was the philosophy of

[10] *Christ Church Press* (New Zealand), 9 August 1952.
[11] 26 February 1957.

religion. But that itself made interest in the world mandatory, for moksha and dharma, spiritual freedom and social duty, were both central concerns of the human being. If at times Radhakrishnan liked to believe that involvement in public affairs was a matter of duty rather than of inclination, contracting out of the world was not either in Radhakrishnan's philosophy or in his nature. His aim was an integrated personality, with a composed mind and a compassionate heart. In one of his early writings he had described man as an amphibious animal living in two worlds, born of matter and entangled in it but with the divine spark:[12] and in his last book he described a truly religious person as one who lived on the frontiers between the sacred and secular, between religion and politics, between being and non-being.[13] So, while philosophy gave his life structure and remained its fundamental impetus, he moved at ease in the world. In a short piece written in 1946 as a foreword to a volume in honour of an old colleague, Radhakrishnan gave noble expression to his conception of the role of the philosopher in society; and, though ostensibly a tribute to another, it was in fact coded autobiography with an undertow of self-reflection. A study of philosophy was to him not an exposition of past and present systems of thought or dialectical thinking about thinking but the reasoned adoption of a way of life, which included the contemplative urge to the knowledge of reality and the practical impulse to weave that knowledge into life. Philosophy assumed a living character only when there was this striving to invest life with significance: 'Every human life should become a poem.' When Plato had said that philosophers should be kings, he had had in mind not the making of laws and the solution of political problems but the philosophic temper of mind, the exalted, calm, noble, dispassionate attitude, unmoved by motives of personal gain, ambition or power, which alone could solve such problems. Philosophy was not a speciality but an integration of specialities and the philosopher, 'travelling in truth and protected by honest thought, ever alive in mind to the ways of spirit', provided the reflection on life's problems. In India the philosopher's duty was to keep in touch with the past while stretching out to the future. The spiritual

---

[12] *The Reign of Religion in Contemporary Philosophy*, p. 431.
[13] *Religion in a Changing World*, p. 110.

life of individuals was inconceivable apart from the society which formed and sustained them; and so the philosopher in India should adhere to its habits while trying to refine society and exceed its forms: 'While it is essential for us to assimilate everything of value which modern life offers us, we must not surrender the master-plan of our life . . .'[14]

This commitment to society, the crusading, urgent tone in his scholarly writings, the modern note in his interpretations of even classical texts, and his intellectual resistance to the deforming pressures of colonialism gave Radhakrishnan even by the late twenties a distinct public image. This was enhanced, of course, by his reputation as a teacher and his prowess as an orator. Over his students he exercised no forbidding authority, tried to build up no school and encouraged them to think for themselves. An hour with him was more than a lecture on a philosophical topic; it became adventure and colour, and spilt over into life. Sometimes a casual manner in class, such as going through his mail while a student was reading his essay, put off a few; once, noticing this, he proceeded to give a precise resumé, establishing that he had missed nothing.[15] Outside the classroom, his public speeches involved the audience in his thought and had the power to move the whole person, the intellect as well as the capacity for feeling. As a broadcaster he was effective; and in his few appearances on television abroad he came across impressively. Unfortunately in his time television had not become a settled fact in India.

His philosophical writings being thus always close to contemporary concerns and reacting to the preoccupations of the time, Radhakrishnan had at no time to make a choice between the contemplative and the active life and bore without any difficulty the double strain. Indeed the clarity of judgement and ability to conciliate with humour and a light touch which distinguished his terms as vice-chancellor were strengthened by his philosophical approach; and he associated philosophy with the promotion of opinion both before and after 1947. Drawing on the resources of deep scholarship and speaking with

[14] Foreword written at Oxford, 10 June 1946, and published in N. S. Sastry and G. H. Rao (eds.), *Hiriyanna Commemoration Volume* (Mysore 1952).

[15] A. K. Mazumdar, 'Radhakrishnan as I Saw Him', *The Statesman*, 4 October 1987.

political sensitivity and a gnawing social conscience, he became
a focus of intellectual and moral authority. In the last decades
of British rule his was the most sophisticated and exalted
analysis of Gandhi's work and thought; and in free India he
provided the ideological armour of Nehru's foreign policy. He
was wholly with Nehru too in the decision to introduce the full
ambit of political democracy and had in fact been demanding
this long before India attained independence: 'I am a great
believer in democracy, not because it is a fine political arrangement but because it is the highest religion.' Both the highest
religion and the highest politics were an emphasis on the role of
the individual: 'The individual is the final fact of life.' If the
freedom of the individual were suppressed, nothing great would
be achieved. In a civilized society, the individual should be able
to develop his mind and spirit and this was the purpose of
education.[16]

His political philosophy Radhakrishnan once summed up as
'civilized individualism'.[17] The civilizing process he had in
mind was economic betterment and equality in social status. He
could, like Ibsen, claim to have within him both the Right and
the Left, for he felt no tension in reconciling commitment to
progress with allegiance to the past. His political awareness
awakened him to social injustice, and he advanced through life
with steadily widening sympathies. He preferred stretching
rather than breaking moulds and saw little to commend in
Marxist theory; but the comfort that conservative opinion derived from this was swamped by his proclaimed support for the
disadvantaged sections of society. Uncorrupted by the compro-
mises of public life and spurning the discreet ways of political
time-servers he consistently and publicly, even when in high
office, criticized the governments of Nehru and his successors
for failing to do enough to improve the standards of living of
ordinary men and women. Such refusal to be enclosed in the
mentality of politics and to be silenced by the seeming needs of
the hour gave style and substance to Radhakrishnan's tenure of
the vice-presidentship and the presidentship. Radhakrishnan

[16] Speeches at Madras, 18 July and 7 October 1938, *The Hindu*, 19 July and
8 October 1938, respectively; speech at Lucknow, 27 December 1939, *The Hindu*,
28 December 1939.
[17] Speech at Cheltenham, *Gloucestershire Echo*, 3 August 1936.

had no hard political intelligence and was not endowed with what Bagehot described as the prowling faculties. He was easily deceived and flattered, could not tell friends from ill-wishers, had not the capacity to manoeuvre. But these very inadequacies gave him a great strength in that he was always himself. His unfailing dignity and unwavering fidelity to high principle lent grace, nobility and moral authority to all the offices which he held.

These qualities of Radhakrishnan were clearly and appropriately reflected in his broadcast on the eve of laying down the presidentship.[18] He declared his unshaken faith in the people of India and in the enduring vitality of Indian culture, the secret of whose staying power was tolerance and understanding. This culture could also pave the way for the real unification of the world. To humanize the universe, man had first to be humanized: 'We have to chart our course by the distant stars and not by the dim street-lights.' In India, national unity had to be built up by community of endeavour and a sense of shared aspiration. Democracy was more than a system of government; it was a way of life and a regime of civilized conduct of human affairs. Monumental self-righteousness was the curse of individuals as of nations. Service at any cost and not power at any price should be the objective: 'It is my earnest hope and prayer that economic growth will be resumed and accelerated, that cleanliness and character will return in a larger measure to our society and the common people of this country get what they so richly deserve—a better life, a more human condition.'

The response of the common people was exemplified by the crowds that assembled at his death. They did not claim to comprehend his thought or even to understand his speeches and writings, which were all in English. But they knew that he had cared. So they came in their thousands—labourers, clerks, rickshaw-pullers, factory workers, party cadres, the unemployed —and joined the well-to-do, the politicians and the diplomats in laying flowers on his body; and they then lined the route to the cremation. But two persons were conspicuous by their absence. The prime minister, Indira Gandhi, and President Ahmed had not the grace to attend.

[18] 12 May 1967, *President Radhakrishnan's Speeches and Writings* (second series), pp. 94–7.

## V

If in India Radhakrishnan evoked a positive emotion, abroad he became by the end one of the best-liked public figures of his time. He earned very early international recognition as a philosopher, and Evelyn Underhill described him, when still in his mid forties, as 'one who must certainly rank among the more important thinkers of our day'.[19] Such respect earned by his writings was enhanced by the influence of his personality, which conveyed a sense of balanced development of the different sides of his nature—physical, intellectual, moral and spiritual. Some idea of this is given by Joad, and the long passage merits quotation in full, if only because it is the first account we have of Radhakrishnan's impact on cultivated minds in the West:

I shall not easily forget dining in company with Radhakrishnan at H. G. Wells's flat. Besides Wells and myself there was only one other person present, J. W. N. Sullivan, the well-known writer on scientific subjects. The talk was continuous and eager; it included science, philosophy, the state of the world, the possible collapse of Western civilization. Radhakrishnan was for the most part silent. He sat there refusing one after another the dishes of an elaborate meal, drinking only water, listening. We others, knowing his reputation as a speaker and a conversationalist were, I think, a little surprised at this silence; surprised, and impressed, not so much because what he did say was always to the point, but because his silence in such a discussion was a richer and more significant thing than any positive contribution he could have made. It was the silence of a completely integrated personality, deliberately absorbing an atmosphere. To suggest an idea to the ordinary man is like dropping a stone into a deep well. One hears the splash of the impact, and then silence. What happens thereafter is unknown; so far as any evidence to the contrary goes, the idea has been completely buried in the bowels of the personality. Certainly it never re-emerges. To talk to Radhakrishnan is not like that. The idea sinks in but only to re-emerge, reclothed and transfigured by the alchemy of a very subtle mind. Assuredly a fruitful and significant experience! I was not surprised at the warmth of Wells's leave-taking despite the silence of the guest.[20]

Soon after the Second World War, national politics, to Radhakrishnan's satisfaction, receded and made room for a

---

[19] *The Spectator*, 22 December 1933.
[20] C. E. M. Joad, *Counter-Attack from the East* (London 1933), pp. 42–3.

universal vision; and Radhakrishnan, an instinctive inter-
nationalist, crisscrossed the world asserting that to regard one's
own country as the centre of the world was outmoded and one
should learn to admit the possible worth of values and ways of
living which were not acceptable to oneself. He never concealed his own Indian identity of mind and spirit. No one but an
Indian could have written his books and he was once described
as 'India personified'.[21] But this very Indianness, in his view,
enabled him to appreciate attitudes and approaches very different from his own. This made him an ideal ambassador of India
to the Soviet Union. He felt that the people of that country were
friendly, that Soviet society was changing, that even beneath
the repression of the Stalin years one could discern an effort to
build something new and decent and that defensive compul-
sions rather than expansionist objectives motivated Soviet
foreign policy. His supple and vigilant mind assisted in the
creation in the world of sympathetic awareness of the Soviet
Union. He brought fresh force to George Orwell's dictum that
an understanding of the Soviet Union requires an effort of the
imagination as well as of the intellect. Himself a philosopher
conforming to Wittgenstein's definition of a citizen who belonged to no community of ideas, he was willing to see good
wherever he found it. He sought to understand the collective
mentality of the Russian people and was intrigued by a statement of Pushkin: 'On the shores of the Baltic stands a great
black oak. Round the stem of the oak walks a great black cat.
When it walks to the left it sings a song. When it walks to the
right it prays a prayer. If you would know the soul of the Russian people, study this cat.' Both Soviet society and the policies
of the Soviet government have in recent years fallen more and
more in line with Radhakrishnan's expectations. In Moscow
his inquisitive friendliness matched with independence was a
novel experience to Stalin and his colleagues, leading to fresh
thinking on several issues and to an acceptance of India's
goodwill.

The reconciling mind that sought to encompass all positions
was Radhakrishnan's distinctive contribution to international
affairs; and his advocacy gained power from both his philosophy and his personality. Russell drew these strands together

[21] By the Lord Mayor of London at the Guildhall Lunch, 21 June 1963.

25

when he spoke of Radhakrishnan as 'a very arresting personality
and a broad-minded philosopher—a man of real philosophical
stature'.[22] To some it was his personality that mattered—
Paul Reps sent a copy of his book *Zen Telegrams* 'to Sarvepalli
Radhakrishnan who is'. To Aldous Huxley both the teaching
and the person mattered and he inscribed one of his writings in
1963 'for Dr S. Radhakrishnan, a master of words and of no-
words'. So too Arnold Toynbee: 'I respect the President of
India because I revere India for all that she has done, and is
going to do, for the human race. But I admire and love the
philosopher Dr Radhakrishnan, and am delighted to see that
even the weight of the Presidency cannot overwhelm him.'[23]
In a post-Christian world where intelligent men and women
have no time for anthropomorphic creeds, religion as postu-
lated by Radhakrishnan seems the most sensible belief.[24] But it
is unnecessary to seek to disentangle the diverse elements in the
persuasiveness of Radhakrishnan's opinions. What is of importance is the cumulative impact. Justice Douglas summed this up
when he requested Radhakrishnan to address the students of
the California Institute of Technology: 'The boys are eager to
learn. And after a week at your feet they will all be world
citizens.'[25]

## VI

Beneath the philosopher and the personality was a very human
person. But the subjective side of himself Radhakrishnan carefully concealed. He shunned all personal revelations as the
public celebration of self and contended that only his philosophical endeavours mattered: 'After all, for a student of
thought, his writings are the best clue to his personality.'[26] He
wrote two autobiographical essays but dealt in them primarily
with his intellectual development and attitudes. The events of

---

[22] 'Talking to Bertrand Russell', *Envoy* (London), May 1956.

[23] A. J. Toynbee to S. Radhakrishnan, 7 June 1963.

[24] Cf.: 'Thank all the goodnesses there is no God in the Vedanta—there is a
That and I feel naturally capable of being a That when I should hesitate long
and shrink from the possibility of being a child of God.' James Stephens to S.
Mackenna, quoted in the *Times Literary Supplement*, 23 December 1977.

[25] W. O. Douglas to S. Radhakrishnan, 18 September 1956.

[26] To C. A. Moore, 21 April 1961.

his life could be of little interest to others; and as 'for the emotions and desires, which make life so intense and interesting, how many of us look straight into our souls?'[27] His gift for friendship was never allowed to gain intensity. Even those in long contact with him knew little about his inner life and could not penetrate the mask of banter. If anything personally sensitive in any area of his life was approached, he quickly put up the shutters and changed the subject with a joke. He rarely gave expression to his hopes, fears, disappointments, elations. What drove him on—a search for the truth, intellectual ambition, a desire to succeed? None of his contemporaries could claim to know.

Yet the personal side was an important and integral aspect of Radhakrishnan's life. His achievement was made possible by the qualities of personal outlook and character. The rootless pattern of his boyhood was soon set right by disciplined scholarship. The poverty of the early years he accepted as an unpleasant fact but did not allow it to demean him. His life was at no stage smudged by a craving for money; and his own experience of deprivation strengthened his social compassion and an unflagging and unobtrusive beneficence to individuals. Endowed with a robust constitution, weakened only in later years by constant use of barbiturates to induce sleep, he took no regular exercise except short walks, but kept in trim by adhering to a sparse but balanced vegetarian diet. By the time of his graduation he had become aware of his intellectual powers and his life now was his work. He developed orderly habits of reading and writing which he did not lose till his final illness; and he was clearly unhappy on any day on which he had not accomplished a sustained piece of writing. This joy in his work, under a sense of divine guidance, helped him to be free of all affectation; and he carried this grace over to the years of his public life in Moscow and Delhi. Patrician by nature, restrained in gesture and emotion, refusing to show such wounds as he had suffered and never appearing to be out of temper, Radhakrishnan hid from the world his sensitivity to pain of all kinds and the fact that his calm and steady detachment had not been achieved without effort.

[27] To P. A. Schilpp, 24 December 1950, reproduced in P. A. Schilpp (ed.), *The Philosophy of Sarvepalli Radhakrishnan* (New York 1952).

Radhakrishnan was reticent also about his domestic affections, and so strong was his sense of his calling that his children sometimes appeared to slip to the edge of his concerns. Further, the frenetic pace of life which he maintained from the thirties, and the constant travelling ravaged normal family life. But the strong and protective ties beneath an undemonstrative front were never loosened. As far as his son was concerned, he had, from the early years, a broad sense of simultaneous awareness:

Long before he was President of India, in the Thirties, Radhakrishnan had a boy at school at Mill Hill. Once after visiting his son he took the boat for France: that evening his son tried to reach a ball that had gone on to the roof and fell 12 feet through a skylight. His temporary guardian and his schoolmasters agreed that a toned-down version of the accident should be transmitted to Papa, a rather anxious parent; but when the guardian got back to his home in Swiss Cottage, he found Radhakrishnan on the doorstep saying 'What happened to my son yesterday evening?' So compelling had been his sudden conviction of disaster that he had turned round and come straight back.[28]

Those outside the family range who had derived from his philosophy an impression of severe authority were soon undeceived at a personal encounter. They found him an extremely sympathetic human being with the charm that stems from spiritual self-mastery and a joy of life. He viewed the world with an inner amusement and a smiling eye. He could be deadly serious without being deadeningly solemn. Auden has written somewhere that to grow up does not mean to outgrow either childhood or adolescence but to make use of both in an adult way. The child in Radhakrishnan vested him with an unmalicious sense of humour and a spontaneity of spirit which was the active side of his tranquil repose. His questing, teasing conversation drew people out and put at ease men and women of all types. With gentle raillery he led them to recognize their weaknesses and inadequacies without stripping them of their dignity. Gorky has said that in Chekhov's presence everyone felt a desire to be simpler, more truthful and more oneself. Radhakrishnan had a very similar effect. Men and women of all classes and many nationalities travelled far to spend even

[28] Katharine Whitehorn, 'Mind Power Does Exist', *Observer* (London), 22 June 1986.

just a few hours with him and talk about themselves to a philosopher confessor. Regarding respect for the individual as the
basis of human decency, Radhakrishnan treated every person
he met as having some significance. He was particularly
generous to broken people living outside the social conventions,
for he had no use for the tyranny of virtue and was unimpressed
by routine respectability. Uncensorious and acting on Goethe's
dictum, 'I see no fault that I might not have committed myself',
he provided those who came to him not with moral judgements
but with the terms of reference through which they could
adjust themselves to their existence. The Hollywood star
Myrna Loy was a member of the American delegation to the
general conference of UNESCO in Florence in the summer of
1950 and came to see him. Radhakrishnan received her informally, lying in bed with his books strewn round him, made
room for her to sit down and went straight to the subject. 'What
is your problem, my dear?' She broke down in tears and
poured out her heart to him.[29] Causing trust to flower in those
who met him, and following their later fortunes with a memory
tenacious of faces and conversations, Radhakrishnan provided
to a large number of persons in all parts of the world a wide
sense of shade and shelter.[30] Such imaginative understanding
he himself regarded, even more than his philosophical and
public contributions, as the best of him.[31]

## VII

All this is not to suggest that Radhakrishnan was an easy hero
or a plaster saint. The philosopher with a well-developed inner

[29] Khushwant Singh in *Illustrated Weekly of India*, May 1975.
[30] One example of his remarkable memory, narrated to the author by P. N.
Haksar, may be cited. In 1934 Radhakrishnan gave away the prizes at the Annual
Day of the Muir College Hostel in Allahabad. Haksar was one of the many prize-
winners, getting his award for table tennis. Radhakrishnan saw Haksar for about
half a minute when he shook hands and handed Haksar the prize. Sixteen years
later, in 1950, Radhakrishnan was passing through London on his way from
Moscow to Delhi, and Haksar, then an official in the Indian high commission,
received Radhakrishnan at London airport. As Radhakrishnan came down the
steps of the aircraft, he said to an astonished Haksar, 'How is your table tennis?'
[31] See the last paragraphs of his essay 'My Search for Truth' in V. Ferm (ed.),
*Religion in Transition* (London 1937), pp. 49–58.

life was in some ways not the most philosophical and spiritual
of beings, and to find perfect consistency in his words and his
actions is to turn away from reality. Radhakrishnan did not
believe in a deadening of the senses: 'With regard to one's
personal life, no repression of emotion is called for unless it
interferes with others' well-being. But with regard to public
conduct, it is a different story.'[32] Radhakrishnan even enjoyed
being double, a religious philosopher luxuriating in the
company of women. This in itself was of no consequence and is
of no interest to anyone except those concerned. But what casts
a shadow is the contrast between the way he conducted his
private life and what he preached to the public. In Calcutta in
December 1942, for example, with his mistress seated in the
front row, he commended the ideal of a faithful, monogamous
marriage.[33] What kind of private accommodation did he reach
to square what he did with what he said? Radhakrishnan's
answer to the charge of hypocrisy would have been that it was
his duty to lay down the highest standards even if he himself
failed to reach them. Indeed he never claimed that he did, and
always refuted the sainthood sometimes wished on him by
others. To a young girl who wrote asking if it were true that he
would one day be compared to the Buddha and Christ he
replied, 'I have no claims to all that your friend said. I am
human, very human.'[34] He had no guru and he did not set
himself up as a guru for others. No teacher could be regarded
as a perfect model of virtue and intellectual efficiency and one
should abide by the maxim of the Upanishads, 'Don't do all
things which your teachers do; whatever blameless acts they do,
follow them but not others.'[35]

Also requiring consideration is whether Radhakrishnan, for
someone who had placed a discount on finite satisfactions,[36] had
been at times too eager and impatient for fame and place. No
one whose intellectual and public achievements have been so
rich and diverse through changing contexts can escape the

[32] To A. J. Shelat, 31 July 1966.
[33] Religion and Society (London 1947), p. 160.
[34] To Harinder Bedi, 10 September 1959.
[35] Speech at the distribution of national awards for teachers, New Delhi, 3
December 1966, President Radhakrishnan's Speeches and Writings (second series),
p. 235.    [36] Indian Philosophy, vol. 1, p. 213.

smears of deviousness, trimming and opportunism. The ambition of the springboard years was legitimate, for the single-minded industry and dedication to the highest standards of philosophical analysis were the fruit not of a chilling careerism but of faith in himself and the pride of patriotism. He rejected safe alleys, did not adjust himself to the British raj, spurned the 'reconciliation with fate' of which Hegel spoke and adopted a public stance of spirited independence. Even after 1947 there is no compromise implicit in the acceptance of offices, and it is a tribute to the prime minister, Jawaharlal Nehru, that he expected of Radhakrishnan no surrender of free judgement. Yet Radhakrishnan was not without his share of the human desire for recognition, giving room, on a very few occasions in a long span of years, for a faint hint of the corruption of expectation.

## VIII

Yet none of this can detract from the quality of Radhakrishnan's genius, and the grandeur of his conceptions and his efforts to bring them to fruition. He lived life fully and at many levels. He was the most variously gifted Indian of his generation and the sheer range and diversity of achievement make it difficult to hold the totality in the mind. It is easier to consider manageable bits. Intellectual activity was itself many-sided: the seminal thinker, the evocative teacher, the virtuoso orator, the writer of stylish vigour, the indefatigable translator and commentator, the prophet soul. Added to this were the interventions in public affairs: the staunch patriot, the constructive educational administrator, the ambassador who won confidence in what was thought to be an uncongenial atmosphere, and finally the dignified presence for fifteen years in Delhi, first building the limited office of vice-president into a centre of national influence, and then converting for five years the presidentship into a civic conscience and a symbol of integrity. At first sight there is even an element of paradox in the various aspects of such a crammed life—a successful philosopher, a man of the world with a devotion to the life of the spirit, an austere believer who had not shut the door on the emotions, a progressive mind within the Indian ethos, a secular Hindu, a

politically committed contemplative. He reminds us of his own
comments on Samkara—'The life of Samkara makes a strong
impression of contraries . . . Such diverse gifts did he possess
that different images present themselves, if we try to recall his
personality.'[37] Yet his thought, his faith, his travels, his patient
and gentle temperament, were all aspects of a coherent life, the
realization of a particular vision. His reading of Hinduism
provided the base for his philosophy of idealism. His efforts to
cleanse Hinduism and restore its vitality were far from chauvinist and promoted social concern and action. His conviction
that Hinduism at its best stood for a religion of the spirit which
encompassed all routes to the same goal prepared the ground
for spiritual bridges and world unity. Like Gandhi, he too was
in the highest degree and at the same time a Hindu, an Indian
and a world citizen; and the three attitudes were not only
compatible but merged into one. It can be said of Radhakrishnan what Sartre said of Proust, that his genius lies in the
totality of his work considered as the totality of the manifestation of the person. His whole life had a single meaning.

What survives of Radhakrishnan? How important was he in
the history of his time, and does he matter at all now? A few
hyenas have gathered round his reputation and it is insinuated
that he was more a plausible than a creative philosopher, a
slick performer of the marketplace, a 'rhapsodic intellect'
churning out rhetorical certainties and not a thinker of intellectual rigour. But such carping cannot effect real damage.
With so vast an output, quality is bound to be variable. His
early works establish a powerful intelligence; *Indian Philosophy*
and *Eastern Religions and Western Thought* convey a sense of
massive scholarship held together by interpretative skill; the
editing of the classics shows his ability to attract lay audiences to
serious subjects. The writings after 1945 are imbued with a deep
purpose. His writings on Hinduism have been criticized for a
tendency to partisanship and the incorporation of new elements
into an old system. But *An Idealist View of Life*, original, distinctive and challenging, gives him a secure place in the intellectual history of the twentieth century.

Radhakrishnan, however, is more than just an undeposed
figure in the realm of pure thought. His comprehensive mind

[37] *Indian Philosophy*, vol. 2, p. 450.

had also turned to most aspects of life and viewed current issues in wide perspectives. In his own country Radhakrishnan is still important, for he brought together two powerful and living forces—pride in the past and faith in the future; 'he represents in himself that great past of ours, the present and the future, all combined.'[38] But he was primarily a philosopher of all the world, in that his work not only shows the influence of the thought of other times and places, but is of interest to men and women everywhere. Although metaphysics, discarded some time ago in favour of linguistic puzzles, has now found its way back and is again respectable, Radhakrishnan's brand of idealism is still out of fashion. But today, when people's minds are awash in doubt and confusion with science no longer offering comfortable certainties, Radhakrishnan's work goes far to meet the spiritual needs of the ordinary person. He came nearer than any other philosopher of his time to resolving the tension between intellectual conscience and the longing for a religious faith. With creeds and traditions losing their hold, his teachings are again coming into their own and helping to assist and enrich life. He regarded his task, in his own words, as not merely to reflect the spirit of the age but to lead it forward, to state the values, set the goals, point the direction and lead to new paths.[39] As was written of him a few days before his death, he, if anyone, could bridge the spiritual chasm between East and West. His lifelong search for insight was a voyage of discovery of himself, a penetration of the depth of his own nature; but he had sharpened this insight from whatever outside sources were available, evolved his own spirituality by applying it to everyday life, and transmitted it to those who would also apply it in their own way and learn from it.[40] A product of his times, he also saw ahead and brought nearer his vision of the international landscape to come. An honorary member of all religions, he maintained that the ultimate truth was one, that every religion shows some traces of it and it is a matter of

[38] Jawaharlal Nehru at the dinner for the prime minister of Mongolia, 10 September 1959.

[39] 'Concluding Survey' in *History of Philosophy: Eastern and Western*, vol. II (London 1953), p. 448.

[40] Clifford Longley, religious affairs correspondent, in *The Times* (London), 7 April 1975.

indifference to which religion we adhere. This objective is now gaining wider acceptance and has recently been clearly stated: 'The pursuit of religious truth together would lead ultimately to mutual transformation within an overall partnership.'[41] More and more Radhakrishnan stands out clearly as one of the great transformative personalities of our age.

[41] Alan Race in *Times Literary Supplement*, 25 September 1987.

# BIBLIOGRAPHICAL NOTE

I have relied much on the private papers of Radhakrishnan, still in the possession of the family. Radhakrishnan maintained his papers carefully, especially in his later years. When items from this source are mentioned in the footnotes, no reference is given.

I have also supplemented the information available in the Radhakrishnan papers by consulting official archives and private paper collections both in India and abroad. Details are given in the footnotes.

A detailed bibliography of Radhakrishnan's writings up to 1952 is available in P. A. Schilpp (ed.), *The Philosophy of Sarvepalli Radhakrishnan* (New York 1952) in the Library of Living Philosophers series. The following are his principal writings:

*The Ethics of the Vedanta and Its Metaphysical Presuppositions* (Madras 1908)
*Essentials of Psychology* (Oxford 1912)
*The Philosophy of Rabindranath Tagore* (London 1918)
*The Reign of Religion in Contemporary Philosophy* (London 1920)
*Indian Philosophy*, Volume One (London 1923); Volume Two (London 1927)
*The Hindu View of Life* (London 1927)
*The Religion We Need* (London 1928)
*Kalki or the Future of Civilization* (London 1929)
*The Heart of Hindustan* (Madras 1932)
*An Idealist View of Life* (London 1932)
*East and West in Religion* (London 1933)
*Freedom and Culture* (Madras 1936)
*Eastern Religions and Western Thought* (Oxford 1939)
*Education, Politics and War* (Pune 1944)
*India and China* (Bombay 1944)
*Religion and Society* (London 1947)
*The Bhagavad Gita* (London 1948)
*The Dhammapada* (Oxford 1950)

*The Principal Upanishads* (London 1953)

*Recovery of Faith* (New York 1955)

*East and West* (London 1955)

*Fellowship of the Spirit* (Harvard University Press 1961)

*The Brahma Sutra* (London 1961)

*Occasional Speeches and Writings 1952–1959* (Delhi 1960)

*Occasional Speeches and Writings 1959–1962* (Delhi 1963)

*President Radhakrishnan's Speeches and Writings 1962–1964* (Delhi 1965)

*Religion in a Changing World* (London 1967)

*President Radhakrishnan's Speeches and Writings 1964–1967* (Delhi 1969)

# INDEX

*(Apart from the entry of his name, throughout this index Radhakrishnan has been abbreviated to R.)*